FROM PITCH
TO PUBLICATION

Carole Blake

FROM PITCH TO PUBLICATION

Everything you need to know to get your novel published

MACMILLAN

First published 1999 by Macmillan
an imprint of Macmillan Publishers Ltd
25 Eccleston Place, London SW1W 9NF
Basingstoke and Oxford
Associated companies throughout the world
www.macmillan.co.uk

ISBN 0 333 71435 0

9 8 7 6 5 4

A CIP catalogue record for this book is available from
the British Library.

Typeset by SetSystems Ltd, Saffron Walden, Essex
Printed and bound in Great Britain by
Mackays of Chatham plc, Chatham, Kent

To the people without whom this book wouldn't exist and I wouldn't have such a satisfying job: my fantastic author clients who give me a reason to get up in the morning; and the wonderful, dedicated and talented staff of Blake Friedmann past and present. Thank you for the stimulation, the motivation, the aggravation and the fun.

Contents

Acknowledgements

As I will repeat more than once in this volume, books are never the work of one person. I therefore want to thank many people who have taught and helped me a great deal: my colleagues Julian Friedmann and Isobel Dixon, who have made numerous invaluable suggestions for this book; Michael Alcock, my original editor, who persuaded me to embark upon it; and Gordon Scott Wise of Macmillan, who encouraged me through the seemingly impossible task of finding time to do it, who actually had to edit it, who was gracious enough to leave in things that he or Macmillan might disagree with, and who kept the faith even through to the third renegotiated deadline.

And most of all to my parents, who succumbed to my wish for a bookcase as my Christmas present when I was eight, and then watched in amazement when I ignored my dolls and spent hours instead 'cataloguing' my books. Look where it's led!

Introduction

This book will not tell you *how* to write: there are many books published that cover the creative process. But it will tell you – if you have talent and enough perseverance – how to get published. It will tell you how to get an agent and a publisher. It will also tell you how to get the best out of them, how to build a good relationship with them, and how to leave them if this is impossible.

Few of the books on how to write fiction discuss what to do with your novel once you've learned your craft. The aim of this book is to turn a creative writer into a professional author, able to get the very best out of the publishing experience, the trade and out of themselves.

According to the cliché, everyone has a book in them. I've been an agent too long to believe that. If it's true, then for some that's exactly where it should stay! I don't believe that everyone has the talent and the craft and the sheer application to become a published writer. But I do believe that those who do possess this combination of qualities will find this book a useful tool to have by their writing elbow. Ignorance is never blissful. The more you know about the publishing process, about what happens on the publishers' – and agents' – side of the desk, the more you can profit from it.

Working with writers is, for me, a source of immense pleasure. Being a literary agent is a deeply satisfying existence. There are stressful and anxious parts of the job, but on the whole it is exciting and rewarding and tremendous fun. I realize how lucky I am to be able to make a living doing something that I enjoy so much. The aim of this book is to achieve that for talented writers too.

The entire publishing industry would be out of work without authors. But writers must necessarily lead a quite schizophrenic life. Closeted away in private while they write, they then offer their manuscript to friends and strangers who will cheerfully tell them (sometimes quite wrongly, sometimes with great insight) what's wrong with it. Or, perhaps even worse, may not tell them what's wrong with it. Then comes a period of limbo while others take possession of their creation, and after that they are expected to turn into sparkling party animals for the publicity and promotion period – then back to purdah while writing the next one. It's not something I envy (as I have had time to discover for myself during the writing of this book!).

But I do love editing and selling the work of writers. The adrenaline rush I experience on the first day of the Frankfurt Book Fair every year (even though I know I'll be totally exhausted, hoarse and probably laid low with 'flu within six days) is like nothing else I can describe. The excitement of discovering and launching a new writer, the exhilaration of conducting an auction, the euphoria of calling a writer to tell them of a big deal: these all amply balance the days when I have to deal with the many and varied problems of the writing and publishing life.

So to all those talented writers out there who aren't yet published: don't give up. Use every setback to spur you to greater effort. Persevere, learn more about your craft and the way the industry works, and use this book to help you find an audience for your fiction. I wish you the very best of luck.

How to use this book

This book is for the writer who wants a career as a published author. It is for writers who wish to manage and make the best of that career and who need to be able to understand the trade. It is therefore not about how to write: there are many good books already published on that subject, some of which I list in the bibliography. I assume that you can write and that you are either embarking upon publication, or are already published. I assume that you want to make sense of an industry that can sometimes, from an author's point of view, seem baffling at best, or obstructive at worst.

The book is organized chronologically, dealing with subjects as a writer would encounter them. The three parts cover, respectively, before your book is sold, from contract to publication, and then publication and beyond.

Part One moves from the initial market research on what to write, through preparing your material for submission, accepting editorial criticism, getting an agent, submitting material, negotiating a deal, and then to a long section on the trade and how it works.

Part Two begins with advice on how to assess a publisher's offer, and moves on to contract advice, work to do on your text before it is published (rewriting, guarding against libel, plagiarism), and then to the publisher's preparation for publishing: decisions on format, jacket and marketing. It also covers how you sell to the publisher's team, how they sell to overseas markets, and how you, your agent and your publisher sell other rights.

The longest chapter, on contracts, is in this section. Once you have an offer from a publisher to publish your novel, the contract becomes vital. Everything that can or cannot be done by the publisher and yourself will be covered by this, and the repercussions of a badly drafted or little-understood contract will stay with you for years. Even if you have an agent who deals with the details for you, I would urge every author to study their contract and only to sign it once everything has been discussed and is understood. So much of the business of publishing and the trade is covered by the contract: a good contract should deal with every eventuality. An author who knows a bit about publishing could well start by reading the chapter on contracts, referring to other chapters to expand on each clause as it is discussed.

Part Three deals with everything that follows publication: publicity (or lack of it), sales (or lack of them), royalty statements (again, sometimes the lack of them), understanding cash flow and dealing constructively with problems with your publisher and agent. And following publication, of course, on to your next book.

Part Four is a section of appendixes including a bibliography of recommended books and lists of magazines, trade fairs and trade organizations. I have not covered areas such as writers' groups, or awards for writers. These change so rapidly that you would be advised to consult an annual directory for up-to-date information.

The sections, and the chapter headings and sub-headings within them, should give you a clear indication of where to find information. An index acts as a further help to finding what you need. The bibliography lists a selection of the many books about writing and the business of publishing. However, this book does not set out to be a directory or handbook of publishing, giving names and addresses. There are very good reference works which list these and I would suggest that an ideal companion volume to this book would be the most recent edition of Barry Turner's *The Writer's Handbook*, which is updated and published annually.

Depending on your present situation, you might want to start reading this book in different places. If you are unsure as to whether you need an agent or not, you could start with chapter 4. If, on the other hand, you have an agent but your current dilemma is that you are unhappy with them, turn straight to the section in chapter 17. If you've sold your book and it's about to be published, chapter 14 on publicity may be of most use. If your book has been published for some months and you've just received your first royalty statement, which looks as comprehensible as if it were written in hieroglyphs, chapter 15, which explains them (royalty statements, not hieroglyphs), will hopefully be just what you need.

I do hope the book proves useful, and helps you maximize the pleasure and the profit of being a novelist.

If you don't find what you need I will be more than happy to hear from you so that I can include the information in the next edition: do write to me either care of my publisher, Macmillan, or at my own agency offices.

Happy reading, and writing!

Carole Blake
Blake Friedmann Literary Agency Ltd
122 Arlington Road
London NW1 7HP
Telephone: 0171 284 0408
Fax: 0171 284 0442

Part One

BEFORE YOUR
BOOK IS SOLD

1   Market research

It is absurd to have a hard and fast rule about what one should read and what one shouldn't. More than half of modern culture depends on what one shouldn't read – Oscar Wilde

Is what you want to write different to what people want to read? – Edwina Currie, speaking at *Woman's Weekly*'s 'How To Make Money Writing Fiction' seminar

What to write?

Are you writing the right book? It's a simple question but it is complicated to arrive at an answer. If you spend time thinking about this before you start your novel, you may save yourself a lot of agonies later. Many writers, whether they realize it or not, are writing primarily for themselves. If you intend to make money from your fiction, you must write what moves you, but you must also write with an eye on the eventual market for your work.

This book is entirely about commercial fiction. I have chosen to concentrate on this for three reasons: because so many people seem to be trying to get novels published, because I love commercial fiction and spend most of my life working with it, and because many of the processes of publishing and selling it (and therefore much of the advice) is so different for literary fiction.

A few years ago, a national newspaper calculated that the average acceptance rate for unsolicited manuscripts by a publisher in Britain or America was half a per cent. That actually seems rather high to me. It's certainly a higher acceptance rate than we take on from the unsolicited manuscripts we receive in our medium-sized agency. Although the total number of books published increases every year, I'm sure the odds against acceptance are just as bad now, if not worse than when the newspaper quoted the figure. It's important not to underestimate the obstacles to publication, but to understand how to overcome them, which is what this book is all about.

Watership Down by Richard Adams, *The Day of the Jackal* by Frederick Forsyth and one of our agency's bestselling books, *Free to Trade* by Michael Ridpath (now translated into thirty-eight languages) were all unsolicited, 'slush pile' manuscripts when they were submitted to their initial publisher or agent.

Life's not fair, so what can you do to improve the odds of getting published? After all, as Steinbeck said, 'Writing makes horse racing seem like a nice stable occupation.'

It's not just how you write. That's vital, of course. But it's also what you write – and how you present it. This chapter deals with how you decide what to write.

Trends and how to spot them

Trying to identify trends is tough. The novels that editors are buying now will not be published for at least a year (if they are bought at finished manuscript stage), or two years (if they are commissioned in the early stages of writing). Starting your novel today may mean that the earliest it could be published is three years from now: eighteen months to write it and then a further eighteen months to sell it and have it published. You would need a crystal ball to know what will be hot in the market place in three years' time. As reliable crystal balls are in short supply, I'll try to highlight other means of identifying marketable areas of fiction.

I am amazed that so many authors start the laborious and intensive work of writing a novel by basing their decision about the subject matter on little more than a whim. Think how much of your time you could waste if you pick the wrong genre or subject, or set your novel in a geographical location that the trade believes just won't sell. It's so hard to break into print that every author should give themselves as many advantages as they can.

If you can write well, your investment in this process – time and money – could be repaid many times over. If you are aiming to be a published writer that's a small price to pay. After all, no one expects any other career to fall in their lap overnight, but it's extraordinary how many people think, 'I could become a novelist if only I had the time', as though talent and hard work were quite incidental!

Don't join a bandwagon that has already been gathering pace for a while: by the time you have written, sold and published your book, the fashion may have produced a backlash. Christian Jacq's bestselling sequence of novels about Ramses began being published in English (having been translated from the original French) in 1997. The first volume was such a success that Simon & Schuster decided to speed up publication of the other volumes. I think they were right. Many other writers and publishers rushed to bring out fiction with an Ancient Egypt theme to cash in on the market created by Jacq's books. Too many titles in the same subject area can saturate the market so that while one or two might sell very well, the rest all suffer from so much competition.

'Write about what you know' is advice often given to writers starting out, but I think this can be misleading. Many writers I know have put good research, way beyond their own immediate experience, to wonderful use. John Trenhaile's first three novels were very classy thrillers set in Russia during the Cold War, published many years before the fall of the Berlin Wall. The rave review that John and I prized most, for *Kyril*, was from the *Los Angeles Times* which began: 'Mr Trenhaile, who obviously knows Moscow like the back of his hand . . .' To this day John has never visited the city. But he is a great professional and knows how to put good research to work. That trilogy of novels was translated into a dozen languages and stayed in print for many years.

I've no doubt that many of the retired civil engineers, dentists and planning officers who write their first novels based in their own field have been told to 'write about what you know'. But can you name novels with those backgrounds, or those professions, which have become popular published books? I can't. As a result, I turn down a lot of fiction from retired civil engineers, dentists and planning officers! These are not aspirational jobs or backgrounds for mass-market readers, so consequently a novel where these backgrounds are central to the story starts life with the odds stacked against it. No matter how fascinating they might be, I've never yet met anyone who dreamed of the glamour of a dentist's drill, or fantasized about the day they would be qualified to wield a theodolite! I don't mean to suggest that these or other professions can never appear within the covers of a successful commercial novel. But if you do use them, make sure that they form the background, rather than the dominant theme, in your fiction.

Now that I've managed to insult at least some of my readers, I'll attempt to explain what I mean. There are some professions that will carry fiction well. Acting, antiques, the art world, fashion, financial trading, horse racing, the law and, of course, the world of the police and private detectives have all been used successfully as backdrops for bestselling fiction. What links them is that they are perceived to be glamorous and exciting, and many people aspire to them, or at least think they would enjoy them more than their own lives. These careers are aspirational: people can dream about them, and backgrounds like these become an advantage to your characters.

An author who turned backgrounds into gold was Arthur Hailey. His novels such as *Hotel* and *Wheels* told the audience everything about running hotels or working in the automobile industry. For a reader, the added value of reading a Hailey novel is acquiring a huge amount of knowledge about a specific business. But he made very sure that his characters were fascinating and the storylines compelling, thus the background did not dominate.

If there has recently been a huge shift of world politics, steer clear of the previous political situation, at least for a while. In the years after the fall of the Berlin Wall, it became very difficult to sell thrillers set against the background of the Cold War. They were regarded as old-fashioned. Readers wanted to believe that the world had become a safer place, no longer populated by spies living in a grey twilight. No matter that one of my spy-writer clients, Ted Allbeury, himself an ex-spy-catcher, knew that the real spy world was busier than ever, public perception had swung against those stories, so thriller writers had to find new arenas for their novels.

Genres

If you choose to write in a genre – crime, romance or science fiction, for example – it is important to know the rules of that genre. Not because you must follow them slavishly, but because if you are going to bend them, it's best to be aware of how and when you are doing so. There are many books on all aspects of how to write, including titles on every specific genre. Seek them out and absorb the information. Also, many genres have well-organized and energetic associations that you can join. Science fiction, crime writing, romance fiction: they all have successful and well-run societies with programmes of speakers and events. You may have to travel to their regional meeting point if you want to attend workshops and talks, but most publish newsletters and some offer a manuscript advice service.

Joining a writers' group can be useful for researching the market too. In a well-run group where the members trust one another, a lot of information is shared that can be of enormous benefit if it warns you away from pitfalls that others have discovered. Writers in these groups share information on what's selling or not, who's buying or not, who's paying what (and sometimes also who's paying late), and they can be helpful with recommendations of editors and agents. At the back of this book you will find details of a wide range of publications and organizations that can be used to brief you on the state of publishing, and what publishers might be looking for. Networking with other writers can be very useful on all levels.

One of the most obvious (and often underrated) forms of research is to read every successful novel you can lay your hands on in your chosen area of writing. Not so that you can copy them, but so that you can analyse why they are successful and what ingredients make them appeal to a wide audience. Also, so that you can identify something for you to include in your novel that will be fresh and original, but will still enable your novel to satisfy the readers' expectations. If you are passionate about fiction you will be reading your competitors' work voraciously anyway. A lifetime's passion for your genre pays dividends if it means you have read all the writers who are your role models, and all the writers whose work warns you what not to emulate!

Don't forget the length: some genres, for example, have strong conventions about the length that they expect novels to be. In general, it is a good idea to look at the length of the books written by writers you might consider would appeal to the same market as yours.

Most successful commercial novels are 100,000 words or so – but I am regularly offered novels that are 50,000 or 60,000 words. Gilbert Adair can publish a beautifully crafted literary novel at that length because novellas work in the literary field, but this is not what a publisher of commercial fiction is looking for. The logistics and the figures of the literary publishing world operate quite differently from that of commercial fiction. Authors who offer insufficient material for the area in which they are working are simply demonstrating to agents and publishers that they can't be bothered to learn the rules of their trade.

Equally, make sure that you do not write too long for the market you are aiming at. The longer your book, the more expensive it will be to print and bind, and this could push up the selling price. If you are a successful writer already, or writing for the fantasy market, say, this might not matter too much. But if you are an unpublished writer it could prejudice an agent and publisher against your work. Salman Rushdie, when favourably reviewing a new and long Don Delillo novel on television said, 'If you're going to write a long novel you have to make the reader feel it is too short; that you have to cram everything in and that you could have gone on for longer.'

There are, unfortunately, times when certain genres fall out of favour. This has happened to historical fiction in recent years, as well as spy thrillers. These restrictions seldom count against an already established writer with a loyal readership, but they can stop a first novelist being accepted if the tide of public opinion (or even simply the perception of that opinion by publishing editors) has moved away from their chosen genre.

Unless you write like an angel, trying to sell material that is not what the market wants is unlikely to succeed: you are creating obstacles for yourself. You can't always be sure of getting it right, but doing some homework before you begin certainly won't do any harm.

Many writers only think about marketing when they are ready to offer their manuscript to a publisher or an agent. By that time it can be too late. If you have chosen a genre that is completely out of fashion, or a subject or background that six well-known writers have used for their latest novels, you will find it extremely difficult, perhaps impossible, to sell your work even if the writing is wonderful and the storyline commercial.

Although it's wise to find a genre or subject to write about that you have a passion for, don't allow yourself to be self-indulgent. It's essential to be self-critical, and it's vital to be open to criticism from others.

The hard work of creating

My advice is always to write about characters and stories that you care passionately about, know something about and enjoy. The strength of your feelings and your connection to your subject will enthuse the reader similarly. When you feel strongly at the outset, passion will carry you through the long and demanding work to completion. This is more likely to happen than if you pick a subject or plot only because you think it will be the next fashionable genre or theme.

Georges Simenon, the creator of Maigret, put it well: 'Writing is not a profession, but a vocation of unhappiness.' For some, 'being' a writer is attractive. Actually doing the work is extremely unglamorous and can come as a shock to the newly initiated. I have an enormous respect for people who write regularly, and who persevere through to a career as a novelist, publishing one good book after another.

I would rather slit my wrists than try to write fiction myself. The idea of spending a year or more in a lonely room, writing and writing, only to deliver the manuscript to friends and critics to comment on it seems like a recipe for hell on wheels. If I'm honest, the process of writing this book hasn't been unalloyed pleasure throughout either! When I was halfway through this book, and complaining to anyone who would listen about how much more I had to do, Michael Ridpath, while commiserating, said to me, 'Most people don't realize that there's an awful lot of typing involved in writing a book.' Apart from the fact that it made me laugh, it also put me in my place. First, I shouldn't have been moaning to one of my clients about my own writing and, second, I should have realized that writing fiction – making it all up – must be more difficult than writing non-fiction on a subject from which I actually earn my living!

The rules

Perhaps writers can take consolation from the fact that first novels are rarely an author's best work. And, as many of you can probably testify, they are often not even their first published work: many first novels lie forever in a desk drawer. But writing them may have been a necessary first step on the way to later publication of another novel.

If you are looking for a career as a novelist (and few publishers or agents will be interested in you if you intend only to write one novel), then the learning process of writing that first novel – even if it remains unpublished – will be invaluable to you in the long-term.

You can win against the tide of rejection if your writing and your storyline are extremely good, you have an original angle, and if you can create characters with whom a wide range of readers want to spend time. No one said it was easy getting published.

A handy (but by no means exhaustive) checklist to apply to your work would include the following:

1. Do I have a clear central character for my readers to identify with?
2. Is that central character fully developed and totally believable?
3. Is the world that I have created in the novel one my readers will want to spend time in even before they know the story or the characters?
4. Does my character grow and develop during the course of the story?
5. Is the pacing – the tension – even, or does it flag in places?
6. Do I have sufficient set-piece scenes as dramatic highlights?
7. Is my story likely to be overtaken by real events thereby making it seem out of date?
8. Are my plot strands too complicated so the readers get confused?

9. Are the stakes high enough for my central character? If not, the novel could fail to capture the readers' imagination.

10. Is there a big dramatic question at the heart of the book? If not, can I inject one? (One crude rule of thumb here is to see if you can sum up the storyline in one sentence: if you can, you have a Big Dramatic Question!)

11. Is the storyline sufficiently high concept to stand out from all the other novels in the market place?

12. Is the ending sufficiently satisfying for the expectation I have set up in the readers? (This presupposes that you have, indeed, set up the expectation!)

Remember that writing fiction is the careful blending together of an art and a craft. It therefore follows that absolute rules are non-existent. All that I, or anyone else in the publishing world, can suggest is that you should try to stack the odds in your favour by doing things that have worked for others. Of course, we will always be able to cite examples of books that have succeeded magnificently despite breaking all the rules. But authors will have done that by a combination of brilliant narrative technique, superb plotting and pace, perhaps an already successful career behind them – and probably a huge marketing budget from their publisher. If you are not sure about having any one of those ingredients, let alone all of them, then I would advise you to stick to the guidelines that most of us in the industry believe in.

There is a careful tightrope to be walked between wilfulness and the market place. There is no point in offering a subject that the market does not want, no matter how strongly you feel about it, unless you can find a really original approach, or if you are prepared for rejection. What the market wants is partly determined by commissioning editors in the publishing companies. They are not always right, so one rejection shouldn't be taken as a reason to give up. But several rejections for the same reasons – for example, the market is not selling this genre, or your characters are not engaging enough – should be taken seriously.

Guard against forcing yourself to write something you have no feeling for just because the market seems to want it: this could result in a cold, sterile and unpublishable manuscript. Take the market place into account, but concentrate on the elements of your book that could lift it above the mass of manuscripts being offered.

Characters

Characters are the most important part of any novel, and the strongest memory that readers carry with them, once they have finished reading, is usually of outstanding characters who have touched them in some way. I would recommend always starting the development process with your characters, even though there are many other important considerations to take into account as well. To make the reader care for your characters and storyline, *you* must certainly care for them. It won't work otherwise.

Self-help

Be sure you understand the sector of the market you are trying to please – read widely within the area you choose. You can learn a great deal by analysing other books and writers in the field. Join a writers' group. If you are given criticism, listen to it carefully. Don't let yourself react negatively to criticism: try not to be hurt by it, try only to learn from it. Even if you disagree with it, think about why the point was made. (See chapter 2 for more detailed discussion of this vital area.)

Read books and magazines about writing. It's fashionable in certain circles to sneer at self-help books, but they contain an enormous amount of useful information. So long as you sift through them and choose what you use, it's possible to benefit from them. Michael Ridpath is on record as saying that he wrote his first novel, the huge bestseller *Free to Trade*, after reading two self-help books, one on plot, and one on character. When their publisher, Robinson Books, heard that, they decided to reprint the two titles in one volume and asked Michael to write an introduction to the new edition. In its new version it's called *How to Write a £illion*.

Join book clubs that offer commercial fiction: their monthly brochures are a very good guide to perennially popular areas of fiction. And reading them over a period of time builds into a useful body of reference of what is popular in fiction.

Enter writing competitions. The discipline and the critiques will be instructive and, should you win, that will be useful information to include in your submission to an agent or a publisher.

The publishing trade press can be very useful: from it you can learn about books being signed up by publishers right now that aren't finished yet and are not due to be published for perhaps two or more years. This is priceless information. Reading the papers and magazines that the trade itself reads can only help you even if, at best, it only helps in identifying what not to write. There is a list of the main trade publications at the back of this book.

Study the bestseller lists that appear regularly in newspapers; subscribe to a range of magazines about writing and publishing, preferably a mix of those aimed at writers and those aimed at the publishing trade; if you have friends who are writers, publishers or agents, then pump them unmercifully for information. Call publishers and ask for their catalogues. Haunt your local bookshop and persuade the staff to chat to you about what is selling, and what is coming in the future that they think will sell well.

Make sure that you see the chart published annually in the *Guardian* in the first half of January. Journalist Alex Hamilton compiles a list of Britain's 100 fastest-selling paperbacks during the previous calendar year. It includes a telling breakdown of figures (retail price, month of publication, quantity sold in Britain and abroad in the British publisher's edition, and total revenue generated for each title). The figures come from the publishers, and the chart, with its commentary, is required reading for people in the trade and, of course, it's a valuable source of information for would-be novelists. Trends emerge as successive years' charts are scanned, and careful reading of the patterns that show up can be enormously informative. But remember, this is recording what has happened, not what is about to happen. Catching a trend before it has peaked requires skilled interpretation of the figures.

An aside: people have wondered whether publishers artificially inflate the figures they quote to the newspaper. Publishing is a small and supportive community. It used to be that a sales rep from Publisher B could easily discover approximately what your sales were with Publisher A by asking competing sales reps or a friendly bookseller a few questions. Now, publishers and booksellers and the companies that chart the bestsellers are so highly computerized that exact sales figures are very easy to obtain. I, and other agents, scrutinize the figures they quote for my own clients, and if they don't match the royalty statement figures on which they report sales and earnings to us, I query them. I'm sure some publishers do round the figures up a little, but if they exaggerated too much it would become obvious, if only to the authors and agents concerned.

Finally, attending writers' circles, book fairs and festivals and talks by people in the industry, can all provide you with contacts and valuable sources of information.

Publishing catchphrases

Catchphrases, so familiar they have become clichés, are bandied about in publishing. Cliché or not, they can sometimes contain helpful advice:

'Local stories for global markets' i.e. concentrate on a small group of characters and construct a tight plotline around them and the world will want to read the book. Maeve Haran's first novel, *Having It All*, did just that: a career woman having difficulties balancing work and family. I remember asking the novel's Polish publisher why she thought it had been so successful in her market. After all, it was set in the world of television in London and might have seemed a long way away from the Polish fiction market in the immediate post-Communist era. She looked surprised that I should have asked and said, 'But Carole, it's obvious. We Polish women have always had to work hard, and run the home at the same time.'

'Big drama in small lives': a similar point. Focus down on to your characters and your readers will want to follow. When Val Corbett (television producer and scriptwriter), Joyce Hopkirk (pioneering magazine editor) and Eve Pollard (ground-breaking newspaper editor and television presenter) were planning their first jointly written novel, *Splash*, we all spent a lot of time talking about what sold fiction in large quantities. When I repeated these two catchphrases the writers seized upon them gleefully. 'But would a Norwegian woman living on a fjord like it?' became the test they would apply to their storylines. They must have got it right because their novels are widely translated too!

'Kill the darlings': this one is a favourite in the film industry. Or as Samuel Johnson put it: 'When rereading your material and you think you have found a particularly fine piece, strike it out!' In other words, don't get so emotionally attached to some part of your work that you can't see what's wrong with it.

'Show don't tell': in order to illustrate a character trait, or a backstory element, demonstrate it with a scene, a snippet of dialogue but please – please – don't have the narrative address the reader like a newscaster reciting facts.

These are a few very general truths about commercially successful writing, but there is more to it than that. Commercial writing is the ability to mix craft with art, and *that* comes with training and practice.

What are agents looking for?

There are guidelines as to what I, and agents like me who handle a lot of commercial novels, want to find.

When I receive sample material from a potential new author, I look for evidence that I am dealing with a *writer* – someone who believes in their material and writes with a sense of conviction. An obvious point, you might think – but too many writers write with tongue in cheek, or think that a gimmicky plot is all that matters. Also, I want to represent writers who are planning a career in writing. I never take on one-off clients.

I look for the writer's ability to involve me quickly in the characters, the atmosphere and the storyline. Good storytelling encourages the reader to relax into it.

In the first few pages, I look for the ability to handle material in a way that suggests the writer could carry off a whole novel and is in charge of the characters and the backcloth. I want to find evidence that the writer has confidence and can handle emotion and pace. I need to see that the characters develop realistically within the course of the story. Characters who suddenly change direction and attitude are seldom believable. The storyline has to be set up in a way that makes their actions wholly credible.

I look for the ability to develop the plot in a way that doesn't raise question marks every few scenes. For example, alarm bells are always set off for me by coincidence. Coincidence at an important point in the story always feels like laziness on the part of the writer. The writer risks that the reader will feel cheated. It's obviously more difficult to construct a plot that twists and turns in ways that reflect the characterization and the world that the writer has already set up, but it's much more satisfying in the long-term. No good plot should rely on coincidence. Small ones can sometimes be justified. Big ones, never, even though I accept that coincidence happens often in real life. Fiction has to be *better* than real life. In life one thing happens after another; in drama one thing happens *because* of another.

Getting readers emotionally involved in your characters is perhaps the most important single aspect of writing commercial fiction today. Creating a tight structure, finding a subject or theme that is relevant: these are vital.

I have a mental checklist when looking at potential new clients. It is concerned with broader issues than just their writing. I like them to have strong convictions but also the ability to listen to constructive criticism.

I want my clients to be commercially minded: writing only for yourself and your favourite aunt is all very well, but I need my authors to be read by large audiences. I don't want to work with people who are too precious. I look for authors who are talented but also have a businesslike and professional attitude to the business in which they – and I – ply their talents.

Novelists must be able to control and manipulate that magical triangle: the relationship between writer and character, writer and reader, and reader and character. Of the three, the most important is the last: the relationship between reader and character. If you forget any part of that triangle you will have an unsuccessful novel on your hands. Manage the triangle well and you *may* be able to produce a novel that will be successful.

Like most professions, the craft can be learned. And it *must* be learned. Some are born with talent. If you have it then you *can* succeed if you are willing to apply yourself to the craft. It is possible for writers with a little talent to get published if they apply themselves to learning their craft, but this will usually only work for strict genres with fans who are voracious readers. Genres such as romance and police procedural can produce examples of mediocre books with a limited shelf life, which find an audience because that genre itself has such a large and enthusiastic audience.

Careful reading of an author's work sometimes leads me to the conclusion that they can write but are perhaps writing the wrong kind of book. One of my clients spent nine months working with me on three drafts of some early chapters of her first book. With each draft it got better, technically, but I liked it less. Eventually I told her I thought she was writing the wrong book because, as I said earlier, she didn't like her characters enough to make me, the reader, like them. It became a heated discussion and I thought our relationship was over before it had properly begun. Some months later she delivered to me a short – and stunning – outline for a novel that got me excited the moment I read it. It became the international bestseller *Having It All* by Maeve Haran. The first novel wasn't working because Maeve was trying to write something that she thought the market wanted but which her heart wasn't in. When she wrote about a subject that she was personally passionate about (babies and the boardroom – the uneven playing field that mothers in business have to contend with) then the characters and the story came alive. This is how that novel, which is now translated into more than twenty languages, had its gestation.

Don't despair. Although we reject most of the 5,000 unsolicited submissions we receive a year – many because they show little or no talent, many because they pay no attention to the market at all – we have also had first novels high in the bestseller lists that I found in our 'slush pile'. This term, by the way, is widely used in publishing circles to mean the piles and piles of unsolicited, unasked-for manuscripts that arrive in the offices of agents and publishers every working day of the year. It wasn't coined by me, it has been in use for at least fifty years and it isn't intended to be derogatory, merely descriptive!

Your preparation for publication should start as soon as you decide you are going to write fiction. The advice in this chapter is intended to help you identify those ingredients that could help your novel to sell, and those that would definitely hinder its potential publication. Time spent thinking about the subjects covered here will be time well spent.

2 Editorial preparation

This is not writing, this is typing!
– Truman Capote, reviewing a Jack Kerouac novel

A bad book is as much of a labour to write as a good one
– Aldous Huxley, *Point Counter Point*, 1928

How to get editorial criticism

There are a variety of ways to obtain editorial criticism before you have an agent or a publisher. Families and friends can be helpful, but more often than not they will tell you what they think you want to hear unless you seriously impress upon them your wish to hear the truth, however unpalatable it might seem.

One suggestion I've already made is to join a writing group. These are numerous: local groups, groups organized by a local education institute or library, or groups that operate by mail. These days there are also a number thriving on the Internet. Reference books, your local library and fellow writers are the starting points. It is essential to remember that you only get out of these what you put in. You must be prepared to read and criticize others' work, and you must have an open mind about the comments you are likely to receive on your own work. Plus you should be prepared to rework your material and submit it again for their comments.

Several organizations will appraise your work, for a fee. The best are those made up of other writers or professionals from the publishing world, preferably those who will have some kind of stake – their reputation, apart from their fee – in your future success. This serves as some sort of guarantee that their advice is impartial and aiming towards helping you achieve your goal of successful publication.

Organizations such as the Romantic Novelists' Association, The Society of Authors or The Writers' Guild will admit you as a member (so long as you qualify for membership), and some run manuscript appraisal schemes. Those that do not will at least introduce you to other writers who may be prepared to read and comment on your work. A professional such as a publisher's editor (who is always working towards the goal of publication) and an agent (whose goal is to achieve a saleable manuscript) will have more at stake when offering you editorial criticism than someone who only prepares a reader's report on your work. Beware of organizations whose reputations you are not sure of, who exist only to appraise manuscripts: their only interest may lie in writing, and charging for, the largest number of reader's reports.

As I've said before, publishers and agents are not welfare organizations: they cannot offer detailed editorial criticism for books they will not publish or represent. Nor can they be expected to become a referral service if they cannot accept the manuscript themselves. No agent can ever be aware of the level of work or the balance of the lists of others and so cannot, and probably should not, offer suggestions of agencies more suited to your material. It would be better for you to do your own homework via a directory of agencies and a number of telephone calls.

If we were to prepare editorial reports for the manuscripts we have to reject every day, we would, quite simply, never have time to work for the clients we do actually represent. It is sometimes possible to offer a few comments to those we reject, but this is not an invitation to enter into a lengthy correspondence or a meeting to discuss the comments.

How to take editorial criticism

Even so, getting people to offer criticism is a great deal easier than accepting it. It's human nature to love something when you've created, nurtured and lived with it. But it remains true that many successful authors owe their success, at least in part, to their ability to accept, absorb and learn from criticism. Writers should be greedy for criticism. It means your reader has engaged sufficiently with your work to want to improve it. It's a smart writer who listens to several sets of editorial criticism and then distils the best of them into a rewrite that turns a good book into a superb book. Who *wouldn't* want to improve characterization, tighten plot, increase pacing and deepen motivation, along with adding impact to the opening and the climax? If you can do that by listening to criticism and then take credit for it all by putting your own name on it, again: why not?

Most of my clients accept criticism very positively. Of course, it is important that the criticism is itself constructive and it's vital to have a trusting relationship with whoever is offering the criticism, be it publisher or agent, family or friends. Most of the writers I work with are confident enough in their talent, and trusting enough of me and of their editor, to be able to accept editorial criticism with equanimity. As Maeve Haran once said to me, 'Of course, I'd rather you rang me and told me you loved it and that it was perfect, but I will revise it if it's going to get better.'

It is rare that an author's words reach the printed page without someone suggesting changes, be it plot restructuring, or line-by-line copy-editing, and it is a wise author who knows that they will get the credit themselves if the novel gets better. It's also the writer – not the agent or the editor – who will be blamed publicly, by reviewers, if there are flaws. It behoves all of us in the process to remember that it is the author's name that appears on the book, and the author must be allowed to be the final arbiter over what advice to accept or reject.

Why do some writers have difficulty accepting comments from others that are intended only to make their novel better? It may be because the manner in which the criticism is offered is tactless. Saying you love a book takes up half a line, but describing in detail a dozen plot infelicities, six points where the characters step out of character, one occasion where the timing has gone awry, an incident where the author has brought a dead character back to life inadvertently and a suggestion for a stronger ending can take ten pages or more. But an editor or agent might need to include all of these comments in one editorial letter. So when I write editorial letters I try to remember not only to point out what I think needs changing, but also to comment on what I think is particularly good. It's surprising how easy it can be to forget that at times. I try to remind myself of the necessity for regular encouragement by remembering what hard work it is to be a novelist!

Agents and editors love working with authors who are open to their ideas. It makes the editor and the agent feel more a part of the book and it bonds them more closely to the writer's career. This could in turn lead to that vital extra bit of effort within the publishing house or the agency necessary to carry the writer on to the next level of success. Agents and editors are always trying to do more than is physically possible within each working day (and during what is laughably known as our 'spare time', which in my experience is likely to be dedicated either to work taken home for evenings or weekends, or spent at work-related social events). We do all work under enormous pressure, so if you can work in a way that motivates your agent or your editor to want to do that bit extra for you, it is you and your career that will benefit. It's human nature, after all, to want to do more for someone you like and admire and whom you feel takes your advice.

One of my clients, barrister-turned-thriller writer John Trenhaile, was superb at this. He regularly received six sets of editorial notes on his early novels. He would get long letters commenting on his manuscripts from his UK hardback editor, his UK paperback editor, his US hardback editor, his US paperback editor, his Canadian publisher and his agent! And he loved it. He would wait until he had all six, analyse them in great detail, picking out the best from all of them, and produce one response letter to all of us, setting out the changes he planned to incorporate into the next draft. If someone's comment on the central character in chapter 5 was not to be acted upon, they would then either argue their case or acknowledge that John was right. John's response to the variety of comments he received from a range of editors was that each one would probably make at least one good suggestion that the others would miss. He saw a definite benefit in having several sets of eyes scrutinize his work.

John is unusual in being able to work with so many editors. I have always thought it had a lot to do with his training as a barrister: he was used to teamwork, but with the knowledge that the team, although expert, did revolve around him, the leader. Barristers have to collate and analyse a huge number of facts in order to produce a clear and cohesive final argument. In John, a barrister's case-winning presentation had become a novelist's technique for improving his final manuscript as much as possible.

Another author I represent, the Irish thriller writer Keith Baker, also embraces editorial criticism with enthusiasm. His editor and I always comment on the fact that Keith doesn't just fix the problems that editing has highlighted, he improves each new manuscript draft dramatically more than is ever asked for in editorial notes.

It is undoubtedly hard to slave over a draft manuscript for months or even years and then to receive a mini-manuscript of criticisms – large and small – from those who seem to criticize rather than create, instead of the bouquet of congratulations and the letter of praise, which is what every writer really wants from their editor or agent. But learning to accept and include in your work the results of well-meaning constructive criticism can be enormously beneficial to your work, and is a major step on the route to becoming a professional writer. I'm not suggesting that any writer should become a slave to their critics: it is the writer who picks and chooses what criticism to act on. But rejecting helpful advice is pointless.

Dealing with rejection

> Not only does this bog down in the middle, but the author tends to stay too long with non-essentials. He seems to have little idea of pace . . . and that puts me off badly . . .
> – on Len Deighton's *The Ipcress File*

> A long, dull novel about an artist
> – on Irving Stone's *Lust for Life*

> You're welcome to Le Carré – he hasn't got any future
> – on John Le Carré's *The Spy Who Came In From the Cold*

All of the above are quoted in *Rotten Rejections* compiled by Bill Henderson (Pushcart Press, New York, 1990), a truly wonderful book that will give encouragement to every writer as it shows critics to be fallible! Mr Henderson started his publishing company after receiving many rejections for his own novel.

> Your manuscript is both good and original; but the part that is good is not original, and the part that is original is not good
> – Samuel Johnson

No one likes rejection. Of any kind, on any subject, from anyone, let alone on the fruits of your literary efforts. But if your manuscript is rejected, you'll be in good company, as you'll see from the quotes above. Take consolation from the fact that almost every successful writer – even those who seem to permanently reside in the bestseller lists – has had to face rejection at some point in their career. Turning rejection to your advantage changes a negative act into a positive one.

Publishers (and agents) will often reject a novel with bland phrases such as 'it's not right for our list', which can be infuriating. Sometimes this isn't just a brush off: it may well be the truth. Did you check what they published (or represented) before sending the material? Did you do your other homework properly? If not, read chapter 1 again! If your manuscript really isn't right for their list then you've wasted their time, and your own, and that of your manuscript. Do some more research. You don't necessarily need to be downhearted about the quality of your writing. If you have submitted your romantic novel to a publisher who doesn't actually publish romantic fiction and they reject it, then it is probably not a criticism of your novel's quality, but rather a straightforward instance of it really being wrong for their list.

Some editors will use that phrase as a get-out. Either they haven't looked at the novel properly, or don't want to say exactly why they are rejecting it, or they simply don't have the time to respond in detail. The sheer volume of the material submitted to agents and to publishers means that, unfortunately, a large proportion of it will be rejected without being read through entirely. This will never change: there will always be many more people writing than can be published. Trying to become a published writer is not for the faint-hearted.

Many writers feel anger when their manuscript is rejected. This is only natural, you've worked long and hard producing something you have confidence in, and for a stranger to bounce it back to you can seem callous and unfair. But look closely at the rejection letter. Does it contain more than a few bland generalizations? If it does make specific remarks about your novel – rather than just how full their publication list is etc. – seize upon those remarks and analyse them. Any comments at all that can be used to make your novel better are like gold dust. Don't let constructive criticism slip through your fingers just because you're unhappy that the editor hasn't fallen in love with your creation.

If an editor says your characterization is thin, maybe the following exercise would be useful: try rewriting your character biographies only from the facts you've given about them in the novel, taking care not to include anything that isn't actually on the page. When you wrote the character biographies in the first place you were including everything that *you* knew about the characters. Did all of that information actually make it to the final draft of the novel? If a scene that demonstrated some vital fact about your hero was cut, it could explain why an editor found the characterization thin. Reinstate it, or get that information back into the novel in another way.

If you see a comment that the novel lacks pace, go through your manuscript and draw a flow chart of each character's actions and appearances within each chapter. I've seen my client John Harvey, creator of the Resnick detective novels and television series, do this for his work. It's fascinating, and extremely useful in spotting potential lulls in the plot or points in the book where you lose a vital character from the scene for too long.

Any and all comments, whether negative or positive, can and should be used to help you constantly improve your manuscript. That's not to say that all comments will be helpful, of course. It's often said that if you put six editors in a room with a manuscript you'll end up with seven different opinions (see the story about John Trenhaile and his six editors earlier in this chapter!). There is never an absolute right and wrong when it comes to fiction. Inevitably you will find editors contradicting each other, often in the most infuriating way if you are the writer. This is another reason for doing homework in advance of offering. As with everything else in life, there are horses for courses. Getting a good match between author and editor is an art form, and something that agents spend a lot of time perfecting.

Recently, we had two different television companies rejecting the same script, one, because the producer liked the storyline but not the characters. But the producer at the second company said she was turning it down because the storyline was poor even though the characterization was particularly well done. Nothing can be learned from those two rejection letters, except that you can't please all of the folk all of the time!

Some of the suggestions for taking editorial criticism can also be applied to dealing with rejection with regard to ego, for example. No matter how much you are infuriated by a rejection letter, I would suggest you should keep it, filed safely. You can then do one of two things with it: use it later, in conjunction with others, to revise the manuscript if you don't get offers meanwhile. Or laugh at it secretly after you've become a successful writer! I would counsel against replying to it with a point by point refutation. The editor didn't love your book: contradicting their reasons won't convince them to love it.

I have never believed that suffering was good for the soul – I'm not that much of a masochist – and ideally I would like all of my authors to be accepted by publishers in the first month of submission. But life's not always like that.

Don't think that agents themselves don't get upset when receiving rejections from publishers. Obviously agents are one removed from the hurt – I didn't actually write the novel – but if I believe in an author's work (and I shouldn't be representing that author if I don't) then it's a blow to see it rejected. It's also a blow to my professional pride (if I know my job, liking a novel should mean I can sell it), and it's then painful to have to deliver the bad news to a client I respect.

Persevere

I write when I'm inspired, and I see to it that I'm inspired at 9 o'clock every morning – Peter de Vries

One particular memory often keeps me hopeful when I'm finding it tough going selling a book. More than fifteen years ago I was trying to sell the first novel by a short story writer I had represented for some time. She had a very unusual storyline, I absolutely loved it, and her writing was superb. But time after time editors rejected it with what the trade calls 'rave rejections'. They praised the novel, but didn't offer to publish it. Letters would arrive which would end with, 'But I just don't know how we would be able to sell it.'

For two and a half years I submitted that manuscript, doggedly aiming it at one fiction editor after another. Every time an editor moved companies, they'd find this manuscript on their desk. I was hoping that the well-known wish to buy something as soon as an editor changed jobs would work the magic for a manuscript that several editors had praised highly. But no. Eventually the author and I put it away for about eighteen months while she carried on writing her very successful short stories for magazines.

We started to talk about it seriously again, four years after I'd first started submitting it. We both felt very strongly that it was a novel that would work one day. We talked about changes to plot and character, and she reworked the outline. Success! The first submission I made after that particular reworking resulted in a modest offer from Michael Joseph, from an editor who had just joined them. Michael Joseph had rejected it twice before, via different editors, and in fact the managing director remembered it from a previous submission and gave the new editor permission to bid for it because it had been so much improved. The fact that the managing director had read it herself, and had remembered it clearly after a considerable lapse of time, says something for the power of the storytelling.

The novel was *Lady of Hay* and the author Barbara Erskine. It was a success as soon as it was published. Michael Joseph's rights department auctioned the paperback rights and Sphere's six-figure advance set a record, at the time, for the highest sum paid by a paperback house for reprint rights to a first book by a British novelist. And it has been in print ever since. A couple of years ago, the eight-year paperback license from Michael Joseph to Sphere ran out (see chapter 13 for an explanation of this) and Michael Joseph auctioned it again. Sphere, now called Warner Books, bid again, as did HarperCollins, Barbara's current publisher.

Funnily enough, the managing director of Warner Books at this time, Philippa Harrison, was the managing director of Michael Joseph all those years ago, when she first allowed a new editor to purchase *Lady of Hay*. HarperCollins won the auction, gaining paperback rights to a novel that was then eleven years old, and the new advance was twelve times what Michael Joseph had paid for full volume rights originally! That track record, and the seventeen translation rights deals that we licensed for this 700-page novel, makes me feel that the four years of hard slog to sell it were more than worth it. And the experience makes me even more tenacious when I hit setbacks with my novel submissions.

But why didn't I find a publisher sooner? Two main reasons, I think, each as important as the other. There is no doubt that it was much improved by the changes Barbara made to the plotline just before we submitted it to Michael Joseph. And it was also genuinely ahead of its time when we began with it. By the time it was published it was hailed as being the first of a new genre, 'the time slip novel'. It is a novel in which several key characters seem to have lived before, and the central character passes (uncomfortably, and not always willingly) from the present to the past and back again. It's a novel that tells two stories, woven together, one contemporary and one historical. During the time I was submitting it, publishers really didn't think that readers wanted this blend of romance and fantasy; they were nervous of the market's reaction. It was clever of Michael Joseph to have bought it when they did: readers were more than ready for it when it was finally published. It has now sold millions of copies around the world, is in print in many languages, and has spawned many imitators.

Another example of this was Carol Shields' marvellous fiction. For several years I offered book after book to every editor I knew at British publishing houses. Finally, Fourth Estate took a little gamble and offered me a small advance for her fifth book. They now publish everything she writes, have bought all the early volumes, and launched their own paperback list with her Booker Prize shortlisted novel *The Stone Diaries*. Editor after editor told me how much they loved the novels but couldn't think how to sell them. Hugely, is the way that Fourth Estate sells them all! Of course, by the time Carol was on the shortlist for the Booker Prize, many editors had convinced themselves that they had loved her books all along. I did indulge in a few 'I told you so' conversations when editor after editor called to tell me what long-term fans they were of her fiction.

If you are sure of your talent, rejection should only make you more determined to succeed. A few years ago I received a letter from an author who was upset that I had not offered to represent him. He wrote:

> I must express my disappointment not so much that you have rejected my work but in the way that you couched your reply. Merely to write that you don't 'feel that strongly' about it doesn't exactly help me. I am a young author who has recently completed my first novel. I wish to have it published and sought your professional help in accomplishing this. Such as constructive criticism; informing me of what the market is looking for. Not necessarily in copious detail but at least giving me a clue.

Sadly I had to reply that I just couldn't prepare editorial criticisms for every author I turned down, and that I felt that not feeling strongly toward a plot and the author's characters was indeed a sufficiently good reason not to take him on as a client.

Don't let rejection make you bitter, for then those who rejected your work will have taken away some of your pleasure in the creation of your novel.

3   Submission to an agent

If you want to 'get in touch with your feelings' fine, talk to your-self. We all do. But if you want to communicate with another thinking human being, get in touch with your thoughts. Put them in order, give them a purpose, use them to persuade, to instruct, to discover, to seduce. The secret way to do this is to write it down, and then cut out the confusing parts – William Safire

Be regular and orderly in your life, so that you may be violent and original in your work – Flaubert

Presentation

Obviously, present your material well. Don't underestimate the value of this. Sending out poorly-printed documents that cause eye strain, curled-up pages or typescripts that have obviously been through many submissions and suffered for it, means that when an agent is choosing which manuscript to pick up next, yours may not be the one that looks most attractive.

Basic skills are not enough. Learn the tools of your trade properly: it is a trade and it requires a serious apprenticeship. With so many people acquiring computer skills, your submission will compare unfa-vourably if you are still using a typewriter, or if you haven't bothered to read your manuscript through to check for typing and grammatical errors. Beware of using a computer's spell checking tool too slavishly. An author I know told me that when checking a document this way the computer stopped on the word 'ful*film*ment'. This was *actually* a mistyping for the word 'ful*fil*ment'. The computer, though, suggested substituting 'ful*movie*ment'. Machines don't think, people should.

Publisher or agent first?

Before deciding on a submission to an agency, consider the following. If you are writing on a specialized non-fiction subject and you can identify likely publishers easily, it's quite sensible to go direct to them. If you're writing poetry, it's quite easy to identify those few publishers that publish poetry and it's extremely unusual to find agents who represent poetry, so again it's sensible to submit direct to publishers.

If you are writing in specialized categories of fiction where it's necessary to conform to fairly strict publisher-given guidelines, such as Mills & Boon romances or the erotic novels published by Virgin and some others, then again you might well choose to submit directly to the publisher. The publishers of these kinds of series are not only very specific about what they want (storylines, length etc.) but tend to be relatively inflexible in the terms they offer authors. They often insist on sticking to their own standard deals, which usually require the author to surrender world rights in all languages to them. This can mean that there would be little leeway for an agent to negotiate and improve on a deal offered by them.

If you are writing general commercial fiction of the kind published by dozens of publishing companies, I would advise you to try agents first. Few general fiction publishers will read unsolicited manuscripts. Of those that do, some shy away from taking on manuscripts that need editorial work. Quite a lot of editorial work is done on first novels by agents these days, and in my experience agents tend to answer their unsolicited submissions rather faster than most publishers do.

When to offer

The obvious answer is to offer your material when it's ready. But how can you tell when the material stands the best chance of pleasing an agent? Should you offer a synopsis and sample chapters? Should you write the whole of the first draft – or revise and rewrite until you can't face it any more?

It's very difficult to make a proper assessment of this when you are so close to your own material. I would suggest the following:

1. Improve your material until, in your judgement, it's as good as you can make it (see chapter 2)

2. Research the potential agents as thoroughly as you can (see chapters 5 and 6)

3. Then seek to manipulate your potential agent as best you can by making a professional presentation and approach (this chapter!)

Improving your material

There are many obvious ways to improve your material. As I have already suggested, you can join a writers' group, or go to evening classes on creative writing, or approach organizations that will appraise your material, such as the Romantic Novelists' Association. They have an admirable scheme that is helpful to many romance writers, whereby experienced editors will critique manuscripts. There are also a growing number of editorial organizations that will provide you with editorial criticism for a fee. In addition, there are 'book doctors' you can hire to provide reports and detailed guidelines for revision, although you do have to check their credentials quite carefully. Not all of the editors and book doctors are qualified. They may not be at all unscrupulous, but people do make money out of authors whose judgement may not be at its most critical when they are paying for value judgements on their own creative work.

Before you enter into an agreement with anyone you are intending to pay for editorial work, I would advise checking them out as thoroughly as you can. Ask them for the names of published authors whose books they have worked on. Ask them if they are prepared to let you talk to an author they have edited. Write to The Society of Authors to ask if they have any information on the work of the person you are considering using. Make sure that you have a clear-cut agreement with the editor as to how much work they will do: how many drafts they will edit, how detailed the editorial notes will be, and how long the editorial report will take to prepare once you have delivered your manuscript.

No reputable agent should ever charge you for editorial work. An agent's function is to send cheques to their clients, not the other way around! If an agent asks you to pay for their editing, you should resist. Point out that the Association of Authors' Agents outlaws this practice and that the agent's commission on the eventual sale should be sufficient recompense for work on the manuscript. If the agent tries to make you pay, it suggests they don't really think they will be able to sell the book profitably and are simply trying to make money out of you without offering a proper agent's service.

There are dozens of good books (and just as many – if not more – bad books) on how to write and how to improve your writing. Two of the best for commercial fiction are *How to Write a Damn Good Novel* by James Frey (Papermac, but sadly now out of print) and *Writing the Blockbuster Novel* by Albert Zuckerman (Little, Brown). The best books to consult for a thorough grounding in grammar are

Eric Partridge's *Usage and Abusage: A Guide to Good English* (Hamish Hamilton) and H. W. Fowler's *A Dictionary of Modern English Usage* (Oxford University Press). Perhaps rather more accessible and easier to digest is Michael Legat's *The Nuts and Bolts of Writing* (Robert Hale), written, he says, after 'a cry of mixed irritation and despair' from his publisher, who was bemoaning the low standard of spelling, punctuation, grammar and presentation in manuscripts he was offered.

The key to getting the best from any of these methods is your own ability to encourage – and take – editorial criticism (see chapter 2). The best advice in the world is useless if you reject it, or feel offended by it. Don't react emotionally and negatively to criticism, even if you disagree with it. The most sensible and professional authors see themselves as a member of a team that has one common goal: the successful marketing of the author's career. The writer is the name spearheading the team, but others can contribute and enhance the value of the 'brand', to borrow a phrase from the advertising world. Agents and editors who offer constructive criticism – criticism that comes from someone already on your side, whose only aim is to improve the book – will be welcomed by smart writers who realize that they will be the principal beneficiary. After all, very few books reach the shops without some – and often very extensive – editing. I firmly believe that the more pairs of eyes that scrutinize material before publication, the better that novel or story will read.

Researching agents

If you know any writers, ask for recommendations. If you belong to a writers' group ask others in the group. Go to talks given by authors in libraries, bookshops etc. Ask booksellers and librarians for recommendations. Writers often mention their agent's name in the acknowledgements of their novels, but before sending off your material, telephone the agency to check the agent still works there.

Call literary agencies and describe briefly the area that your novel falls into: the receptionist will probably be able to tell you if it is likely that they have an agent who would be interested. Read the trade press for news of deals recently finalized by agents. These will all give you information about what areas an agency works with.

Meetings organized by The Writers' Guild, The Society of Authors and the various genre associations are good places to pick up recommendations. And they often have speakers who are agents too: stick around after the talk so that you can meet the speaker.

Professional presentations

I get very irritated when first-time novelists send me only a synopsis for the novel they plan to write. Without a few chapters, I cannot possibly form an opinion as to whether they can actually write. I also dislike receiving sample chapters without a storyline. I can't judge whether a novel sets up the characters and the plot well if I don't know what the writer's intentions are for the plot. I also hate receiving complete novels as an initial submission: neither my staff nor I can afford to read entire manuscripts speculatively, nor do we have room for them. And please do remember to send return postage. If we had to pay postage on the manuscripts we return to authors we cannot represent it would cost us many thousands of pounds annually.

This tells you two things: what agents don't want, and that I can be pretty short-tempered.

What agents and publishers do want is a package that enables them to judge content and style as quickly as possible. Then, if they like it, they will ask for the full manuscript. I believe that an ideal submission package consists of:

1. A brief blurb (one or two paragraphs)
2. Biographies of your main characters (perhaps two or three paragraphs per character)
3. A synopsis of the whole novel (say four to ten pages)
4. The first two or three chapters
5. An author biography (one page)

The blurb whets my appetite. The biographies introduce the people I am going to care about. The storyline tells me what is going to happen to them. The chapters show me if the writer has the talent to make it work. The author biography is because I like to know a little about the people I may choose to work with, and if there is anything about them and their life that makes them saleable or interesting. An interesting or relevant life is helpful, but a quiet life does not count against you if your material is good.

People read fiction in order to live vicariously. Readers wish to relate to characters and situations that they might not come into contact with in their own life. Whether consciously or subconsciously, they wish to see themselves in the dramas they read about. So it follows that the preliminary package you submit to an agent or a publisher must convey that you can achieve this for your reader: it must show that you can create credible characters, who inhabit a world we can believe in and wish to share.

I think of the synopsis and chapters as being two sides of a graph. Together they will demonstrate the qualities of content and style that the writer is able to bring to the book. One without the other isn't sufficient.

Blurb

Here you must sell it, not tell it. Imagine it as the text for the back of the paperback cover, without the hyperbole of which copywriters are so fond. This is not the place to cover every twist of the plot, nor should you make extravagant claims or compare your writing favourably to a range of bestselling novelists. Simply produce one or two paragraphs that indicate the genre, the period and the world you are creating, in a way that will persuade a reader to open it now and know more. Your blurb should set up expectations about the plot, but it shouldn't tease as much as a paperback publisher's blurb: yours will be read by professionals keen to know how you resolve your plot.

Character biographies

These should contain the key personal traits and characteristics and background details that will dictate the behaviour of your main characters. The biographical notes should not contain parts of the plot: save that for the synopsis. But past events that take place before the action of the novel begins can be touched on here if it is important for us to know them, and if they are important in forming the character of your players.

If, for instance, you have a character who will show extreme mistrust in a relationship, then it is valid for us to know that they may have been betrayed by a lover some time in the past. It may not be part of the current plot, but is an incident that has produced a character trait.

Tell us briefly in their biographies what they look like and how old they are at the start of the novel, their relationship to one another, their position in society, if they have a career etc. This is the place to give a thumbnail sketch so that the reader can picture them not only physically, but also psychologically. Putting the essential biographical details of your characters in this separate part of your submission document enables you to keep your synopsis – the storyline – uncluttered. If you have already written twenty-page biographies for your characters, and/or long monologues (perhaps to find the voice of your characters), keep these to yourself for now. Once you have an agent or a publisher these may become useful. Detailed character research always pays off in the long run for the writer, but doesn't have to be shown to the agent or editor when you are first submitting your material.

Synopsis

Unlike the blurb, which should sell it, not tell it, a synopsis *must* tell it.

A synopsis should provide answers to the following key questions:

1. *Whose story is it?*
   In other words, is it clear who your central character is? A weak central character, or no obvious central character, spells disaster in commercial fiction.

2. *What do they want, and what stops them from getting it?*
   Do we know what the central character is setting out to achieve, and what they are up against while they try?

3. *How do they get it?*
   Is the plot compelling and page turning?

The synopsis not only informs the reader of the journey you plan for them and for your characters, it also performs another equally important function: it helps you organize your thoughts and shows that you can think ahead. Keeping all the plot points separate from the character biographies makes it easier for you and the person reading it to analyse your storyline. Because you don't have to describe each character as you introduce them into the plot (this has already been done in the biographies), you can describe the action in a simple straightforward way. This is very helpful for agents and editors analysing pace and tension.

Lay out the plot in the order you will write it. If you are using flashbacks, describe them in the position where they will occur. For example, I once received a synopsis that began in 1950, describing the upbringing of a post-war baby. But the opening chapter of the novel took place in 1975. The character was a young married woman, and it was only in the second chapter that we were told, in a flashback, about the incident that happened when she was a child in 1950. The synopsis must mirror the plot sequence in the novel.

Much commercial fiction is plot-based and writers who do not plan a plot in advance may be storing up future problems for themselves. A truly satisfying ending for the reader can only be achieved when the writer knows at the beginning what they are aiming for – not to plant heavy signals ahead of the action, but to seed, early in the novel, pieces of story that will deliver their pay-off much later.

The synopsis is thus not only your selling document, but also your map for writing the novel. It is a skeleton whose covering is built up, layer by layer, as you write the chapters. A surprising number of writers are either nervous of writing a synopsis or feel that an agent asks for one simply to read less than the whole manuscript. But I have met so many writers over the years who say that having a synopsis actually makes it so much easier for them to write the novel (as well as the help it affords agents and publishers' editors in assessing the work). So I'm going to stick to my guns and say that I won't read chapters from a potential new client unless I also have a synopsis.

So many potential plot problems can be ironed out while working on a synopsis that it's easy to demonstrate how much rewriting time they save later. Occasionally a prospective new client who has already completed an entire novel will approach our agency. I still ask for a synopsis because initially I can't commit myself to the many hours of speculative reading that a whole manuscript would entail. Having a synopsis makes it much easier to analyse the use of characters in the plot, the pacing and the tension, because these things are clearer in a ten-page synopsis than in a 500- (or 1,000-) page manuscript.

Sometimes, having completed the whole novel, the author declines to produce a synopsis, or finds that another agent will read their manuscript without one. At that point I wish them well and send the material back. Life is too short for me to spend dozens of hours reading material I may not like enough, by a writer who doesn't want to take what I think is tried and tested advice. Writers who make their long-term decisions about taking on an agent, based on the short-term wish not to write a synopsis, are perhaps not thinking as clearly as they ought about their representation.

Some writers worry that a synopsis written before the manuscript is completed will tie them down to a plot structure they may wish to change later. There is no need to feel that you can't revise your storyline when you come to the actual writing. No agent or publisher will object to you making alterations later if they improve the novel. Of course, if you have accepted representation by an agent, or a contract from a publisher, based on a synopsis that promised a pacy, plot-based thriller set against today's politics in South Africa, and the delivered manuscript is a character-based relationship novel set against the backdrop of village life in southern France, you are going to have to explain yourself to puzzled publishing folk. A publisher who has contracted for a novel that, when delivered, proves to be substantially different, may have the right to reject it.

I do have sympathy for those writers who genuinely feel that, having written a synopsis, they no longer have the same feeling of excitement about writing the novel itself.

I used to be very unsympathetic to writers who said they couldn't write synopses, thinking they were just not wanting to do the work, until my client Kay Mitchell wrote a more detailed synopsis than she usually did for one of her detective novels. (Her editor wanted to be able to brief the designer for the jacket before the novel was finished.) Kay then hit a terrible writer's block that took her some time to work through. She felt so constrained by her outline that her creative writing dried up for months. It was only much later, when we were chatting over lunch, that I came to understand the depth of the problem she had faced. Kay was writing two series of detective novels, one under her own name featuring Chief Inspector Morrissey, and another under the pseudonym of Sarah Lacey featuring amateur detective Leah Hunter.

I'd always been amazed that Kay could work on both at once. When we were talking about the problems she had faced after producing the detailed synopsis for one of her novels, Kay told me more about her work methods. She keeps two desks, with two different word processors – one for each series – and can write alternate chapters by turning from one desk to the other. She sees the plots in her mind's eye like a series of rooms, opening one from the other, with each room being a chapter. Her characters beckon her from one room into the next, and that's how the storyline evolves. An outline seemed to halt this flow.

I was astonished: I'd never heard of a work method like it. But it worked well (Kay seldom has to do much rewriting or reworking on her novels) and so I was anxious that she shouldn't try to change it. On the basis of 'If it ain't broke, don't fix it' I was keen for Kay to stick to what suited her. She hasn't been asked to write a detailed synopsis since. If I hadn't heard this story from someone I've worked with for a while and whose novels I love, I don't think I would have believed it! But I still believe that for those who can write them and still face writing the novel later, a synopsis is a useful instrument.

Sample chapters

Never send random chapters, or worse, random pages (we do regularly receive packages of each of these!). Make sure all the main characters are introduced in these opening chapters, and that you have introduced the theme and set up the major action, the reason for the plot. If these elements don't all get going in a satisfactory way within your first few chapters, then you should ask yourself why anyone should keep reading. Go back and revise once more until everything is properly set up at the beginning. In commercial fiction in particular, there is no excuse for dull or slow opening chapters.

I did once receive a submission where the covering letter from the author said that he was sending the first chapter and then two from further into the novel '. . . because the first chapters aren't the best'. Well all I can say is that they should have been. If they were not, he should have reworked them until they became so. There is so much competition in the commercial fiction market place that only the strong win – and strong means offering characters who involve readers in the story right away, exciting plots that make readers want to turn the pages and a world that enthrals.

I can think of no better way to illustrate this point, than these opening sentences from novels by authors whose careers have begun with Blake Friedmann:

> Lying back on their big double bed, Allegra Boyd watched her husband Matt remove his socks with one hand, the other still firmly holding on to the sports' section, and drop them to the carpet where they would remain as if rendered magically invisible by some male chauvinist genie until she or Mrs O'Shock, their Irish cleaning lady, picked them up.
> – *Scenes from the Sex War* by Maeve Haran (Penguin)

> I had lost half a million dollars in slightly less than half an hour and the coffee machine didn't work. This was turning into a bad day. Half a million dollars is a lot of money, and I need a cup of coffee badly. – *Free to Trade* by Michael Ridpath (Arrow)

> Orgasm. It was the most perfect word. Eliciting all it could, easing meaning out of every syllable O . . . a large perfect Oh, the softly parted lips, the promise of the never-ending union. Gas . . . gasp, a shuddering intake of breath, a sensation to savour and the arching curving back as you sink into the mmmmm . . . the bliss. Yes, it was a great word, Amy thought.
> – *Love: A User's Guide* by Clare Naylor (Coronet)

Author biography

I don't want to know your school examination results, but I do want to know anything relevant about you that will persuade a publisher to buy your book. If you are seventeen or seventy-five, say so: both extremes can be selling points. Clare Naylor was only twenty-four and assistant to an editor I knew and worked with when she sent her manuscript to me. Both facts intrigued me. If you are a trader of stocks and shares and have used the financial world as a background for your thriller, tell me, as Michael Ridpath did in his submission letter when he sent me *Free to Trade*. It will make me more likely to believe that your novel's background will be authentic.

If you have reached a level of prominence in your career, say so, no matter that it may not be writing-related. It will establish a level of professionalism that will create a favourable impression in the publishing trade, and achievement in any field augers well for your other ventures. Maeve Haran was a very successful television producer who had just had her second daughter and was dying to be able to stay home with her, rather than go back to the studios, when she wrote her first book.

If you are a single mother with triplets, writing every night while the children sleep, say so. It suggests tenacity and a passion for writing. Many writers send covering letters that describe their novels as 'light airport reads' or 'a romance for the beach'. While that may have been sufficient to allow the novel to be taken seriously a few years ago, the competition to be published now is so fierce that agents and publishers look for evidence of more commitment to their work from new writers. It's better to describe the warmth and emotional intensity of the characters, the credibility and excitement of the plot. It's vital, too, that the preliminary material you send lives up to your promises.

I, and most agents I know, want to represent writers who are planning a career in writing. I never take on one-off fiction. The effort of placing a first novel is often so great, that both agent and publisher – and author – will be looking for more of a return than just a one-book contract. These days, it's quite common for a publisher to offer a two-book contract when first signing up a writer. This is evidence of enthusiasm and excitement for the writer's work, but it's also practical: the publisher wants to know that the money invested in marketing the first book can be amortized over the selling of another. Since they want to be sure that the writer isn't a one-off, they want to protect their investment in the launch of the first one by knowing they have the second under contract. It's not necessary to have written a second book, or even to have started a second, before approaching an agent or publisher. But they will probably ask you if you are planning a second and how long you think it will take you to complete it, so be prepared.

How to offer

Your submission letter must sell you and your work. Take great care when composing it. It has to speak for you to a professional who has little time to spare. Don't make extravagant claims: it prejudices people against you. Don't write ten-page letters: life is too short, and certainly mornings in the office are too short to read long and wordy letters with unsolicited manuscripts. Unless you are really sure that you are funny, don't write jokey letters.

By the time I've read something like these quotes which follow, for the tenth time in a week, I'm ready to scream:

> I know you receive many useless manuscripts but this really is different.

This simply invites the reader to think the book will be as bad as all the others that come in with letters with extravagant claims.

> It will appeal to a huge international audience because the action takes place in New York, London, Madrid, Nairobi and Tokyo.

You've completely misunderstood what constitutes international appeal: having your hero spend most of the novel on planes or trains doesn't add up to a page-turning plot.

> It is ideal for a Hollywood film.

It will be hard enough to sell it to a publisher, let alone to a film company, especially a film company in Hollywood.

> You'll be turning down a fortune if you let it get away!

This shows too much arrogance at the beginning of the submission process.

> I will telephone you in three days to arrange a meeting to discuss my novel.

Not with me, you won't! Anyone with so little respect for the work levels within most agencies, and showing such pushiness, will rarely receive more than a form rejection letter from our agency.

> I'm faxing [or e-mailing] you my manuscript as postage costs are so high.

You don't want to spend your money on mailing costs, but you expect me to spend my company's money printing out your manuscript!

Don't start your letter by telling the recipient what is wrong with modern fiction. Don't write a three-line letter asking for a meeting tomorrow so that you can bring in your manuscript. Don't offer a 'fictional manuscript' (we do have prejudices against overwriting and ungrammatical use of the language).

I would also advise against including copies of other publishers' or agents' rejection letters, even if they do contain phrases of praise. All too often an unsophisticated author is simply sending out copies of a company's standard rejection slip without being aware of it, but another publisher or agent will spot it straight away. It will only alert the reader to the fact that you have been to – and been rejected by – others already.

Here's a direct quote from a letter received by our agency:

> X [a well-known publisher] turned this down. I think the sentimental style of writing was too much for them. However, it is the way I write, am I supposed to change my style to suit the market? I hope not as I might as well stop now. I felt they missed the point. The story moves very slowly, and has to be read in its entirety in order to appreciate its subtlety.

I can't be alone in thinking that this demonstrates unrealistic expectations of one writer wishing to change the market to suit themselves.

Saying that your mother and aunt have read the material and thought it wonderful only tells me that you have a polite family, unless your mother is chief executive of a publishing company and your aunt runs a bookshop. It's important not to be overly modest, but it's just as important not to be unnecessarily pushy. Be as critical of your autobiographical sketch as you are of your chapters: read it and try to imagine the character being described. Don't fictionalize it, but do look for ways of presenting the facts as positively as possible.

My postbag produces evidence of all of the above points regularly. Don't do any of them. They will mark you out as an unworldly amateur, unlikely to appeal to agents.

I favour a short and informative covering letter, preferably no longer than one side of a page. Our agency, which is not one of the largest by any means, receives between a dozen and twenty-five unsolicited submissions a day, many more if the agency has received recent publicity. Imagine how pleasing it is to read a letter that imparts information without padding, gimmicks, too much boasting or whines about other writers! A submission letter is not only selling your work, but yourself too.

Personal promotion is a vital part of the publication package these days, and your own profile, and the way you put yourself across, is very important indeed. Publishing people look for evidence of professionalism in their new authors: dedication to writing, to producing a book a year or at the most every eighteen months, the ability to take criticism, the ability to learn how publishing works and how you can help the publishing process. Most of all, publishers look for authors who are willing and able to put themselves over to their audience (whether it is the publisher's own staff, booksellers or readers) in an attractive and helpful way. So starting that process by thinking carefully about how you put your personality over to your potential agent or editor right at the beginning is obviously time well spent.

I sometimes receive letters from would-be clients that tell me very little about why they are writing, who they are, what their expectations or hopes are for their writing. A six-line letter saying you are enclosing early chapters from your novel and you hope the agent will like it is tantamount to putting your book on sale in a bookshop without a cover, title or author's name. You have to set up some expectations in your audience (as true for your story as your submission letter) or there is no motivation for the agent to read on. If you have written a medical novel and you were once a nurse, say so. If you are writing a financial thriller and you are a bond trader, say so. If you have won a writing competition (even years ago), say so. Every piece of information that suggests you know your subject and have been successful in the past should be included.

Many writers like to include a stamped self-addressed postcard for the agency to acknowledge receipt of their material. This way you do know it has arrived safely at the agency, although in our experience the mails are actually extremely reliable.

I've not mentioned the more obvious dos and don'ts of submitting material: it goes without saying that you should keep a copy of what you send out, and that you *should*:

— have a title page

— put your name and address on the manuscript

— cross-reference your real name and any pseudonym on both letter and manuscript (These points are all essential because material must be easily identified within the agency or publishing house. We all receive so many submissions that anything that helps prevent muddle is useful.)

— number all pages sequentially rather than starting each chapter with page 1 (Editors can tell the approximate length of a manuscript by the number of pages it contains. Also, if the manuscript was accidentally dropped, all those page 1's from each chapter would make it very difficult to put it back together again correctly.)

— double space your typescript with at least a 1 inch margin on all four sides (There must be room for editing marks. It's terribly frustrating for an editor to run out of room for comments on the text.)

— make sure your typescript is legible: no faint or tiny type (Editors and agents have such heavy reading schedules that it's not surprising they are loathe to read typescripts that are hard on the eyes.)

— punctuate your dialogue correctly

— be consistent in spelling, headings, paragraph indentation, capitals etc.

— read it through when finished for spelling and typing mistakes (These last three points demonstrate that you have a professional approach to your writing. If you can't be bothered to get these details right, why should an editor or agent spend time teaching you?)

— *type* your script (Too obvious to mention, you might think, but I receive handwritten manuscripts occasionally. Most editors and agents refuse to read handwritten pages: it's just too much hard work.)

— enclose return postage and an envelope big enough to take your material

And you *shouldn't*:

— use staples, binders, paper clips, string or ribbons. Just two rubber bands – one north/south, one east/west (My staff has ripped their fingers on staples. Trying to read a manuscript that has every chapter separately paper-clipped is very irritating. Binding often is so tight that you can't read the whole line length. And I like to read single chapters at a time in cabs on the way to lunch, in the bath, even on the exercise bike at my gym!)

— send miles of connected zigzag computer paper (The most irritating of all! Don't make it hard for an editor to read your material: the odds against acceptance of your novel are already high enough.)

— send manuscripts with traps built in to test if all the pages have been turned over, such as stapled-together pages, or bookmarks in certain places (This simply shows paranoia and a mistrust of the professionals to whom you have submitted your novel. If I am feeling particularly stressed when I find these little traps they will often make me reject the material straight away.)

— send manuscripts that smell (As a life-long non-smoker I have sometimes reeled at the smoky smell given off as a manuscript is unwrapped from its envelope. I could never take a cigarette-smelling manuscript to my home to read, I would find it too unpleasant.)

— pack your manuscript so securely that unwrapping it is akin to breaking into Fort Knox (See the point above about staples etc. Physically injuring your potential reader is not a good way to make friends.)

Look at your letter and manuscript with a critical eye. The better it looks the better the chance it will stand. It is human nature to feel more kindly towards a clean, clear, well-typed manuscript with page numbers, than one which is on flimsy, curling, smelly paper, punched with holes, cluttered with rusting paper clips and tied in a faded pink ribbon, which shows evidence of having been all around town before it reached me.

Another give-away is failing to check for previous submission letters to other agents or editors that might be tucked into the manuscript. Editors often use the submission letter as a bookmark and they can be left there. Check through a returned manuscript before resubmitting it.

Years ago, I was given as a present a slim and ancient volume entitled *How to Write Saleable Fiction* by George G. Magnus (which carried a copyright line for 'The Cambridge Literary Agency' but no year of publication). It finished with this advice: 'No MS. should be sent out in a travel-worn condition, for the Editor is not the least observant person in the world; and when a MS. shows signs of the sloven [sic] outside, he knows what to expect inside.' Quite.

How long to wait?

How long should you wait for a response? Certainly it's not practical to expect an answer in less than two weeks: the quantity of submissions can mean that it takes us four to six weeks to respond to the initial material.

By all means *politely* chase the agency a few weeks after making your submission. It's extraordinary how rude some authors can be on the telephone. The ruder a caller, the faster I reject material. I suppose the caller is getting a result, but if they want to be taken on by the agency, it's perhaps not the result they were aiming for!

After you've received an initial favourable response from an agent who has read your synopsis and sample chapters, the next round may take longer. Reading a full manuscript obviously takes much longer than reading a short sample and, because of the detailed analysis and number of readers needed, as you get closer to acceptance by an agent, each new stage may well take longer than the previous one. Patience will be required.

Remember that an agent is not working *only* for love of writing: we are running a business. We are not obliged to provide critiques of work by writers who are not our clients. We can't possibly read all the way through all the manuscripts that arrive – unasked for – and give detailed constructive reasons as to why we can't represent them. I will always, personally, look at every book submission that comes to our agency. But no agent could ever offer specific advice on every one.

I know that it must seem unfair that your work, which you feel is as good as much of that published, is rejected by agents. Luck and timing are involved – bad and good – and I would advise tenacity. Keep at it. Resubmit work that has been revised, write again if you feel the market has changed in your favour, or if you discover that staff have changed, or if you know that the agent has lost a client who writes in a similar field to yourself. Faint hearts do not win fair ladies – or agents!

You shouldn't expect a meeting with an agent before they have read some of your work. After all, it's your words that we must make a judgement on, not your pretty blue eyes.

4   How to get an agent

First of all, you must have an agent, and in order to get a good one, you must have sold a considerable amount of material. And in order to sell a considerable amount of material, you must have an agent. Well, you get the idea – Steve McNeil

In a perfect world authors don't need agents – and that's why they do – Jonathan Lloyd, Managing Director, Curtis Brown

Do you need one?

When you're a bestselling author you'll be fighting off approaches from agents, although you might be able to manage without one. When you're starting out, and you most need one, even getting to meet one can sometimes be an insurmountable obstacle. True or false?

Well, a bit of both.

Established authors are often approached by agents, even if they are already agented. The Association of Authors' Agents has a strict Code of Practice (see Appendix) governing the behaviour of agents towards clients of other agencies, but even so, some agents do try to poach clients from others. I have mixed feelings about this. I would never approach agented authors myself, but banning such approaches severely curtails an author's right of choice, which I believe they must have. I take the pragmatic approach and try to maintain strong relationships with my clients so that they don't want to leave me for another agent.

It's not true that an established author doesn't need an agent. Well, I would say that, wouldn't I? Yes, but I do believe it. A successful author will have several books published or on offer in many markets and languages, in multiple formats, editions and versions, and they all need monitoring. No author alone can expect to acquire the amount of information available through a good agent and that agent's network of co-operating agents worldwide, or the amount of experience an agent accumulates spending a whole working life negotiating deals on behalf of many authors.

Why should a writer try to learn every skill and fact about an industry that an agent has already spent their career amassing? It would be far better to form a partnership with an agent so that you can write, and they can deal.

Unpublished writers, or newly published but not – yet – successful writers, often find it incredibly difficult to obtain agency representation, even once they have a publisher. Do they really need an agent? Probably, but not necessarily. Much of the rest of this book will help you cope without one, whether you have decided to do without one, or find it difficult to acquire one.

Writers in some fields will always find it hard to get an agent. Very few agents find it worthwhile to represent writers of educational books, or poetry, for example. These areas either don't bring in much income, or don't have a wide variety of publishers competing for the same books, and seldom provide much room for manoeuvre in the deals themselves. However, the international fiction market is so competitive that writers must try to stack odds in their favour whenever they can. Having an agent means you have a professional on your side, whose role is to put all their professional expertise and knowledge of the trade at your disposal. I'm an agent, so you would expect me to take this view, but I was also a publisher for many years and I believed it then too. If a writer has an agent, a publisher knows the writer has passed through at least one level of screening, and that another professional in the trade, the agent, believes the author has a future. The agent's reputation says something about the author's abilities, too. As a publisher, I saw how good agents improved the profile of their clients within the publishing house, how they pushed for promotion budgets, argued for good publication dates and fought for their clients' views on covers.

If you are an author with a publisher but no agent, then your editor is your closest ally. Most editors fiercely champion the cause of the titles they acquire. But remember: no matter how much they love your work, they work for – and get paid by – the publishing house. Making profits for the company – not you – must be their main priority. They change jobs, or move on to other jobs within the company, which can mean passing you over to another editor. Sometimes this can happen smoothly, other times it can become a nightmare.

An agent work for – and get paid by – their client, the writer. And they get paid only if and when that writer gets paid. I find it concentrates the mind wonderfully!

Does an agent need you?

An agency is a business that, like any other, must trade at a profit to survive. The commission an agent charges a client must pay for the direct work they do for that client (the career planning, the editorial work, the submissions, and the negotiations), plus contribute to the fixed and variable costs of the business. These include rent, rates, staff salaries, attendance at book, film and television trade fairs, entertaining publishers, editors and producers, foreign sales trips, and mailing of manuscripts, proofs, books and publicity material around the world. The commission must also cover that commission which the agent pays to their co-operating sub-agents in the overseas markets. (A fuller list of tasks performed by agents on behalf of their clients will be found later in this chapter under the heading 'What an agent does'.) So when an agent assesses your work and your career, they have to feel confidence in you long-term, as well as admire your work.

Liking the way an author writes is a vital first step, so when I'm looking at a new submission, in addition to assessing the writing, I think about the following:

— *Is this a regular writer? Will there be a career to nurture?* One-off books are less attractive to agents and publishers. It's rare for a first novel to earn enough money to provide a real income for either party, so agents have to think long-term, knowing it will cost more to represent an author at the beginning of their career (when they are usually earning very little) than it will once they are established (when their earnings will be higher).

— *If it is someone with more books to come, are their other ideas in related areas without repeating themselves?* Re-establishing a writer in a different area is as difficult as launching a new career.

— *Is the writer seriously committed to a writing career?* Submitting six totally disconnected projects suggests someone who isn't very committed to any one idea.

— *Does the writer have reasonable expectations of what can be achieved?* A submission letter that claims the book will be an automatic bestseller and should sell quickly to Hollywood with the author insisting on writing the script does not come under the heading of 'reasonable expectations'.

— *Once I've met the writer, do I think I can work with them for several years? Do we get on well enough to survive the inevitable pressures of a difficult career? Do we have the same aims for their career?*

How to get an agent

It's pretty obvious that without authors, an agent would be unemployed. This may sound like a sick joke to those writers who have received dozens of rejection letters from agents. But if you put yourself in the place of the agent you are approaching, you might change the information you provide, or the way you present it.

Once you've decided whom to approach, make a list of the important and interesting facts you will want to tell the agent. Think about how to present yourself and your work, because you may only have a brief telephone conversation with a member of the agent's staff (it is unlikely you will speak to the agent unless you are already an established writer). This brief time span must be put to good use to convince the agent that you have something interesting and marketable that the agent will be able to sell.

Present your ideas and your work with clarity and brevity. Say how much you have already written and how much you have ready to read now, whether it is a chapter and a synopsis or an entire manuscript. Say if you are on the fifth draft or the first. Say why you wrote it and who you think your audience is. How long is it? Give an estimate of the word count.

If you have been published or had an agent before, give details. I always like to know the names of the individual agent or editor. If your experience with them was not successful, be honest and say that you feel it is time to start afresh with another. The agent will discover this, anyway, if you eventually work together. It's so much better for the information to be offered at the beginning. It sets the tone for direct communication and honesty. All information that you give to an agent under these circumstances should be treated as confidential.

If the material you are offering to the agent has already been submitted to publishers, say how many, when and to whom.

If you were recommended to the agent, say by whom. But make sure that the recommendation does come from someone the agent knows, or at least knows of. I'm always surprised by the number of letters that tell me the author has been recommended to me by someone of whom I have not heard. It achieves nothing.

How we assess new material

All unsolicited book submissions to our agency come to me first, after they have been 'logged in'. Receipt of manuscripts used to be recorded manually into lined, bound books: now, of course, it's an entry in a computer file, which makes tracing any particular manuscript (by date, title or author's name) so much faster and more accurate.

I could delegate the first 'tasting' of submissions to others but I've learned through experience that it's best for me to do it myself because I know that there is a maximum quantity of clients our agency can successfully handle. I also know what I like, and what I want for the agency. I am perhaps (or certainly!) more cynical than those who work for me.

I weed out many at this stage. Because we always have a full client list, I am basically looking for reasons to turn submissions down. I only want to consider those that I think are really exciting. I sift through the piles once or twice a week, and the rejects move to a huge pile awaiting answers. An assistant sends out the replies regularly, working through the piles in chronological order, and we aim to respond to most within two or three weeks of receipt by the agency. If an author has not sent a stamped self-addressed envelope for return of their material, we send them a reply but ask for stamps if they want their material returned.

We do use a standard rejection letter because of the sheer quantity that need to be sent out to deal with the submissions we receive.

A maximum of two or three a week might be retained for further reading. Those that reach this stage are allocated to someone else within the agency who will read and report on them for me. At this point, we are usually only reading a synopsis and a few chapters. This reading can take three to six weeks depending on the workload at the time. If the staff member liked the material and writes a good report, I will then read it. If they didn't, it's rejected at this stage with a slightly differently worded, but still standard, rejection letter.

If it is passed to me for reading, it is at this stage it is really likely to get held up. I always have a huge reading pile (as I'm writing this chapter I am forcing myself not to look at the pile in my study which stands at well over a metre high). My reading priorities have to be as follows:

1. Delivered manuscripts and part-manuscripts by agency clients who are already commissioned (i.e. contracted) by publishers. My colleagues or I must read (and often edit) these before

they are delivered to the publisher who already owns them, or at the very least, at the same time as the commissioning editor. They are always top priority, and often go through several drafts (and therefore several readings).

2. Speculative work by our published authors: manuscripts, part-manuscripts, sample chapters and synopses. All these may go through multiple drafts too, and often require editing.

3. Speculative work by our unpublished authors. Material as listed in 2, and with the same last sentence, only more so!

All of the above concerns work with material by authors who are already clients of Blake Friedmann. Only after that can I tackle:

4. Unsolicited material from authors who would like to join us. Within that category there is another sub-division: published writers and unpublished writers. Naturally published writers, who have a track record (whether it's good or bad) are easier to assess and they do get looked at ahead of the unpublished writers.

If I like the reader's report and the unsolicited material, we will ask for the rest of the manuscript. The consideration process begins again, bearing in mind that a detailed reading can take longer: a full-length manuscript never takes less than three hours, often as much as twelve or more. Up to this point, all our work (and all the people-hours it entails) is speculative: we have no agreement to represent the author and no right to sell the material yet.

You can see why it can take time. If I see a huge reading pile ahead of me, I will sometimes write to promising unsolicited writers to warn them of the expected length of the delay and will offer to return the material if they don't want to wait. This may happen around the time of a trade fair or other times of the year when any of our staff are away from the office. The reading piles that build up around the time of the Frankfurt Book Fair in October, or summer holidays, or the close-down for Christmas and New Year – and our recent office move – would have to be seen to be believed.

There is a risk, of course, that an unsolicited writer will lose patience and go to an agent who has been able to read their material more quickly. I have sympathy with this and so long as the author tells us they are approaching other agents, there will obviously be no hard feelings. But if the author knows that several of us in the agency have spent many hours reading their material, I do feel they owe us the consideration of waiting for our reply before approaching other agencies. I do not like our staff spending time on material that is also on submission to other agencies. It's a waste of our time that could be better spent on our existing clients. I feel that an author must be honest when offering material and must make it clear, at the outset, if it is on multiple submission. Then it is up to the agent whether to spend time on it, and to decide how long to work on it and to hold on to it.

Personally, I don't worry too much about competition from other agencies in this regard. Not because it doesn't exist – there are many very effective agencies in competition with us and we watch them carefully – and not because I'm smug (I hope!), but because when it comes to taking on unsolicited, first-time authors, there is a limit as to how many our agency can accommodate. Launching a new writer is very labour intensive and having too many at any one time would drain our resources. We must keep a balance between our established clients who are earning income regularly, and our unpublished authors who have to be launched, who often require intensive reading and editing time, and who are not earning anything, yet. This means that we will often read unsolicited material from a published writer rather faster than the sequence above suggests if I know, from their career to date, that the writer is of interest to us. This is because they are more likely to know several agents and may well be receiving approaches from them too, if it is known they are seeking new agency representation. This may seem unfair to unpublished writers who have to wait longer for a response, but remember, running an agency is a business, not a charity. We must make money for ourselves as well as for our clients or we're no use to authors at all!

I think this is as honest a way of dealing with material we haven't asked for as I can devise, but we are still sometimes castigated by writers for holding on to material too long and thereby spoiling an author's chances of selling it elsewhere, or for returning it too quickly, which makes the author believe we haven't looked at it. Sometimes you just can't win!

If we like all the material we have read, I will then set up a meeting with the writer, often with my partner, Julian Friedmann, who will eventually, with colleagues on his side of the agency, be responsible for selling film and TV rights to the material if we do take on representation for the author. These meetings are rarely less than an hour, often longer. Sometimes we get on well, sometimes we don't. If we do offer to represent the writer we always suggest to them that they should think about their decision after the meeting rather than agreeing on the spot.

I suppose we take on about six or eight new clients a year. Of those, perhaps one to three at most comes from the unsolicited submissions, which gives you an idea of the attrition rate. It also gives you an idea of the enormous amount of work we do (and have to pay for) in return for those one, two or three clients a year from the slush pile, who may or may not sell, once we have taken them on.

We are only one of many agencies. There are dozens of reputable literary agencies, and publishing houses. Perseverance should pay off if you have talent, have done your homework about the market, have revised your material until it is as good as you can make it, and have polished your submission material and letter.

How to find the right agent

If you're an unknown author, your agent's reputation will be the first thing that an editor knows about you. It's therefore a very good idea to research agencies to find out how good their reputation is. How do you go about it?

There are directories that list agents (*Writers' and Artists' Yearbook, The Writers' Handbook, Cassells Directory of Publishing*) but agencies seldom list their specialities, or the areas they are not interested in. This is probably because most agents want to keep their options open. Fashions in reading change and agents have to move with the times and markets. Few directories list the agents' clients. And the directories are just that: they give information but they do not comment about levels of performance. *The Writers' Handbook* does offer more commentary than the other directories, and it lists some of the authors represented by the agencies.

You can call a literary agency and briefly describe your novel: some will tell you immediately if they do not handle certain areas of work. Some may be prepared to recommend agents who specialize in genres such as science fiction, crime or romance. On the whole, people in the writing business tend to be fairly generous with information and contacts. But don't expect them to hand out telephone numbers, contact names or addresses: you must be prepared to do your own research.

The Association of Authors' Agents, while not strictly speaking an information service for the public, do nevertheless have names of agents who specialize in, say, children's books, or science fiction. The officers of the AAA give their time to the organization on a voluntary basis: they are themselves all full-time agents with their own agency work to do. Remember this if you contact them, so as not to take up too much of their (unpaid) time.

The Society of Authors can be extremely helpful to writers looking for agents. They have conducted surveys of agents (the last one in 1998) and through their author members and their own work in the trade have a pretty clear idea of the capabilities and reputation of most of the literary agencies. If you describe your work, the Society may well be able to recommend several agencies.

If you know writers with agents, or you know some publishers, ask them for recommendations. And always ask them who that agent already represents. If you are looking for an agent to represent your romance, you would do well to go to someone who already works in that area, because the agent will already know the editors who buy romance, the magazines who print romance stories and extracts, and the foreign publishers who buy translation rights in the genre.

However tempted you are to sign up with the first agent who offers you representation, be cautious. If at all possible, meet before signing up with an agent, or at the very least talk at some length on the telephone. An author–agent relationship can be a close one, combining business and friendship, loyalty and trust, over a long period of time. I represent some clients who joined me in the 1970s when I first became an agent: I'm very proud of that. Every author has a right to expect their agent to be someone they can get on with, someone they feel can empathize and sympathize with their aims and expectations. And you will be more comfortable in the relationship if you believe the agent will sell you enthusiastically.

A writer friend of mine (not a client, he works in an area that I don't handle) was once complaining gently about his agent and mentioned to me that she was shy. He was astonished when I laughed and suggested his agent was in the wrong job. What good is a shy agent? When part of the job description is enthusiasm and confident selling, shyness is definitely not an asset!

But if you yourself are gentle and not overconfident, you'll want to make sure that your agent isn't brash and overbearing or you'll never get a word in edgeways. A meeting or a conversation is essential to establish a rapport between you.

Other ways to get recommendations to agencies are through writers' groups, staff at a local university, local reviewers, and bookshop staff who will also know the local sales representatives for publishers. Read interviews with writers in the press, read the acknowledgement page in the books of authors you admire, listen to book programmes on the radio and television – they may all mention the names of relevant agents. The main trade reference books can be helpful, also the publishing trade press such as *The Bookseller*, and *Publishing News* in the UK, *Australian Bookseller* in Australia, *Quill And Quire* in Canada, and *Publishers Weekly* in America. There is no equivalent trade publication in South Africa. Some of the trade papers report publishing deals done by agents, which can be helpful in revealing the kind of clients they represent.

Go to book festivals and readings in bookshops, join the societies formed around many genres (Romantic Novelists' Association, Crime Writers' Association). Then call the agencies and say what you are writing and a little about your expectations and ask for the name of the most appropriate agent in that agency. Write in first; don't insist on speaking to that agent right away. Busy agents can seldom be expected to accept 'cold calls', and browbeating the person who answered the telephone is not the way to make friends and influence people at an agency you would like to join.

'Time spent in reconnaisance is seldom wasted'

It is as true when looking for a literary agent as it is in the spy world that coined the phrase! My strongest recommendation by far, when deciding to be represented by an agent, is to take time to find the right one. The commitment that a client and agent make to each other should be long term and should result in a close relationship that is more than just a business relationship. It can be painful to sever ties between client and agent, and writers can find it immensely upsetting to have to change their representation. It is far better to spend more time at the beginning making sure, as much as you can, that you and your potential agent are well suited to each other.

When you do talk to or meet with an agent, ask them to describe their work methods, how they deal with the various subsidiary rights areas and how much of the publishing process they are involved in. Questions might include:

- *General*
- — How many agents work for the agency and where does your agent stand in the hierarchy?
- — What writers do they handle?
- — Are they members of the Association of Authors' Agents? If not, why not?

- *UK deals*
- — If the agent takes you on, will your negotiations in the UK market be handled personally or will they be handed to another staff member? If so, whom? Can you meet that person now?
- — Will your manuscript be sent out on single submission,

multiple submission, or will it be auctioned? What is the reason behind their answer?

— How long are they prepared to go on submitting projects before giving up?

— Do they handle, and solicit commissions for, short stories? (And journalism too, if that's another writing area that interests you.)

- *Editorial input*

— Does the agent expect to be involved in the planning process for your next book? Will they advise you on marketable areas before you start writing?

— Will they read and comment on synopses?

— Will they read, comment on and edit early chapters and whole manuscripts?

— Once you are contracted to a publisher, will the agent still read your material or rely on the publisher's editor for a report?

- *The publishing contract*

— Does the agency use its own contract with most publishers? If not, does it have a specially negotiated agency boilerplate contract with the big publishers?

— What is the agency's stance on royalties on high discount sales?

— Do all the agency contracts contain non-assignment clauses? (If you're wondering about these three points, by the time you've read chapter 9, 'How to Read a Contract', you'll certainly have a view on them!)

- *Marketing, sales and publicity*

— Will the agent make sure that you see the cover design in time to pass comment on it?

— Will they become involved in the publisher's marketing planning? Will they ask for a promotion plan?

— Will they also monitor it and make sure that everything promised is actually carried out?

— Will they talk to your publicist and monitor progress on the publicity front?

— Will they get you regular updates on sales figures in the first few months after publication?

- *American and translation rights*
- — Does the agent intend to offer single territory rights to publishers in each market, or offer world rights in all languages to the first market they sell?
- — Do they get personally involved in selling these rights or does someone else handle that? Who? Do they think they can place your work in other markets?
- — Does the agency have co-operating agents around the world? Ask for a list of the agents and the territories that they cover.
- — What arrangements do they have for handling American rights?
- — Do they attend the Frankfurt Book Fair and other trade fairs? If not, who covers them for the agency?

- *Film and television rights*
- — Does the agency have a film and television department? Will this department know about your book before it is published?
- — Have they been successful in selling film or television rights to books in your area? What are they?

What an agent does

Norman Lebrecht, writing in the *Daily Telegraph* on 15 June 1996, said, 'Blaming agents for raising fees is like accusing mosquitoes of bloodlust. It's their livelihood.' He was talking about the music industry, but the same point applies to authors' agents.

In the film *Tootsie*, Dustin Hoffman (playing an out of work actor) asks his agent why he isn't getting him any work. The agent is outraged and replies that his job is not to get work, his job is to 'field offers'. I laughed so much at that line that I missed the next minute of dialogue. A literary agent's job is not as simple as that.

An agent's role is to manage a career based on the combination of talent and craft. The agent decides, in consultation with their client:

- — when to offer
- — what rights to offer to publishers in which markets (does the publisher get serial rights, export rights, more than one market?)
- — whether to make a single or multiple submission (i.e. whether

to show it to more than one publisher at a time in any one
market)
— whether to auction the book
— whether to recommend a single book deal or a multiple book
deal
— whether to recommend the author should accept an offer

All the final decisions are made by the owner of the rights – the author
– but it is the agent's task to sift and sort, to manipulate and improve
the offers, and to explain the implications of all aspects of the offer or
offers to their client.

Recommending that an author take a particular offer isn't always
or necessarily, or only, a matter of looking for the largest amount of
money. An agent has to bear in mind what an author wants: short-
term gain (the largest advance) or long-term financial stability (perhaps
much better royalties or a publisher famed for their marketing abilities).

How agents sell

Agents sell. When they do, they get paid. As and when monies come
in for the client, the agent takes commission, which should only be
commission from the amount that has come in for the client. If for
any reason a payment is not made, the agent loses as well as the
author. Bad debt is actually rare in publishing, thank goodness. If
agents don't sell, or if they don't collect the monies due, they don't get
paid. Sometimes I think the job description of an agent must be a mix
of nanny and brothel keeper: kind, supportive and protective (to the
writer) and procurer and exploiter (when luring the editor to the
novel). Not every one of my workdays is as stimulating as that though.

Joking aside, agents must both protect and exploit their clients:
protect their rights, exploit their work. To this end, good agents spend
all of their working week (and a great deal of their so-called spare
time!) talking to editors, negotiating with publishers, reading contracts
and manuscripts, attending prize-giving ceremonies and writers' conferences, giving talks and writing articles, reading trade magazines and
pitching their authors' books at trade fairs and on foreign visits, and
breakfasting, lunching, dining and drinking with clients and customers
alike. This means they know what's selling, who's buying, what the
current rates and fashions are, and who's looking for what.

Those bits sound interesting. Unfortunately, these social and stimulating parts of the working week are not all that agents have to do. That attractive list is balanced by a range of less glamorous activities: chasing overdue payments; checking royalty statements, publication dates and whether the author has received their free copies; arguing with an editor over a manuscript's acceptability; telling the author that the book needs rewriting, or sometimes that their editor has turned the new book down.

Agents vary a lot in the amount of editorial work they are prepared to do. We get paid for our sales, not our opinions, but our agency takes the view that the better we can make the manuscript, they better the deal we can do for it, and the better the long-term prospects for the writer. So we throw the opinions in free, even though reading the manuscripts and then editing them is the most time-consuming part of the job.

Once the first deal is made for a manuscript (usually, but not always, a book rights' contract in the author's country of origin) the agency starts to work in several additional areas at once. The agent will monitor the relationship between the author and the publishing company, not only to make sure that the author and the editor are working well together, but also to keep an eye on the author's relationship with the copy-editor, the publicity department and the marketing department. In some cases the author may not have any contact with these people. Authors seldom meet marketing executives if there isn't a substantial marketing budget allocated to the book, for instance, and should beware of pestering for marketing input on books that don't warrant it, and which are likely to be review- and PR-led. But a good agent should know these people anyway and be ready to promote their writer to them at every opportunity.

I have several times had to step in and gently mention to the acquiring editor that they might take a close look at the manuscript that has just come back from the copy-editor. It is unusual, but not unknown, for copy-editors to sometimes exceed their brief and start rewriting an author and changing their style. Inexperienced authors, or simply those without a liking for confrontation, will sometimes become very upset at this kind of situation, and if they don't know how to handle it will talk first to their agent. It's then easy for me to speak to the commissioning editor and ask them to deal with the copy-editor. Not only does this preserve the author's voice in the text (which, after all, is what the publisher demonstrated they wanted, by purchasing it in the first place), but if the publisher will reinstate the original text, it also saves the author all the work of doing it.

If the deal agreed gives the publishing company subsidiary rights to exploit (book club, serial, large print almost certainly, American and translation rights perhaps), then the agent should make sure that the editor has briefed the publishing company's rights department well. If the agent has interesting biographical material on the writer, or reviews for earlier books, or rights sales information for earlier books, it's only sensible to provide that for the rights and publicity departments. A good editor will do that automatically: a good agent will remind the editor or do it, and will make sure the same material goes to the publisher's key export offices around the world, or to the person in the head office who is co-ordinating the publisher's export efforts. (For an explanation of the major territories for English language publishers, see chapter 12.)

Simultaneously with monitoring the home market comes the beginning of the overseas work. Offering the manuscript to American publishers and translating publishers around the world, whether direct or through the agency's co-operating agents worldwide, and starting to work on film and television submissions is always exciting. I love the knowledge that I've sold a book once but can sell it all over again – dozens of times, hopefully! (For a full explanation of how overseas rights are exploited on behalf of authors, see chapter 13.)

We circulate our client list, with details of all our current books, very widely, and I issue a new one every month so that rights sales information is kept up-to-date. Every new sale is listed so that publishers in markets that are still free can see the calibre of publishers who have signed up for the book so far. I send a long chatty newsletter to all my foreign agents about three times a year in addition to mailing them manuscripts, proofs (of books and covers), and finished books and press cuttings with reviews, and sales presenters and advertisements and catalogue pages from my authors' publishers. The newsletter keeps them up to date with all the latest news about our writers, including film and television options and sales, manuscripts delivered or delayed, entries in the bestseller lists around the world, new clients who have joined us, clients who may have left, and snippets of information about our own staff. That's a lot of work, but it pays dividends in the way that our agents feel connected to our writers and to ourselves. And the more my overseas agents know about my writers, and about the agency, the better they can – and do – sell them.

All of this, including mailing costs but not including actually purchasing the text (copying manuscripts, buying proofs and finished books from the publisher) is covered by the commission we charge. We check that the client is happy for us to copy manuscripts (we do it in the office and charge at cost) and will authorize us to purchase proofs and books, and we charge the cost of these items against monies we are sending to the client. We do not send invoices to our clients for monies owing unless there are payments to set the charges against, although I believe some agencies do.

Now that it's so easy to e-mail manuscripts around the world we spend less time and money on mail and courier deliveries. We only e-mail manuscripts to scouts, agents and publishers with whom we have made a prior arrangement to do so: companies in publishing do not like receiving unsolicited manuscripts by e-mail. Authors should be careful not to antagonize agents and publishers by sending material in this way, or by disk alone. It is a courtesy to enquire first if text is welcome because of the cost and time taken to print it out.

Our agency's film and television staff compile newsletters too, which they mail around the world to film and television producers, directors and broadcasters before the major film and television festivals and markets. These carry news of all our books optioned or bought for audio-visual rights, films distributed or television work broadcast either from our books or from scripts by our scriptwriters. When our first film and TV newsletter is produced in each calendar year, usually for MIP TV in Cannes in April (the international television market, which is quite different from the better-known film festival which is held in Cannes in May), I also mail that to our overseas book agents and do a wide mailing of it to English language publishers. This is more for general information on the agency's activities than anything else, because the relevant publishers will already have been informed, as a matter of course, where film or television deals have been struck for books they are publishing.

Although there are far fewer magazines publishing short fiction now than there used to be, we do try to persuade our novelists to write some short stories so that we can place them to coincide with the novel's publication. There are few magazines serializing novels now, but a short story will often carry with it a mention of the author's latest novel. Every little bit of publicity helps. And while the fee for a short story sold to, say, a British magazine, is never huge, if it's possible to sell it to other markets as well, such as Australia, South Africa, the Scandinavian countries and Holland, the accumulated fees, plus the publicity generated for the author's novel, make the writing of it worthwhile.

Short stories have proved quite lucrative for some of our clients. Teresa Crane and Barbara Erskine both began their writing careers by concentrating on stories for women's magazines. Some years ago, when Barbara Erskine's publisher was worrying about the fact that she wouldn't have an Erskine novel in the next calendar year (Barbara's novels are long and often require a lot of research so it takes her almost two years to deliver each new one), I suggested rather diffidently that she could publish a volume of Barbara's stories. I say I suggested it diffidently because the publishing trade has always believed that 'short story volumes don't sell'. The stories I was offering had all appeared in print in magazines over a period of years. The publisher jumped at the chance. They published a large hardback of more than forty stories (*Encounters*, now a Fontana paperback) and, having retained serial rights, we sold six of them to six different women's magazines to coincide with publication of the volume. I was particularly pleased about the magazine sales because this meant these stories had been paid for three times in the UK alone – by a magazine first, then by the publisher and then by another magazine: deeply satisfying. Barbara now has a second volume of stories, *Distant Voices*.

More recently, Maeve Haran's German publisher, keen to publish her more often than she could write full-length novels, also raised a contract for a volume of her stories. These stories will be published in German in book form without appearing in book form in English first. Another translating first has been achieved for Barbara Erskine because of her short stories: the first time any of her work appeared in Japanese it was a collection of her stories which a Japanese publisher put together by making a selection from Barbara's two English language volumes of stories.

By the time we get to the first publication date for a novel, we hope to have several overseas sales. So when we send finished books to our agents, and the publishers who will be translating, we give them news of the editions signed up so far.

Once the books are published, we collect press cuttings (and extra covers) for our authors' books from their publishers around the world, and send everything from every market, to each publisher who has bought the book. The covers are particularly useful because publishers in the smaller markets (such as Norway, Denmark, Estonia and Poland) don't always want to commission artwork themselves in order to generate a new cover, and often couldn't afford to do so. By showing them the range of covers that have been designed by publishers in the larger markets (UK, USA and Germany, for example) they can choose one and buy the right to use that artwork from the publisher, usually purchasing a colour transparency, perhaps with a disk linked to the art files, which enables them to separate design from lettering.

At the same time, we send all the press cuttings to our agents in markets that have not yet bought the book. It's a lot of work and expense and occasionally I wonder if it's worth it. But at every book fair I have ever attended at least one publisher has told me that getting all the press for an author regularly is very valuable to them. They can pick up on marketing ideas from other countries, use favourable review quotes on their covers, and brief their own sales people more widely than if they were ignorant of what was going on in other markets. So we still do it.

The author–agent agreement

This protects both parties, and I would be suspicious of any agency that does not offer one to their clients. Having an agency take you on is the beginning of a business relationship, and writing down the rules is only common sense so that both parties know what to expect from that relationship.

The agreement sets out what commission rates the agent charges for a variety of rights sales (usually from 10 to 20 per cent); what rights the agent is, or isn't handling for the client, what charges may be deducted from the clients' monies, and makes it clear that the representation is exclusive.

The text of our agency agreement is in the appendix. It is based on wording recommended by the Authors' Agents Association. We have expanded the text to include information about our co-operating agents overseas, and our own staff members, and we have added a sentence to make it clear that clients may leave at any time.

Beware of any agency that asks you to pay for editorial advice, or any other expenses that should be part of their normal office overhead such as phone calls, faxes and mailing of packages. It is common for courier costs – if approved by you – to be deducted from your income. In our agency we don't charge our client for costs incurred by couriering initial submissions: that is our choice and we pay. But once a book is sold, if the author wants us to courier subsequent drafts of the manuscript to publishers at home and overseas, then we do, after discussion, pass on this charge to our client.

Don't allow an agent to be paid a royalty by the publisher in addition to the commission earned on your deal; one agent did this some years ago and was forced to leave the Association of Authors' Agents as a result. The Association took the view that an agent who was being paid by the publisher as well as the author cold not be impartial, and might not be representing the interests of the client solely.

Don't sign agreements that tie you to an agency for a set period of time, or for a particular number of books, or that call for an unduly long notice period should you wish to leave: authors should be free to leave when they want to.

When moving agents, be sure that your agency agreement is clear on the matter of which agent handles foreign sales on your earlier titles: are they staying with your previous agent or is your new agent taking them over? And if you expect your agent to handle work in addition to books, such as short stories or journalism, check that the agreement is clear as to the commission rate charged, and that you know which person at the agency will be responsible for those sales. Make sure that you are always sent copies of your fully signed contracts, and that you receive your (checked) royalty statements reasonably quickly after the publisher sends them to the agency. If you are not happy with any aspect of your agency representation, say so. An agent is supposed to look after your business affairs and if they are not doing so efficiently, you must tell them you are unhappy. If your complaints are not rectified, you may feel that your only option is to change agencies. There is a section dealing with this in chapter 17.

Instead of an agent

If, for whatever reason, you decide not to have your work handled by an agent, there are other organizations that will check your contracts and advise you, to varying degrees, on practice in the trade. But none of them will operate in all the areas covered by literary agencies.

The Society of Authors

The Society of Authors is a long-established and respected body that offers remarkable value for money. Officially they describe themselves as 'an independent trade union offering business advice to writers in all media, particularly in the area of publishing'. Their annual membership fee is low, and in my opinion worth it for *The Author* alone, their quarterly publication. This is a very professionally produced magazine full of useful news and feature articles on the trade and all aspects of the writing life. The magazine highlights current concerns for members and publishes the results of their surveys. In recent years it has published surveys among others, on what their members think of their publishers, their agents, a survey organized by the Association of Authors' Agents on the content of publishers' royalty statements, and a survey of the speed with which publishers supply royalty statements. They do not mince their words and the surveys make fascinating reading. I comment on the two surveys on agents in detail in chapter 7.

The news section of *The Author* keeps members abreast of moves among publishing companies' staff, but because of its quarterly publication it cannot be as up to date as the weekly trade magazines *The Bookseller* (which it credits as the source for most of its staff moves information) and *Publishing News*. But I read *The Author* with great interest for its feature articles, which are pertinent and useful. It regularly carries articles on 'My First Book' by well-known writers, in-depth pieces on copyright, libel, new technology, and warnings to others about problems that have beset members. In one such incident a national newspaper suddenly started demanding to own copyright in articles it printed by freelance writers: the paper backed down.

The Society will read, check and comment on contracts free for their members and offers advice on how to negotiate points an author may wish to change. They will also sometimes instigate, at their own expense, legal proceedings on behalf of a member if they believe the issue is an important one for their membership. This is another area in which the cost of membership could be recouped many times over.

Although the Society will not *sell* the work of its members, they do act as an agent for a variety of authors' estates, managing the rights and negotiating contracts for work by authors who have died. They also administer a wide range of literary prizes, which culminates in a sparkling party every May when the awards are announced and the prizes handed out to their recipients.

The Society will advise authors about publishers and agents, and give advice on what is, and what isn't, accepted trade practice. They also publish an invaluable series of *Quick Guides*, free to members, on subjects as diverse as publishing contracts, copyright and moral rights, libel, income tax, permissions, indexing your book, literary translations and authors' agents.

One major area of their work is, together with the Writers Guild, negotiating with publishers to produce documents that are known as the Minimum Terms Agreements (MTAs). Each one is personal to the publisher it is agreed with, and each has taken a considerable time (years in some cases) to negotiate. Indeed, it's a major step forward every time they persuade another publisher to enter into negotiations in the first place.

If an author has no professional adviser, and may not have seen many other publishing contracts if any, they will have no means by which to judge the deal they are offered. By agreeing minimum terms in areas of a deal such as royalties, subsidiary rights income splits, royalty accounting periods, the percentage of royalty income that can be held back in case of returns, the Society believe they are achieving a level of protection for their members that they would otherwise not have. If you are a member of the Society they will provide you with copies of all the current Minimum Terms Agreements on request.

This is one of the few areas where my thinking is not entirely in accord with the Society. Certainly the MTAs protect unagented authors. But too often agents find that publishers are offering to the agent the MTA levels of royalties or subsidiary income splits and treating them not as minimum levels, but as normal, or maximum, levels. On these points my arguments must be with the publishers who misuse the figures as norms rather than minimums. Publishers also try to insist that other areas of a deal, which are accepted by the Society and the Guild and which have been enshrined in that particular publisher's MTA are, once again, the norm rather than the minimum. It can take a lot of arguing by an agent to persuade the publisher that the agent's client is at a stage in their career where they deserve better than the minimum. I suppose that as an agent I subscribe so whole-heartedly to the principle of individual negotiation that the idea of collective bargaining is anathema!

I think that the Society does a fine job on behalf of their members and do recommend my clients to join if they want to meet other authors, or if they just want to have a broader view of the publishing industry. I know some agents who actively discourage their clients from joining the Society. I think that's a very defensive posture only likely to be taken by a less-than-professional agent.

The Writers' Guild

The Guild defines themselves as 'a TUC-affiliated trade union, and represents writers in all media, particularly in broadcast media'. Most of their activities are concerned with film and television and their members are predominantly scriptwriters. They negotiate, with bodies representing producers and broadcasters, the rates for minimum terms for film and television writing work, and these rates are used through-out the film and television industries in Britain.

Their publication, the *Writers' Guild Newsletter*, covers news and features for scriptwriting members and keeps the membership up to date on issues, arguments and rates of pay. The *Newsletter* regularly carries book-oriented features. The Guild organize programmes of seminars and workshops for the membership and there are regional groups around Britain so that everything isn't focused only on London.

There is a Books' Committee (which I sat on as adviser for some years), which answers queries from members about book contracts and trade practice. It is the Books' Committee that co-operates with The Society of Authors in negotiating Minimum Terms Agreements with a range of publishers.

If you are a scriptwriter who occasionally writes books then membership of the Guild would be advised. But if you are mainly a book writer I doubt you would find the Guild alone sufficient for your needs.

A contracts agency

There are few literary agencies that will negotiate your contract for you if you are not a client. If you were to find one that did, they might still want to charge you a commission, as opposed to a fee. But there are contracts agencies that will negotiate your contract for you, for a fee. You will have had to sell your book and obtain the initial offer, but a contracts agency will negotiate final terms for you and check and negotiate the contract. One such agency was established some years ago by a highly experienced publishing executive. Roger Palmer had been head of the Hodder & Stoughton contracts department and I had always enjoyed dealing with him because he was always fair and knew more about his subject than most publishing company contracts managers I had to deal with. His company specialize in contracts for all media, and his staff are very experienced. They will give you an estimate of their fee before they do the work. They will not monitor progress of your book after the contract, and they are not lawyers, but they do know trade practice. They are called Roger Palmer Ltd and are based in London.

A lawyer

Lawyers and contracts are synonymous in some people's minds. There is no doubt that lawyers can help to produce a tight contract. But if you are using a lawyer to advise you on a publishing contract, be sure that the lawyer has detailed and up-to-date knowledge of the trade and current accepted trade practice. If you engage one who knows little of the trade, you may find yourself paying for a protracted negotiation while the lawyer tries to renegotiate issues that are absolutely standard throughout the industry.

Lawyers charge you by the hour, which can become very expensive. I have seen lawyers spend a lot of fruitless time arguing with publishers over items that are absolutely normal and accepted by authors and publishers throughout the industry, while at the same time missing the significance of vital clauses that can make a big difference to the authors' earnings, such as retention of royalties for returns and the levels at which the royalties on high discounts kick in. These are not legal matters but depend on knowledge of the way the trade works.

If you do have a lawyer negotiate your contract for you, it is therefore wise to question them about how much experience they have with publishing contracts, and to ask for an estimate of the cost before they work for you. One difference between having a lawyer act for you on a contract and working through an agent is the method by which you pay them.

An agent takes commission on the book for the life of that contract, which, if the book is very successful, might amount to a considerable sum. A lawyer charges a one-off fee for their time, which could be less. But lawyers charge a single fee no matter what the book will eventually earn (on a small publishing deal it could eat up most of your advance) and do not go on to monitor the publication of the book (and all the complicated royalty statements) in the way that agents do. Lawyers may also charge a high fee for negotiating a contract on a high-earning deal because a mistake would be more costly to them if they had to claim on their professional indemnity insurance.

Using a lawyer instead of an agent means you probably have to do the initial negotiating yourself, and you don't have someone by your side to guide you through the publishing process. Hopefully this book could help with that. Once the lawyer has finalized the contract that is the end of their involvement with it and your book.

Alternatively you could have them check the contract and send you a list of points for you to negotiate yourself, if you feel sufficiently confident.

But, with apologies to my lawyer friends, I do think that The Society of Authors will serve an unagented author better than most lawyers when it comes to negotiating with publishers. So much knowledge of current trade practice is gained by negotiating regularly with publishers that unless a lawyer specializes in publishing work they are unlikely to be as up to date as any agent or the Society.

A last word from a client of mine – Teresa Crane was with another agency before coming to us and, for a short while, during the transition, wasn't technically represented. She said that, 'Having no agent was like going out without underwear: exciting but quite scary and not very comfortable.'

5   Submission to a publisher

You've done your homework about what to write, you've worked on your preliminary material until it is as good as you can make it, having taken comments and criticism from others into account, and you have either been taken on by a literary agent who is about to offer your work to a publisher or you have decided to submit to a publisher yourself. How should this happen?

Obviously, the best way to sell something is to make it easy to buy: simple to say, hard to achieve. Much of the advice I've given in chapter 3 about submitting to agents applies here too: good presentation, revising until you feel the material is as good as you can make it, carefully researching the authors and genres that the publisher handles. Look at the publisher's name on the spine of novels you think appeal to the same audience as your own and approach them. As with agents' names, authors sometimes mention their editor in the acknowledgements of their book: again, check that the editor is still with the publishing company.

Call publishers for their catalogues so that you can check what they are about to publish. Read the trade press, look for talks given by editors to writers' groups, or at book fairs and festivals.

Single or multiple submissions?

Some agents won't read material if it's on offer to other agents at the same time. This is simply self-preservation: we have so much to read that the idea of reading material speculatively, in competition with others, is very undesirable. But many authors and agents do make multiple submissions to publishers. That seems unfair but at least the publishers' editors are being paid while they are reading. (At this point my editor put a note in the margin of the first draft of this manuscript: 'Unless they are reading at home in the evenings or at weekends.' Point taken! The point I am making though, is that agents' earnings come directly – and only – from deals they do on books they sell: editors are part of a team within the publishing house that works on a range of books: it's difficult to relate an editor's earnings to specific books.) Agents don't get paid for doing anything that doesn't result in a sale.

If you make a multiple submission, it is important and courteous to say so in your submission letter. Whenever I make multiple submissions to publishers, I always tell them so. If an author makes multiple submissions direct to publishers, they should allow at least three to five weeks for an answer. I'm afraid that single submissions to publishers could take a lot longer to receive replies for the simple reason that competition might engender a sense of urgency.

If you are making a single submission to a publisher, I would suggest you include that in your letter, and say that you'll be happy to give them four weeks for an exclusive look at it: any longer and you'll feel free to show it to others. A well-run publishing house ought to be able to respond within that time if an editor thinks your material is interesting. If you don't hear within your specified time frame, and you have chased them once for a response, then you can honourably submit to others.

If you have submitted to several publishers at the same time and you receive a favourable response from one of them, inviting you to send in the whole manuscript, or inviting you to a meeting, you should let the others know and tell them you therefore require their answer within, say, a week. The point of this is to persuade everyone to respond within the same time frame. If you can do this, then you stand a chance of being able to choose between several interested parties without keeping anyone waiting an undue length of time. You may even be able to benefit from the competition.

Occasionally an author will receive an offer or offers and then feel they need an agent to progress the negotiation. Agents will sometimes step in after offering has begun, and can usually produce a better deal for the author than the author would have managed alone, but deals like these are seldom as good as those begun by an agent. If particular aspects of the deal were not made clear enough at the start, each party may have made different assumptions about crucial areas such as territory or period of licence, and publishers can become irritated at being asked to start negotiations with a third party when they thought they had almost finalized a deal directly with an author. This is not a good reason to hold back from asking an agent to finalize negotiations for you, but it is a good reason to get an agent on board at the beginning, if you can.

Auctions

An auction is a structured way of creating and benefiting from competition between several publishers. Agents choose to auction material when they feel there is sufficient feedback from the market place to suggest that several publishers will be prepared to bid against each other for publication rights. I would not recommend that an unagented author should try to run an auction unless that author had considerable experience of negotiation, publishing deals and contracts.

Auctions can be minefields, even for agents. When I was President of the Association of Authors' Agents, I received more complaints about agents from publishers on this subject than on any other. Some agents are nervous of auctions, and some have sometimes got themselves – and their authors – into muddles through improperly run auctions. It's no wonder that I strongly advise unagented authors to steer clear of trying to auction their own book.

I will describe the procedure in an auction in some detail because when they are run well they are very straightforward and they can produce extremely good results for the author. When they are not run efficiently or honestly, they produce bad feeling in the trade, and the auction result and the mood in which it leaves the participants can have a detrimental effect on an author's career. Also, so many tactics are involved in an auction that lessons can be learned for any negotiating procedure. Auctioning book rights can be exhilarating when you achieve the desired result – a big deal with a good publisher and a happy author and editor. They can though, also go wrong and therefore be nerve-racking and exhausting. But there are several well-established and proven reasons for putting an author's work up for auction:

1. To move from a publisher you no longer respect or like and whom you suspect will not outbid other publishers in an auction (if they do last – and win – the chances are you will at least be better paid). This can only be done after you have fulfilled the terms of any option clause in the previous contract. It may mean showing the new manuscript to your previous publisher and then turning down any offer they make. This can be worrying, as you have to do so before approaching other publishers so you need to be very sure of the saleability of the material.

2. To discover the author's real market worth, perhaps after several books published by one publisher have only produced small increases for each succeeding contract. Again, you must get out of any option clause honourably.

3. To change terms in other ways. For example, in the markets granted: to make Canada a separate market (from Britain or America), or to sell just British rights to the British publisher when your previous contracts have specified world in all languages, or to withhold serial rights in the new contract, after the last contract had granted them to the publisher, or to get better promotion guarantees or better royalties.

A warning: If you or your agent takes the bold step of auctioning a first novel, you need to be very excited indeed about its saleability. With no previous track record for the author, it is the seller's reputation and knowledge of the market place that will be put to the test during the auction. If you read the market wrong, you may get no offers; or you might find yourself selling the book for less than you could have got if you had offered it on a single submission. In an auction, publishers will often start out by offering much less than they are prepared to offer later, because they expect to have to offer through several rounds of bids. If there is no or little competition, an editor could win the book with a first or second round bid, which might be much lower than they think the book is really worth.

The seller – be it agent or author – should be clear at the outset about exactly what they are trying to achieve, because the whole approach to eliciting offers will depend upon their intentions.

Preparation

Homework is the key to a successful auction. At Blake Friedmann we spend a great deal of time – weeks or months (in one case nearly two years) – setting up auctions: talking enthusiastically to get publishers interested, putting together impressive presentations and press kits, editing and re-editing the material we plan to show (which can range from a two-page synopsis to a full draft manuscript, depending on the circumstances). The author's wholehearted commitment to this plan is necessary.

Homework is essential when deciding which publishers to include in the auction. The most interested publishers might be those who need you most because they have a weak list; they will be the last publishers you'd want to end up with, even if they do bid more than everyone else. Some agents will include such publishers for the sake of pushing up the final price, but hope that someone better will offer more. It's a risky gamble – and can lead to publishers feeling 'used' – which won't help you next time you really do want them to bid for a book. When auctioning, don't mix apples and pears: have a list of publishers competing with each other who are all hardback publishers, or all hardback and paperback partnerships.

A precaution: don't invite anyone to the pyjama party that you're not prepared to have breakfast with later. If you are not prepared to sell to a particular publisher, *don't* involve them in the auction. If one such publisher asks to be involved, you must find a tactful way of telling them that it is not possible. I think this is much easier for an agent to do on behalf of their client than for the author to do themselves.

Look carefully at authors who would be your direct competitors on each publisher's list: should you include those publishers? Certainly include publishers who may have recently lost authors and who might therefore be prepared to pay over the odds. Editors in new jobs often want to make an impression by bringing in new authors and therefore may bid high in auctions. Newly set-up companies might 'overspend' as a pump-priming investment, to stock their 'front' list.

When to offer a work by auction depends on the status of the author, topicality of material, the amount of material you have available and the time of year. (Christmas, high summer and around the Frankfurt Book Fair in October aren't ideal times for publishers to get an editorial board together, although just before these periods of activity can be good times to sell because editors like to acquire before leaving the office.) A first-time author should not expect to get a big response when offering just a synopsis at any time!

Publishers and auctions

Publishers have mixed feelings about auctions. If a manuscript is offered to six publishers, by the auction's end, five of those publishers will know they have wasted their time. Five of them will have had several members of staff read it, will have had people assessing it, discussing it, and doing sales estimates and costings – all for nothing. Only one publisher can end up with the property. But a property that is offered in an auction may be by a writer who was not previously available to that particular publisher, and an auction may give a publisher an opportunity to buy a high profile book that acquires extra visibility precisely because of the auction. Auctions themselves can become news, often in the trade papers, sometimes (less often) in national newspapers. My first Michael Ridpath sale was an auction and the news of the outcome was reported on the front page of the *Observer*.

Never change the rules during an auction. Upset publishers help no one and today's loser could be tomorrow's winner. *Never* let one publisher bid for more territories, rights or books than another publisher is bidding for, and don't extend the bidding date just because one publisher isn't ready.

Auctions that go wrong

One should never rush into an auction without considering the negative possibilities. Although publishers sometimes spend more money in an auction than at other times, remember that you can't *choose* your publisher when the top bid will win. A failed auction (the wrong publisher wins or you get few and low bids or – devastatingly – none at all) can be humiliating to author and agent and can prove a setback to an author's career. If you word your submission letter carefully, you may be able to choose the best overall package at the end of your auction and not be tied simply to accepting the highest advance offered. I favour this approach because if the royalty levels are higher from a publisher who is offering a slightly lower advance, it may be in the author's long-term interest to accept that because royalty earnings may eventually produce more income. If you receive a relatively low advance offer with an excellent marketing plan and budget, that could be more to your advantage than a higher advance with poor marketing plans.

This kind of choice does have to be made carefully, and the decision making can be nail-bitingly fraught for agent and author.

If you are tempted to exaggerate to other bidding parties the size of the last bid in an auction, don't. Apart from the importance of ethics and morals, publishers do talk to each other. There was a case some years ago when a British auction was called off very publicly because one publisher discovered he had been falsely induced to bid higher than he needed to top the under-bidder. That story even made the front pages of several Sunday newspapers. In that case it was a hardback publisher auctioning paperback rights to other publishers.

In the summer of 1997, a shocking case came to light in America. An American agent concluded an auction for over half a million dollars: the novel went to Dutton, an imprint within the huge Penguin group. Publishers like to talk to each other when an auction is over and Dutton discovered, in one of the post-auction discussions, that the agent had greatly exaggerated the size of the other bids in the auction.

The agent had lied to Dutton. The head of Dutton complained publicly, withdrew her offer and initially said that she wasn't prepared to buy the book at all. Eventually she relented, but ended up purchasing the book for a fraction of the previous auction figure. The story was splashed over the American publishing trade magazine, *Publishers Weekly*, and the agents' association in America condemned the agent's actions. I can't imagine how that agent can continue in business.

This result is tough on the writer. A well-run auction might have produced a better result. The author must be left with ambivalent feelings towards his agent after such public condemnation by her peers. He probably also has grounds for a lawsuit against the agent.

The auction submission

I should say here, for people who are confused about the location of publishing auctions, that these do not take place, like fine art auctions, with all the participants sitting in the same room, watching each other bid. Agents do not call everyone to their office and stand in front of them, wielding a gavel. Material is mailed or messangered to the publishers, and the offers are made by telephone, e-mail or fax. The publishers who are bidding may well have a fairly good idea of their competitors in any one auction, but the identity of the bidders (and who made what bid) is always kept secret until the auction is over.

Don't feel foolish if you thought they were conducted face to face in one room. Just before the Frankfurt Book Fair in October 1997, I received a telephone call from the Publishers' Association who were expecting a Minister from Britain's (then) new Labour Government to visit the Fair. This was the first time a Government Minister had ever wanted to see the most important publishing trade fair in the world and Britain's book business was very pleased that he was prepared to devote two days to us. The Publishers' Association wanted to put on a good show for him and asked if he could come to our stand at the Fair and watch me run an auction. I explained gently that in terms of a spectator sport, it was about as exciting as watching paint dry. Even the PA staff didn't know how publishing auctions were conducted!

Setting up the auction

In an auction, agents must always send the *same* material and information to everyone at the *same* time. In their own interest, agents give publishers as much information as possible about the book, the author and the author's track record: how they like to work, how often they produce books, press cuttings and reviews for previous books, and, if the author is good at publicity, they say so. Film sales, wide publication overseas: information like this is all helpful when the publisher is putting together a bid. If book sales on previous titles have been good, say so and give details. If they haven't been anything to shout about, keep quiet about details. Publishers may ask for sales figures later so it is best to be prepared to confess to them at that point. There is absolutely no point in lying or massaging the figures. Apart from honour, and maintaining credibility, sales figures can easily be checked. Life is much simpler when sticking to the truth, however unpalatable.

It is vital to decide the conditions of an auction *before* it starts, the most important areas being what rights and what territories are on offer. The seller must decide if they want a hard and soft offer (hardback and paperback editions coming from the same publisher, or two publishers buying together: this can give the author greatly enhanced royalties, especially on the paperback edition, which then does not have to be split with the hardback publisher), or if the auction is to be conducted among hardback-only publishers, who will sell the paperback rights to another publisher later. In these days of group publishing, this is becoming a rarity.

Will you insist on author cover approval as part of the contract? Do you want a promotion plan included, perhaps also with a minimum guaranteed publicity and promotion spend? Do you want a clause in the contract that gives you the right to break the contract if the purchasing editor leaves the publishing house before the manuscript goes into production? Are you looking for a one- or a two-book contract? Will serial rights be included in the publisher's package? Is the deal intended to be for the publisher's own territory alone or will you allow them broader rights (which involves them licensing other language rights around the world)?

In the submission letter, the seller will set out the date for offers, what time on that day each first offer should be in by and the minimum size of the increments, if that seems appropriate. This last item is often left until the first round bids are made so that the agent can assess the right level for future increments. If new rules are set once the auction has begun it is vital to communicate them to every party affected simultaneously.

Floors

Before the auction starts, you must have decided if you are accepting a floor bid. This is an offer from a publisher, made before the auction begins, which, in return for making it, confers a privilege upon the publisher and an obligation upon the seller.

The privilege is that it buys the publisher 'pole position', to use a sporting phrase. That publisher will be able to sit back while the rest of the bids are elicited. A floor holder has the satisfaction of knowing that having established a floor will have made all the other participants just a bit uneasy.

Motivation for offering and accepting floors is quite straightforward. The publisher who offers a floor wants a preferential place in the auction; the author who accepts a floor does so either because any offer on the table is a comfort, or because the figure is a high one that they fear might not be offered under normal circumstances in the forthcoming auction.

There are two different kinds of floors, and two quite distinct categories: first in, last out versus topping rights, or high versus low.

First In, Last Out vs. Topping Rights

'First in, last out' is shorthand to describe a situation in which the floor holder does not bid during the rounds but has the right to bid against the 'winner' from the rest of the bidders. The winner and the floor holder then bid against each other until one clear winner emerges. In other words, the floor holder stands aloof throughout the entire auction until one top bid has emerged from everyone else. Only at that point will the next stage be actioned, in which that winner and the floor holder start to bid against each other. Personally, I would only be prepared to accept a floor under these circumstances if the floor was exceptionally high (high enough to be acceptable as the winning bid) because other potential bidders find it so off-putting. It can be wearisome for publishers to battle through one sequence of bids only to have to embark upon another. They find it dispiriting and this can have a detrimental effect upon the way they view the auction and therefore make their bids.

Topping rights means again that the floor holder does not bid in the rounds but has the right to top the bid of the 'winner' from the rounds by an agreed percentage. The floor holder will establish their floor, and then agree with the seller that the topping privilege will be, usually, 10 per cent of the otherwise top figure. For example, if the floor holder had established an accepted floor at £20,000, they would wait until the rest of the auction had finished. The bids may have got up to, say, £95,000. If the topping percentage was agreed at 10 per cent, then the floor holder would be able to win the auction by bidding £95,000 + 10 per cent (£9,500) which equals £104,500. Sometimes the floor holder will exercise that right, and sometimes they decide it is too expensive and they won't. Either way, it can also be a deterrent to other bidders to know that however valiantly they fight the auction, someone else (whose identity they do not know during the auction) may win by making the last bid. This situation has stopped a number of publishers bidding in auctions. But of course it has also produced some spectacular advance figures.

High vs. low floor

A seller will not be likely to accept a low figure as a floor because it will suggest to other potential buyers that the seller is nervous and would rather accept a small, guaranteed figure, than go into the auction with no offer on the table. The agent who is selling must, of course, discuss any floor offered with their client and if the client wants to accept it, the agent must bow to their wishes – another reason for the agent and client to have discussed all aspects of an auction before embarking upon it.

I think that the only reason for accepting a floor is because it is a substantial enough sum *that you could imagine being happy to accept as a final offer*. Please note the italics. If you accept a high floor, you must also accept that it may make other bidders feel uneasy: which is all part of the psychological warfare of an auction. That's precisely *why* the floor bidder offered that sum: they want to scare off the opposition. If a high floor is offered in an auction I am conducting, I talk it through very carefully with my client because I want them to be aware that this could be the only bid we receive. If it does what the floor holder intends, it will indeed scare off everyone else. That can leave an author and agent feeling very flat indeed.

Picture the scene: agent and author have been working towards the auction for months. Homework done, material edited and honed, editors primed, material copied, letter drafted and redrafted. Just before it goes out to everyone, Publisher A offers a fairytale figure that is, after discussion, accepted as a floor with 10 per cent topping rights.

The material is sent out, a couple of weeks pass while the publishers read, assess and do their figures.

The day of the auction arrives and by the appointed hour, say, 11 o'clock in the morning, no one has offered. Several have called to say they found the floor a bit steep and as it obviously signalled very serious intent on the part of the floor holder, they thought they couldn't put up any opposition. Reluctantly, Publishers B, C, and D will not be bidding. Publisher E has forgotten that today is the bidding day and asks for an extra couple of days. You have to tell them no. During the day, agent and author have spoken to each other several times, always trying to guess at the final outcome and, probably, reassuring each other that it will be fine. By lunchtime on auction day they have to face the fact that there will be no other bids and the floor holder has acquired the book for their floor bid. Everyone will, inevitably, feel despondent, including the floor holder.

Why should this be, when they agreed before the auction that the floor figure was also acceptable as a final offer? The author is miserable because they wanted to see publishers fighting over their manuscript.

The agent is not entirely happy because they put the case for an auction in the first place, and also recommended accepting the floor, and they may feel a bit guilty for letting the author believe the book was worth more than the floor figure.

And the publisher – even though they are the winner of the book – probably has the sneaking suspicion that if they hadn't offered this floor, and scared off all the other potential bidders, that they might have got the book for less than they are now committed to paying for it. It's a tough scenario for everybody.

I feel very strongly that it is unfair to the other publishers if the seller accepts a floor after the auction submissions have been sent out. Not all agents agree with me, but I do not believe that the seller should move the goalposts after the game has begun. I will only accept a floor if it is offered before an auction package has been submitted. If the agent is doing their preparation for the auction sufficiently well, then the publishing community becomes aware that an auction will take place at some point in the future. It is at this point that I will sometimes consider accepting a floor.

But in general, I am against accepting a floor. If it is high, it can stop everyone else bidding so the floor bid wins the book. If the floor you accept is low, you look desperate for having accepted it. If you are desperate, maybe you shouldn't be selling this book by auction.

Floor bids are also rarely the highest bid a publisher is prepared to make: publishers nearly always have something else they can produce if the competition gets fierce. But some publishers do risk putting in their highest bid as a floor offer in order to scare the opposition away from the start, which is not in the author's interests.

The bidding

Say how you will accept bids. Alternatives are:

1. The second round of bids (i.e. after everyone who is going to, has made their first offer) can be made in the same order as the bids came in during the first round.
2. The size of the publisher's bid in the first round can determine their position in the order of bidding for the second and subsequent rounds – i.e. the lowest from round one bids first in the second round.

Once bidding starts, keep everyone informed of what they need to know to make their next bid. Make sure you get as many details as possible from everyone, and to everyone about:

— the size of the advance
— the stages in which it will be paid
— the royalty scales for different editions
— publicity plans
— proposed position on the publisher's list (e.g. will it be a 'lead' title with all the marketing and razzamatazz that entails?)
— the identity of the proposed editor

All these can be negotiated and improved while you (the seller) are in a position of strength during an auction.

Make sure that you get an answer from everyone during every round. If you have five publishers bidding in round one, call all five at the beginning of round two and ask them for another bid each. Write down the exact details (I also put the time and date next to each new offer), noting not only the advance, but any improvement on payment stages, royalties, subsidiary rights splits etc. If anyone declines to make another bid, they are then out of the auction and you note that down too. As each round progresses, publishers will drop out until you have just one left.

Finalizing an auction

Most auctions end naturally with one clear winner.

If the bidding goes on so long (lucky you!) without publishers dropping out, and perhaps with the increments and improvements becoming smaller and smaller with each round of bids, you can bring it to a conclusion in one of several ways.

Asking for a blind bid final round is one way of coming to a swift conclusion but it's anxiety-ridden for seller and buyer alike. You establish the so-far best bid and tell the details to all parties (without revealing who made that bid). You then ask them all to make one last 'sealed envelopes' blind bid. It will be the last bid any is allowed to make and you bind yourself to accepting either the highest offer or the overall best package. Like all the other rounds, bids are made on the telephone. It is entirely unacceptable ever to ask anyone to bid again after a blind bids round, unless that blind bids round ends in a stalemate with two or more editors making *exactly* the same bid. In which case you can either go through the process again with just the top bidders, or you can choose the best package if there are differences in detail. Either, I suggest, should be done after discussion of the predicament with all the affected bidders and, if an agent is handling it, the author too.

When preparing their final blind bid, publishers must try to outwit their competitors. The bidders all know the value of the bid they have to beat, but what they don't know is who they are bidding against or how much higher the other bidders will go now. Some very odd figures emerge at this stage. Some publishers will obviously offer big increases in their bids in the hope of being the winner. But if they all offer round figures (e.g. in thousands) there could be a stalemate. Hopeful of avoiding the problem of coinciding with another's bid, publishers will offer £107,500 rather than £105,000, or £251,000 rather than £250,000. A couple of auctions I have conducted have been won by such tactics.

If you began your auction with a floor, then however the other bidders are sorted out, you will be left with two publishers: the winner from the bidding rounds, and the floor holder. At this point you go to your floor holder and tell them all the details (except who made the bid) of the best offer that the bidding produced. They must then decide whether to top it in whatever way was established when you accepted their floor. If they do use their topping rights, they win the book. If they don't, the winner from the bidding rounds wins the book.

Whatever the outcome, it is courteous to go back quickly to the highest bidder from the rounds and tell them whether they have won the book or lost it. At this point you can reveal the names of the other editors and publishers who were bidding. The other participants, who dropped out earlier, will also appreciate a call with information about who won the book, and thanks from the seller for their participation.

Make sure every single item in the deal is crystal clear between yourself and the buyer before you say done. You have more cards in your hand before you close the auction than once you've clinched the deal.

Now the auction is over and you have a winner. Confirm all details in writing immediately. I prefer to do this by fax for speed and efficiency. And a fax carries a signature, unlike an e-mail.

Other reminders

There are other things to remember which can make for better auctions:

1. Remind .publishers of the date of your auction a couple of days before, perhaps by sending them more press cuttings, or hopefully news of a film sale. I sometimes hold a little information back at the beginning in order to have something more to add just before my auction date.

2. Stay in all day on auction day: be available to bidders (and, as an agent, be available to your client too).

3. Keep meticulous records of every bid: the time it was made, the size, the order in which it was received, etc.

4. Improve all the points in the deal (not just the advance)as the auction progresses.

5. If you are the client and your agent is auctioning for you, don't call the agent every ten minutes. I often arrange that I (or my staff) will call my client at appointed times during the day to tell them of progress. In fact, I always try to call clients between each round of bids. But if the bids are coming in slowly and the client is in an agony of anticipation at home alone, I know that a call every few hours will be appreciated, even if it is only to say that there is no change since I last called.

The outcome

What can go wrong? The 'wrong' publisher (i.e. one you didn't wish to end up with) emerges as the winner, or a low offer wins, or no offers come in. All of these suggest you didn't do enough homework because the state of the market into which the material is offered can be researched in advance. And if the wrong publisher wins, it's your fault for inviting them to bid in the first place. It's sheer greed to open the bidding to a wider range of publishers in the hope of driving up the price if you are not prepared to be happy about the outcome whichever one of them wins the book. If you have strong feelings about who should publish the book, better to risk a lower final figure by excluding some publishers at the beginning.

What can go right? Everything, if the book is as good as you said it would be and the auction produces the right partnership of author, editor and publisher and deal. In which case we usually turn to a bottle of Moët et Chandon shared with our client. We then immediately start telling all our overseas agents and the publishers' scouts about the outcome so that the trade 'buzz' on the book will spread to other markets. If appropriate, an announcement to the publishing trade press is another way of spreading information quickly.

6   The art of negotiation

Whatever you think it's gonna take, double it. That applies to money, time, stress. It's gonna be harder than you think and take longer than you think.
– Richard A. Cortese, *On Starting Your Own Business*

A definition

A good deal is one that pleases both parties. A touch idealistic perhaps, but essentially true. Negotiation is a social skill as well as an art. Something of the art can be taught, but nothing beats practice. The best way to refine your technique is to negotiate again and again, learning from each encounter. I think that good negotiation is usually a combination of subtlety, grace, a little flattery at times and controlled aggression. And, un-politically correct as it may be to say so, a little flirtation can be useful!

> A tourist in New York is trying to find the famous concert hall.
> *Tourist:* How do I get to Carnegie Hall?
> *New Yorker:* Practice, man, practice.

The same is true of negotiating. The best way to refine your technique is to negotiate again and again and to learn from every encounter. Analyse how you succeed, and why you fail. When you do win a negotiating point, look closely at the conversation or sequence of correspondence that led to it and see if you can spot the turning point, the moment when the person you were negotiating with started to show signs that they were going to compromise. If you fail to persuade the other party to give you what you want, again scrutinize the exchange to pinpoint where their attitude hardened and what you may have said that caused it. Did they then stand firm entirely, or did they – or you – offer a compromise? If so, who gave way most?

What to aim for

All negotiations are forms of compromise. The art is in making your partner in the negotiation give you more than you give them and, through persuasive communication, for you both to be pleased with the deal at the end of the negotiation. The end of the negotiation is also the beginning of your collaboration on the publishing of your novel so don't make an enemy of the publisher at the outset.

Negotiation of a publishing deal should be based on the win-win theory of negotiating where both parties end up with most of what they set out to achieve. You both know you want to work together, not just on this negotiation but for a period of time following the negotiation. The 'win-lose' style of negotiating, where the negotiators see themselves in battle and think they can only win by making the other lose, creates a situation in which it can be very difficult to work together amicably afterwards; not something to aim for in the publisher–author relationship

Decide what you are selling

Before establishing a price, you must decide what you're selling. Before you begin negotiating, give some thought to what you are trying to achieve. Decide how many titles, what rights, what territory and what period of time you are prepared to license. A larger rights package, a world rights deal rather than only one market or language, will obviously be worth more. But you must weigh this against what you could sell the other rights and territories for later, if you were to keep control of them yourself to sell separately.

If you sell two or three books to the publisher, then obviously the deal must be richer than if you are selling just one. But here you must weigh up what you could sell book two and book three for if you did these deals later. A single book contract now might be wiser in the long run, but you would receive less initially because you wouldn't have the signature money from the multiple book contract right away. For example, if Publisher A was offering £10,000 for a one-book contract, they might be prepared to offer £22,000 for a two-book deal or £36,000 for a three-book contract. The reason for the increased figure per title is because it can be worth the extra outlay for a publisher to have the security of knowing they have bought three books ahead. This way they know exactly what each of the three books has cost them, and they know that they have a guarantee that they will be able to publish the author for three books and several years ahead.

With a £10,000 contract for one book you might expect to receive £2,500 on signature (if the payments were to be made in four equal stages on signature of the contract, delivery and acceptance of the manuscript, first publication in hardback, and first publication in paperback). But if you accepted a three-book contract at £36,000 (an advance per book of £12,000), with similar proportional payment stages for each of the three titles, the least you could expect on signature of the contract would be £9,000. And if your negotiating skills were good, you might be able to argue for even more. So the cash flow looks good initially if you accept a multiple book deal. But you won't be able to negotiate another contract that increases your advance per book with this publisher until you have delivered all three books under contract. Even if the first book in the contract becomes a major bestseller and sells hundreds of thousands of copies, you are still obligated to write the next two for the figure previously agreed. Of course, you might receive extra money from the royalties your bestseller will earn, but royalties take a long time to arrive.

A similar weighing up has to take place when you are deciding whether to sell, say, just British and Commonwealth rights to a British publisher, or whether to let them buy world rights in all languages. They ought to pay more for a bigger rights package (they then sell translation rights to publishers overseas), but the publisher who owns world rights usually keeps all the income from selling these rights until the total advance they contracted to pay you has been covered. After that, it is paid to you, less the percentage that the publisher keeps for doing the deal. (For a detailed description of the way advances and royalties and subsidiary income works, see chapters 9, 13 and 16.)

If you retain the right to sell translation deals yourself, or through your agent, then although you might receive less initially from the British publisher, you do have the chance of making more, long-term. If you sign contracts with translating publishers, all of the income from these additional sales will come straight to you, after deduction of your agent's commission. There will be no unearned advance from your British publisher to swallow up the overseas rights income.

If you have an agent, you will obviously want their advice here. Agents who are well-connected internationally will often advise selling only British rights to the British publisher, Australian rights to the Australian publisher, American rights to the American publisher and so on. But there is sometimes an argument for selling world rights in English, or world rights in all languages, to just one publisher and then letting them sell the other rights on. This can be either because you or your agent does not have the means to exploit these rights well yourselves, or because the publisher is offering such a large guaranteed advance that you think you'll do better selling this way. Or it could be because you are short of funds and need money now, rather than later. These are all perfectly legitimate reasons for selling a large rights package to one publisher, but you must be clear about the trade-off.

Points to consider include:

1. The publisher may take a larger cut than your agent would have done from the international rights sales.

2. You will probably have less control or approval over whom you are sold on to in the other markets and almost certainly less direct contact with your overseas publishers.

3. Unless you specifically negotiate otherwise, the subsidiary rights income from your book will be set against the original advance paid to you by your primary publisher, so you won't receive any extra income until your first advance is earned out. Not only advances from foreign publishers but also earned royalties will reach you much more slowly. This is a serious consideration when you realize how many markets can be reached by a commercial novel; the record in our agency at the moment is thirty-eight languages, all contracted direct with the author.

4. Again, unless specifically negotiated, even if the primary publisher's edition goes out of print, they will be able to resist reverting rights to you by virtue of the fact that they have subsidiary contracts that are still valid.

The initial offer

Once you have established what you are selling, what happens when a publisher makes an offer?

It's human nature, and a basic concept in negotiation, for them to start offering at a lower figure than they are eventually prepared to pay. So how do you get them to improve their initial offer?

If you have offers from other publishers too, you can play them off against each other (see under 'Auctions' in chapter 5). If you have only one publisher offering, you must be more subtle, and old-fashioned market place bargaining comes into its own here.

It's extremely important not to become emotional when you're negotiating; not to lose your patience or your temper or to insult the person you are negotiating with. It hardly ever achieves what you are aiming for and can lose you ground. If you are feeling threatened or bullied by the other party's negotiating tactics, look for ways to strengthen your own. Speak more slowly on the telephone, or make copious notes if the negotiating is taking place face to face. These both buy you more time for thinking. Stand up, even if you are talking on the telephone. Odd as it may sound, it can make you feel more assertive.

Express disappointment: 'To be honest, I was expecting a higher figure. Can you improve on that? I'm finding it hard to accept the present offer.' Note that, unless you intend to reject the offer outright, phrasing your response like this keeps the offer current and the negotiation proceeding. Be careful not to say no at any point, unless you really mean it. Once you have said no, the whole offer is deemed to be taken off the table, and it is then entirely up to the publisher whether they re-offer at all. Keep the offer 'in play'.

Areas to negotiate

Final offer: something a veteran negotiator makes just prior to making concessions
– Jim Fish and Robert Barron, *Great Business Quotations*

It's important to be aware how many areas of an offer can be improved and in what order it is best to negotiate them to produce the optimum deal. (For a more detailed explanation of the many points raised, see under 'Subsidiary Rights' in chapter 13.)

First, always make sure you and the publisher are talking about the same thing by asking them to be specific about the following areas when they first make their offer:

— the advance
— the stages in which the advance is paid
— the territory
— the licence period – full term of copyright or a fixed licence period?
— the rights package
— the split of income between you and the publisher on major subsidiary rights controlled by the publisher (paperback, US translation, serial, audio, film, TV, electronic where applicable)
— home royalties, hard and soft

- export royalties, hard and soft
- special royalty provisions:
  on high discount sales
  on small reprints

Because these special royalty provisions are always to an author's disadvantage, if a publisher doesn't mention them when first offering, don't introduce them yourself. But if a publisher's offer includes mention of them, make sure they come with specific definitions and try to improve upon them along with everything else. For further explanation of these points, see chapter 9 on contracts.

Obviously the first area to address is the advance. Often a large portion of the time taken to negotiate a deal is concentrated on the advance figure. Stuart Krichevsky, a New York agent who represents many bestselling clients, was once asked by a publisher what kind of figure he wanted for a particular book. Mindful that he didn't particularly want to name a figure, Stuart replied, 'I want you to make an offer that you think will buy this book.' Wonderful!

Once the figure is agreed (and it will usually be a compromise!) look at the way it will be paid. Traditionally, advances were paid over to the author in thirds (signature of contract, delivery of manuscript, first publication), but increasingly publishers have been looking to make payments in quarters (signature of contract, delivery of manuscript, first publication and then later paperback publication) with some even adding a fifth stage on big money deals: six months after paperback publication.

I can see the attractiveness to the publisher of spreading out the payments (it helps cash flow and puts payments to the author closer in time to the point where they can start getting payments in from booksellers). But I work for my clients and longer payment periods hit individual authors harder than they do publishing companies. My authors may have very few other sources of income – if any – and they do have grocery bills and mortgages to pay. I think it's especially important for authors and agents always to resist contracts that call for income to be paid after publication, although allowing that can be a favourable negotiating point if you want a more drawn-out payment process in order to increase the total figure of the advance. You should look for every way that you can turn a potential disadvantage into an actual advantage.

Once the advance figure and the payment stages are established, you should try to reduce the rights package and territory controlled by the publisher. Every piece you keep, provided you have the means to sell it, can improve the amount and flow of cash you receive from your book.

There are many areas for negotiation in a contract. For instance, we represent several South African authors. It therefore follows that if we are selling the Commonwealth rights package to a British publisher we always try to negotiate special royalties for copies sold in South Africa (i.e. the same level as 'home' royalties rather than have the author accept a lower export royalty). Or even better, we might try to separate out South African rights and sell them direct to a South African publisher. I would expect a local publisher of good standing to do as well – if not better – than a UK publisher, even if the UK publisher had their own local sales force. And a book by a local author might do particularly well in that author's home market (not least because the author will be available to promote it). So any improvement in the royalty percentage could result in a significant actual increase in income for the author.

Sometimes, oddly as it must seem to those outside the trade, it can even make sense to do separate deals with two pieces of the same company. If a worldwide, or Commonwealth-wide English language publisher uses their own company in South Africa to sell the books there that are published from London, you might feel safe in assuming that you can sell the whole market to the London portion of the company. But there are often good reasons for selling, say, South Africa, direct on a separate contract to the South African office. Because this way it will be viewed as a 'South African published' title by the South African office, rather than one of many titles bought thousands of miles away in London which the South African office is expected to sell as the export agent for the London office. The degree of enthusiasm and energy accorded to the title can be markedly different, reflected in sales and marketing time and money expended – or not. Of course, it's difficult to separate relatively small markets unless there is some reason for the title or the author to appeal to that market in particular. But if you can do it, you might increase earnings for the title in a dramatic way.

Most publishers offer royalties on a scale that goes up as the book sells more copies. The figures at which the royalty goes up to the next level – known as the break points – can be negotiated downwards, which have the effect of bringing forward the point at which the author earns a higher royalty. A publisher has to recoup initial costs (the advance, paper, printing and distribution) on the book, which depresses the profit on early copies sold. Although some costs will continue at the same level no matter how many copies are sold, the cost per copy does diminish as the sales increase, thereby increasing the publisher's profit per copy. It is only fair that the author's income should rise too.

Royalties can be aggregated in preference to non-aggregated, i.e.

home and export sales added together so that the author reaches the higher royalty level sooner than if the royalty scale were applied to home sales and export sales separately. (A reminder: for explanation of all these terms, see chapter 9 on contracts).

Marketing budgets and promotion plans can sometimes be made to form part of the contract. Extra payments can be negotiated as escalators or bonuses depending on the performance of other rights, for example, an extra figure is paid if a film based on the book opens, or if a television series is broadcast, or if the book appears in specific positions on named bestseller lists.

If a contract is for more than one book, then you need to negotiate whether the advance is for joint or separate accounting. As with aggregated royalties (see above), separate accounting for each title in the contract allows you to receive extra earned income earlier, whether it be from royalties on the publisher's own edition or subsidiary income from rights the publisher has sold to others. 'Separate accounting' means that although the contract covers two or more titles, each title will have a specified portion of the total advance allocated to it, and each title will be the subject of a separate royalty account. For example, if a two-book contract was for £50,000, each title might be allocated £25,000 as its advance. When the hardback of book 1 is published, the royalty earnings accrue to that title's account, and the same for subsidiary rights income and paperback royalty earnings, and audio tape too if that edition has been published or licensed. Once the earnings have reached £25,000, the author will be eligible to receive extra royalties: much preferred to having to wait for extra royalties until the whole £50,000 has been earned back.

Changing from joint to separate accounting in a multiple book contract can make a big improvement to your cash flow. For this reason agents argue strongly for separate accounting. For the same reason, publishers fight against it.

If you are selling world rights in all languages to one publisher, negotiate a clause that automatically brings all unsold rights back to you if they remain unsold after a certain period, for instance, a year after publication date.

Above all, make sure that your negotiation covers every aspect of the final deal, so that everything has been dealt with before you move to the contract. There is nothing worse than a negotiation that leaves important points to be discussed after you have accepted that the publisher owns the book.

As each piece of the deal is finalized, be sure to confirm, verbally at this stage, or in writing if you are exchanging letters or faxes, each step that has been agreed before you move on to the next one.

When you get to the end of the deal, confirm every single tiny detail that has been agreed and ask the other party to contact you immediately if their understanding is not the same as yours.

When the deal is done, stop. Don't be tempted to move the goalposts. Don't be tempted to think or say, 'I've just thought of something else . . .' And remember to be positive about the deal that you've just struck: you're going to have to live with it and work with the person you've been negotiating with for a long time, so you want to go into the deal with both parties feeling satisfied and pleased with their part in the negotiation.

Sometimes a deal will be negotiated in good faith but then be held up for many months at contract stage while points of law or principle are argued with the contracts department. This is more common when one publishing company is selling to another, and their differing policies clash on issues such as which country's law will predominate, how warranty clauses can be made to fit with two different insurance policies etc. It is not uncommon for contract arguments to go on for so long that the book is published before the contract is agreed but this does happen more often when companies are dealing with companies, rather than with authors. If you are in any doubt about the wording of a publisher's contract, ask to see a blank one before signing the deal.

General negotiating tips

If you are intending to negotiate your own deal without having an agent work for you, don't ever believe a publisher who tells you that they have standard contracts that are non-negotiable. I have negotiated contracts with thousands of publishers and never found one who stuck to that. Every contract is negotiable and if you find a publisher who truly won't negotiate, I suggest you walk away from them even if they are offering to publish your book. If they are as inflexible as a non-negotiable contract suggests, imagine how little influence they will allow you to have on other aspects of your publication. The thought of querying a royalty statement with a publisher like this is appalling!

Of course there are some clauses that will be non-negotiable. Once you have read chapter 9 on contracts you should have a good idea of what can be negotiated and what can not. One area in contract negotiations that can cause a lot of irritation and bad feeling (and can result in the publisher becoming less flexible on other points) is if they find themselves negotiating with someone who clearly knows very little about the publishing business. I have seen this quite a few times either from an author who hasn't bothered to find out the first thing about the way the trade works, or – more often than it should happen – from novice agents or lawyers who are not experienced in the book world. In each case it can result in lengthy, drawn-out negotiations and explanations in which the publisher can feel as though they are having to give a seminar on the trade to negotiate points that are standard throughout the industry. Negotiating with an experienced agent means that the publisher knows the agent won't try to vary points that the whole trade views as normal and standard. Knowledge of trade practice means that the negotiators don't have to spend time arguing over things that will never be altered anyway and can spend more time on the items than can actually be varied and of benefit to the author.

Of course, you aim high when negotiating because the other side will never offer you more than you try to negotiate for. If you show ignorance of the business by asking for unreasonable levels (of royalty, for example) you will lose respect from the person with whom you are negotiating, and that could be detrimental further along in the negotiation. The more you know about the business and the way publishers put their offers together and the way the trade sells and operates, the greater the chance you have of negotiating a good deal for yourself. You waste time if you don't know what the parameters of the variable elements are.

Remember that you must keep the whole deal in mind while you negotiate every individual point. If you forget the way that the elements knit together, you run the risk of ending up with an unbalanced contract where you may have won some small concessions but had to give way on much bigger issues. You must never offer concessions to the publisher yourself: they should be prised out of you in return for some gain somewhere else. Once a publisher has made their initial offer, I usually draw up a checklist for myself of the areas I want to – and think I can – improve upon. I then work through them, tackling the biggest first and ending with the least important. If I find the publisher unwilling to concede my third item, I will sometimes mention my last (and least important) item and say that I would be willing to forego that request, i.e. I will trade it in return for the agreement I'm looking for on my third point. Thus I am conceding a small point in return for success on a larger one.

It can often be worth negotiating for more items than you intend to settle for (so long as they are not unreasonable or unworkable) specifically in order to have points you can trade with, points you can concede in order to win something else. This also makes you look reasonable and civilized, which in turn can persuade the publisher to feel more generous.

As I mentioned earlier, you can buy yourself a lot of time for thought and reflection by speaking more slowly than you would normally. This has the added advantage of seeming to confer an air of wisdom upon the speaker too! Contrast the speed of delivery of a stand-up comedian, or a group of people gossiping at a party, with the measured tones of a practised speechmaker. This same advice is always given to people doing radio broadcasts, or any form of public speaking: speaking much more slowly than normal conversation makes you sound like an expert.

If the publisher says flatly that something is impossible, throw the negotiating ball back at them by saying, 'Well what can you offer in return for me backing down on that one?' and then keep quiet while they think about it. And continue to keep quiet until they offer a concession.

Silence, used sparingly and at the right times, can be remarkably effective as a negotiating tool. It is easier to do this on the telephone than face to face, although if you can bring yourself to use this technique in a meeting, it can unnerve another party pretty quickly! Most people jump in to fill a silence and often will give away information or negotiating points unwittingly. If your negotiating partner is using silence as a weapon in their armoury, you must be very careful not to fall into the trap yourself.

Having used the words 'weapon' and 'armoury', I do nevertheless normally try to stay away from confrontational language, which is why I have refrained from calling the publisher your negotiating 'opponent'. Keep the 'win-win' theory of negotiating in mind at all times! Another way of doing that, and of engendering friendly feelings during the negotiation, is to remember to compliment the other party every time they make a good point. Phrases such as 'I can see that will work well' or 'Yes, I'm prepared to concede the point there, that's only fair', actually make you sound strong rather than weak. And they can help you win other points too, because the publisher feels generous towards you rather than antagonistic.

One negotiating ploy that buys valuable thinking time is easier for an agent to use than an author negotiating for themselves. If the publisher raises something particularly knotty, or that I hadn't foreseen, and that I don't want to react to immediately, I can always say in reply, 'I really think I have to discuss that with my client.' Whether I do discuss it with my client or not at that time, it nevertheless buys me time to think through the point and try to find a solution that I like.

Human beings are territorial animals and we all function best on home ground. Most publishing negotiations take place with everyone in their own office and communicating by telephone, or fax, or e-mail, but if you do have to negotiate face to face try to get the publisher to come to you. Failing that, meet on neutral territory. Agents and publishers spend a lot of time negotiating in restaurants! If you are negotiating face to face you have to remember all the signals that body language can give away. There are some fascinating books on body language but actually most of it is plain common sense. Everybody knows, for instance, that crossing your arms over your chest is defensive. Don't do it when you are negotiating because the person you are negotiating with will rightly deduce that you don't feel sure of yourself on whatever point has just arisen. Allowing your eyes to slide away from theirs when you are speaking suggests you might be being less than totally truthful. Alternatively, deliberately looking past them to the far distance, sighing slightly, and creating a pause after they have made a point suggests you are thinking deeply, and probably wisely, about it. Never mind that your mind might be panicking: creating a calm impression is always helpful. Make sure you can carry this off well, though, otherwise you run the risk of giving the impression of boredom!

If you are in any way nervous about negotiating, I would strongly advise against doing it face to face. You risk losing too many points by letting the publisher see your nervousness. Confidence – or at the very least an air of confidence – counts for a lot.

Make promises only when you are on sure ground. Delivery dates are sometimes sore points: publishers want manuscripts early so they can plan their list, their publication strategy and marketing, while authors always need more time to write them. I find that saying something like, 'My author needs time for research and revision, so why don't we add on another three months. If she can deliver before the deadline you know she will' not only buys the author more valuable time, it also makes her sound extraordinarily professional. And if she does indeed deliver before the contracted date, everyone will think her even more professional. So much better than delivering on exactly the same date, but being a month later than the agreed revised date.

Learn to listen for other people's hidden agendas. If you can pick up on something that the publisher wants very much but doesn't want to ask for outright, then you can use that to your advantage by blocking it time and again in return for concessions that are useful to you.

It is quite common in publishing negotiations to find the editor or contract department assistant you are negotiating with either doesn't fully understand the implications of a point you are making, or feels they are being pushed to the limits of their own responsibilities or jurisdiction. I will sometimes say, in as helpful a tone as I can, 'Would it help you to sound out someone else on that? Perhaps you'd like me to draft some wording for the clause and fax it over?' When you hear the rush of relief as they say, 'Yes please' you realize it was the right thing to do. It doesn't necessarily mean you win the point, but you have created another bridge of understanding between yourself and the publisher's negotiator that may be paid back by a concession further on.

Editors will also sometimes become extraordinarily conspiratorial with an agent if they want to be able to concede a point but fear their superior will not sanction it. I have often been asked by an editor to send a particularly stern, or angry, or hurt fax protesting a point that the editor does not have the authority to concede. The editor then shows the agent's fax to their superior and is able to argue the point within the company without looking like they are opposing their boss or company policy themselves. I'm always happy to oblige if it wins me a point for my author!

Psychology plays a large part in negotiating and it is enormously useful to know the person well, or to have negotiated with them before. This is something that is more likely to occur if an agent and editor are doing a deal than an author and editor. No matter how prolific an author, it is unlikely that he or she negotiates as often with that editor as an agent with a fair-sized client list will. The editor will know that they have to negotiate again with that agent and will want to leave the negotiation in a reasonable mood. And they will know that the agent is a practised negotiator. Many publishers do try to bulldoze authors into accepting points that they know agents would never allow in a contract. They play on the fact that it is unlikely that the author is a skilled negotiator with a wide knowledge of what is, and what isn't, common in book business contracts.

I don't like overreacting in negotiations, but if used in a controlled way, strong reaction can be effective. Listening to a point made by the publisher and then responding with a very loud 'What?' expresses as much outrage as is usually needed, perhaps backed up with 'I can't really believe you expect me to accept that.' Concessions have been known to follow if the publisher has been made to feel really bad. That only works on certain kinds of personalities, as you can imagine.

Preparation pays, and nowhere is that more true than in the area of negotiating. It's only sensible to try to stack the odds as much in your own favour as possible. The only place where you'll encounter success before work is in a dictionary! You've made a start by buying this book. But don't think you'll know all you need to know about negotiating a publishing contract just by reading this chapter. You need to read the whole book to set it in the context of the trade as a whole, and you'll need to read one or two books specifically on negotiating – and then practice and practice – before you will be skilled at it. It's such fun when you are!

7 The trade and how it works

A cottage industry meets big business

This is a huge subject and could be a separate book. I shall attempt to cover the many aspects of the diverse publishing industry even if it must be quite brief. I'll describe the various parts of the trade in the order that an author, and a book, will meet that part, starting with agents, progressing through publishers to booksellers, then to book clubs, mail order and other special sales' sections of the trade.

The agents

Authors' agents are pretty much an English-language phenomenon. They do exist in other language markets, but it is still unusual for writers working in German, or French or Italian to be represented by a literary agent. They will more likely contract direct with a publisher in their own country who will control all rights in all languages. In other words, the publisher will be responsible for trying to sell the book to publishers in other languages and territories.

But in the English-speaking world, literary agents are thick on the ground (and it seems to me on my more cynical days that everyone who gets fired from a publishing company sets up as an agent the next month). It is often an advantage for an agent to have worked on the publisher's side of the desk, so long as their publishing expertise is relevant to the work of an agent. An editor, for example, might not be skilled at negotiating; a marketing manager might never have seen an author's contract. But a publisher turned agent who does have the required skills can be invaluable: knowing how your opponent in negotiation is putting their offer together, or planning their negotiating strategy can be extremely useful.

Apart from the fact that inevitably there are good and bad agents, there are three kinds of agencies, defined by size. But there is no easy way to identify the right agent by size alone: small isn't always beautiful and big isn't always bad. One reasonable precaution, when deciding which agents to approach, is to restrict yourself to those who belong to their country's agents' association. In Britain, America and Australia, for instance, membership of the associations implies a certain level of professionalism, of knowledge of the industry. And it does mean that if something goes badly wrong you have a body you can take your complaint to.

So much is dependent upon the personality of the agent (particularly if they are a sole trader), their experience, how they are organized within their company (particularly with the large agencies, see later) and what international contacts they have, that the size of the agency tells you nothing about how good they are likely to be. It also doesn't always mean that the larger the agency the more clout they have: some smaller agencies carry an awful lot of weight (in prestige) because publishers respect their knowledge and expertise in certain areas.

Taking size only as a criterion though, let me define the three groups.

Agents: sole traders

These are either agents who are starting out and haven't yet grown beyond a one-person company, or the agents who prefer to work very closely with their clients and customers and want a hands-on approach at every level. The positive aspect of a company this size can be personal attention to every detail: the principal of the agency attends to everything with perhaps just one or two assistants. A negative aspect can be when they become so busy they can't attend to every detail any longer. If there is no one else to do the work some things are not dealt with at all. Their contacts might not be as broad, worldwide, as agencies that are larger. But for an author starting out, this kind of close personal attention can be invaluable.

The sole-trader agent owns their own agency and should be totally committed to their success, which makes for very high motivation when working for their clients. But business trips or holidays away from the office can leave clients and their books unattended.

Agencies of this size can sometimes prove vulnerable once their clients achieve fame: the clients may yearn for broader contacts, and other, bigger agencies can sometimes be predatory. Sole traders often find it difficult to grow. They must either stay the same size, or change their structure radically.

The most positive aspect of being represented by an agency of this size is the close relationship formed between client and agent involving intimate knowledge of each other's work patterns. Each client represents a large proportion of the agency's business and so attention to detail should be scrupulous.

Many successful agents of this size do not welcome unsolicited approaches from would-be clients because they do not have the time or staff or inclination to deal with a large slush pile.

Two of the most successful agents of this size are Deborah Owen and Christine Green.

Deborah Owen is an American who has lived in Britain for many years. She represents a handful of extraordinarily successful clients such as Delia Smith, the Ellis Peters estate and Amos Oz. Her philosophy is based upon representing a small number of clients and doing everything for them. But understandably, this approach rules out a large client list.

Christine Green handles all her clients personally, and has a stable of clients who have been with her for years, including the extraordinarily successful Maeve Binchy. To use a shopping analogy, agencies that operate like this represent the 'designer boutique' style of agent.

Agents: the groups

These are a fairly recent phenomenon, having appeared in the last ten years or so, almost always growing from an old-established agency.

The attraction of a large agency, for a client, is that they wield a lot of clout. Because they handle so many authors, publishers prefer not to offend them, and if an agency of this size takes a stance on a particular trade issue, they can make themselves heard very effectively. A problem with large agencies is that sometimes authors can feel themselves to be just one of a crowd, and if they are not one of the biggest clients in a large agency, they can feel – and sometimes actually are – overlooked.

Authors can be attracted to a large agency because they have heard good things of the principals, only to find that the agency designates a younger, less experienced agent to work on the author's titles. That is why it is important for authors, when first joining an agency, to discuss exactly who will do what for them.

Agencies of this size may be owned in a variety of ways. Most originated as agencies owned by the proprietor-agent or agents who started the company. Most now have some additional agents who do own shares, but many of the agents who handle their own list of authors within the agency may not own shares in the company.

Agencies of this size often employ a profit-share scheme for their agents, share-owners or not, which either gives them bonuses related to the overall profitability of the whole company at year end, or which rewards them related to their own performance during the year.

A. D. Peters, started by Mr Peters more than seventy years ago, was one of the oldest literary agencies in Britain. It became Peters, Fraser & Dunlop when the Fraser & Dunlop Agency was absorbed; and when it took over the June Hall Agency it was known for a while as Peters, Fraser, Dunlop & Hall which made it sound a little like some of the advertising agencies of the 80s! It now seems to have gone back to styling itself as Peters Fraser & Dunlop (PFD).

I always think of Curtis Brown as a group even though, for the most part, it has grown organically, rather than taking over other agencies. Curtis Brown employs more than a dozen agents and so, to continue the shopping analogy, presents itself rather more as a department store than a designer boutique. Like all the larger agencies, it has a great deal of talent to call on and, like all the older agencies, many lucrative estates, that it continues to handle. In this context, 'estates' are the work of dead authors, still in copyright, whose work can be managed – licensed and reissued throughout the world – often very lucratively. These can be very big business indeed for the agencies that represent them. Agencies with estates to handle tend to be the older established agencies that have been going for many years, and which represented the clients when they were alive. Estates can be attractive as a business proposition, but the unattractive side, for the agents, can be dealing with lawyers for the estate or family members, who often know little and care less about the literary aspects of the work, so long as the income keeps flowing.

The main attraction of an agency as large as Curtis Brown or PFD, for the clients and for the agents who work for the agencies, is the range of experience represented by the variety of agents employed, and the use of specialized departments to place certain rights such as translation, film and electronic.

Agents: medium-sized

There are many of this size, and here I would put my own. Bigger than sole traders, not group sized, we and many like us have a small number of primary agents. We have four: myself and Isobel Dixon handling book rights and Julian Friedmann and Conrad Williams handling film and TV rights and scripts, and a staff of seven other people to supplement our work. I feel we are small enough to deal with everything personally, but big enough to have worldwide contacts and a wide range of experience.

We are large enough to have a reputation for strength in certain areas but can we continue to give our clients enough personal attention? My feeling is that agencies of our size offer the best of all possible worlds: experienced agents, personal attention, a small friendly staff, and a big enough reputation to be able to get what we want for our writers. The success of this depends upon keeping a close eye on client and staff numbers (and client and staff relationships) and, like all agencies, taking care not to represent more clients than can be properly handled. Balancing this is vital, for any sized agency.

Surveys on agents

At the end of the day it is up to each author to select the kind of agent they feel most comfortable with, or who offers them the best service. I realize that this is often only known after an author has joined an agency, which can be too late if the wrong decision has been made. Independent judgements of agencies have been made by *The Author*, the magazine of The Society of Authors. They have carried out two surveys about how their members felt about their agents. The surveys were each completed by too small a number to rate as a real cross-section of authors, but their findings were published, and the resulting analyses and articles by Michael Legat made fascinating reading, for authors and agents (and publishers) alike.

Their most recent survey on agents, for example, conducted in 1998, was based on 507 questionnaires containing thirty-eight questions each, returned by their members who were reporting on ninety-eight different agencies. At the time, the Society had approximately 6,000 members, of which about half were unagented. The analysis was 'a considerable labour' as Mr Legat remarked. He also commented that authors seemed to remain loyal to their agents and many had been with the same company for over thirty years. In the previous survey, completed in 1994, one of David Higham's clients had actually been with them for 'almost sixty happy years since the firm's foundation in 1935'. What a wonderful testament to how they look after their writers. The 1998 survey produced one author who had been with their agent for fifty-three years!

Forty-three per cent of those responding had worked with no other agent and 32 per cent had had just one previous agent. Michael Legat commented that some authors had changed agencies only because the earlier agent had gone out of business or had died or had been taken over, which means that in an even larger number of cases the relationship seems to be rather more permanent than modern marriage.

The two surveys make interesting points about what authors want from their agent. First in importance, as was to be expected, was selling the author's work and negotiating contracts. Next came friendship, support and encouragement, followed closely behind by advice, editorial judgement and provision of ideas. Then came acting as a buffer between author and publisher, the agent's experience and knowledge of the market, communication and availability, and the continuity which agents provide in a changing market place.

The 1998 survey discovered that the section that received most praise from authors for their agents was with regard to accounting: 93 per cent said they were satisfied that money received and due to them was properly accounted for. There was general satisfaction over the time taken to get the money to the client (with more than 200 authors using words like 'immediately', 'quick' and 'a few days') and only twelve authors commented that they felt the time lag to be 'too long'. There were few fears that agents were sitting on their clients' money.

In 1994, the Society then listed twelve agencies (out of the 106 covered by the questionnaires that year) as 'highly commended' because they received at least five reports with no negatives. I'm pleased to say that we were one of the twelve. If you want to look up the survey, it appeared in the spring 1994 issue of *The Author*. I might have reprinted it here but one of the agencies that was not favourably mentioned has taken great exception to it and the Society felt it would be unwise to reproduce it in full.

In the 1998 survey (which appeared in the winter issue of the magazine) only three agencies received such a good result: John Johnson with eight reports, and Felicity Bryan and Gregory & Radice each with five reports. A. P. Watt with fifteen reports received only one negative verdict, and then eleven agencies were listed as receiving 'very respectable ratings', of which we were one, with eleven reports. The Society's commentary went on to say: 'Obviously, the more reports received about a given agency, the more reliable the results should be, but I think there is an element of luck involved in all of them . . .'

My feelings about our showing in the 1998 survey is that, while we have no room for complacency, given the rate at which we have grown in the four years between the surveys, and the larger number of our clients who replied, we've no cause for panic either. The more clients who report on their feelings about an agency, the greater likelihood there is that someone will have some cause for complaint. But I do intend that the Society's next survey should show us as entirely blameless again, if possible!

A final word on agents: when an author is seeking an agent, nothing is better than a personal recommendation from an author already represented by that agent. Yet another reason for agents to cherish their existing clients!

The publishers

Publishers come in every variety of size, energy, competence and efficiency, and areas of specialization and ownership. I have chosen to focus on them via ownership, because I think that defines the way that authors respond to them, and vice versa.

Independent

There are many fewer of these than there used to be. But it is encouraging that publishing tends to be cyclical. After a few years of seeing the big groups relentlessly swallow up all their smaller competitors, one usually sees a few enterprising individuals who have had enough of working for the big companies, and who are determined to start their own. The pleasure, for an author or an agent, of working with an independent publisher is that they can make their own decisions without having endless meetings. They can move fast when they want to, unencumbered by a huge bureaucracy, and they are sometimes able to buck the trend and make a success of something the bigger companies wouldn't dare to try because the bigger the publisher, the more cautiously they often behave.

The problem of working with an independent is that while they can be quick, they can also sometimes take forever to make decisions. (But it's easy to nag them because it's usually simple to discover who is handling a particular project; there just aren't dozens of people to delegate to.) They can find themselves with cash flow problems precisely because they are small, and if they do make a surprise success of a particular title they are sometimes too small to keep it going.

Because it is so difficult to be a mass-market paperback publisher if you are independent (size does matter, at least when it comes to paperback publishing!), most of the independents publish in hardback and/or trade paperback. This means that if their books are suitable for mass-market paperback publication they will sell the rights to a paperback house, usually keeping 40–50 per cent of the income themselves before passing on the rest to the author. If that paperback goes on to sell well, the author must accept that a large proportion of the income continues to be retained by the original publisher.

This can lead to independent publishers losing some of their most successful authors to larger publishers who publish both hardback and paperback themselves. The author then receives 100 per cent of the paperback royalty rather than only 50–60 per cent of it.

Souvenir Press and Piatkus Books are two examples of long-term independent publishers. Souvenir and Piatkus both publish quite a variety of titles, Souvenir concentrating on non-fiction, Piatkus publishing non-fiction and fiction. Piatkus Books have, relatively recently, established a mass-market paperback line that seems to be bucking the mass-market trend by being both small and successful. Their first year-end figures published since the start-up of the paperback line looked very good, even though, not surprisingly, company profits dipped a bit due to the cost of the new list's launch.

Fourth Estate is a hugely successful publisher (albeit partly owned by the *Guardian* newspaper), which publishes upmarket fiction and non-fiction that regularly gets their books into the bestseller lists. Like Piatkus, they are unusual in being still independent but big enough to publish their own mass-market paperback list. Bloomsbury is another independent house with their own paperback imprint. These are rare examples.

Because publishers' publishing profiles, like their ownership, can change from season to season, it's always sensible to research a list at the time you are planning to approach them.

The groups

These are companies that control a range of imprints, many of which may, in the past, have been independent publishers. They publish in a variety of formats – hardback, trade paperback, mass-market paperback, educational editions, audio cassette, CD-ROM – and often they are multinational (see Global below). Hodder Headline is a prime example: one of the few UK publishing groups that is neither owned by an overseas publisher, nor owns a US publishing house. The group publishes under many imprints in the UK – Edward Arnold, Coronet, Delta, Headline, Hodder, New English Library, Review and Sceptre – and also under some of these imprints in Australia. But although they have very effective distribution agreements with other companies in Canada, South Africa and Europe, they do not own publishing houses there.

These companies have enormous muscle, wield a lot of power in negotiations – with authors, agents, booksellers and printers – because of their size, and are capable of huge marketing campaigns. They can publish a title in several formats within their own group – first as a hardback, then paperback, perhaps simultaneously as a single-voice reading on audio cassette – and the author will usually receive full royalties on all editions. Because the group has bought the book for several of their imprints at the outset, the contract with the author will specify the level of royalty for each of the editions planned, and it all goes to the writer, to be set against the initial advance which covers all the versions and editions.

The advances are often larger than an independent could afford, and the groups are sometimes able to be generous when agreeing payment stages as they have more flexibility with their cash flow than smaller companies.

Large groups can spend huge budgets promoting certain authors. This is great if you are one of them, but other authors may feel quite forgotten as they languish on a massive publication schedule with no marketing spend for their particular title. A marketing campaign, and a design strategy, planned by a large publishing group can be used for several different editions of a book and also for the audio tape, CD-ROM etc. when the group publishes and sells all of them. This can be tremendously effective as a way of 'branding' the author in the market place.

However, the publishing groups' internal systems can become bogged down in red tape: try getting an agreement to revert rights back to you on your out-of-print book from Random House, say, and you'll see what I mean. But because of their size and diversity, no group is all bad, or all good.

Some groups are so large that it is quite common for an agent to be conducting an enormously protracted discussion, escalating into a row, with one imprint, but to be basking in the glory of a bestseller, beautifully and cleverly and expensively marketed, and lovingly looked after, by another imprint within that same group.

All the groups operate in slightly different ways but most of them have rules and systems to prevent their imprints bidding against each other for the same book. If a book is being sold by multiple submission or auction, most groups are happy for their imprints – in any combination – to offer for any book. But if, towards the end of an auction, two imprints in the same group are the only ones left bidding, most groups have rules that say that one of them must withdraw. A senior executive in the group can decide which imprint can continue bidding by either examining the figures each editor has prepared – their top offer, their estimates for sales – or by listening to each editor pitching as hard as they can for the book. Whatever method they choose, the groups try to protect themselves against a situation in which their investment in a book is escalating because two of their own editors are competing with each other, yet drawing the money from the same bank account.

There are few publishing groups these days that operate only in one territory. As one looks at ownership, so it becomes increasingly clear that the bigger the group, the more likely it is to be multinational. Orion is a UK based and -owned group (Orion, Weidenfeld, Phoenix House, Cassell and Gollancz) that grew quickly and became very successful, despite operating only in the UK. But this changed in 1998 when Hachette, the French publishing giant, bought into Orion. In its new incarnation, Orion is looking west toward America and I would expect that in the not too distant future it will have bought, or set up, a company in the States.

Multimedia and global

When publishing houses were being frantically bought and sold in the late 70s and throughout the 80s, the buyers were sometimes from the same country as the company that was being purchased, but often not. There was a lot of very excited talk of 'synergy' at the time that these multinational groups were being formed. The *Oxford English Dictionary* defines synergy as 'joint working, co-operation'. The idea was that a company that owned publishing houses in, say, Britain, America, Australia and Germany, would be able to buy world rights to a book and publish it successfully in all these markets and languages.

The intention was that they would be more successful because they could co-ordinate the timing of publication worldwide, co-ordinate packaging so that the book's cover would be the same worldwide, which would promote 'product recognition'. This is what happens in the music industry where an identical product – a compact disc or record – can be marketed around the world, simultaneously, with one cover. But the music industry doesn't have the problem of having to translate its work into a range of languages: music is (or is marketed as) an international product.

Global publishers reasoned that if they also owned a record company, or a film company, or radio or television stations, that same 'product' (which began life as a 'book') could be turned into a film or a television series, the music from which would be sold as a record or compact disc, the film poster or book cover could be sold as a poster. Many products with a single image could be marketed together to create even greater product recognition.

It didn't happen. Why? Because human nature and the idiosyncrasies and logistics of publishing meant that it couldn't. First, buyers and markets are not the same the world over. People do not necessarily want to buy the same book, at the same time, around the world. And following that thought through, the editorial directors and publishers who run the publishing imprints in different countries (even though for the same owner), cannot always be persuaded to like the same books at the same time, whatever the wish of the corporation.

Of course, sometimes it does work, wonderfully. A case in point was when the Bertelsmann group (Bertelsmann in Germany, Bantam Doubleday Dell in America and Canada, Transworld – Bantam, Corgi, Doubleday, Anchor, Black Swan – in the UK, Transworld in Australia and South Africa) bought world rights to *The Horse Whisperer* by Nicholas Evans. (This was before Bertelsmann had bought the huge, multinational Random House.) A first novel, *The Horse Whisperer* was bought at auction for high figures and published very successfully by the group's publishers around the world. But this kind of success came about because the editors at the imprints who published it genuinely thought the book right for their own company and country: they didn't have to be coerced into publishing it. This novel was bought individually by different parts of the groups, and they co-operated closely with each other over publication dates and covers and marketing.

Groups who force their publishers into publishing certain titles because they have bought worldwide rights can sometimes regret the decision, if the book flops in some of the markets.

Bertelsmann astonished the book world in 1998 when, without anyone being aware that negotiations were taking place at all, it announced that they had bought the entire worldwide Random House group from their American owners, the Newhouse family. Random House itself (Arrow, Chatto, Ebury, and many others in the UK; Random, Crown, Knopf, Vintage and others in America) had bought the commercial imprints of the Reed group (Heinemann, Mandarin, Minerva and others) from Dutch-owned Reed-Elsevier just one year before, and were still in the process of integrating the companies. Change is the only constant in the corporate ownership world. Most company sales and purchases in the publishing industry are heralded by intense gossip and rumour, sometimes for many weeks or months before an announcement. Bertelsmann's purchase of Random House was unusual in two respects. First, the sheer size of the buyer and the bought; and second, the secrecy with which it was accomplished. This was only possible because Bertelsmann and Random House were both privately owned: no shareholders or large boards had to be consulted. It is said to have been finally agreed between two men at the birthday dinner of one of the Newhouse brothers.

One odd event that took place close to the purchase by Bertelsmann of Random, centred around the publication of a John Grisham novel. Random House UK was the British publisher and part of their exclusive territory was South Africa. Doubleday, one of the Bertelsmann imprints in America, was the book's American publisher. American copies (published by Doubleday) seeped into South Africa, controlled by Random House. So Random House South Africa found themselves lodging an official complaint against Doubleday, whose German owners had just bought Random House! Global publishing can be complicated.

Another hitch to a simple plan for publishing the same title on a worldwide scale is that authors and agents are not always convinced that big is beautiful. If I judge a company in America as the right publisher for one of my clients, it doesn't always follow that their sister company in Germany or Britain will also be the right publisher for that client.

And there's one other objection. Although many agents are happy to sell world rights in all languages to one publisher, and then let that publisher sell rights on to other publishers around the world, I, and many other agents like me, do not favour this approach, except in very few circumstances. If I am representing a highly-illustrated book, then it probably does make sense for the publisher to handle all rights around the world. They can then set up international co-editions and, by printing together, be able to afford a level of sumptuousness in the production of the book that might not be viable for one edition alone.

A co-edition is several publishers printing all their copies in one print run for economy of scale. Each translates into their own language, with only the black plate, for the text, changed for each edition. An illustrated book – the usual kind of book for a co-edition – is printed using four or six different colour 'plates', each plate taking one colour ink. If so set up, the text can affect only the black plate so that is where all the language changes occur, leaving the other plates (for the colour illustrations) unchanged. Each publisher takes care to fit their text into the same area and shape on the page, around the illustrations. The participating publishers all benefit from lower prices per copy printed because the printer produces one long print run, with all the colour plates printed at once. A lot of money per copy is saved on titles with a high colour content by only changing the black text plate from one publisher's edition to another. Because separate printings, involving separate start-up costs for each language edition, would be much more expensive, co-edition printing, while complicated to organize, is very attractive to publishers when it can be done. It's possible, but tricky, for agents to co-ordinate this. On the whole, most agents I know are happy to let the publisher do it so long as the author gets the right level of royalty and is kept informed of progress at every stage.

But with fiction – text only, no illustrations and no tricky layout problems – production of the physical book is straightforward. So unless the publisher is offering my client truly silly money for world rights, I think it is my duty to sell my writer's book, language by language, to separate publishers. I believe this is almost always in my clients' best interests because they then contract directly with each publisher and receive each advance as each contract is signed. They don't have to see each new contract's advance held by their initial publisher to pay off that publisher's advance to the author.

Silly money would have to be so much that I couldn't imagine being able to gather in a similar amount for my writer by selling rights individually to publishers in each market.

Of course, if an author needs a large amount of money right away, selling all rights to one publisher at the beginning can be easier than selling each right individually. And the author gets the security of one large advance, guaranteed at the outset. So there can sometimes exist a need to sell a larger package of rights to one publisher in order to maximize the deal for the sake of the author's short-term cash flow. The richness of a world rights deal depends on the status of the author and the marketability of the book itself.

If an author needs a lot of money at once, a world rights deal with one publisher is sometimes the only way to achieve that, because usually you need to wait for a complete manuscript before you can sell translation rights. I have sold fiction on only a proposal and a couple of chapters to overseas publishers, but the books – and the authors – do have to be exceptional. One novel – and a first novel at that – that we were able to do this for was the remarkable literary novel *Lempriere's Dictionary* by Lawrence Norfolk. Knaus, an imprint of the Bertelsmann group in Germany, bought that novel when only four chapters were written. The German editor said to me when he was offering for it, 'This will be a bestseller for me.' At the time I took that to be normal publishing hyperbole. But when Knaus published it four years later (when the 700-page novel had been completed and translated into German) it quickly became a bestseller, achieving a sale of 100,000 hardback copies within a few months of publication. Ongoing sales in hardback, a book club edition and a paperback edition have multiplied the German sales to several times that number by now.

Other circumstances that make a very early translation sale possible are successful sales of the author's previous titles in a particular market. Glenn Meade, a thriller writer I represent, had his first two novels published in Japanese very well by Futami Shobo. They were very keen to own *Sands of Sakkara*, his third novel, and made a substantial offer for it (based on a synopsis) about ten months before he finished writing it. We were happy with what they had done for him so far, and the offer was good so Glenn accepted the Japanese deal and signed the contract before he'd completed the novel.

The publishing groups that made fine speeches about international synergy and global marketing at the end of the 80s have changed their minds in the last few years. They have seen that buying a worldwide rights package (which usually means an expensive high-figure deal at the outset and can be hard on their cash flow) and then forcing that title on all their publishers worldwide doesn't guarantee success in all those markets. And it can severely de-motivate their own publishers, who may be made to feel that they are losing their autonomy, and losing the right to back their own judgement.

These days, the multinational groups tend only to buy world rights if several of their companies want to publish the book anyway. Under those circumstances some very fine publishing *can* take place.

There are many multinational groups in publishing now, in addition to those I've already mentioned. Others include:

> **HarperCollins** (the eponymous imprint in the UK, Australia, Canada and the USA, plus Flamingo, Fontana, Fontana Press, Thorsons, Times Books and Voyager), owned by Rupert Murdoch's News Ltd
>
> **Little, Brown** (publishing under that name in the UK and the USA, plus Warner, Abacus and Virago), owned by America's Time Life group
>
> **Holtzbrinck** (the German newspaper and publishing group

which owns Fischer, Rowohlt, Wunderlich, Droemer and others in Germany; Macmillan, Boxtree, Picador, Papermac, Pan and Sidgwick & Jackson in Britain; Macmillan, Pan and Picador in Australia; St Martins Press, Henry Holt and Farrar Straus & Giroux in America), owned by the Holtzbrinck family

Size can be their attraction in the first place: it can also produce some of the obvious problems of dealing with them. Their contracts departments might be slow because of the quantity of work expected of them, and they can be less flexible in negotiations as they use their muscle to enforce unpalatable clauses and conditions upon authors. I have sometimes spent many months arguing just a single contract clause with large publishers, as they try to use their size and power to force authors and agents to accept clauses that we consider to be unfair and publisher-biased.

Self-publishing and vanity publishing

It's unfair to classify these together really, but I want to discuss them together in order to contrast them. These two terms, often mistakenly believed to be interchangeable, mean very different things.

Self-publishing is just that: an author deciding to publish for themselves and take control of the whole process. 'Vanity publishing' is a widely used and derogatory term for a branch of the trade that has a dubious reputation and sometimes deserves it.

Vanity publishers are companies that offer to publish an author's work (often representing themselves as conventional publishers) but require the author to 'contribute' a sum towards the book's publication. This can involve the author financing the publishing of their book to the tune of many thousands of pounds, and vanity presses have been known to promise marketing and selling skills that are never put into place. They promise active publication, whereas what they often do is simply print the book using the author's cash. This is where deception can creep in.

The difference between self-publishing and publishing with a vanity press is epitomized by the expectations of the authors who embark upon either of the options. Self-publishing is usually quite straightforward. Authors decide to self-publish for a variety of reasons, often it is frustration with the publishing establishment, as for Jill Paton Walsh when she self-published her novel *Knowledge of Angels*. Fourteen publishers, including her regular publisher, would not accept the manuscript. So she went ahead on her own, and was vindicated in her decision when she saw the novel shortlisted for the 1994 Booker Prize.

When Timothy Mo self-published his novel *Brownout in Breadfruit Boulevard*, it was because trade publishers did not offer a figure that he regarded as the right advance for the book. Although he must have known he would not make as much money by publishing himself, he determined to do so in order to control every aspect of his book's publication. And perhaps he had it in mind to prove to the publishing industry that they were wrong in their assessment of the figures they offered him. As his figures are not available for scrutiny, a comparison cannot be made between what he was offered and what he ended up making, but the view in the trade is that he would have made more money by accepting the figure that had been offered to him by a publisher.

These authors were probably aware of the expenditure they were committing themselves to before they began the self-publishing process.

Our agency took on an author who had successfully self-published his own memoir of growing up in the 1930s in Manchester. Wilfrid Hopkins not only sold several thousand copies of *Our Kid* in his local area, but enjoyed the process of self-publishing so much that he set up a small company called The Limited Edition Press to help others do the same. He is not publishing books for these other authors, but instead is helping them to publish themselves: to edit and design the book, to obtain competitive printing estimates, to decide on the quantity to print, to distribute it and sell to bookshops, and to publicize. Self-publishing is often a very satisfying outcome for many writers so long as they are realistic about what can be achieved.

We met Wilfrid Hopkins because he sent us his memoir and became our client, hoping that his local success could be repeated on a broader scale. After his own local publication of the book, Isobel sold *Our Kid* to Headline for publication in their Review imprint, first as hardback and later as paperback with book club and large print rights sold as well, thus achieving national distribution for a book originally sold only locally.

Other authors who have self-published include David Caute, Susan Hill, J. L. Carr, Beatrix Potter, Walt Whitman, Virginia Woolf and James Joyce. Any author would be proud to count themselves among a group such as this.

Vanity publishing, on the other hand, often begins with an author expecting – and being promised – much more than they end up with. Vanity publishers are so-called because they appeal to the vanity of the author concerned. These companies will often write fulsome letters of praise, ostensibly about the manuscript they have just read. I have seen at least a dozen letters, sent to different authors over a long period of time, from one particular vanity press. They pretend to refer to splendid plotting and pacing, poetic language and a very commercial storyline. A telling fact is that these letters always contain only extravagant praise: there is never a hint of criticism or any suggestion of editing or revision. In fact, the letters are standard, and are customized on computers. Modern technology has a lot to answer for.

The letters are designed to flatter authors into believing that if they come up with a cheque 'as a contribution towards the publishing expenses' their book will be properly and professionally published. I have heard heart-rending stories of people being tricked out of their life savings by believing that they can make a profit on their investment. They are told that the vanity publisher will publicize and sell the book, and that they might see handsome sales that will be very profitable for the author after the first print run has sold out. Few of the vanity publishers have staff experienced in any aspect of publishing as we expect it to happen: all that they do is to print the book and deliver copies to the author, sometimes many fewer than originally promised. Over the years, there have been a number of investigations – by individuals, authors' associations and occasionally by the police –into particular vanity publishers, but so long as there are people happy enough to pay for their own book to be 'published' there will be a market for this kind of business and the possibility of these kinds of problems.

One vanity publisher in Canada called Commonwealth Publications disappeared in 1998, leaving approximately 100 authors, mostly American, organizing a legal action against it. Apparently, Commonwealth had signed contracts with more than 500 writers over a three-year period, promising to print and publish 10,000 copies of a writer's work in return for payments of between $3,000 and $5,000. In fact, most authors received fewer than 100 copies of their book, with little or no marketing, publicity or distribution. The contracts signed meant that when the company ceased trading (owing money to its staff and printers, paper suppliers and a design company) the rights to the manuscripts were controlled by Commonwealth – a sad and worrying story.

If you self-publish you retain control of the costs yourself and if you go into it wisely, you will not end up with any nasty shocks. I would strongly advise against ever getting involved with a vanity press unless you can afford to lose all the money it will cost you.

When you self-publish you must be sure that you know as much as you need to about the practical aspects of what you are taking on.

You also need to ask yourself why you are doing it, what you expect to get out of it, if you can really afford the time and the money required, and whether you are able to face selling and pitching your book yourself to booksellers and potential publicity outlets. It can be a chastening experience to meet a bookseller who refuses to buy a copy, or to approach a newspaper or radio station who refuses to interview you or review the book. Quite apart from the shock of receiving a bad review, if you are lucky enough, or persistent enough, to see reviews at all.

There are easily accessible guides to self-publishing and I would recommend any author contemplating such a course to read at least one. One I can certainly recommend is published by The Society of Authors, and the magazine *Writers' News* published a very good series of articles of advice about self-publishing in their issues throughout autumn 1997 to spring 1998.

Disquiet with the vanity publishers has produced a new kind of company, which came to the attention of the trade when it started to advertise widely early in 1998. Citron Press took whole page advertisements, some in full colour, in the national press in Britain, mounted a successful PR campaign that resulted in large space articles in the publishing trade press, and did a wide mail-out of expensively produced, well-designed colour brochures to many companies in publishing.

Their ads in the national newspapers were aimed at authors frustrated at receiving only rejections from publishers and agencies. Styling itself 'Britain's most unique [sic!] publishing company', they offered authors the chance to join their New Authors' Co-operative and to have their works 'printed and aggressively marketed to the public, through the Citron Press Book Club'. They stated, 'We are not a vanity press, nor are we a traditional publishing house. We are the publishing concept of the future' and quoted a range of impressive and successful authors, including Martin Amis, 'Patron of Citron Press'.

The whole-page article on them in a February '98 issue of *The Bookseller* was headlined, 'Citron adds sparkle to the slush pile'. They went on to explain that the owners of the company, Nikki and Steve Connors, were inviting unpublished authors to pay £400 to join the writers' co-operative, and to submit their manuscript on disk with a 100-word synopsis and short biography. Editors would read the first two chapters; rejected manuscripts would be returned to authors together with a full refund and an explanation as to why the material had been rejected. Accepted work would be printed to a high standard and the authors would receive a royalty of 7.5 per cent of the retail price of £5.99, with the books being marketed through their Readers' Club. Membership of the club would be made up of the authors themselves and 'members recruited through national press advertising'. Members would be asked for feedback on the books, which would be relayed to the authors themselves as well as being used 'for approaches to retailers and mainstream (publishing) houses'. They promised a deal with 'a big Internet bookseller to be announced soon'.

While many respected figures such as Waterstones' marketing director Martin Lee, and authors such as Mavis Cheek, John Mortimer, Penny Vincenzi, Melvyn Bragg, Jeffrey Archer, Josephine Hart, Sheridan Morley, Wendy Perriam and Michael Holroyd are all quoted in the company's literature as applauding the scheme, the secretary of The Society of Authors, Mark Le Fanu, was quoted as sounding a note of caution. He said, 'I wish them luck, but I am slightly sceptical, because there are so many worthy operations of this kind that start out with the best of intentions.' He was most unsure about Citron's ability to sustain a market for the 1,500 titles it aims to publish annually.

Citron mailed more than 1,000 expensively produced colour promotion packs to the 600 writers' groups registered in Britain, and to 400 publishers and agents. The package addressed to me came with a letter urging me to send on referral cards supplied, to all the authors we rejected. 'Why not give new authors a second chance and insert these cards in any future rejection letters you send out?' The pack enclosed consisted of a sixteen-page full colour, well designed and printed brochure pitching the company as a bridge between amateur writers and professional authors. The text sympathized with authors whose material was rejected, stressed that Citron were not in competition with the mainstream publishing houses, and that they 'will NOT [their capitals] take clients from literary agents. And we are NOT a vanity press'. The February '98 letter to me from Nikki Connors included a PS: 'I will be contacting you direct to discuss the concept further. Please accept my call.' I did not hear from her by telephone. Instead I received another letter in April, which told me that they had received enormous support from publishers, agents and the media and had received enquiries from around the world. The letter then quoted again all the supportive comments from authors (which had already been in the first letter) and promised that the book club would be launched 'in the next few months so there is still time for manuscripts to be considered'. The letter offered to send me more referral cards.

In the autumn of 1998 I telephoned to request information about their publishing service: I gave my own name and my home address and telephone number and was assured a package would be sent to me. Nothing has ever arrived.

Their publicity promises that good critiques from readers will result in approaches to mainstream publishers or agents, but they don't mention if, or what, they charge for this service.

I have quoted this correspondence and press coverage at length because I am intrigued by it. I have, as yet, no reason to suspect Citron will not do what they promise, and if they do, I – along with many others already, it seems – will applaud them. So why do I sound sceptical? Probably – like Mark Le Fanu – because experience has led me to realize that the gullibility of frustrated authors (who in many cases do not have the talent to be rewarded by commercial publication) supports an industry that feeds off their vulnerability.

I hope my suspicions are unfounded and I will follow the fortunes and performance of the Citron Press closely. They seem to be concentrating on new writing only so may intend not to publish more than one book by any one author. In November 1998 it became a public limited company.

I am left wondering why Citron require the authors' £400 before reading the manuscript, even though they say they will refund it if they reject the work. Why not ask for the payment only when the manuscript is accepted for publication? They are unusual among 'vanity presses' in that they have spent a lot of their (presumably) own money on advertisements and the PR was very professional and effective. I haven't sent on their referral cards to authors whose work I reject, because that would suggest I am recommending Citron Press. Until I see more of their performance I'll reserve my judgement.

The booksellers

Booksellers and authors' agents are at different ends of the publishing chain of events and are probably the two groups that know – and see – each other less than any other groups in the industry. When I first started meeting booksellers we eyed each other warily, due no doubt to understanding little of what we each did. I decided that one way to understand bookselling better (one part of the industry I have never worked in) would be to attend the annual Booksellers Conference. I found it so interesting that I now go every year and am often the only agent in attendance. The conferences are extremely useful, not only because the business sessions give me an insight into the daily concerns of the bookselling community, but because networking – with publishers as well as booksellers – between the sessions and during the social events always benefits my clients.

Booksellers and agents can help each other in many and varied ways when it comes to promoting authors and books. I'm reminded of one incident in particular that might have ended very differently had I not known the head of the Waterstones chain. A large London publisher was very late in getting a cover design mocked up for a big-selling novelist I represent. She didn't love it and I didn't either but that was not our prime concern. What did the main booksellers think of it? The publisher, obviously keen to press ahead with that design, because to design a new one would cause more delay and pressurize their publication schedule horribly, assured us that booksellers expected the book to sell well and had seen the cover design and all had liked it. He then couldn't resist adding a further persuasive sentence: 'Waterstones, who are very important for this author, really love it.' That did it, we were convinced and my author agreed to the design.

That very evening I was at a publishing dining club I belong to and by coincidence my guest was that author. During dinner we were engaged in conversation with a variety of people on the table. At one point I found my author – normally most civilized – prodding me in the ribs with her elbow. I listened to the conversation she was engaged in with the man opposite, the head of the Waterstones shops. He was saying that he was looking forward to reading her next novel but was rather disappointed with the cover her publisher had shown them a few days earlier ... Next morning I was on the telephone to the publisher as soon as I reached my office. Needless to say, the cover was changed and I think that publisher will think twice before telling us such fibs again!

Basically booksellers fall into two different categories: the independent stores and those owned by the bookselling chains. Again, as with publishers, I am separating them according to ownership. Independents and chain booksellers are fundamentally different in their structure and aims and philosophies, if one can talk about philosophies in the retail sector. And the biggest difference that size makes is to their buying power and the size of the discounts they can command from publishers.

The discount (off the recommended retail price set by the publisher) that a publisher allows a bookseller can be based on the total level of purchases made by a particular chain from that publisher during a fixed period of time. Or – and sometimes in addition – it can be based on the size of the order placed for a particular title. The old adage in the real estate business (and the joke about tattoos) that everything depends on 'location, location, location' can be extrapolated to the size of discounts in the book retail business: everything here depends on 'volume, volume, volume'. The only difference is how it is calculated. Chains of bookshops – with central ordering – obviously use their muscle to demand bigger discounts from publishers. Independent booksellers, who lack the ability to order thousands of copies at a time, may make up for that by developing a speciality – by subject or genre – that allows them to bargain with particular publishers whose titles their customers favour.

The chains

The bookselling chains – of which there are only a few – are very important to publishers. They have enormous buying power, with big orders coming from just a few sources. Support for a book from a chain – either in the form of a large order, or guaranteed window or in-store displays, or themed store promotions – can turn a book into a bestseller. Publishers will therefore do special deals with bookselling chains, both on the levels of discount they afford them and with regard to exclusive promotions for a particular chain on specific books.

It's a curiosity that in 1997, for instance, a tough year in general for the publishing industry, many of the bookselling chains announced plans to expand and to open more shops. What did they base their optimistic outlook upon? Did they believe the trade was facing a period of rapidly expanding book sales? Or were they motivated by the need for a bigger market share for their own chain of shops? I believe it is the latter, and as each chain announces, as they do regularly now, that they are now opening the biggest shop in Australia or Britain, their aim is to try to damage the opposition, and leave the field to themselves, rather than simply expand the market for book sales in general. The opening of more and more, larger and larger bookshops is an indication of competitiveness among the chains, not only a wish to service the consumer.

The biggest chain of booksellers in Britain for many years was always W. H. Smith. Not a books-only chain, but a retailer that also sells music, toys, stationery, papers and magazines. For many years they were famous – or notorious – for central buying, and for a policy of rotating the buyers from one product area to another, which saw music buyers suddenly switched to books, book buyers moved to stationary, etc. When Smith's bought the Waterstones stores from Tim Waterstone, they announced that they would not fold Waterstones in to their central buying system – 'Waterstones will not be Swindonised' (named after the location of W. H. Smith's huge head office) – but of course they did eventually. The amount of power they control is extraordinary. They buy such a large proportion of the UK's commercial fiction in paperback that they have a quite unhealthy ability to manipulate publishers, not only in the area of high discounts for their purchasing, but also in refusing to stock a book if they don't like the cover. Publishers of paperbacks regularly change cover designs to suit Smith's.

Shortly after Waterstones was 'Swindonised', things changed again, with Waterstones becoming part of the HMV Media Group, which aligned them with the Dillons bookshops.

Anyone who has been afforded a tour of Smith's Swindon headquarters and warehouse can hardly fail to be impressed. It is highly automated, runs like clockwork (well, most of the time) and is dedicated to moving large quantities of books around the country, continuously. They take in deliveries from UK publishers on a continuous basis, separate out the stock and then ship it to their many stores. They have a highly sophisticated computerized system to track and analyse the sales of individual titles across the chain by volume, retail value, store, rate of sale and supplier.

Smith's say that they should get big discounts from publishers because of their central buying system: publishers receive one order, only have to deliver to one location, and Smith's take care of distribution from Swindon out to their stores around the country and Europe. Smith's maintain they are saving the publishers money that the publishers would otherwise have to spend on shipping books to each and every store if they were not able to deliver to one central warehouse.

Publishers' concerns centre around the huge power that the chains have when negotiating for discounts with the publishers: even chains that don't order titles centrally do negotiate their chain-wide discount from head office. Publishers are frustrated at not being allowed to sell to managers of individual shops within the chains' ownership. Nevertheless, one big order, so long as there is still some profit in it, is a boon to a publisher. The other side of the coin though, is that if a buyer for a chain decides they will not be taking a particular title, that is a huge blow to the publisher and to the author whose career may suffer enormously because of a decision made by one person.

Whether a chain's scale of operation can justify discounts that can be as high as 55 per cent off the retail price, and which have been rumoured to touch 65 per cent on some titles, is open to argument when you think that the remaining 35 or 45 per cent of the selling price has to pay and profit publisher, printer, binder – and author. (For discussion of the way that retailer discounts impact on authors' royalties, see chapters 9 and 15.)

One aspect of the power of the large chains such as W. H. Smith, which might not be apparent to the general public, is their stranglehold on the mass market. If one or more of the bookselling chains decides not to stock a particular title, then that title will find it very difficult indeed to achieve substantial sales. And it will be virtually impossible for a title to get into the bestseller lists if it is not stocked by most of the major chains. Entering a shop that is part of one of the chains can give you an impression of enormous choice: books everywhere, well displayed, some offering price promotions, etc. But in fact, for many years at W. H. Smith, the number of titles was strictly limited, usually either to books where the chain was able to drive a hard bargain over the discount, or to books that they couldn't afford not to stock, such as titles tying in to a current television series or film, or to well-known and bestselling authors.

Smith's are now broadening their range of books stocked, but such are the quantities of titles published every year that no chain could hope to stock anything but a small proportion of new books, let alone a fair representation of backlist (i.e. previously published) books.

There are many other bookselling chains in the English-speaking world, most of them selling books only, or some with a range of gift items and stationery as well. While their operations may vary from W. H. Smith's in many ways, Dillons, Ottakars and Waterstones are in essence pretty similar. They don't all buy centrally from their head office, but they do use their multiple stores to buy in quantity from publishers, thereby maximizing the discounts they can achieve. They mount promotions to sell these books on to the public, including price promotions offering titles at less than the recommended retail price.

The chains compete fiercely with each other. They vary a lot from one chain to another as to the level of stock they hold in their shops. Smith's, which for many years had actively concentrated on a relatively low number of individual titles, hold less stock in their shops than almost any of the chains. Waterstones and Books Etc. (now part of the even larger, American-owned, Borders group) are stockholding booksellers with an impressive range of titles in each store. They make a point of impressing with the sheer quantity of stock and thus become 'destination stores' for book buyers, stores that a buyer will go out of their way to visit because they will know the chances of finding what they want is high.

Ottakars, once a relatively small south-of-England chain, has become the fastest growing chain in Britain in recent years and it will be fascinating to see how far they will, or can, go in challenging the larger groups.

The chains are good at promoting themselves to the public on the whole. They all mount a range of promotions in-store, some of the biggest, inevitably because of their size, coming from W. H. Smith. Their annual 'Fresh Talent' promotion for first novels in paperback is responsible for several authors' careers being kick-started. Their annual 'Thumping Good Read' promotion features a range of paper-back titles, of which one is then voted the winner by a panel comprised of members of the public. It can add many tens of thousands to the sales of the selected writers during and after the period of the pro-motion in every one of Smith's stores nationwide.

But don't assume these promotions are entirely financed by the booksellers. The publishers whose titles are chosen by the chains for promotions must contribute to the costs themselves: many thousands of pounds in each case, so these titles have to pass two tests. First, in order for their publisher to put them forward for selection, they must be judged, by the publisher, to be worth the money it will cost if they are selected, and second, the title has to convince the bookseller that it will repay the bookseller, with large sales, for having been selected.

Apart from these special nationwide promotions, publishers also have to pay for special display sites in the bookstore, for having their titles appear in the chains' Christmas catalogues etc. I do find myself wondering if the chain booksellers haven't pushed publishers just about as far as they can go. With huge discounts off the recommended retail price now the norm, and every display space in the shop carrying an extra cost to the publisher, the level of profitability on many titles is dangerously low. A publisher who makes little profit on a title will think very hard before buying the next book from their author.

Superstores

A relatively recent development in the bookselling world has been the emergence of 'superstores': gigantic stockholding shops that become destination stores by virtue of their sheer size and breadth of stock. New stores are getting bigger and ever bigger, and almost every month in the publishing trade press we see notice of 'the biggest bookstore in the country' opening in America, or Australia, or Britain.

When the US chain Borders first announced their purchase of the UK chain Books Etc. (in my view one of the very best booksellers for actively selling books) they also announced plans to open Britain's first really vast bookshops. These are in the American style with long opening hours that extend until late in the evening, really good coffee shops, some with restaurants, live music, busy programmes of author visits and promotions etc. They offer social events that happen to include books, often looking like a lot more fun than book promotion events in the past. All the groups that are opening 'superstores' are doing this now and they have become a fixture in the local singles scene! And they all owe their inspiration to the American bookselling style. I think this is a wonderful innovation. When I first visited one of the Barnes & Noble superstores in Manhattan many years ago I never thought that shops as big or as attractive as those would ever be part of the British or Australian bookselling scene. I'm glad I was wrong.

Independent booksellers

The brave, idiosyncratic, sometimes eccentric owners of independent bookstores have to be very good at marketing themselves if they are to compete with their larger cousins, the chains and the superstores, and if they are to make a profit. Because their volume of purchases from publishers is small compared to the chains, they cannot command discounts at anything like the rate of Smith's or Borders. They have to be so much more innovative at selling themselves and their service to the public.

It is independent bookshops that will stock titles according to the taste of the owner, or the local area, or clientele. And it is the independents that will often know their regular customers well enough to be able to recommend unusual titles that might appeal to individual purchasers. Times are tough for independently owned bookstores everywhere, and becoming only tougher. Publishers need independent booksellers because independents can often be effective in selling titles that the chains ignore. But publishers can't give big discounts on small orders, the independents often can't – and shouldn't – order a large quantity at a time, so the independents often have to accept smaller profit margins per book sold, even if they do eventually sell a large quantity of a particular title. But because they might order a small quantity several times over, their discount stays small even though the total quantity might eventually be large. Without big discounts from the publisher, a bookseller can't reduce the recommended price to the consumer. An independent bookstore selling a title at a higher price than their nearby chain bookseller knows that many potential book purchasers will be happy to walk around the corner if they can pay less for the same title.

Where the independent bookseller can come into their own is when they make an idiosyncratic choice of book to highlight to their customers. There are many books, from Dava Sobel's *Longitude* to Louis de Bernière's *Captain Corelli's Mandolin*, that have benefited from this kind of 'hand-selling' – personal recommendation from an opinionated bookseller who really knows their customers. In an ideal world every bookseller would work like this. But as urban centres become more crowded, and rural areas cease to be able to support an independent store, good independent booksellers who can make a living by servicing a regular clientele are becoming an endangered species, more's the pity.

Independent stores, which can't offer thousands of titles, or huge discounts, can nevertheless inspire a devoted following. This makes me think of some of my personal favourites among smaller stores in north London where I work and live, such as Compendium or the Regent Bookshop, both close to my office in Camden Town, or Backstage, the performing arts bookshop in Chalk Farm, or The Owl Bookshop in Kentish Town, or – and I never have enough time to browse in this shop which I love – Daunt's Bookshop for Travellers in Marylebone High Street, which shelves travel guides and travel literature and fiction by geographical region. Every time I go on safari to Africa I buy new guides, maps, narrative travel writing and novels from the same bookcase. Marvellously convenient, and logical, and unusual! And very seductive: I always buy more titles than I went in for. An example of the way that independent bookshops can sometimes win over the chains in creating destination shopping locations.

Supermarkets

In Britain, supermarkets are relatively new retailers of books in any quantity. They stock mostly fiction, mostly in paperback, and mostly for women. Just occasionally they will stock some hardcovers. The fact that they concentrate almost exclusively on bestselling fiction should make supermarkets of particular interest to readers of this book! Many supermarkets buy their books from wholesalers.

They became big retailers of books once Britain's Net Book Agreement disappeared in 1995, making it legal to sell books at less than the retail price set by the publisher. When discounting from the retail price was allowed in stores in Britain, the supermarkets realized there was money to be made. For the most part, they were (and still are) only interested in a few titles that could be bought cheaply from the publisher (at very big discounts indeed) and sold on to the customer while they – usually she – shopped. Thus the stock is usually paperback (lower prices), usually fiction directed at women (because on the whole it is women who shop for groceries), and always titles aimed at the 'bestseller' market (in order to achieve high volume sales and therefore profits).

Supermarkets offer a small range of titles, and by purchasing a lot at once, get large discounts that enable them to sell to the public at anything from 20 to 40 per cent off the recommended retail price. The books are displayed as 'treats' for the shopper, an inexpensive boost for her after the chore of necessary grocery shopping. The cover is all-important when books are sold in supermarkets. A wholesaler who supplies supermarkets once told me that the longest time that buyers take to select a product in a supermarket is fifteen seconds. Therefore, to quote him, 'It's vital that the clarity of the proposition comes over immediately.' (Bob Wilmot, commercial director, Thomas Cork.)

As an agent for commercial fiction, I applaud any initiative that gets books to buyers and in principle I think supermarket selling is wonderful. One problem for authors though, (and therefore their agents) has been that as supermarkets demand bigger and bigger discounts, publishers have been trying to renegotiate royalty levels with their authors down, even long after a contract is signed. They will argue that they can only fulfil a larger order from a supermarket by supplying at a huge discount, and in order to do that they must ask the author to accept a lower royalty.

The conundrum for the author and the agent is to work out if they believe the order will only be forthcoming at that level of discount and, if so, is it worth selling many thousands more even though the royalty per copy is unusually low? I have had many a conversation on that topic with publishers and with authors. It is impossible to give one answer to this frequently occurring puzzle: each deal has to be thought through from the point of view of that book and that author and the market place at the time the order arises.

There's another problem to be tackled with supermarket selling too. When my clients write novels that sell heavily through supermarkets it can be disappointing when they don't show in the bestseller lists, despite the high overall sales reported by the publisher. Supermarket sales, until recently, were not taken into account by the compilers of the bestseller lists.

Peter Harland of Bookwatch, one of the companies that compiles bestseller lists (and who provide their lists to the *Sunday Times*) told me why. When supermarkets first started to sell paperbacks enthusiastically, everyone in publishing expected these retail giants to be tracking their stock in a much more complex way than bookshops could, even with EPOS (see page 129). After all, we knew that supermarkets were able to track their food product lines in a most sophisticated fashion. But in the early days of bookselling in supermarkets, it seemed that they lumped all books together – as 'non-food product' – which is why their sales data was useless in compiling bestseller lists, which were only interested in sales figures for specific titles, not in the total of all book sales.

Bookwatch had been working to improve their data and in April 1997 printed the first lists to combine bookshop and supermarket sales. They get their supermarket figures from A. C. Nielsen (very expensively I understand) and the terms of their contract prevent them from stating either the extent of the sample or the numbers sold through it. Peter Harland is the first to admit that much analysis and testing has still to be done on these figures and they will not be included in the lists printed in the *Sunday Times* for some time to come.

Bookwatch make the point that the sums that the grocery trade spends on a research contract – say £50,000 a year by a baked bean manufacturer – put publishers' marketing budgets in the shade. And until book publishers can put themselves into the same spending league, the major grocers will not be prepared to encode all their book sales on an individual title basis. The problem for the publishers, of course, is much lower profits than baked bean manufacturers! Bookwatch started their supermarket sales watch by tracking a limited range of titles, fifty a month, and so are relying on their own ability to spot potential bestsellers in these outlets. It's an interesting beginning that everyone in the trade will watch with interest.

The book buyer for Tesco told me some time ago that when a particular cookery book featured in the bestseller lists with sales of 9,000 copies showing, Tesco alone had actually sold more than 10,000 copies, which shows how dramatically the supermarkets' sales can disprove the bestseller lists!

Direct sales

This is the area of sales where a middleman will buy in quantity from a publisher (big discount for big quantity) and then sell on to the customer without owning a retail outlet themselves. The most successful direct sale company in Britain is called The Book People and they have a unique operation that employs some 300 freelance reps to visit a large number of companies: 30,000 is the figure I have heard quoted. They visit offices, shops, factories, fire stations, 'everywhere that has someone sitting behind a desk'. They effectively turn people's workplaces into bookshops, taking orders for the books shown from among the 2,500 titles they carry a year. When books were still subject to retail price maintenance, one could understand the appeal of this kind of purchasing on the grounds of discounted prices, but now, when books can be sold at discounted prices in any bookshop, the appeal has to be sheer convenience, and the attractiveness of the books themselves. The titles sold tend to be hardback rather than paperback, and rather more non-fiction than fiction, but the range is very wide. The trade views these sales not as competition for bookshops' sales, but as extra to them. They can produce spectacular sales figures, but because the discounts to The Book People are very high, the royalty to the author on each copy sold is correspondingly low. If they really are extra sales, which would not be obtainable from any other source, perhaps that's acceptable for once.

Internet selling

The newest – and to some people in the book trade the most alarming – development in bookselling has been the advent of companies that now sell books on-line. Why alarming? Because selling via computer links takes no notice whatsoever of territorial boundaries.

Historically, British and American publishers have tended to share the English-speaking world between them, and their contracts with authors will allow them to sell to specific territories, but not to enter each other's except for the territories that are meant to be shared. When booksellers sell over the Internet they receive orders from around the world; computers know no territorial boundaries unless they are programmed market by market. The proprietors of Internet bookshops say they will always try to sell only to markets licensed to the publisher of the edition they supply, but understandably they sometimes transgress as it is often difficult to discover which publishers holds the rights for a particular geographical region. Publishers are wary of signing a contract with an author that gives them certain territories on an exclusive basis, only to find that territory invaded by copies from another publisher's edition. This is a growing problem for which the publishing industry has yet to find a solution.

Internet booksellers can offer an awe-inspiring selection of titles because they don't have to hold stock of all they offer. At its simplest, they can order from the publisher in small quantities as they see orders coming in from customers so they can offer practically every book ever published that is still in print. Those operating from America have the advantage of working in a book market approximately seven times larger than the United Kingdom and American books are accordingly much cheaper than UK editions.

The first to set up, in 1995, was Amazon, or 'www.amazon.com' to give their full address. They call themselves 'Earth's Biggest Bookstore' and given that there is no limit to what it can 'offer' – browsing the Website revealed 2.5 million titles in early 1998 – they could well be right. They operate from America where retail prices of books are lower than many other territories, they offer many titles at large discounts from the retail price, and one gets the instant satisfaction of placing an order, paying by credit card, if you can locate the book you want.

Does this kind of purchase represent instant satisfaction? Given that the book still has to be mailed, it can either take several weeks to be shipped by sea, or cost quite a lot of money to be sent by air. That can still be more satisfying than calling or visiting a number of shops which can't provide the book you are seeking.

The possibility of credit-card fraud when paying over the Internet stops some people from buying this way. Despite an 880 per cent growth rate in 1997, Amazon has yet to make a profit. (Source: Books and the Consumer Conference 1998.)

In addition to Amazon and other Internet-specific booksellers, many bookselling chains and independent shops now offer an ordering service via a Website. They, too, can receive orders from customers around the world and have to make both a legal and an ethical decision as to whether to supply to customers a copy of a book available to them, which has been ordered by a customer within the exclusive territory of an overseas publisher.

Internet selling is hard to control or police: it's almost impossible to discover when a copy is supplied by an Internet bookseller to a territory it shouldn't be selling to, and publishers do not really wish to offend booksellers who are their customers. The trade has to find a way to deal with this problem but at the time of writing there are no viable suggestions as to how to do it. There's no doubt at all that buying books over the Internet appeals enormously to today's consumer.

Distribution

When I first came into publishing in the early 60s, the salesmen who visited stores on behalf of the publisher were called 'travellers', which sounded rather genteel. They were trusted by the booksellers, they knew their own lists and the selling pitch often sounded more like good advice from one friend to another. True or false? It was probably never as soft as that but compared to the mid-70s, when I became marketing director for the mass-market paperback publisher Sphere Books, the market place in the 60s was very gentle indeed. Sphere was relatively new, and we certainly intended to be very aggressive and planned to fight hard for every sale. We did still have 'travellers', except that they were now called 'representatives' and they fought hard to compete with our more established competitors. There was much competition among the reps to beat their own targets, and enormous competition between publishing houses. But looking back on that period from today's vantage point makes it look very tame indeed with regard to the fight for market share, for discounts, for shelf space.

Now that there is so much central buying, and many publishers regard a 'rep' on the road all day as a terrible waste of manpower and resources, most publishers' sales teams are head office based, with a small core of 'key account managers' who maintain contact with a targeted list of buyers from certain booksellers.

When the bookshop trade was more diversified, before chains and central buying, the orders a publisher acquired prior to publication – the 'subscription' as it was then called – usually came in early, many months before publication date, and would allow the publisher to plan the print run in a relatively safe and leisurely fashion. For some years, the print run could usually be safely reckoned as twice the size of the subscription.

Today, with a huge proportion of the pre-publication orders coming from just six or seven sources, (and often coming in perilously close to publication date), much more risk has to be taken by the publisher. This is mitigated only by the fact that current technology means that reprints are not as expensive as they used to be and can be supplied more quickly than in the past.

Now, the initial print run is much less indicative of a publisher's enthusiasm, or of the eventual total sale, than it was even ten years ago. Then the first print run often was the only print run, but it was probably bigger than it is today for most books. Now, many more authors see their books reprinting yet the total quantity sold may be smaller than in the past.

Wholesalers

The pattern of selling by publishers has moved from dealing with numerous individual bookshop accounts, to dealing with fewer, larger accounts. To reach many of the outlets for books not serviced by these larger accounts (including some of the newer outlets), publishers deal with wholesalers. A wholesaler is a middleman who buys in bulk from the publisher (and expects a good discount for doing so), stores the stock in their own warehouse, and then sells on to outlets like motorway services stations, stores like Woolworth's and local newsagents.

Wholesalers sell at a price that builds in profit for themselves, but has to allow their customer to sell at a profit too. The service they offer is their knowledge of the books that they will match to their customers' outlets. Paperbacks (and readings on audio cassettes) are common in motorway service stations; non-fiction books about health are usually found in health food shops. The wholesalers will often be entirely responsible themselves for the individual titles the outlets take and sell: the shops leave it to the wholesaler to stock their racks. And if the wholesaler gets it right they make more sales. Their expertise creates a market for books that motorway service stations, for example, don't want to spend time to explore themselves.

The outlets that are serviced by wholesalers are not particularly author-oriented. They rarely organize author events in the way that bookshops do because their clientele spends little time shopping there: customers are passing through and the books will be impulse purchases bought because they are conveniently to hand, not because the customer went into that shop with the specific intention of finding that book. These are sales that the publisher would find it difficult and expensive to service themselves, which also include booksellers' quick, small and mixed reorders (the publisher supplies one order, deals with one invoice, makes one delivery rather than five or six) for fast reorders around rush periods such as Christmas, and for individual customer orders. Wholesalers thus achieve high-volume low-income sales for publishers and authors. The unit sales can be very high, but the royalty to the author, and the profit to the publisher can be low on each sale.

EPOS and stock control

EPOS stands for Electronic Point of Sale. It is a method of recording details of a specific sale at its point of purchase, and the computer records details that include title, author, quantity, price, location of sale, and the number of that title left in stock at the store in which it was purchased. This is done by means of a bar code printed on the back of the book that is electronically read by the register when the book is paid for. It means that bookstores with EPOS record each and every individual book's sale from the till point that processes the transaction. This is fed to a central system that can tell how many of that particular title and edition are in stock, and where, at any given time, and will alert the store as to when to reorder, what the *rate* of sale has been and therefore what the size of the new order should be, and when the order should be placed, taking into account how long the book has been published and how fast it has been selling. It's heady stuff, and a long way removed from the publishers' 'traveller' advising the local bookstore about the size of their next order!

EPOS has had an interesting effect on the trade overall. Previously, a publisher expected most of the total sales of most titles to be ordered before publication. They were then able to print for the orders they had taken plus a little in hand. They only had to warehouse a small proportion of the print run as the rest went out to bookshops as soon as it was delivered from the binder. This meant relatively low risk and good cash flow for the publisher. With EPOS giving bookshops far greater information about, and control of, their stock, the booksellers don't feel the need to buy a large quantity of any one title at a time, secure in the knowledge that they can reorder small quantities from the publisher as and when they need them. Lower risk and better cash flow for the bookshop, which means that publishers must now bear the cost of warehousing the stock and the risk of setting the print run without very much feedback from the shops.

Publishers believe that EPOS has dramatically affected the pattern of buying in stock for bookshops. Not only can booksellers order little and often if they wish to, but being able to look back at the total number of books taken in by a shop and the number returned to the publisher once sales slowed down, can often mean that a bookseller will order very conservatively when the author's next book is offered. If, for instance, a shop had initially ordered 100 copies of a particular title, reordered thirty, but was left with – or returned – twenty copies, a publisher might hope for an initial order for that author's next book of maybe 120 – a little above the 110 total sales of the previous title.

But a bookseller, looking at the same figures, might prefer to order ninety . . . They can always reorder, after all. That might not matter too much if the pattern of sales out of the bookshop were to remain the same as with the author's previous title. But customers these days have grown used to seeing piles and piles of the latest bestseller in a bookshop, and the large display can be a persuasive factor in an impulse purchase. So it could be argued that by buying fewer, the shop is influencing sales in a negative fashion – fewer on display means fewer then that will be sold. And so the pattern of sales for that author goes down with each book published.

A simplistic and rather doom-laden scenario I know, but I have heard publishers comment very bitterly that EPOS persuades booksellers to order in an ever downward spiral because of the wish never to be left with unsold stock.

There is no doubt that as a stock control tool EPOS is invaluable in the hands of retailers who use it to maximize sales. The problem is when it is used negatively. Eric Lane, who runs the independent publishing house Dedalus, was quoted in the *Writers' Guild Newsletter* back in 1996 as saying, 'Many booksellers have developed a tendency to send books back almost as soon as they get them and use EPOS and bar codes, not as a way of ordering books, but as means for not buying in sufficient quantities to give the book a chance to sell.'

Many publishers feel, perhaps cynically, that books are no longer bought by bookshops, but instead are ordered, held for a while, and then returned for credit, often before the initial invoice has become due for payment.

Discounting

Two different kinds of discounts operate in the book trade: the discount that publishers and booksellers negotiate between them (35 per cent off the retail price used to be normal; now 50 per cent is more usual), which produces the selling price from the publisher to the bookseller, and the discount from the recommended retail price that the bookseller offers to the consumer who buys from a shop.

The first has always been with us – but the figures are changing dramatically. The latter – selling to the consumer at less than the retail price set by the publisher – is relatively new in Britain, but common in many other markets, notably America and Australia. Until September 1995, Britain's book trade voluntarily operated under Retail Price Maintenance, and so book prices were fixed at the price printed on

the book's cover by the publisher. The Publishers' Association promoted the Net Book Agreement as central to the health of the British
book trade, and mounted vigorous defences of the system whenever it
was challenged. It was an anomaly in British retailing where no other
products except pharmaceuticals had fixed pricing, and I think it was
inevitable that it would have crumbled at some point. But the manner
of its going was surprising and sudden.

On one day at the end of September 1995, several of Britain's
largest publishers (among them Random House, HarperCollins and
Penguin) suddenly announced their intention of opting out of the
voluntary Net Book Agreement scheme.

This changed the face of British publishing literally overnight. By
the next morning, publishers and booksellers were talking bigger levels
of discount than had ever been heard of, and agents were already
fielding calls from publishers anxious to negotiate authors' royalties
downwards to accommodate the smaller slice of the retail price that
the publisher was retaining.

Journalists wrote many on the whole, superficial and ill-informed
– articles suggesting that books were entering an age of consumer
heaven, and that nasty profiteering publishers had now seen the light
and books were at last to be priced within the reach of ordinary
mortals, and that book buying in Britain would soar upwards, along
with the income of all writers as retail prices for books fell dramatically. I wish! None of these improvements have been seen.

Many bookshop chains rushed to promote titles they were selling
more cheaply than their rivals. Owners of independent bookstores,
fearful that they couldn't buy the kinds of quantities that would
qualify for huge discounts from publishers, predicted their own
demise.

Now, several years on, everyone seems to have been disappointed.
The total quantity of books sold has not increased. Many sales have
simply changed to the titles being discounted. People who did not buy
books before still don't buy books: people who were already book
buyers seem to be shifting their book buying to titles that are price
promoted. Because it's only the well-known names that will sell in the
quantities necessary to support the discounts, the big names are selling
more, and the authors who didn't sell many are now selling even less.
So fewer and fewer titles are being price promoted, despite retail prices
having risen – exactly the opposite result than everyone expected and
hoped for.

But haven't retail prices gone down on the whole? No, because
publishers have increased the recommended retail price to make room
for a discount below it. Many recommended retail prices have been

artificially increased by the publishers, and many so-called 'discounted' books are actually selling at the same price that they would have before the NBA was removed.

Aren't the authors of discounted books reaping fortunes? Sometimes, yes, if the extra sales generated have been colossal. But because the royalty per copy on discounted titles is often much lower than the regular royalty on non-discounted titles, if the extra sales are not enormous, the author may earn less money from royalties altogether despite a larger number of books being sold.

Many of the bookstores that wholeheartedly embraced the philosophy of discounted selling prices initially have now quietly dropped the idea, or are only interested in price promoting very few titles.

It is exciting that publishing now has another tool for selling and promotion – the price to the final buyer – because booksellers can be creative in the way they use pricing. Not only are they simply reducing the price on a particular title, but offering three books for the price of two, one book (the cheapest) free when a buyer pays for five, and so on.

But one legacy of the Net Book Agreement being so harshly abandoned is that in the resulting scramble for sales, publishers became so competitive that levels of discount were given to booksellers that seriously squeeze the already small portion of the final selling price that finds its way to the author. The author is, after all, the creator of the book upon whom every other part of the trade depends. Discounts to booksellers only ever seem to get bigger, and the royalty to authors smaller. I've never seen it moving in the other direction!

This is not just the perpetual moan of someone who is paid to be on the authors' side. The analysts Key Note said in their 1998 *Market Review: UK Publishing*, 'Book publishers have ceded too much of their profit to retailers – a state of affairs unlikely to be reversed in the near future.'

High discounts that squeeze profit levels to new lows for publishers are ultimately detrimental to authors too, if it means publishers cease to invest in the authors.

Another fear, voiced by some booksellers and the journalists writing in the book trade press, is that the kinds of books that will never attract large sales or large discounts – the minority interest titles, the specialist books – will find it harder and harder to be stocked, or perhaps to be published. If so much more of the profits in publishing are to be concentrated on the bestsellers, how will publishers finance a first novel, or a scholarly history, or a biography of a little-known seventeenth-century composer? This kind of publishing offers great choice to book buyers: reducing choice to just a narrow range of titles because they appeal to the masses would be seriously detrimental to literary health.

●

I have attempted in this chapter to outline the main workings of a very diverse industry. Of necessity I have had to skim swiftly over some fairly complicated explanations of who does what with whom, but do remember that it is a trade in constant change. This book will take many months to be published once it has been delivered to the publisher, so by the time you read this some aspects of what I have described may have moved on yet again. I hope though, that this long chapter has given you a snapshot of how authors, agents, publishers and booksellers interact.

Part Two

FROM CONTRACT
TO PUBLICATION

8 How the publisher puts the offer together

No man but a blockhead ever wrote, except for money
– Samuel Johnson

When offers are coming in, you want to be professional, but
what you want to ask is, 'Do you really like it?'
– Former Houghton Mifflin head Joe Kanon on his first novel

They like it!

The editor who has read your manuscript – we'll call it *Freddy's First
Fiction* – likes it, and likes it enough to want to make an offer. This is
a wonderful moment for the editor, and for the writer, who doesn't
know about it yet. What happens next, before the editor calls the
writer (or the writer's agent)?

First, there will be other people in the publishing house for the
editor to convince about the purchase. As soon as they have decided
they are keen to buy a book, a wise editor will persuade others in the
company to read it in the hope that they, too, will think it worth
publishing. People from sales, marketing, rights, publicity, and perhaps another editor – they will all be helpful in adding their weight
when the editor brings the book up at the next editorial meeting and
preparation at this stage can be very helpful to the editor later. At the
editorial meeting the editor will hope to receive approval to take the
book to acquisition stage The editor will pitch the book to the editorial
board and others present, which will include staff from a range of
other departments such as sales, marketing, publicity and rights.

If the book doesn't get shot down in flames at that point, and the
consensus is that it should be taken further, others from the meeting
will be asked to read it too, and the editor will start to prepare a
submission for the acquisition meeting. The editor may at this point
tell the author or agent that they like *Freddy's First Fiction* and are

planning to 'put it up at the next acquisition meeting'. Most authors start to have palpitations during this period. So do agents, even though they try to seem very cool indeed!

More readings in-house may be solicited at this point. If the book is thought to be 'big' enough, the author important enough, or the potential price high enough, the sponsoring editor will want, and often need, senior executives to read it too.

The next step involves the editor preparing a set of costings, which requires input from the sales department. See how useful it was to have someone from that department read it early (so long as they, too, thought it worth publishing)? The estimates will be educated guesses, but they will probably be broken down into the different markets the editor wants to include in the offer. For the sake of this illustration, I'll assume our enthusiastic publisher is British, which means they will probably be offering for Britain, Australia, South Africa, perhaps Canada, Europe, and for the right to sell their English language book in the 'open market', the territories in the rest of the world commonly shared with American publishers.

The markets they will try to define first will be broken down into home (the British Isles for our British publisher) and export (which itself breaks down, for British publishers, into the major export areas of Australia, Canada, South Africa, and Europe) and 'the rest'.

If the purchase price of the book is expected to be high, or the author already has a profile in the trade, the publisher may well courier the manuscript (or e-mail if they have it on disk) to their Australian, Canadian and South African offices or agents so that their estimates can be based on a local reading of the material in each major export market. More likely, especially for first novels, the sales department in Britain will base their estimate of sales on a guess, which itself will be based on sales of similar novels.

Once the estimated sales figures are available, the editor has a basis for beginning the costings. Most houses these days have costing models on their computer databases that allow staff to feed in the variables. The computer will then do the rest of the calculations based on figures for the publisher's overhead and a contribution to profit that the publishing company has decided is necessary.

The costings

Doesn't that sound simple? The reason why it isn't simple is the number of variables. There are certain fixed costs in the process of publishing a book, meaning they are always present. But there are many variables because every book and its publication plan is different.

Printing and binding

The length of the book and the length of print runs vary enormously. The printing, binding and shipping costs for a novella of 200 pages are going to be rather different to that of an 800-page saga. A book whose print run is 2000 copies is going to cost more per copy to print than one whose print run is 100,000 copies. The larger the print run at one time, the cheaper the unit cost even though the total paper and binding costs escalate as the print run lengthens. It can take longer in machine time and staff time to prepare to print a few thousand books than the actual printing time itself, so the cost per copy becomes less, the more copies you print. But the more you print, the more it costs you to warehouse the books, particularly if they sell slowly. Overall, the unit costs diminish as the print run increases, because start-up and fixed costs can be amortized over a larger number of copies.

Publishing the book in a larger format – a larger page size – increases your paper and binding cost. Every book has to have a cover and artists and photographers must be paid anything from £500 to £2,000. These are fixed costs. Typesetting costs may be £4 per page. Authors who deliver a computer disk to the publisher in addition to the manuscript can make a difference here in the time it takes to reach proof stage. When authors first started to deliver manuscripts on disk there were many discussions about how to persuade publishers to pay for them as it was assumed it saved a lot of money in typesetting. But it does seem to be accepted now that quite a bit of time has to be spent, by someone paid by the publisher, in reformatting, correcting and styling a manuscript on disk, thereby eating up much of the money it was assumed could be saved.

Publishers also allocate a particular percentage of a book's costs towards their own overheads, the cost of staff and premises being the largest components.

Publicity

Publicizing the book – even one without a specific budget for advertising or point-of-sale material – costs money. One publisher told me that their twice-yearly catalogue cost £30,000 to produce and mail each season. Each book has to contribute towards that cost, as well as the cost of mailing free books to reviewers. Here the quantity can be anything from thirty to several hundred depending upon the book and the publisher. And even books that are not given their own promotion budgets – money that the publisher will spend solely on that particular title – will usually be allocated to a member of the publicity staff in the publishing company. They will spend time compiling a list of potential reviewers, obtaining quotes in support of the book (perhaps to be used on the paperback cover later), calling journalists and broadcasters in the hope of persuading them to interview the author, writing and mailing a press release.

If advertisements and posters and dumpbins and bookmarks and a publicity tour are contemplated, they have to be built into the costings. 'Point-of-sale' material is a catch-all phrase that covers all the publicity and promotion material offered to booksellers for display, i.e. at the point where the sale takes place. It can be surprisingly costly. Point-of-sale items include posters, shelf-liners (cardboard strips advertising the title and author), 'wobblers' (stand up cardboard and spring concoctions!), counterpacks (they hold a book upright for display on the counter, say, next to the cash register), give-away bookmarks, 'dumpbins' (a less than attractive name for the heavy duty cardboard holders that display six or nine or twelve books face-out to the customers, sometimes with a 'header', a cut-out or plain promotion piece that stands on top), and anything else that a bright publicity department can think of that can possibly be used to catch a buyer's eye.

This kind of publicity material is only produced for authors who are already established, or for books for which the publishers are paying a high advance, because publishers need to recoup their high outlay. This kind of marketing spend will have been factored into the figures when they first put their offer together, and money spent in this way is exactly what helps to make the authors into 'brand names' recognized throughout the world.

Is there anything else for the editor to build into the costings? Yes, on the debit side a royalty to the author for each copy sold, and, for credit, an estimate of which subsidiary rights might contribute income. This will enable the editor to calculate the total amount of earnings the book might produce. The editor, and the editor's boss, then must take a view as to what proportion of that figure it is reasonable to offer to the author by way of a guaranteed advance.

So, now the editor has the costings, having taken a reasonable guess at what the first print run might be, and brings the whole project to the acquisition meeting. If the costings, based on a sales estimate that both editor and sales department think is a reasonable one to achieve, show that the book makes a sufficient contribution to overheads and to profit, then the meeting may decide to allow the editor to make an offer to the author or the agent.

Putting the offer together

A new regulation for the publishing industry: The advance for the book must be larger than the cheque for the lunch at which it was discussed – Calvin Trillin

At its simplest, an advance is arrived at by the following equation: copies sold (perhaps from the first printing only, or calculated over the first year's sales), multiplied by the recommended retail price divided by the royalty equals the advance. Plus earnings from another edition if more than one format is planned, hardback followed by paperback say, and perhaps they might include an amount to be earned from exploitation of some subsidiary rights such as serial rights sold to a magazine or newspaper. In practice, because of the many variables, it's not quite as simple as that, but let's stick with this example for the time being.

Trade sales

Freddy's First Fiction is thought to be viable both in hardcover and paperback. Say the sale of the hardback was expected to be 1,500 copies at a retail price in the UK of £15 (I know publishers still stick to pricings that all have 99p on the end and are so hard for mental arithmetic, but I'm trying to keep this simple!). If the publisher is planning to offer the author royalties in the home market of 10 per cent of retail price to 2,500 copies sold, 12.5 per cent to 6,000 copies and 15 per cent on sales thereafter, then the royalty per copy sold on the first 1,500 will be £1.50 per copy on books sold in the 'home' market – the United Kingdom and the Republic of Ireland.

Royalties paid to the author get higher per copy as the total sales increase because the publisher's costs in getting the book into print in the first place diminish as it orders reprints. The initial costs are hopefully amortized over the first printing, and that will leave a little more for the author as the sales grow past that point. The royalty 'escalators' or 'break-points', the points at which the royalty increases, are major points of negotiation between publisher and agent. The actual royalty levels (for hardback, 10 per cent rising to 12.5 per cent and eventually to 15 per cent) are accepted throughout the trade, even

though some authors may not be offered a rise above 12.5 per cent
and some may be offered no rise at all beyond the initial 10 per cent.

Export sales (copies sold outside of the 'home' market) usually
attract half the home sales rate. Publishers vary in the way they like to
express export royalties: some will offer exactly half the UK rate tied
to the UK retail price (on our illustration that would produce 5 per
cent UK retail price to 2,500 copies sold, 6.25 per cent to 6,000 copies
and 7.5 per cent thereafter). Agents prefer this method because it is
clear and easy to check. Publishers prefer to pay export royalties based
on 'price received' or 'net receipts', i.e. based on what they receive
from their customers, the bookshops and the wholesalers. Agents
don't like this method because the higher the discount that the
bookshop manages to negotiate with the publisher, the lower the
author's royalties, and it is hard to police because no publisher will
reveal what discounts they are currently giving booksellers. They keep
these discounts secret from their competitors and between booksellers
to maintain their market edge, but that's no comfort to authors trying
to check their royalty level.

Traditionally, export royalty levels have always been lower than
home sales royalty levels because publishers have allowed higher
discounts in the export markets, and sometimes also have to pay for
shipment to faraway territories. Nowadays, discounts to export markets can be as high as 80 or 85 per cent of the selling price. Competing
with lower priced American books in the export markets means
everyone's profit margins are shaved. For this reason, publishers are
putting more and more pressure on authors and agents to accept
royalties based on the price received, and often to accept an export
royalty at one flat rate with no rising rates.

As a rough guide, expect an export sale to yield a royalty of half
that of a home sale, but in practice it can be much lower. For the sake
of arriving at some concrete figures here, we'll assume the best: our
export sales from this 1,500-copy sale of hardbacks at 5 per cent of
£15 will produce 75p per copy for the author.

At this point someone has to estimate the balance of home and
export sales: this will vary greatly depending on the book. I am
assuming that three-quarters of the 1,500-copy sale will be in the
home market, and one quarter will go to export.

Another variable is the royalty level on high discount sales. Booksellers and wholesalers expect and negotiate for extra levels of discount for larger purchases. At the simplest level, this involves the
bookseller ordering a large quantity of a single book and receiving a
bigger discount in return for that large order. The more complicated
model requires the bookseller (or bookselling chain, or wholesaler) to

guarantee a certain high level of business with a particular publisher, over a fixed period of time, in order to qualify for a higher level of discount across all the purchases. As you can see, this could mean that the bookseller was acquiring perhaps a tiny quantity of one particular title, but buying it at a deep discount because of the level of their overall business with the publisher. The author might not have the satisfaction of a large order, but would see a few sales to that bookseller, invoiced at a low rate, and earning a low royalty.

All sales to supermarkets – a relatively new area for bookselling in Britain, and almost exclusively involved with paperbacks – are at very high discounts. They are only made viable by the large quantities that these outlets usually take.

The slice of the pie to be divided is now much smaller. Publishers do not like to shoulder the burden of high discounts alone: they want the author to share in the reduction of income. They will negotiate with authors and agents for a sliding scale royalty that goes down, with the percentage to the author becoming smaller as the discount to the bookseller becomes larger.

This area of negotiation became the subject of a bitter dispute between agents and publishers some years ago, when I was President of the Association of Authors' Agents. It dragged on for ten months, with most of the larger agencies refusing to sign contracts with publishers until the issue was settled to our satisfaction. Naturally we had to have the agreement of our clients: I'm pleased to say that all of my clients understood the enormity of the problem and were solidly behind me during the negotiations. We were still doing deals with publishers and agreeing sales, but the contracts – and therefore all payments – were held up pending the outcome of the dispute on this particular issue.

Most publishers wanted authors' royalties, on high discount sales, to switch over to 10 per cent of the amount received. High discounts were usually defined as a discount of 50 per cent or higher on hardbacks and quality (or 'trade') paperbacks, and a discount of 52.5 per cent or higher on mass-market paperbacks. Agents wanted the royalty on high discount sales still to be expressed as a proportion of the recommended retail price: I'm pleased to say that we did win this particular point. The generally accepted royalty for high discount sales with most publishers (not all; there are still some renegades out there intent on fighting this over and over again) became, and still is, 'four-fifths of the otherwise prevailing royalty'. In other words, on our particular illustration, if sales for the hardback edition haven't yet reached 2,500, you would be receiving a 10 per cent royalty. But when sales are made at a rate that brings the high discount provision into play, then the royalty you receive will be four-fifths of 10 per cent, which in real terms is 8 per cent of recommended retail price.

Let's continue with our figures for *Freddy's First Fiction*. Home sales will have produced the following figures for royalty income:

Hardback home sales

£15 retail price @ 10 per cent royalty = £1.50 per copy
£1.50 × 1,125 copies (three-quarters of the total sale of 1,500) = £1,687.50

But 800 of those copies were at a high discount, so the royalty will be four-fifths of the price

Four-fifths of £1.50 ≐ £1.20 per copy
Difference in royalty per copy is 30p (£1.50 − £1.20)
Reduction in royalty is 800 copies × 30p = £240
Estimated royalty for total home sales is £1,687.50 − £240 = £1447.50

Hardback export sales

Export sales were estimated at 375 copies at a royalty rate of 5 per cent of UK retail price

£15 retail price @ 5 per cent royalty = 75p per copy
75p × 375 copies (one quarter of the total sale of 1,500) = £281.25

I'm not going to assume a reduction of royalty for high discount sales because most agents take the view that an export royalty is already reduced to take account of the higher discounts given to buyers in the export markets: we fight against publishers who wish to apply a reduced high discount royalty to an already reduced export royalty. But be warned: many publishers, including some of the most reputable, do apply this practice which reduces income from export sales even further, and authors without agents will find this difficult to negotiate.

So far we have the following expected income from the hardback edition:

Home sales	£1,447.50
Export sales	£281.25
Total sales	£1,728.75

Now we do the same exercise for the paperback edition, which will usually be published anything from six to twelve months after the hardback edition. Let's assume an expected sale of 15,000 copies at a UK retail price of £6. Whatever the scale of royalties offered (and the point at which a paperback royalty level increases from 7.5 per cent to 10 per cent varies more than the variable points in hardback royalty rates, anywhere from 15,000 to 50,000), it is more than likely that a

15,000 sale will not take you beyond the starting royalty level of 7.5 per cent of recommended retail price. Paperback export rates are (preferably) 6 per cent of UK retail price while the home royalty is 7.5 per cent and 8 per cent when the home rate is 10 per cent. Less happily for authors, some publishers calculate export rates on the amount received when the percentage should be much higher, of course.

Paperback home sales

£6 retail price @ 7.5 per cent = 45p per copy
45p × 11,250 copies (three-quarters of the total sale of £15,000) = £5,062.50

But if 6,000 of those sales were at high discount, the royalty will be four-fifths of the price

Four-fifths of 45p = 36p per copy
Difference in royalty per copy = 9p (45p − 36p)
Reduction in royalty is 6,000 × 9p = £540
Estimated total for home sales is £5,062.50 − £540 = £4,522.50

Paperback export sales

Export sales were estimated at 3,750 copies at a royalty rate of 6 per cent of UK retail price

£6 retail price @ 6 per cent royalty = 36p per copy
36p × 3,750 copies = £1,350

Figures so far show

Hardback	home sales	£1447.50
	export sales	£281.25
Paperback	home sales	£4,522.50
	export sales	£1,350.00
Total trade sales royalties		£7,601.25

Subsidiary rights

How can this income be increased? It could be increased by a sale to a book club, a serialization or sales of large print rights.

Book Club

In practice, few first novels are bought by book clubs, and the author's income from book club sales is pitiful. Assuming a hardback retail price in the trade of £15 as before, a book club will want to offer the book to their members at three-quarters of the trade selling price, i.e.

£11.25, and will want to buy it from the publisher at one quarter of the trade retail price, i.e. £3.75. The royalty to the author will probably be 10 per cent of the price at which the book club buys copies, so the royalty income per copy for the author on a hardback sale from the book club to their members will be 37.5p. Publishers and book clubs defend book club sales by saying that book club members are not regular bookshop purchasers and so the sales must be viewed as extra to the trade sales; they don't decrease the volume of sales through shops.

I'm not sure this is entirely true, but as long as the clubs are able to increase a publisher's print run and therefore the publisher's profit (the larger the print run, the lower the cost to produce per copy), publishers will want to go on selling to book clubs. Publishers also argue that a book club offering is good exposure for the book. It certainly is if the clubs use it in their full colour display advertising in magazines and newspapers. But this hardly ever happens for first novels, and even when the club does take a book from a bestselling author, why is this exposure helpful when, first, it is offering the book cheaply with hardly any profit for the author, second, (to use the publishers' argument) it's not selling to people who go into bookshops anyway and third, it is in the main exposure of books that are already selling well?

The method of working out a book club royalty is unfair in my opinion. While a publisher can often demonstrate that they are not making a huge profit on the 2,000 copies sold to a book club, if the costings for that book were to be scrutinized it is likely they would show that the addition of 2,000 copies to the print run increased the profit margin for the publisher. Occasionally authors will take a stand against book club sales: Jeffrey Archer did once by saying that he was taking a stand in favour of booksellers. He refused to allow one of his novels to be sold to the clubs.

Jeffrey Archer can afford gestures like this, and he sells so many books that he doesn't have to worry too much about offending one portion of the trade. I think he only did it once, and chose to announce the decision in such a way as to obtain maximum publicity from it within the publishing trade. In practice, most authors and agents will accept whatever book club sales their publisher can generate for them. But I'm not supposing a book club sale for *Freddy's First Fiction* because book clubs seldom buy first novels.

Serial

Other potential income could be from serial rights, but how much fiction gets serialized these days? When I was rights manager at Michael Joseph back in the early 70s, I could sell serial rights in fiction to about a dozen different magazines and a few weekend papers. At that time they all published short stories and nearly all serialized a book in every issue as well. Almost all of those publications have either ceased publication themselves, or stopped serializing fiction. Now, although there are many more magazines being published, there are fewer that run a fiction serial, and only a few that publish short stories. Very occasionally weekend newspapers will take a fiction extract, but none of them serialize fiction regularly.

When we sold Michael Ridpath's first novel *Free to Trade* to the *Daily Telegraph* for six days of extracts, it was the first time that paper had run fiction in its history, and the newspaper was founded in 1855! The resulting coverage was extremely good for publicity and the paper paid five figures for the rights too. The agency had kept serial rights out of the publisher's contract. If the publisher had controlled those rights (and managed to sell them) then probably 90 per cent of what the paper paid would have been credited to the author's royalty account to be set against the advance. By selling to the newspaper on behalf of the author, we received the whole payment within a month of the paper's publication date and paid it straight over to our client less our commission.

Selling serial rights for fiction is so rare that we can't assume the same for *Freddy's First Fiction*.

Large print

The publisher usually has the right to sell large print rights. These are books printed in very large type for use by the partially sighted. They sell almost exclusively to libraries, residential homes for the elderly and hospitals. Advances range between from £300 to £1,000 usually, but can go much higher for well-known authors. Again, few first novels are bought by large print publishers so we'll leave this income out of our estimates too.

Escalators

When agents feel an advance offered by the publisher is too low for their author to accept, it is sometimes possible to add to an offer promises of extra future income, dependent upon particular events in the life of the book. These are called 'escalators' and editors and agents can be quite creative in thinking up new versions of them, and agents even more creative in persuading editors to include them in deals! They usually take the form of a named sum, say £1,000, of extra advance (i.e. it's regarded as an advance to be earned back by royalties, it is seldom an ex gratia payment) to be paid as and when specified factors come into play.

The more common types of escalators are:

— bestseller escalators, which are sums paid over when the book has reached a certain position in a particular bestseller list, or stayed there for a fixed number of weeks

— bestseller escalators that are dependent upon the book having sold a certain specified quantity, at which point the extra advance is paid

— escalators based upon the sales performance of the author's previous book

— escalators payable when a film opens or a television series is broadcast. These usually specify how many cinemas the film must open in to qualify, or how many episodes a television series must contain. The television option often also specifies terrestrial, i.e. broadcast television rather than just cable or satellite broadcasting.

Escalators are usually only negotiated when the publishing house really wants to sign the author, but cannot add to the guaranteed advance at the time of buying. It can be a way of improving one offer over another when an auction has reached stalemate and no house bidding can improve its advances. But escalators are seldom offered for first novels outside of hotly contested auctions.

Negatives

If we can't increase our estimated figure of £7601.25 earnings for *Freddy's First Fiction*, is it likely to be decreased for any reason? Most certainly. If this is the maximum figure the editor can calculate as likely earnings from sales for the book, it is very unlikely they would be allowed to offer it all as a guarantee to the author. Remember, these figures are being calculated anything from one to three years before the book is likely to be published in its first hardback edition, and two to four years before the publisher can think of seeing any income from the paperback edition.

The cost of money has to be taken into account (the interest payable on the publisher's borrowings), and also other areas where the figures could vary. The average returns rates (the unsold books that booksellers can return to the publisher for credit) in the trade could increase; the subject of the novel could become deeply unfashionable (or over-published) in the time between the publisher buying it and publishing it; hardback fiction could cease to sell entirely. (Every year since I have been in publishing I have read articles predicting the demise of hardback fiction sales.) A gloomy picture, but a realistic one. That is why the publishing house is often likely to authorize the editor to offer only half to three-quarters of the estimated royalty income to the author as an advance.

Negotiables

The following are almost always negotiable and should form part of the offer that the editor specifies during the negotiation:

Payment stages

— the whole amount on signature of the contract (virtually unheard of in the English language publishing world, but still normal for translation rights sales to foreign language publishers)

— half on signature and half on first publication (probably only ever offered when the manuscript is already delivered and the publisher intends to publish only in one edition, say, an original paperback, or as a hardback when the publisher does not own their own paperback house)

— a third on signature, a third on delivery of the manuscript and a third on first publication (fairly normal, but not as often offered as the next example)

— one quarter on each of the following performance points: signature of contract, delivery of manuscript, first publication in hardback, first publication in paperback. This is the most usual form of payment now that most publishing groups publish themselves in all formats.

If *Freddy's First Fiction* attracted an offer of £4,500 as an advance, we might find that the amount offered on signature of the contract varied from £1,125 to £1,500.

Royalty levels

Home and export royalties on hardbacks and paperbacks produce many variables. If the publisher contemplates publishing in two different paperback formats, there might be two different paperback royalty scales, one for the larger format trade paperback, and one for the smaller format mass-market paperback.

Territory

This can vary from British Commonwealth, to world English language (the publisher may sell rights to America or publish themselves in America through a related company), to world in all languages (in addition to world English language the publisher may also license translation sales around the world). Or they can be smaller than the full Commonwealth, breaking out territories such as Ireland, Australia, Canada or South Africa.

Subsidiary rights

This involves the inclusion or exclusion of serial rights, audio rights and others, as well as the income split on American and translation rights.

Licence period

Some publishers are prepared to accept less than the usually expected full term of copyright (seventy years after the author's death), and will offer for a fixed term licence. Foreign language contracts may often be for as short as three years in some markets; English language publishers are seldom happy to settle for less than ten or twenty years, with the right to renew dependent upon certain specified sales levels in the years preceding the renewal.

Is it acceptable?

> Money, it turned out, was exactly like sex; you thought of nothing else if you didn't have it and thought of other things if you did. – James Baldwin

> Money is like a sixth sense: you can't make use of the other five without it – Somerset Maugham

Freddy's First Fiction, which may have been the fruit of a year's hard work or more, might be offered an advance of £4,000 to £5,000. Is this realistic? It's certainly likely: in fact, a great many novels are bought by publishers for less than these figures. Whether the deal is enough to compensate for the work that the author has put into it can only be decided by each writer. But you can begin to see why I spend a lot of my time advising my clients not to give up their day job.

Authors and publishers have always differed over advances. When Trollope was selling *Barchester Towers*, his publisher, Longmans, offered him £100. He said no, he would leave them and take it elsewhere. They argued that surely their name on his title page was worth something? Trollope replied that it was better at the bottom of a cheque.

One often hears of huge sums offered by publishers to novelists, to celebrities, or for a suddenly sought-after first novel. It can be in a publisher's interest to pay much more for a novel than it can ever earn for itself. This might be because the publisher really believes in the long-term worth of the novelist and will pay a premium to get the writer on to their list, or the publisher may be encouraged by competition to pay more than they might have done if they were offering alone.

Large figures paid for novels as the result of auctions between several publishers are similar to transfer fees paid for footballers: not always related to their expected earnings, but worth the expenditure to the publisher for the publicity value. A high advance paid to one author can attract other authors to the publishing house. It can alert other agents to the fact that the publisher is in a buying mood. It can attract celebrity authors. And the fact that other publishers are losers in an auction for a book can gain them another manuscript, as agents realize the publishers have a large advance unused!

Large advances that make newspaper headlines can kick off publicity, not only in the publishing trade press, but sometimes also in the general press, which the publisher can capitalize on when they come to publish.

Of course, there are other forms of offers too, but available only to the bestselling authors who are already household names. There is a persistent rumour in British publishing circles that one particularly famous author, already very rich, had his jaded palate tickled by an offer from his publisher that was not expressed in monetary terms at all. The story has it that the deal carried no advance in cash, but took the form of a racehorse. The publishing company has always denied the story so I don't know if it is true. But I do know that the author in question is keen on horse racing, and the details of his contracts are inaccessible to the publisher's staff . . . and no, it's not Dick Francis!

Stephen King and Clive Barker have each agreed deals with their

American publishers that were unusual, and which the publishers each liked to call 'partnership deals' in which the authors did not receive advance payments, but instead were guaranteed very high level royalties on sales. For the publishers, this gets around the problem that these authors were regularly being paid multi-million dollar advances that stretched the cash flows of their publishing companies. The authors in question were not desperate for a cheque to pay the next electricity bill and were confident of huge sales so could afford to gamble on receiving the money later. With royalty payments spread over a long period of time, it may have been beneficial to the authors tax-wise too. But these options are only ever offered to hugely bestselling authors. It is only those authors who could afford to take them up anyway.

I heard of another highly innovative offer put together by a small, independent US publisher who was desperate to buy a book attracting high offers from his bigger competitors. The publisher was at a disadvantage because neither did he own a paperback publishing company nor did he publish in paperback himself. Therefore he would be faced with publishing in hardback himself first, then selling paperback rights to another publisher, and splitting the paperback income with the author. Traditionally, this was divided 50:50, but these days it is sometimes much more in the author's favour, often 70:30, sometimes, in rare cases, higher than that.

This publisher offered an advance of $150,000 (very high for his company, low compared to offers of more than $1million from other publishers), but he made his offer unusual in several ways. First, he offered royalties of 20 per cent on all copies sold of his own hardback edition. Next, he offered the author a 75 per cent share of the paperback monies, 'not applied to the advance', in other words, as and when the hardback publisher received advances and royalties from the sale of rights to a paperback publisher, 75 per cent would be paid directly to the author without being held to cover the advance of $150,000 that the hardback publisher was offering the author.

When these figures are examined, it becomes clear that once the paperback income goes beyond $1million (quite possible in the American market) this offer is likely to benefit the author more than the higher advances from other publishers that came with lower royalties, even though they were paying the author 100 per cent of the paperback royalties.

The agent who was handling that deal in the end had to advise the author to accept one of the higher advance offers from a bigger publisher. The author hadn't much money at that stage, had several children to put through school, and couldn't afford to gamble on receiving income later, even if it would prove to be larger eventually. That book isn't published yet, but I am going to watch its sales very closely and I'm sure the small American publisher who lost it, despite his clever offer, will too.

Authors react to a publisher's offer in different ways. Some are just glad to be published (and so don't perhaps negotiate as hard for themselves as they might); others are affronted and see a low offer as an insult to their work; and others – those keen to be seen as professionals – will try to drive a hard bargain but at the same time be realistic about the book's sales prospects.

I often discuss with clients whether a different publisher would offer more, whether we should gamble on submitting again later when there is more of the manuscript completed, whether a one book, or two book, or three book offer is better for the author. All of these areas must be explored when deciding if an offer is acceptable, but many of them should have been discussed and decided (by author and agent) at the time the material was submitted, well in advance of when an offer has to be assessed. When the author is weighing up the pros and cons of accepting an offer, they – or their agent – should have done their homework well enough to know the publisher's capabilities with regard to editing, publicity, marketing and sales. So the author is left to make a decision that is partly hard-headed business and partly emotional: do they want to be published by this publisher and can they agree the deal offered?

Whatever the advance agreed, it is only part of the offer. It may appear to be the main topic of conversation during the sale of a book, but other aspects of the contract are just as important. The next chapter deals in depth with all aspects of a publishing deal and contract and not all of them are negotiable: some aspects of the deal and many aspects of the contract will be company-wide policy from which the editor is not allowed to deviate.

At this point I will assume we've agreed to accept the £4,500 advance and sell *Freddy's First Fiction* to the publisher. The next step is the contract.

9 Contracts

God is Love. But get it in writing – Gypsy Rose Lee

A verbal contract isn't worth the paper it's written on – Samuel Goldwyn

Why do you need a contract?

Your publishing contract is pivotal to your career. It's also vital to your bank balance: without one you'll not get paid! But don't rush into signing the first document your publisher offers you just to get your hands on the first cheque: when you do sign it you want it to be a good contract. I make no apologies for the length of this chapter: apart from the quality of your work, your contract is the most important part of your career. It affects every aspect of it.

Your contract might be current for a couple of years only (if your book goes out of print quickly and you then claim the rights back from the publisher) or it can be valid for your lifetime plus seventy years (if the book either stays in print in the original edition for many years, or if a license between the original publisher and another remains current).

Although Sam Goldwyn's quote above is, at first glance, as garbled as many of his famous one-liners, it strikes to the heart of this chapter. Publishing famously relies upon good relationships and communication – between author and agent, between author and editor, between agent and publisher, and between one publisher and another around the world.

No matter how friendly you are with your publisher, no matter how good your agent, it's every author's responsibility to understand the contracts that they sign. Only two people are the principals in the publishing contract: the licensor (the proprietor, the owner of the rights, the author) and the licensee (the purchaser, the publisher).

In a contract, an author and a publisher are each accepting obligations and undertakings for actions that they will perform with regard to each other and the manuscript in question. The contract shows that both parties are prepared to be bound, legally, by its terms. A professional author will take care to read the contract carefully and ask questions about any matters that are unclear before signing it.

Don't read it only to understand what's written down within the contract: look for a range of clauses that should be there for your own protection and make sure that they are. If you find, for instance, that there is no clause obligating the publisher to publish within a certain period of time after signature of the contract or after delivery of the manuscript, ask for one. I will deal with this and all the other important areas of a publishing contract in this chapter. A word of advice: this chapter can only contain a sample of the kinds of clause that might appear in a publishing contract, and agents have different views on the relative importance of different areas of a deal. Use this chapter to familiarize yourself with the items that will be dealt with by your publishing contract. But remember that only professional advice, based on your specific deal, can be sure to make your contract work best for you.

Authors sometimes ask me for advice based on the wording of just one or two clauses in their contract: this can be very dangerous. Never read a clause in isolation. Contract clauses are like pieces of a jigsaw: you only get the full picture when you have all the pieces together.

It is the publisher's job to get the best deal for themselves. No matter how good your relationship with your editor, they are not working for you, the writer, they are working for the publisher, their employer. If you find after you've signed the contract that there is something you don't like about it, you've only yourself to blame if you didn't read it carefully at the beginning.

Most agents – and publishers – are happy to explain a contract in detail to a first-time writer (or indeed to any writer, no matter how many contracts they have signed). Publishing contracts are much more complicated than they used to be: don't be afraid to ask for explanations. Question your agent or your publisher until you feel happy that you understand all the implications of the contract offered to you. You are the seller of the rights, it will be your signature on the contract. You owe it to yourself to understand it fully.

If you don't have an agent, I would strongly recommend asking The Society of Authors to vet your contract for you. It employs specialized lawyers, they have many years of experience in negotiating publishing contracts and they are very author-friendly. The membership fee to join is a worthwhile investment for a professional author, including those who do have agents. The contract vetting service is free to members.

In common with many other agents, I am not wildly enthusiastic when a client of mine tells me they plan to have their lawyer vet the contract I've sent to them. If I've sent the contract on to the client, then I have vetted it and approved it. I have spent years negotiating our agency boilerplate contracts with publishers, and I am, by virtue of sending it to the client, recommending its signature.

Naturally I wouldn't dream of telling a client not to show a contract to a lawyer if they wished, but it can suggest that there is less trust than there should be between client and agent and also suggests to me that the agent might face, in the near future, a conversation with the lawyer that involves the agent giving the lawyer a seminar on publishing practice.

Some lawyers, as I have already said, are well-versed in publishing contracts: it's the others that can be time-consuming for the agent and expensive for the writer.

Boilerplate agreements

Where an agent and publisher have been dealing together over many years, each new contract is based on all the previous years of experience and negotiation, against the background of accepted trade practice. In case this sounds too cosy, and you fear your agent and publisher may be working too closely together, rather than one of them working for you, remember that they are always negotiating, always trying to better their own positions. An agent betters their own position by improving the contract for the author.

A boilerplate contract is essentially a series of preconditions accepted by both parties. It saves time because the negotiating parties don't have to discuss every tiny point with every new deal, and so more time can be spent on the variables. Both negotiators will know that anything not specifically negotiated will be as in the agreed boilerplate. Items covered by the boilerplate might include the quantity below which the 'small reprint' clause comes into effect; the parameters of the 'royalty on high discount' clause; the percentage and time period in the 'reserves for returns' clause, and many others. This does not mean that these areas can never be negotiated differently; but it does mean that if they are not negotiated differently in a particular contract then the boilerplate provision will apply.

If a contract is generated by your agent, you can be sure it's more in your favour than if it's generated by the publisher. And most agency boilerplates with publishing houses will be considerably better than the boilerplates agreed between publishers and The Society of Authors and The Writers' Guild, commonly called 'Minimum Terms Agreements'. The two writers' associations do splendid work on behalf of their members, but even so, their boilerplates tend to be just that bit softer than most agencies'. Many publishers have refused to negotiate a boilerplate with the Society or the Guild. But they have to have boilerplates with agencies or their contracts departments would sink under the weight of negotiations if every new contract with an agency were fought over, clause by clause.

Publishers prefer to do without boilerplates with the Society and the Guild because they like to press their own so-called 'standard' contract on to unagented authors who make up a significant proportion of the membership of the two associations. Let me tell you there is no such thing as a 'standard' contract. All that this means is that it is the contract that the publisher wishes to use: it is a contract that suits the publisher and so is probably very much in their favour. If you do not have an agent, scrutinize that contract extremely carefully. I guarantee there will be clauses omitted which, if they were included, would be to your advantage.

Your right to negotiate

Contracts reflect a deal, and every deal is different. Every contract can, and should be, negotiated. A publisher might well wish to offer what they consider to be standard *terms*: that is quite different to a refusal to negotiate over the wording of the clauses in the contract. I have dealt with literally hundreds of publishers around the world and every one has been prepared to listen to reasoned argument. If you ask for changes that the publisher will not agree to, you have not lost anything. If you ask for changes that the publisher agrees to incorporate into the contract, you have improved your deal. Your publisher will certainly not think less of you if you take a professional attitude to the contract between you. And it might make them behave better toward you during the rest of the publishing process if they respect your professionalism.

Exchanging contracts

The process of exchanging agreed contracts so that each party signs the same documents should be relatively straightforward, but even with today's ease of communication, packages can get lost in the mail, and people do sometimes make changes to contracts without pointing them out to the other party (bad business practice and I am shocked to say that it happens even in otherwise well-run publishing companies). Both parties should sign identical sets of documents: in duplicate if author and publisher are each to have a copy, in triplicate if the agent is to keep a copy as well. (If it is a foreign language contract and a second, subsidiary agent is also involved, four copies will be needed. If there is more than one author – less likely with fiction than with non-fiction – then correspondingly more copies will be needed so that all signatories may keep a copy with original signatures.)

This is what I do when I draft a contract: if there is one author and no other agent involved, there will be four sets made initially: three to be signed and one to be my file copy for reference while the others are being signed.

It will be drafted with reference to the agreed boilerplate that I have with that publisher, taking into account any special precedents we may have agreed in previous contracts between that publisher and that author. Obviously, the particular terms of this deal are inserted. I will send them first to the publisher in case they request changes. This often happens: contracts and contract law are constantly evolving but no major deal points should be changed at this stage. So three copies are sent to the publisher.

When they are returned to me I check they have not made unauthorized changes, that any agreed changes are identical on all three copies, and that all three copies are signed in all the appropriate places (at the foot of each page, next to any agreed changes, and in the main signature box towards the end of the contract). The three copies signed by the publisher are then sent to the author for signature with instructions to keep one for themselves and send the other two back to me. When I receive the two that are now fully countersigned by both parties, I keep one for our agency files, return the other to the publisher, and invoice them for the amount now due on signature.

The contract

I'll now go through a publishing contract, mentioning all the clauses that I think should be present and explaining their purpose. Remember, when reading a contract, and this bears repeating, no single clause should be taken out of context. Although many clauses may seem to exist quite separately from the others, it is important to read the contract as a narrative to make sure that clauses do not contradict each other. Certain clauses need to be looked for in pairs: for instance, if your grant of rights to the publisher specifies 'world rights in all languages' then you will want to look for a part of the subsidiary rights clause that spells out your income when the publisher licences American or translation rights. Likewise, if the subsidiary rights clause does lay out these percentage splits, make sure that the grant of rights clause does indeed give the publisher all the rights mentioned in that clause, or it will not be able to licence the rights.

With practice, one gets used to the sight of one clause triggering off the need for other specific clauses.

I have divided the clauses into five sections after the preamble: rights acquired by the publisher; publisher obligations; author obligations, author protection; and payments. Contracts are not necessarily laid out like this (but perhaps should be). Dealing with the contract like this makes it easier to find your way around it and also makes it easy to check that your contract has all the requisite protections and obligations.

It is not possible, in this book, to cover every contractual possibility and variation. I have included a version of most clauses that you would want to find in a contract between an author and a publisher for a novel but every negotiation and deal is different, and few contracts will ever look exactly like the one I am taking as my example. If, despite the length of this chapter, you are keen to know more about publishing contracts, I recommend two excellent books: *Understanding Publishers' Contracts* by Michael Legat (Robert Hale) and *Publishing Agreements: A Book of Precedents* edited by Charles Clark, Lynette Owen and Roger Palmer (Butterworths). The latter is written for publishers; the former is more accessible for authors.

The preamble

This will state the date of the contract, the parties who are signatories, the terminology used throughout the contract for the parties and the title of the work. An example:

> MEMORANDUM OF AGREEMENT made this [xx] day of [Month] [Year]

Between [Author's Name] (hereinafter called the Proprietor) for themselves and their successors and assigns of the one part c/o [Agency's Name and Address] and [Publisher's Name and Address] (hereinafter called the Publishers) for themselves, their successors and assigns of the other part.

Whereby it is mutually agreed as follows concerning a work (hereinafter called the Work) presently entitled: [the title] by: [author's name].

Some publishers wish for 'successors and assigns' to appear after the agency name. I prefer it to follow the author's name, so that it is clear that only the author is enjoined in this way. Otherwise, even though the agency is not a signatory to the contract, it could be argued that it might be liable for some of the obligations.

Most agents prefer 'successors and assigns', which comes after the publisher's name here, to be omitted; most publishers strongly prefer it to be there. The reason for wanting it out is because the author has chosen to sign up with that particular publisher – not with someone the publisher might sell themselves to at a later date, and not to someone that the publisher might wish to assign the contract to in the future. More of this below when we come to the 'non-assignment' clause.

Rights acquired by the publisher

Grant, territory and licence

This clause tells the publisher whether the contract is a licence or an assignment of rights. A licence, which confers permission upon the licensee (the publisher) to exploit rights owned by the licensor (the author), is preferable. An assignment implies that ownership has passed to the licensee and leaves the author with far less control.

The clause sets out the language or languages that the publisher is acquiring and it defines the territory. It also defines the period of time during which the publisher may exploit the work: either the full period of copyright or a shorter term, ten years, for example.

It sets out exactly what rights are included in the publisher's package. For instance, some publishers own their own audio cassette divisions and like to obtain these rights. I will only include these rights if the publisher will give the same undertaking to publish in audio as they do for book rights, i.e. they agree to produce the cassettes and to produce them within a specific period of time. Almost always, book publishers will issue the audio version in an abridged form. Unabridged audio rights are then retained by the author and we sell those direct to unabridged audio publishers: the markets are quite separate. More about this under 'Subsidiary Rights'.

Such a clause, in a contract with a British publisher might, for instance, read as follows:

> The Proprietor hereby grants to the Publishers for the full period of copyright the sole and exclusive license to print, publish and market the Work in volume form in the English language exclusively in the territories in the schedule attached and non-exclusively throughout the rest of the world except the USA, its territories and dependencies and the Philippines.

This clause means that the publisher

a) may exploit the work for the full period of copyright, provided they publish within the period provided for in the later clause headed 'Publication', and provided they keep it in print. To make sure of this, it is essential to include a clause dealing with out-of-print situations, so that if the book goes out of print and the publisher does not reprint it within an agreed period of time, rights will revert to the author. See the explanation for the 'reversion of rights' clause under 'Author Protection'.

If it has been agreed that the license will run for a fixed period it will be stated in this clause, often with provision for a renegotiation at the end of the fixed term. If it has been agreed that the contract will be for the full period of copyright, there can sometimes be a provision for a review of the terms at an agreed date in the future. A review clause should be specific about the date of the review, naming the period of time and when it dates from (e.g. 'ten years from the publisher's first publication of the work'). This is discussed in 'Author Protection'.

b) has a licence rather than an assignment.

c) may publish in volume form (as a book: a hardback, trade paperback, or mass-market paperback or possibly all three). It is possible to limit publication to any one or two of these formats if that's the way you have negotiated the deal. Although certain rights may not be covered by publication in volume form, the subsidiary rights clause may extend the rights granted.

d) has the right to publish only in English and in the territories listed on the schedule of exclusive territories page, which is usually at the end of the contract. This wording usually means the British publisher's market is exclusive throughout the British Isles, Australasia and South Africa, and sometimes Canada and the European Union.

e) may in addition publish non-exclusively throughout non-EU Europe and Asia – i.e. the rest of the world except those territories listed, and excluding the territories usually licensed exclusively to an American publisher.

Variations on the territories could mean that the publisher has world rights in the English language, i.e. they can publish in the British market and the American market (or license to an American publisher); or that they have world rights in all languages – i.e. they can publish or license throughout the world in English and all other languages. This means that they would have the right to license translation rights to other publishers.

In contracts with British or American publishers, Canada should be mentioned somewhere in this clause: either it will be included in the British publisher's exclusive market and excluded from the market you license to an American publisher, or it will be specifically excluded from the British publisher's market so that you can include it in the American publisher's market or license separately to a Canadian publisher.

If the British publisher has the whole of the European Union and EFTA as an exclusive market, when you license separately to America you must take care to exclude these markets. (For more information, see chapter 12.)

Variations on rights granted to the publisher are many and various: rights granted can include electronic, film and television, audio tape etc.

As a second paragraph under the 'grant, territory and licence' clause our agency's contract has the following:

No abridgement of the Work shall be issued without the consent of the Proprietor, such consent not to be unreasonably withheld.

This means that if the publisher wishes to publish a shorter version (perhaps after publication of the original edition) the author must be consulted and their consent obtained. Quite separately the publisher may have the right to license, say, to Reader's Digest Condensed

Books. This is dealt with under 'Subsidiary Rights', as are all the other rights that the publisher may license to others.

There will always be a page listing the specific territories that are licensed exclusively to the publisher: this is often the last page in the contract. Here is an example of one for a contract that gives the publisher the UK and the Commonwealth, but not Canada, and not European exclusivity:

SCHEDULE OF THE EXCLUSIVE COUNTRIES

Ascension	Native State of India
Australia	New Zealand (including Ross)
Bangladesh	Nigeria and the Cameroons
Botswana	Northern Ireland
British West Indies, comprising:	Pacific Islands, comprising:
Bahamas	British Solomon Islands
Barbados	Tonga
Bermuda	Western Samoa
British Honduras	Naura Islands
Guyana	New Hebrides
the Caicos, Cayman,	Gilbert and Ellice Islands
Leeward, Turks and	Union Islands
Windward Islands	Norfolk Island
Brunei	Papua New Guinea
Burma	Pitcairn Island
Cocos Island	Pakistan
Cyprus	St Helena
Falkland Islands	Seychelles
Fiji	Sierra Leone
Gambia	Singapore
Gibraltar	Somali Republic
Ghana	South African Republic
Hong Kong	South West Africa
India	South Yemen Republic
Irish Republic	Sri Lanka
Jamaica	Sudan
Kenya	Swaziland
Kuwait	Tanzania
Lesotho	Tasmania
Malawi	Trinidad and Tobago
Malaysia, comprising:	Tristan da Cunha
the Malayan Union	Uganda
Sabah	United Kingdom
Sarawak	Zambia
Malta and Gozo	Zimbabwe
Mauritius (including Rodrigues)	

If Canada is to be part of the publisher's exclusive territory it would be included in this list; likewise if the European Union were to be included in the exclusive territory, each and every individual country would be listed here. I also favour putting an asterisk by each of the European Union countries and adding the following to the bottom of the schedule of exclusive territories:

> * Additional countries to be treated as the Home Market with regard to royalties

Many of the territories forming part of the UK or US publishers' licence are traditional: Empire countries that may no longer be constituitionally tied to Britain, ex-protectorates. This explains why British publishers still regard Hong Kong as part of their market (although American publishers are now arguing against that) and why the Philippines are part of the American market. Many old trading patterns still show up in the split territories between English language publishers.

Subsidiary rights

Subsidiary rights are additional rights granted to the original publisher, which the publishing house will not exploit directly themselves but will sell, licensing the rights to others in return for payment that will be shared between the author and the original publisher (see also chapter 13). Payment to the author for these rights will normally be made into the author's royalty account, and will be paid according to the agreed schedule, usually twice a year, although it is possible to negotiate for earlier payment of specific income (see under 'Payments').

Whatever rights the publisher does control, make sure that they agree to give you approval over the deals they do before they finalize each one. With today's speed and efficiency of communication, written approval is no longer as cumbersome as it used to be and I favour this where possible. Publishers will often ask to add the phrase 'not to be unreasonably withheld' to any clause that requires the publishing company to request approval. I recommend trying to resist its addition, as it dilutes your right to deny agreement to the deals they put before you.

But take care when exercising this right: denying the publisher the right to do deals that will earn back the advance they have paid you will cause problems in your relationship with your publisher unless you have a very good reason indeed to turn down the subsidiary deal. One reason why I am so keen for my clients to have approval written into their contracts is so that we are told every aspect of the deal before it is agreed. I seldom recommend that my clients turn down a subsidiary deal completely, but I do often persuade the publisher to improve the terms in my client's favour.

It is precisely on items like this that co-operation between author and publisher can become strained. If the publisher's rights department has been working hard on a deal that the author then quibbles about unnecessarily (in the publisher's view) then the author might find relations cooling with their editor.

If you are contracting with a publisher who publishes in both hardback and paperback, it may not be appropriate at all to include (a) or (b) below, although publishers will always argue for the right to license rights on to others, for example, to a library reprint publisher who may want to reissue the book in hardback long after the original edition has gone out of print. Serial rights, which allow a newspaper or magazine to print extracts, are sometimes omitted from a publishing licence and the author or agent places the rights themselves. This is a deal point that should be agreed before the contract is finalized. Publishers may also ask for audio cassette rights. My view on this is that if they issue audio cassette recordings themselves, then the specific rights (abridged audio rights usually; few trade publishers issue unabridged audio cassettes themselves) can form part of the license to the publisher if they obligate themselves to produce an audio cassette version in the same way as they obligate themselves to publish in book form. If they will not do this, I see no reason why they should control these rights. I usually then keep them out of the book contract and we place these rights on behalf of the author. But if you do not have an agent you might prefer to let the publisher handle these rights on your behalf.

Always think of the practical implications of granting or withholding rights. If you do not have the means to exploit the rights you are withholding, either seek out a specialist who can do so for you, or let the publisher handle the rights on your behalf, after negotiating an acceptable split of income from their eventual sale.

A typical subsidiary rights clause might read as follows:

> The Publisher shall have the sole right to license the following subsidiary rights in the language and territory granted herein, subject to the written approval of the Proprietor or his/her agent,

and shall pay the Proprietor the indicated percentages of the gross amounts due from such sales:

(a) Publication of a hardback edition by another publisher: 80%

(b) Publication of a paperback edition by another publisher: 60% on income up to £5,000, 70% thereafter

(c) First serial (i.e. serials or extracts published or beginning before first publication): 90%

(d) Second serial (i.e. serials or extracts published or beginning after first publication): 75%

(e) It is acknowledged that the Proprietor retains all serial rights in the Work, but the timing of publication of extracts or serials from the Work shall be mutually agreed between the Proprietor and Publisher and will not take place earlier than one week before publication

(f) Publication of a large print edition: 60%

(g) Publication in a set, omnibus volume or anthology by another publisher: 50%

(h) Publication of full length or condensed editions of the Work by a book club or similar organisation in which the Publisher has no financial interest: 50%

(i) Publication of full length or condensed edition of the Work by a book club or similar organisation when they take sheets or bound copies from the Publisher: 10% receipts

(j) Should the Publisher arrange for an Australian edition of the Work published in Australasia either under the Publisher's own imprint or by arrangement with another Publisher, the royalty payable to the Proprietor shall be mutually agreed

(k) In the event of the selection of the Work by an American book club the Publisher shall be at liberty to license the said book club to distribute copies of their edition to its members in Canada on the basis of the book club accounting to the Publishers for the royalties payable on such copies and all monies received being equally shared by the Proprietor and the Publisher

(l) The Publisher shall be entitled to authorize free of charge the recording of the Work in Braille or as a Talking Book for the blind, such authorisation to be given only for non-commercial use

(m) Any commission due to an agent acting on the instructions of the Publisher in respect of the sale of rights as set out in this Clause shall be deducted from the Publisher's share of income

All of these income splits are subject to negotiation. Obviously the better established and more successful authors have more room for negotiation than authors at the start of their publication career. If the publisher is acquiring world rights in the English language, then included here would be a sub-clause dealing with the division of income on a sale of rights to an American publisher; similarly, another clause dealing with translation rights sales if the publisher were acquiring world rights in all languages. Any other rights that the publisher may control, such as film or television rights, would be listed here too.

Some points worth noting are:

Preamble of subsidiary rights clause: this is where you want to build in wording regarding author approval. Some publishers will argue that it is too time-consuming, and that they risk losing a deal while waiting to hear from an author or an agent. The counter argument is that modern methods of communication provide for almost instant response. And few of these rights have to be dealt with in a matter of moments: there is usually plenty of time (provided the subsidiary rights staff are efficient in communicating with the author or agent) for approval to be sought and obtained.

Requiring approval means, at the very least, you do get to know about the deal and so can look out for the income on your next royalty statement. If your contract does not call for approval, it is possible that you might not be told about a right that has been licensed by your publisher to another company. You could lose income and information, and you might not be able to acquire a copy of the book in that format.

There is one publisher I know of who is notorious for insisting that they sign up authors for world rights deals in all languages, and then seldom informs the author of the deals they have agreed. It is unprofessional, and frustrating for the author.

Some of these rights and payment splits are major deal points that will have been negotiated before the deal is agreed, such as serial rights, or the right to license paperback or American or translation rights to another publisher; others, such as large print and anthology rights, are pretty standard throughout the trade.

   (a) Publication of a hardback edition by another publisher: 80%

   (b) Publication of a paperback edition by another publisher: 60% on income up to £5,000, 70% thereafter.

If your publisher intends to publish first in hardback and later in paperback, or perhaps to produce both editions simultaneously, I would take these clauses out, to avoid the implication that they also have the automatic right to license these editions to others. Inclusion could imply that they can pull out of publishing a hardback or a paperback themselves without further discussion with you. A compromise might be that if (a) and (b) are to be included in the contract, instead of agreeing the income split, you take the percentage figure out and substitute 'to be agreed', which provides for discussion *at the time* a license is contemplated.

If (b) is included, I favour a sliding scale such as I have suggested, rather than a single split of 50 or 60 per cent, which is favoured by publishers. The monetary figure of £5,000 that I have included refers to the monies from the paperback publisher who licenses those rights from your original publisher. In this clause, once there was more than £5,000 worth of income from this license, the proportion to the author increases from 60 per cent to 70 per cent. The break point at which the proportion to the author goes up might logically be the same as the advance paid by the original publisher to the author. Once that has been reached, the publisher has recouped a large portion of the money originally paid to the author, so there is no reason why the author's portion should not increase.

(c) First serial (i.e. serials or extracts published or beginning before first publication): 90%

(d) Second serial (i.e. serials or extracts published or beginning after first publication): 75%

Serial rights are not always included in a publishing license. They should always be discussed before a deal is finalized. If a publisher is making an offer based on the assumption that serial rights will be part of the license granted to them, they will probably have included some estimated income from serial rights in the offer they made to you. If these rights are not available to them, it would reduce the value of the property and they would wish to reduce the advance they are offering you.

The income splits can vary enormously so, again, it is important to negotiate them as early as possible. Some publishers like to keep 15 or 20 per cent of first serial, or 50 per cent of second serial. It is common to allow the publisher a greater proportion of second, or post-publication, serial than of first or pre-publication. Publishers have successfully argued over the years that their publication and distribution of the book contributes to the attractiveness of post-publication serial to a newspaper or magazine. But as post-publication rights regularly attract far less income than pre-publication, I'm not sure that this argument can be upheld!

(e) It is acknowledged that the Proprietor retains all serial rights in the Work, but the timing of publication of extracts or serials from the Work shall be mutually agreed between the Proprietor and Publisher and will not take place earlier than one week before publication, nor will the serial contain more than 50% of the text of the Work

This sub-clause would not be included in the contract if you had allowed the publisher to have control of the sale of serial rights. When the author retains serial rights, some publishers require an undertaking from the author that consultation will take place about the timing of a serial publication. The timing of publication of serial rights must be co-ordinated with the publisher's publicity and promotion. A badly timed serial publication, or one that uses a very high proportion of the text of the work, could harm sales of the published book, rather than enhance them.

(f) Publication of a large print edition: 60%

Large print editions are for the benefit of the partially sighted and are usually published by specialist publishers for sale to hospitals, old people's homes etc., although a small quantity do make their way into bookshops. The percentage to the author is usually 50 or 60 per cent.

(g) Publication in a set, omnibus volume or anthology by another publisher: 50%

This covers rights that sometimes bring in very little money and can be costly for the publisher to administer. 50 or 60 per cent is the norm here.

(h) Publication of full length or condensed editions of the Work by a book club or similar organisation in which the Publisher has no financial interest: 50%

(i) Publication of full length or condensed edition of the Work by a book club or similar organisation where they take sheets or bound copies from the publisher: 10% receipts

These are two different ways of granting a book club license. In (g) the book club is taking a license and will print the books themselves, usually paying an offset fee to the publisher in addition to the license

fee. (An offset fee covers their use of the publisher's original typesetting, whose copyright rests with the original publisher.) The usual
proportion of income would be 50 or 60 per cent. In exceptional
cases, say, for a very successful author, a higher percentage can
sometimes be negotiated.

In (i) the club would be buying printed copies from the publisher,
which the publisher would either add to their initial print run or print
at the same time as a reprint for themselves. Printing a book club
edition separately could be unnecessarily costly and is therefore to be
avoided unless the quantity ordered is sufficiently large to bring the
unit cost down. The publisher will usually quote a monetary figure to
the book club for their copies, which will include manufacturing cost
and royalty. The proportion to the author is usually 10 per cent of
this figure but 12.5 per cent or even 15 per cent can sometimes be
achieved. Another possibility is to agree a sliding scale, with the
percentage to the author increasing after an agreed level of income
from the club edition has been reached.

> (j) Should the Publisher arrange for an Australian edition of the
> Work published in Australasia either under the Publisher's own
> imprint or by arrangement with another Publisher, the royalty
> payable to the Proprietor shall be mutually agreed.

If your UK publisher proposes for their Australian office or distributor
to print a separate edition in Australia, it suggests they have big plans
and expect a success. A separate printing would be uneconomic and
unnecessary if the figures were small. I prefer for the income split to
be left out of the agreement so that one can argue at the time with
knowledge of the facts of the specific case.

> (k) In the event of the selection of the Work by an American book
> club the Publisher shall be at liberty to license the said book club
> to distribute copies of their edition to its members in Canada on
> the basis of the book club accounting to the Publishers for the
> royalties payable on such copies and all monies received being
> equally shared by the Proprietor and the Publisher.

This affects a British publisher who has Canada as part of their
exclusive license and it provides for the situation that arises when an
American publisher has licensed book club rights to an American
book club and wants to allow the American book club to supply
books to their Canadian members. The American publisher will ask
permission, usually from the author (via the author's agent if there is
one) from whom they hold the license. If this occurs with a client I

represent, I let the UK publisher know about it and they usually agree on the terms stated in this clause. The US publisher will pay these royalties to the UK publisher in return for being allowed to license rights that encroach on part of the UK publisher's otherwise exclusive market. The UK publisher will then, in turn, show these royalties on the next royalty statement it sends to the author after receipt of the income.

(l) The Publisher shall be entitled to authorise free of charge the recording of the Work in Braille or as a Talking Book for the blind, such authorisation to be given only for non-commercial use.

This is a pretty standard sub-clause allowing the publisher to authorize rights for the blind or partially sighted. These rights are always allowed free of charge provided the material is not sold for commercial gain, and provided the right is exploited directly by the company authorized to do so: they may not themselves license the rights to anyone else.

(m) Any commission due to an agent acting on the instructions of the Publisher in respect of the sale of rights as set out in this Clause shall be deducted from the Publisher's share of income.

This provides for the fact that the proportion of income due to the author in the other sub-clauses is free of any deductions. If the publisher chooses to use a sub-agent they must pay for the agent themselves out of their proportion of the income: they may not take the agent's fee 'off the top' and then divide what is left according to the proportions stated. This has to be policed very carefully: another reason for requiring the publisher to provide copies of all subsidiary contracts (see under 'Publisher Obligations').

Where your original publisher acquires the right to license foreign publications – say the British publisher being allowed to license American and translation rights – I would favour adding a clause to the effect that any unsold rights in these areas revert to the author after a specified period of time. The time period can range from one year from delivery of the manuscript, to one or two years from the publisher's first publication date. Obviously, from the author's point of view a shorter period is preferable.

In my experience, both previously as a manager running a subsidiary rights department within a publishing company, and now as an authors' agent, rights departments in publishing companies tend to be understaffed, overworked, and seldom allowed to travel to the markets they are selling to. It is not uncommon for rights departments to only be able to concentrate on selling rights for the titles in their current publication season or year. It is difficult for them to sell rights in such a way as to build an author's career in each and every language market as an agent can. This is partly because of the lack of resources, and partly because they may only control rights in one or two of the author's titles if the author moves from one publisher to another. So taking the precaution of requiring unsold rights to revert to the author after an agreed period of time allows you or your agent to take over the selling effort at a time when the publisher's rights department may have stopped offering them anyway.

Publisher obligations

Publication

This clause obligates the publisher to publish (a rather necessary function of the contract but I have seen several publisher generated contracts, some from large and respected companies, which do not include this obligation!), and to publish in certain formats within specified periods of time. The time periods may start from the date of the contract itself (if the manuscript is delivered at the time you sign) or from the date of delivery if that is after signature of the contract.

If the publisher is to publish more than one edition – say, a hardback followed by a paperback – don't sign a clause that only obligates them to publish the second edition a certain period after publication of the first. The effect of this can be that if the first edition is delayed for any reason, the publication obligation for the second edition is also automatically delayed. Although a publisher might argue that if a hardback publication date is delayed, then there *should* be a similar delay in producing the next edition, I would always rather have the contract provide for publication dates all to be timed from the contract or manuscript delivery. This is because if there are payments to be made by the publisher to the author on each of those publication dates, those payments should still be made to the author on the originally agreed dates (provided the wording is correct in the 'advance' clause), even if the publication date itself is delayed. An important consideration if cash flow is vital to the author!

I also like this clause to obligate the publisher to consult the author on blurb, cover design, author photograph and biographical information used on the book; to make sure that any advertisements contained in the book are for books published by that publisher; to tell the author the quantity of books printed; to show the author a finally edited typescript before it goes to the printer; to indicate what they expect the retail price to be; and to agree that they will publish effectively in the markets granted to them.

This last may surprise you. Our lawyers once pointed out to me that very few publishing contracts require the publisher to publish *well*. Although this may sound like a bland statement to include in a contract, there can be occasions when it is very useful to include it. For instance, I was once negotiating with a British editor for a contract for a second novel by one of my clients: the first had been published a couple of months before this negotiation was taking place. The editor said she wanted to ask for something extra this time: she wanted to have Canada as part of their exclusive territory. There was an ominous silence and I said very quietly, 'But you have Canada on the first novel.' Somehow she had informed her sales department that they did not control the Canadian market and no sales had been solicited from Canada, or any copies shipped there.

This was a serious error that cost the company – and my author – sales and income. If the author had wanted to sue he could have done so, because of the 'publish effectively' sub-clause. Like many authors in his situation he actually chose not to, but we were able to pressurize the publisher into spending more time and energy and money on marketing the paperback of the first novel and got quite a few concessions out of them in other areas too

Here is an example of the clause dealing with publication:

(a) The Publishers shall, unless prevented by circumstances beyond their control, publish the Work in hardback form at their own expense within twelve months of receipt by them of the complete Work and in paperback within 24 months of receipt of the complete Work. Except if otherwise expressed in this Agreement, all details as to the manner of production, publication and advertisement and the number and destination of free copies shall be left to the sole discretion of the Publishers except that the Proprietor has the right of consultation on proposed cover design and cover copy.

Notwithstanding the above, the Publishers undertake:

(b) to consult the Proprietor about blurb and jacket design and to obtain the Proprietor's prior agreement to the use of any drawing or photograph of the Proprietor or biographical material;

(c) not to print advertisements other than for books published by the Publisher in any edition of the Work or on any cover or dustjacket of the Work whether issued by the Publishers or their licensees;

(d) to inform the Proprietor regarding the number of copies printed in each impression or edition;

(e) to use their best endeavours to publish the Work effectively in all significant markets;

(f) The published price will be approximately £00.00 in the first instance for the hardback edition and approximately £00.00 in the first instance for the mass market paperback edition.

(g) The Publisher will use its best endeavours to show to the Proprietor for approval a copy of the final edited typescript at least 14 days before it goes to the printer or typesetter.

Points to note include:

(b) Consultation on cover design and cover copy: some authors might be surprised that I don't automatically ask for my client to give 'approval', rather than the milder 'consultation'. I think that so long as the publisher agrees to consult properly (with enough time to take the author's views into consideration and enough time to make changes if they are agreed by the publisher) that should be enough. The cover is the single most important selling tool in the publication process; it is the central image that every other part of the selling and marketing process is built around. I firmly believe that the publisher should listen to the author's views, but I also believe strongly that it must be a process of consultation. The publisher, with years of experience of selling to the trade, must be allowed the final word in this area. With good communication, consultation can result in all parties being pleased with the outcome, without the need for one party to dictate to the other on image or style. (For more discussion of this point, see chapter 10.)

(c) I think it is perfectly reasonable for a publisher to be allowed to advertise other titles that they publish in the pages at the end of your novel. After all, this could mean your book will be highlighted in other novels. But I do not think it reasonable that they sell advertising space to other companies. This happens more in America, where it is common to see advertisements for self-help courses or insurance printed on tear-out cards in the middle of paperback novels: I think this is inappropriate. Most publishers are happy to agree this sub-clause.

(d) This information is quite straightforward and no publisher argues that the author hasn't a right to it but several have asked that the beginning of the sub-clause be amended to read 'to inform the Proprietor, *if requested*' so as to put the onus on the author or agent to ask for the information. This doesn't bother me: in practice we ask for the information whenever we want it.

(e) I have commented on the need for this earlier in this chapter.

(f) A simple matter of information.

(g) This ensures that the author will see the copy-edited manuscript before it is sent for setting. Many publishers would, out of courtesy, do this anyway, but many have to be reminded.

If part of your negotiation involved the publisher undertaking a promotion guarantee (that it would spend no less than a certain sum on promotion) or a publication guarantee (that your book would be a lead title in the month of publication), wording would need to be added to this clause to specify exactly what had been agreed.

Libel reading

I always try to obligate the publisher to obtain a libel reading and be obliged to pay for it themselves. Many publishers insist that the author should pay for a libel reading (they argue that this instils a far greater sense of responsibility in the author not to libel anyone in the manuscript: a large part of the warranty clause deals with an author's obligation not to libel anyone). A compromise is for the cost of the libel reading to be shared between author and publisher. If so, the libel clause should reflect that. Under these circumstances, I prefer for the publisher to pay for it initially (after consulting the author over the size of it) and then have the publisher take the author's portion out of the amount payable on publication of the book. Even if an author is liable for costs, I try to set up a contract in such a way that they are taken out of monies due to the author, rather than that the publisher should send the author an invoice.

A libel reading clause where the publisher pays the cost of the libel reading might read as follows:

> The Publisher shall have the Work read for libel at their sole expense if, in their reasonable judgement, the Work requires it. The Publisher shall not alter or delete any passage without the

prior written approval of the Proprietor. However, in no event shall the Publisher be obliged to publish the work if, in the opinion of their Counsel, it violates the common law, copyright or other rights of any third person or contains libellous or obscene matter.

It's not common for fiction to need to be read for libel, but it is wise for authors to understand the risks and take extreme care if basing characters on real people. With regard to the last sentence of this clause, it is obviously not possible to insist that a publisher should publish a text their lawyers have advised to be libellous. But if the lawyers are unsure about the risk of libel, some publishers might be prepared to take more risk than others. (For more discussion of libel, see chapter 10.)

Review

This is a clause in which both parties agree to review the terms of the deal at a later date (usually ten or twenty years after publication), if the contract is still active.

If this has been agreed in the original negotiations, the details need to be clearly set out. But beware: these clauses seldom specify that royalty levels will only be renegotiated upwards. The terms are seen against the background of the trade at the time of the review. As the author's royalty (the author's share of retail price) seems continually under pressure, the inclusion of a review clause could be a double-edged sword: you could find yourself being pressurized to accept a lower royalty rate at the time of a review, because trade practice has reduced royalties since you first signed the contract.

This clause is usually used to review royalty levels but there is no reason why any other aspect of the contract could not be renegotiated if both parties agree to do so.

A sample clause might be:

> On every fifteenth anniversary of the publication date (or within a reasonable time thereafter) either party may give written notice to the other that he/she would like specified terms of the contract to be reviewed, in which case those terms shall be considered in the light of comparable terms then prevailing in the trade and shall be altered (with effect from the date of the notice) to the extent that may be just and equitable.

Items to take into account when negotiating a review would include the rate of sale and the current state of the author's reputation (the higher either of them, the greater chance you have of increasing the terms and also arranging another 'top-up' advance). If the author's current titles were still published by the same company, and the terms of the newer contracts were significantly better than the contract in question, you might well succeed in improving the contract to the level of the newer contracts.

Supply of subsidiary agreements

If a publisher had the right to license an author's work to others, then they should supply proper paperwork so that the author or agent can keep track of what rights have been licensed and when, and what monies are due and when. This is the kind of clause that few publishers offer willingly but most will agree to include if you ask for it. A typical clause might read:

> The Publisher undertakes to supply to the Proprietor within 14 days of receipt a copy of all contracts relating to the sale of rights specified under Clause XX and, if requested, copies of relevant royalty statements.

Some publishers argue that it is difficult for them to remember to supply copies of contracts and that they wish to amend the first line to read:

> The Publisher undertakes to supply to the Proprietor *if requested* a copy of all agreements.

This puts the onus back on the author or agent to make the request. I don't object to doing this because I always ask for a copy, but I object to the principle of having to ask. If some publishing companies (Headline and Hodder stand out as shining examples of this) can be efficient enough to have their subsidiary rights staff automatically supply copies of signed contracts to their authors or authors' agents there is no reason why others should not also do so.

Examination of accounts

This clause gives the author the right to have an accountant examine all the records of the publishing company relevant to the author's title. It might read as follows:

> The Proprietor or his/her authorised representatives shall have the right upon written request to examine the accounts of the

Publishers insofar as they relate to the sales of the Work, which examination shall be at the cost of the Proprietor and settled in account unless any errors in the sums paid to the Proprietor are found to his/her disadvantage in which case the cost will be paid by the Publishers.

It is common for publishers to ask to limit in some way their need to pay the costs of such an examination. Some will only agree to pay up to the cost of the amount found owing to the author; some will only pay the cost of the examination if it discovers errors of more than 2 per cent of the monies paid to the author; some will limit the author's right to order this kind of examination to no more than once in any calendar year.

These examinations do not take place very often and an author would want to have strong grounds for believing they would find discrepancies in their favour before entering into an accounts examination. Because of the detailed paperwork that has to be examined, such an exercise can be time-consuming and costly. It has to be undertaken by qualified accountants, preferably familiar with publishing book-keeping and trade practice.

The Society of Authors has examined the accounts of several publishing houses over the last few years and has found an interesting, non-confrontational way of doing it. Its members who are willing to participate have their names put into a group from which one is chosen at random. That author's publisher's accounts are examined by the Society and a report published in *The Author*. They make fascinating reading, although give little comfort to those who favour conspiracy theories. Although the Society's examinations have found mistakes, most of their reports have concluded that they are genuine mistakes due to human error, rather than wily publishers who are trying to steal income from their authors.

Presentation copies

This clause sets out how many free copies will be supplied to the author. The quantity varies from publisher to publisher: some give fewer of the hardback than the paperback, some still rather meanly stick to half a dozen of each edition, while some publishers are more generous. I think if they realized how much it means to an author to have copies of their own titles, publishers might be more generous. I have known some authors be more upset at the provisions of this clause than publishers might realize. It would cost them so little to improve the numbers, but could buy them so much goodwill from authors. On the whole, American publishers are more helpful here than others – it is not uncommon for American publishers to offer twenty or even fifty copies of paperback editions.

A sample clause might read:

> On publication the Publisher will forward direct to the Proprietor at [author's home address]10 (ten) presentation copies of each of the Publisher's editions, and the Proprietor shall be entitled to purchase further copies at a discount of 50% (fifty percent) from the list retail price. Additionally, the Publishers will provide the Proprietor's agent with 2 (two) presentation copies of each edition. It is further agreed that the Publishers shall send 2 (two) copies to the Proprietor and 1 (one) copy to his/her agent of every sublicensed edition of the Work.

Some publishers supply extra copies of printed books to authors and agents at a less generous discount than 50 per cent, 33 per cent being quite common. But with discounts to booksellers being so much higher these days than in the past, I think it's only reasonable that authors buying extra copies should not pay more than booksellers for their own titles! Hodder Headline include wording to the effect that an author can be supplied with extra copies at a higher discount if they pay at the time they send in their order, thus passing on cash flow savings to the author. I think this is quite reasonable.

Return of typescript

Since most authors now store their material on computers, there is less need for this clause than in the past, although many writers do still like to have their original material returned. A sample wording might be:

> The Publishers shall return the original typescript to the Proprietor within ninety days of publication of the Work.

Again, as with the requirement for the publisher to supply copies of subsidiary agreements to the author, they will sometimes ask for the words 'if requested' to be added to the end of this clause, putting the onus upon the author to ask for the return of their material.

Other clauses relevant to publisher obligations include 'accounts' and 'reversion of rights', which are discussed under 'Payments' and 'Author Protection' respectively.

Author obligations

Warranty

There is a great variety of warranty clauses, those drawn up by publishers being the longest (and, inevitably, the more onerous upon the author), those drawn up by authors' agents being the shortest (and deliberately, the most vague). The purpose of the warranty clause is for the publisher to receive a series of undertakings from the author: that the author owns the rights they are granting, that the work is not illegal in any way, and that the author should indemnify the publisher if the publisher is sued under any of the areas mentioned, for example, libel or copyright infringement or obscenity. It is, of course, the publisher who is most often sued, so it is understandable that they should require some reassurance, in the contract, from the author.

The clause in my contract is pretty short, as you would expect, and is as follows:

> The Proprietor warrants that he/she has the sole and exclusive right to dispose of the rights granted herein to the Publisher; that to the best of his/her knowledge according to the laws of England the Work contains no matter libellous or obscene, or infringing upon any copyright or right of literary property or otherwise contrary to law; and that with respect to any adverse claim which is finally sustained as to any of the foregoing warranties that Proprietor shall defend, hold harmless and indemnify the Publisher.

Many publishers object to the phrase 'to the best of his/her knowledge' because it does weaken some of the undertakings that the author gives in this clause. Try to avoid accepting warranty clauses that indemnify the publisher against 'any claims'. This would mean that you indemnify them against claims that fail to be proved: that's why the wording of the clause I have quoted includes 'adverse'. Many publishers argue against its inclusion on the grounds that even claims that prove unsustainable in law can be expensive to defend.

Other requirements of publishers' warranty clauses may include a statement that:

— the work has not been published or distributed before in the territory covered by this agreement

— the work contains no breach of confidence

— all statements purporting to be facts are true and that the work contains no instructions or recipes that, if a reader were to act upon them, would cause damage or injury

— the work has not been the subject of any complaint or legal proceedings

— the warranties given will survive the termination of the contract

— if either party to the contract receives a claim or complaint concerning breach of the warranties given, they will immediately inform the other

— the work does not breach the Official Secrets Act or similar legislation

— if the author is proved to be in breach of any of the warranties, the publisher may withhold payment of sums due to the author under the contract until the claims are settled or disposed of

— if the publisher asks the author to remove material that contravenes any of these warranties and the author refuses to do so, the publisher may withdraw from publication

Delivery

If the manuscript is already delivered at the time the contract is signed, this clause should make that clear, and should also make clear that the manuscript is acceptable to the publisher.

If the manuscript is not delivered but the publisher has made their offer on the basis of an outline, or an outline and some sample chapters, then again this clause should make it clear both that the outline and the chapters have been delivered, and that they are acceptable.

Then the clause should go on to provide for the agreed delivery date by which the author will deliver the manuscript to the publisher, the approximate length of the manuscript in words, and should state whether the author must supply photographs, diagrams, maps or other illustrations. This clause also usually obligates the author to obtain permission, from the copyright owners, for any quotations from other works that they are including in their manuscript and to pay for the right to use anyone else's material that is quoted.

For example, our clause might read as follows:

(a) The Proprietor has delivered an outline which the Publisher finds acceptable.

(b) The Proprietor undertakes unless prevented by reasons beyond his/her control to deliver to the Publisher a copy of the typescript, which in style and content is professionally competent and fit for publication, by [date]. The said Work shall be approximately XXX words in length. At the same time the Proprietor shall supply at his/her own expense all photographs, pictures, diagrams, maps and other illustrations as shall be mutually agreed in writing by both the Proprietor and the Publisher to be necessary to the Work, and also any quotations contained therein. In respect of any such illustrations and/or quotations the Proprietor shall obtain from the copyright holders written permission to reproduce such material and shall be responsible for any expenses in connection therewith.

It is quite possible that at the time the deal is negotiated your agent may have provided for the publisher to pay some or all of the copyright fees or illustration fees. It is also possible that the publisher would agree to write and send the request letters for such permissions as well. In all of these cases the clause would be varied to be explicit as to what had been agreed. (For more discussion of permission requests, see chapter 10.)

In this clause and the clause dealing with payment of the advance due on delivery, beware of the publisher asking for the right to 'accept' – or not – the manuscript. If such a clause is included, be sure that you also include precise definitions for what is acceptable, and a provision that if the publisher does not accept the manuscript, they must provide a detailed critique (consisting of a minimum of, say, 250 words) within a specified period of time (for example, twenty-eight days from taking delivery of the manuscript) setting out why the manuscript is not 'acceptable'. If you allow the publisher to 'accept' or not the manuscript, it might be wise to include a detailed description, in the contract, of the book they commissioned, including a description of the material they saw before offering for the book (for example, a synopsis and two chapters). It's only too easy, months or years after the signature of the contract, to forget exactly how much of the material they had seen at the time they gave their commitment to publish. If you describe or attach the material that existed at the time of the contract, it could be helpful if you find yourself later in an argument as to whether the manuscript is acceptable or not. If the publisher is seeking to reject the manuscript by saying it doesn't conform to the original outline, it can be very helpful to be able to produce the outline. And if it is attached to all parties' copies of the contract, there can be no dispute about it.

The Hodder Headline group have a clear and fair clause dealing with this:

> An 'acceptable typescript' is one which fulfils the specifications and complies with the warranties in this agreement and is in style and content professionally competent and fit for publication. The Publishers may only decline to accept the typescript delivered on the grounds that it fails to satisfy those criteria; and if the Publishers do decline to accept the typescript they will set out their full reasons for doing so within thirty days of receiving the typescript, in a written notice of at least 250 words.

If you get to a point where you know that you are going to be late in delivering your manuscript, it is good manners and good business to inform your editor as soon as you are aware of the fact. The more notice a publisher receives of such a delay, the better. Once you agree a substitute date, either exchange letters, which you will both file with your contract acknowledging the change of date, or draw up a formal addendum to the contract.

Beware of delivery of manuscript clauses that include the phrase 'time shall be of the essence'. This has the effect, under English law, of putting the author in breach of contract immediately the delivery date has passed. In other words, by the very next morning after the date of delivery, the publisher could repudiate the contract and request the return of any monies paid.

Some books might require time to be of the essence: if you were contracted to write a novelization of a film or television series, it would be fairly pointless to deliver it too late for it to be published to coincide with the film's release or broadcast date of the series. If you were writing a book to tie in with a sporting event, it would be vital to have it in the shops to coincide with the event itself.

But this kind of timeliness applies little to fiction and I see no reason at all why a publisher should use such onerous wording in an author's contract. I have no objection to including informative wording in this clause that makes it clear that the publisher wishes the author to work to the agreed delivery date if at all possible, and if not, is required to give the publisher a reasonable period of notice that the author will be late. I have a wording like this in one of my boilerplate contracts now with one of Britain's biggest publishers.

An additional requirement of the contract with regard to delivery of manuscript might be that you guarantee to deliver it to the publisher no later than you deliver to any other English language publisher, and that you should keep the publisher informed of the publication dates of the work in any other market. This is a consequence of the Australian copyright law. (For more details, see chapter 12.)

Correction of proofs

'Proofs' is the term for the text once the publisher has had it set in type. There are several kinds of proofs. The most common being the flat paged proofs that arrive first and are used by the author and publisher to check for corrections. In my early days in publishing, authors used to be sent proofs that were on long, thin sheets, two or three times as long as an A4 sheet, with text run straight through without being divided into pages. They were called galley proofs for obvious reasons. They were horrible to deal with. Now, few authors would expect to see proofs that were not already paginated. Bound proofs, which resemble paperback books, are sales tools for use by publishers and agents to sell to booksellers, book clubs and foreign publishers among others, and are sometimes sent to reviewers.

As the author of the work, you have both the right to see proofs for publication and also the obligation to read and correct them within a specified period of time. I think that twenty-one days is about the right length of time in which to expect an author to correct proofs and return them to the publisher. If a publisher asks for a shorter period, say, fourteen days, I would argue for longer because if they were to arrive on Christmas Eve, say, then your Christmas and New Year holiday would be rather overshadowed by the work you had to do! Also, make sure that you stay in touch with your editor so that you know when to expect them. Again, if they were to arrive on the day before your wedding, it might cause the first row on your honeymoon!

Publishers want to caution authors against trying to rewrite at proof stage (because it is expensive) so there is usually a financial penalty if you make too many changes other than correcting errors of typesetting. While some publishers will set any extra costs against your royalty account (meaning they will not send you a bill straight away), more frequently they try to protect themselves against unpaid bills by invoicing the author, because if they do agree to set the costs against your royalty account, they will not be repaid if your book does not earn more royalties than the advance they paid you.

A compromise would be for the publisher to agree to take any costs for proof corrections out of the portion of the advance to be paid to the author on publication of the book. In this case you would want them to inform you of the figure within a specified period of time after you return the proofs, rather than, as I have it in my sample clause below, after publication, but before production of the first royalty statement (which would normally be six months or so after publication).

Some publishers' contracts contain a provision that if they do not receive proof corrections from the author within the time period provided, they can assume there are no corrections. This is a reasonable requirement because the publisher has a publication schedule to adhere to, but if you have a good relationship with your editor you ought to be able to ask for a few days extension if you need it. And you ought to expect a call from your editor if they do not receive your proofs, before they go ahead. It is always a good precaution to call your editor to be sure that your returned proofs have indeed reached the publishing house if you returned them by mail.

If you have provided your publisher with a computer disk containing your text (which is compatible with their system), you should find there are relatively few errors (providing your disk was error-free to start with). When texts were typeset from hard copy by a printer, new errors could be introduced. Computer typesetting is much speedier and often much simpler. But I have heard horror stories of incompatible computing systems producing unintelligible proofs!

I like the correction of proofs clause to include an obligation on the publisher's part to provide at least two sets of proofs to the author (so that you can keep one with your corrections on it as a record of what you've sent back to them) and I also like to have an undertaking that the publishers will also pay someone to read the proofs. At least one major publishing group has recently refused to take any responsibility for proof correction. I find it extraordinary that a publishing company can take so little pride in the books they produce, that they are willing to put their name on the spine of books they have not themselves checked for errors.

Here is a sample clause:

> The Proprietor shall correct, revise and return the proofs of the Work within 21 days of receiving them. The Publisher shall provide the Proprietor with two free proof copies of the work and further copies at cost. The Proprietor shall be responsible for proof correction costs exceeding 10% (ten percent) of the cost of composition of the Work, providing that such corrections are not the result of errors by the Publisher or the Printer or made at the request of or with the agreement of the Publisher. The Publisher will notify the Proprietor of any such excess expenses within 90 days of publication and any such costs shall be set against the

Proprietor's royalty account. The Publisher undertakes to have the proofs read by an experienced proof reader.

If a publisher does charge you for the cost of corrections, with a clause worded as this one is, they will have to show you their invoice for the cost of composition, because the author is only responsible for costs that exceed 10 per cent of that figure, if that's the percentage agreed in the contract.

Promotion

If your publisher intends to use you as part of the publicity and promotion, it is possible they might want to include a clause that requires you to be available at the appropriate time. Be sure to include wording that makes it clear they will pay all expenses incurred. Here is the text of a clause I have for one of my clients in a contract with Macmillan:

> Upon reasonable request by Macmillan, the Author shall make herself available to promote and publicise the Work. In particular she shall make herself available during the week of publication of the Work and subsequently in any week of reissue of the Work or issue of a new edition of the Work. The Author shall be entitled to reimbursement of reasonable costs incurred during such promotion.

Option

An option clause obligates the author to show part or all of their next work first to the publisher who is publishing the work that is the subject of the contract. The reason for this obligation is that publishers argue that they are investing in an author, not just in one book, and they are adding to the 'brand value' of the author with each publication so they wish to benefit from this by having first chance to buy the author's next work. Setting aside the argument that this suggests that a publisher who publishes an author badly should perhaps be required to forgo their option rights, some enlightened publishers now do accept that an author should be free to move publishers as they wish, and they are prepared to accept contracts without option clauses, relying instead on their own ability to do a good job for the author and so keep their loyalty through efficiency.

It is ideal to have no option clause in your contract, so as to keep as much freedom of choice as possible, but many publishers do still wish to include them.

There is a wide variety of wording and obligation among option clauses. The best (for the author) simply call for the publisher to have first look at the next work; the worst provide for an endless circle of delivery and continuing options that the author can never be free of. Option clauses should never tie the author to having to accept any particular terms, such as territory or multi-book deals: all of the terms of the next deal should be subject to the fresh negotiation.

And take care that the option clause does not require you to deliver the whole of your next manuscript before the publisher will make a decision on it. If they have bought one book from you, they know how you write. It should therefore be perfectly possible for them to decide upon your next book based upon a synopsis and two sample chapters. This clause should therefore state exactly what material they will require before making a decision.

If you can, try to avoid the inclusion of a clause that means the publisher does not have to make a decision on your next book until some time after your current book is either delivered or published. These clauses are only in the publisher's favour, either to help their cash flow (they can decide – and therefore pay – later) or to help them delay a decision until they have other people's opinion (booksellers' or the consumers', if they wish to wait until after publication). In order to publish regularly, all writers have to – or should – start writing their next book before the previous one is published and publishers know this. Everyone in the publishing process knows they have to take a leap of faith every now and then.

Before agents were so widespread in publishing, it was usual for an option clause to be very onerous on the author. Publishers now generally accept that the most they can expect is first sight of the next work, or part of it. I have though, within the last year, seen publishers' contracts (which have been signed by unagented authors) that included an option clause that required the author to promise two option works to the publisher (presumably when the author signs the contract for that first option work, that too would include a two book option clause) and one where the option clause was worded so as to require the author to accept the same terms for the next book. This was particularly unfair as the publisher had not paid the author an advance, and 'the same terms' for the next contract would have presumably meant including the same option clause, again.

Each of these examples would result in an endless circle of contracts and continuing obligations upon the author that was intended to keep them with the same publisher for ever.

A fair option clause might read:

> The Proprietor agrees to give the Publisher the first option of publishing the Proprietor's next full length work of fiction on terms to be mutually agreed upon. The Publisher will give their decision to exercise such option within four weeks of the delivery to them of a synopsis and two sample chapters of said Work.

This states clearly that the option is for fiction and for a full-length novel, i.e. for a similar book as that which is the subject of this contract. I do not think it fair for the option clause to simply ask for 'the next work' because if the author writes, say, a historical biography next, it might be appropriate to approach a quite different publisher. This can also give some protection to the publisher as well, for if the author does write a quite different style of book after the novel that is the subject of the present contract, perhaps a scholarly work on a little-known poet, which the publisher might not wish to publish, the publisher would lose their option on the author's work if they turned it down. By stating in the option clause that the option only covers the next novel, the publisher can be sure of seeing the next novel even if it is not the next book that the author finishes.

Lawyers don't like option clauses because they point out that 'an agreement to agree' isn't binding under English law. An option clause that states that terms are to be agreed is just such an agreement. I suppose authors could take comfort from that if they find they have an option clause worded in that way, which they later want to contest.

Agency

Strictly speaking, this is as much of an 'agency protection' clause as 'author obligation', but it is also simply informative. It informs and authorizes the publisher to pay monies to the agent on the author's behalf. And it is confirmation that at the time the author signed the contract, they intended the agent to be part of it, and to receive income from it.

Take note that this does not bind the author to remain with the agent for the life of the contract. The agent remains 'the agent of record' for the entire period that the contract is valid, but the author may leave that agent and take future work elsewhere. The agent is not a signatory to the contract between publisher and author and so can therefore only be part of it while the agent carries the authorization from the author. But it does instruct the publisher of the author's intentions at the outset and, unless the publisher received contrary instructions from the author later, all monies and statements will continue to be sent to the agent.

The next part of the clause, which does not appear in all agency agreements (but is part of Blake Friedmann's: see chapter 4), goes on to provide for the eventuality that the author might, at some later date, wish to leave the agent and have the author's portion of income from the contract be paid by the publisher direct to the author. It states that, if this happens, it is the publisher's obligation to inform the agent and to pay the agent the commission amount on future earnings under the contract.

Because the agent is not a signatory to the contract, and because the contract can only be varied by agreement between those who are signatories to it, this alone would not stand up in a court of law. Neither could an agent sue an author for their commission if the author chose to leave the agent and instructed the publisher to pay 100 per cent of all future earnings direct to the author (unless there is an agreement between agent and author to the contrary), nor could an agent sue a publisher for their commission. There exists no contract between the agent and the publisher and it is the author who pays the agent, not the publisher.

If the agent had a 'terms of business' agreement between the agency and the author (discussed in detail in chapter 4), that document would allow the agent to sue the author for their commission on such a contract. Adding wording to the agency clause of the author/publisher contract, which states what an agent would wish to happen if they parted company with their client, might persuade the publisher to tell the agent that the publisher had received instructions to vary the payment procedure, even if the author had not chosen to tell the agent. The agent would then have to take steps to recover the commission amount from their now ex-client.

I have never wanted, or needed, to sue a client under these (or indeed any other) circumstances and hope I never shall. But it is only prudent, if one's remit as an agent is to look after the business interests of the authors who are your clients, to also look after your own.

So our agency clause reads thus:

> All monies due under this agreement shall be paid to the Proprietor's agent as specified in the Preamble of this Agreement, whose receipt shall be a full and valid discharge of the monies received and the said Proprietor's agent is hereby empowered by

the Proprietor to conduct negotiations with the Publisher in respect of all matters arising in any way out of the Agreement, but the authority given to the Publisher under this clause may be revoked by the Proprietor at any time on giving written notice to the Publisher who shall then upon notification to the Proprietor's agent pay direct to the Proprietor all monies due under this Agreement less XX percent commission which shall be paid by the Publisher to the Proprietor's agent at the same time the remainder is paid to the Proprietor, and in such cases none but the Proprietor's receipt shall be a full and sufficient discharge to the Publisher.

For more on agents, see chapter 4.

Author protection

Copyright

Like libel, copyright laws differ from country to county, sometimes simply in the number of years that copyright runs for, sometimes in more complicated ways. In Britain, as in most of western Europe now, copyright runs for seventy years from the end of the year in which the author died. Britain adopted the seventy-year period relatively recently (January 1996), having had a fifty-year period prior to that. There are many variations on this and copyright law is immensely complex (especially with regard to books that had ceased to be in copyright, but which came back into copyright when the law changed from fifty to seventy years). Most authors reading this book will not need to be involved in the more complicated aspects of it. There is further discussion of copyright under 'Permissions' in chapter 10.

In general, this clause should make it clear that the author owns the copyright (authors should never be required to surrender their copyright in fiction; some non-fiction work, say pieces supplied as part of a large encyclopedia, might well have their copyright resting with the publisher), the publisher will print a copyright line in all the appropriate places, and they will pass on this obligation to anyone to whom they license any rights. The copyright line is printed in the book (usually on the verso – the back – of the title page). This makes it clear that the work is protected in every country that is a member of the Universal Copyright Convention.

The obligation for the publisher to surrender copyright in their editorial work is a protection against an editor later claiming some rights in the work. It's not widely used, but I do have it in our agency contract. Obviously, publishers would successfully argue against this in cases where they were investing substantial work and expense in producing edited and annotated editions of classic works, where their substantially altered work might qualify for a new copyright date. But we are dealing here with new novels by current authors, so this is unlikely to apply.

This clause, which also deals with credit provisions for the author of the work, might read:

(a) The Publisher warrants that the name of [Author] shall appear in due prominence on the title page, cover and binding of every copy of the Work and on all advertisements issued of the Work by the Publisher or their agents, and that every copy of the Work shall bear the following copyright notice:

© [author's name] [year*]

[*this will be the year of first publication anywhere in the world in any language]

(b) The Publisher warrants that they own the copyright in all editorial work to be carried out on the Work and hereby assign it to the Proprietor.

(c) The Publisher further warrants that they will pass on these undertakings to all licensees and agents. The copyright of the Work shall remain the exclusive property of the Proprietor.

You should note that in contracts for translated editions, it is right and proper that there exists another, separate, copyright in the *translation*. Either the overseas publisher, who has commissioned the translation, will own it, or the translator will own it: this will be determined by the contract between the foreign publisher and the translator. They will not be able to exploit their rights in the translation without also having the rights in the underlying work: your novel. All translated editions of your novel should still carry your original copyright line as it appeared in the first edition to be published: your copyright dates from its first publication anywhere in the world and keeps the same copyright date for as long as copyright in the work subsists. The copyright in the translation is an additional line that usually appears below yours.

Moral rights

Moral rights became part of British law when they were incorporated into the Copyright Act of 1988. They confer upon authors (including scriptwriters, translators and illustrators) a number of rights; there are two key ones that are relevant here: the right of 'paternity' and the right of 'integrity'. The right of paternity means that the creator of a work must be properly credited as such; the right of integrity protects authors against having their work altered or, in the words of the Act, it gives the author the right to object to 'derogatory' treatment of their work. Another of the moral rights covers the right not to have a work wrongly attributed to you. There are few conditions to claiming these rights. The right of integrity is automatic. The right of paternity comes into being once the author has asserted their right to it. This is covered initially by a clause in your contract with the publisher, and further by a statement that appears alongside the copyright line at the front of the book.

Such rights do not exist in all countries – Canada and Australia, for example – so this clause would not appear in contracts with publishers in those countries without them.

In British contracts it is sometimes necessary to waive the 'integrity' part of moral rights in order for the publishers to be able to license specific rights that they have been granted. Licensing condensed book rights to Readers' Digest, for example, guarantees that the work will be altered – it will be reduced quite considerably. Licensing abridged audio cassette rights has a similar effect on the work. These could be said to be 'derogatory' treatments of the work under the terms of the Copyright Act, but of course the author is usually in favour of such rights being granted and so will usually agree to the waiver.

However, you do not have to waive the right of 'paternity', your right to be credited as the work's author.

In France, where the notion of these rights originated, none of the moral rights can be legally waived (which can cause a problem for French authors when they wish to sign contracts for the sale of film rights to their work). The licensing of dramatic rights usually requires the waiving of the right of integrity. Adaptation of the work for use as a film, a television play or serial, or a theatrical production always involves altering the work. In these circumstances authors seldom, if ever, get consultation or approval rights of the adaptation of their work, and these contracts will hardly ever be signed without a waiver. A bestselling novelist may be consulted over the adaptation of a novel, but this is unusual. For more detailed discussion of moral rights as they are affected by film rights see *How to Make Money Scriptwriting* by Julian Friedmann (Intellect, 1999).

The wording of some companies' moral rights waiver clauses can sound alarming. Macmillan, for instance, when introducing their new form of contract a few years ago had the moral rights clause worded in such a way as to ask the author to waive their moral rights so that Macmillan could 'authorize derogatory use of the manuscript'. I pointed out that this would set off alarm bells with any author reading it, who would probably visualize a Macmillan staff member gleefully altering their prose, changing the plot of their novel, shredding the pages or setting light to them. It was only there, of course, so that Macmillan could legally license rights on behalf of the author, such as condensed book rights, or serial rights! They argued that the clause was valid because it followed the wording of the Copyright Act. Yes, well, that may be so, but was it *clear* what Macmillan wanted the clause to achieve? No. So why don't we reword it so it is more reader-friendly? I encountered more opposition until I suggested that if they really wanted to keep the offensive wording I would tell every one of my clients who queried its meaning that they should telephone either the contracts director or the managing director of Macmillan, who would be pleased to explain it personally. The wording was changed to the following, which I have no objection to:

> The Author, on written request from Macmillan, undertakes to waive his moral rights as provided for in section 80 of the Copyright, Designs and Patents Act 1988 to the extent necessary to allow the exercise of any of the rights granted to Macmillan under this Agreement.

This is fairly standard wording for the paternity moral rights clause:

> The Proprietor hereby asserts to the Publishers and to their licensees his/her moral right to be identified as the author of the Work and to have a notice to this effect printed in each and every copy of the book.

These clauses usually appear in the contract as part of the copyright clause, or as a separate clause close by.

Film quit claim

This is a clause that is helpful to have in your publishing contract in case your novel is made into a film. Any film company that acquires rights in your work will insist on the right to use extracts, and/or a summary of the plot for advertising purposes, either within the film trade (in order to sell distribution rights to other territories) or to the consumer. It is as well to provide for this in your original contract with the publisher so as to save time and energy later.

A sample clause might look like this:

> In the event of the disposition of the motion picture or other performance rights by the Proprietor, the purchaser of such rights shall be free to publish or cause to be published in the Publisher's exclusive territory excerpts and summaries of the Work not to exceed in the aggregate 10,000 (ten thousand) words for advertising and exploiting such rights, provided such excerpts and summaries shall not be sold to the general public.

If your novel is particularly short, a publisher might ask that the length of such an extract be reduced to, say, 7,500 words, so as to make it likely that someone reading the extracts provided by the film company might still want to buy the book.

Although this clause is often headed 'Film Quit Claim', strictly speaking a 'quit claim' is a separate document that you will still have to obtain from the publisher at the time you sign a contract with a film company. At its simplest, a quit claim states that the publisher does not own film rights and has no claim upon the film company. You (or your agent or lawyer) will have to send this document to each and every publisher of your novel once you have sold film rights, in order to deliver signed copies to the film company. This should be straightforward, but in practice can be extremely tedious and time-consuming, particularly if film rights have been sold many years after the novel's original publication. We have often found ourselves trying to get quit claims signed where publishers have been bought and sold and the identity of the publisher is no longer clear; where the author's editor has long since left and the publisher simply doesn't respond; where the publisher has gone out of business but we need to prove that to the Hollywood lawyer of the American film production company.

The film industry is nervous because of the huge amounts of money invested in making any film and because of the litigious nature of the business. Without a clear chain of title, the insurers will not allow the production to go ahead. A quit claim is therefore necessary and useful in case a film contract is later negotiated.

Remainders

It is an unfortunate fact of publishing life that publishers must sometimes pulp, or sell off very cheaply ('remainder'), books that aren't selling fast enough to justify the cost of keeping them in the warehouse. This clause provides for a royalty to be paid to the author if copies are sold above their cost of manufacture (which is actually quite rare). It sets out the minimum period of time the book should have been in the shops before it can be remaindered, and provides for the author to be told of the intention to remainder and be allowed to buy copies at the cheapest rate.

The second paragraph of the clause deals with the situation that arises when remaindering puts the book out of print: rights must revert to the author if the publisher does not have another edition in print, and does not intend to reprint within a specified period of time. Publishers do sometimes remainder only a portion of their stock: this would not lead to an out-of-print situation and therefore it would not be appropriate to ask for a reversion of rights.

An author-friendly wording might be:

> No remainder copies shall be sold within a period of two years from the date of the Publisher's first publication of the Work except with the written consent of the Proprietor. On remainder copies sold the Proprietor shall be entitled to 10% (ten percent) of receipts on copies sold above cost. The Proprietor shall be given the option for 28 days from receipt of the written notice to purchase copies at the remainder price. When copies are remaindered the Publisher will send to the Proprietor 25 copies free of charge.
>
> In the event of the Publisher putting the Work out of print by remaindering their stock this Agreement shall automatically terminate and all the rights hereby granted shall revert to the Proprietor subject only to the subsisting rights in force of any sub-licence of the Publishers hereunder and to the continuing rights of the Publisher to their share of the proceeds of any sub-licence in force properly entered into by the Publisher hereunder.

It is common for publishers to ask to be able to remainder less than two years from publication: a period of eighteen months or a year is often requested. Resist if you can.

Instead of paying 10 per cent per copy only on those remaindered copies sold above the cost of manufacture, some publishers more generously offer 5 per cent on *all* copies remaindered, whether above or below the cost of manufacture.

If you are offered copies at the remainder price, do reply promptly: the publisher may go ahead with the remaindering and sell off all the stock and then you may have lost your last chance of buying your book, which is now going out of print. These copies will be very cheap and it's often worth buying as many as you can. If the book does then go out of print entirely you have copies you can show with a view to selling it to another publisher (either in the original language or in foreign editions). When the rights then revert to you, you can sell the copies yourself for full retail price and therefore legitimately make quite a profit on every copy sold.

Most publishers have efficient systems for informing authors and agents of remainder operations that are about to go ahead: some do not. If you have a requirement in your contract for the publisher to inform you, and to allow you to buy copies, you can protest vigorously if they fail to do so. I have heard of one case in which an author sued a publisher who did not give him the chance to buy the last remaining copies of his book. He won and was awarded damages. Obviously, few authors would wish to go to such (potentially expensive) lengths. If you see from your royalty statement that sales are slowing, or have stopped altogether, it is a reasonable precaution to contact the publisher to ask exactly how many copies they have left. Even if they haven't already started the process toward remaindering, they might be open to an offer from you to purchase their stock at a very reduced price.

Always ask for a quantity of copies to be supplied to you free if and when the publisher prepares to remainder. They will usually agree because by this time the value of the book to the publisher is very little, but copies that you own can bring you a profit.

I like to have the second paragraph attached to the remainder clause so that if all copies are sold off and the book becomes out of print as a result of remaindering, rights will *automatically* revert to the author. However, some publishers require that this not be automatic but that the author must request a reversion. For further discussion of the reversion of rights process, see the next clause.

On a lighter note, Clive James wrote a marvellous poem called 'The Book of My Enemy Has Been Remaindered'. The second line of the poem is 'And I am pleased.' There speaks an honest man.

Reversion of rights

This clause seeks to apply a principle I believe in strongly: if a publisher is not actively exploiting rights in a book, they should no longer hold the rights. Ideally, it should provide for rights to revert automatically (i.e. without any action required by the author) and should come into play when the book is no longer available in the publisher's own edition or if the publisher is at fault with regard to any of the obligations required of them by the contract.

Some reversion clauses preferred by publishers allow rights to revert to an author only if all editions of the book are unavailable, but I would argue that it is unfair for a publisher to hold on to all rights granted under the original contract if their own edition is out of print, simply by virtue of the fact that they had licensed another edition (say, large print, audio or paperback) that was still in print. The wording that I reproduce below makes it clear that if rights revert to the author because the publisher's own edition is out of print, the publisher may continue to receive the agreed proportion of income from the licensed edition that may still be in print. I think this is equitable: the author gets all the other rights back (and may therefore be able to license some other rights for themselves, thereby retaining all the income); the original publisher, who is no longer actively publishing the book themselves, gives up all the other unsold or inactive rights as well as their original volume rights, but does retain some income from rights they had properly sold prior to the reversion, which are still active.

This means that if, for instance, a large print license was still active, but the original publisher's own edition was out of print, rights would still revert to the author and the publisher would no longer have the right to license more rights to others.

If a film or television series was later made from the novel (whether the film or television rights were sold by the publisher or the author, before the reversion of rights or after) the author could still offer paperback rights to another publisher – or indeed, back to the same publisher – for publication at the time a film or television series was released or broadcast, thus achieving a new contract and another advance. If the author had failed to obtain a reversion of rights, and the original publisher still controlled the rights at the time a film was released, the original publisher could choose to publish their own paperback edition to tie-in with the film, no matter how long their own edition had been out of print. The author would of course receive royalties for this new edition but not another advance. And if the original advance was not earned, those royalties would be set against the original unearned advance and the author might never see any more income from book sales.

These are all good reasons to be vigilant about both the reversion of rights clause in your contract, and later monitoring of your publisher's sales and printings!

Our clause also provides for rights to revert automatically if the publisher fails to provide payments or accounts information as required by the contract, after giving them time to repair the omissions. The clauses referred to at the end of the first paragraph deal with, respectively, the advance payments, the royalties, and subsidiary rights.

The second sub-clause cannot always be included if the publisher does not have their computer programme set up in such a way as to provide this information. And, sadly, even some of the publishers who do sign contracts with this clause included often fail to provide the information. As I've said earlier, it is always wise to keep a close eye on your royalty statements and to stay in touch with your editor, to stay up to date on sales and printing activity.

My suggested wording for this clause would be:

(a) If the Publisher fails to publish their edition of the Work within the time specified in Clause X, unless such delay shall have been approved in writing by the Proprietor or if the Publisher's edition at any time goes out of print or off the market (but it is understood that the Work shall be considered to be in print if it is on sale in a paperback/hardback edition under the Publisher's own imprint, or if the Publisher shall default in accounting or in making payment to the Proprietor as herein before provided, and if after written demand from the Proprietor the Publisher does not within one month express their intention to publish the Work or issue a new edition or settle all accounts due, then this Agreement shall immediately terminate and all rights granted herein shall revert to the Proprietor, without prejudice to any monies due or to become due by reason of sales made by the Publisher prior to the date of such termination subject only to the Publisher being liable to pay and making all the payments provided for in Clauses X, XX and XX.

(b) Should the Publishers at any time allow the Work to go out of print, they shall state that fact on the next royalty statement due.

The clauses refer to advance payment, royalties and subsidiary rights.

I think it is likely that the definition of 'out of print' will have to change dramatically in the near future to take account of the changes in printing technology. Now that facilities exist for publishers to 'print on demand' they no longer need to keep books in warehouses. With centres expected to open shortly that will offer a ten-day service or a 24-hour service that can produce and even distribute books, and with publishers themselves acquiring the technology to print any book, individually, as it is required, books might never again actually go out of print. These facilities will initially be used more for academic titles than for general books, and I don't expect novels to be supplied in this way in the near future, but because the technology is available, agents need to find a new definition of 'out of print'. If we don't, or if we do suggest wording that publishers will not accept, we could find that even though a publisher is no longer actively selling the book, and may not have copies available in shops or in their warehouse, an author can never obtain a reversion of rights because technically the book is still available and can be supplied in response to a single order.

Liquidation

If a publishing company becomes insolvent, or goes into liquidation it is vital that the author's book does not remain an asset of the company, and perhaps get tied up for months, or sometimes years, in legal arguments. To make doubly sure of being able to enforce the rights conferred under this clause, it is important that a 'non-assignment' clause also be included in the contract (see below).

A suitable clause might read:

> In the event of the insolvency or liquidation of the Publisher through any cause whatsoever, other than for the purpose of reconstruction, all rights herein granted shall revert to the Proprietor and the Proprietor shall for 90 (ninety) days thereafter have the option of buying any plates and/or remaining copies of the Work bound or unbound at the fair market value thereof, this value to be determined by agreement or by arbitration.

As production processes become ever more computerized, the language for the production material that an author might have the right to purchase would change – from 'plates' to 'disk', for example, but the principle remains the same. It is certainly worth including an option for the author to be able to purchase stock of unbound or bound books in the publisher's warehouse: if rights revert automatically at such a time, the author can then sell such copies themselves.

Non-assignment

Because of a couple of high profile and taxing situations I have been involved in on behalf of my authors, I regard this clause (often misleadingly headed, or referred to, as the 'assignment clause', which couldn't be further from the truth!) as one of the most important, albeit most overlooked, clauses in a publishing contract. Boiled down to its basics, it means that the company that acquires the license to publish from the author must not 'assign' – pass on those rights it has acquired – without the author's written consent.

Take care to understand the difference between assignment – which we do not want to allow – and the legitimate licensing of subsidiary rights that all contracts contain and are, for the most part, entirely in the authors' interests.

Assignment of a contract happens when the original acquiring publisher wishes to dispose of the contract entirely and to pass on all the rights and obligations to another company: for instance, if the original publisher is sold, or if it goes bankrupt and the accountants wish to treat the contract as an asset and to dispose of it for cash.

It can never be in an author's interest to have their contract passed on to another company with whom the author has not chosen to do business, or signed a direct contract. The non-assignment clause, short as it is, can make the difference between getting your rights back under your own control, or having them passed, without your agreement, to a company you might know nothing of or, worse still, might well know much about, but all of it unpleasant.

My preferred wording is simply:

> This licence is granted to the Publisher solely and shall not be assigned or otherwise transferred without the written consent of the Proprietor.

It is likely that your publisher will ask for an extra sentence making it clear that if the entire publishing company, or a substantial portion thereof, is sold, that this clause cannot be applied. Strictly speaking, if an *entire* company is sold, then you have little option but to see your contract go with them because your contract is still probably with a part of the company, which is now owned by someone else. This means that no assignment would be needed or sought.

For instance, my original contract for this book was signed several years ago with Boxtree. Boxtree was then bought in its entirety by Macmillan. I had no qualms about being published by Macmillan instead of Boxtree: indeed it probably benefited me, despite my harsh words about their contracts! Boxtree's editors – and the company itself – benefitted from the purchase by Macmillan by becoming part of a company that had a much larger marketing, sales and distribution system, more resources and a higher marketing profile. My contract was signed, before Boxtree was owned by Macmillan, on my own agency's contract form. But in fact I couldn't have done anything about it if I had objected: Boxtree was now entirely owned by Macmillan (who were themselves owned by the German Holtzbrinck group: another company I'm quite happy to do business with) and my contract was not affected and I was not required to agree to an assignment.

An assignment would be requested though if only *part* of a company was purchased. For instance, when Reed-Elsevier (an Anglo-Dutch group with huge scientific publishing holdings) sold off part of its trade publishing imprints in the UK and Australia (keeping the scientific publishing), the purchasers, Random House, did need Reed authors to agree to assign rights to Random House as the contracting party from Reed was not purchased entirely by Random.

For example, one of the Reed companies sold to Random House was Secker & Warburg. Random acquired 100 per cent of Secker: Secker could be argued not to have changed. Only Secker's owner changed. Authors whose contracts were with Secker did not need to be asked to agree to assignments of their contracts because they were not needed. Random now owned their contracts and assumed the obligations within their contracts.

But Reed had reformed and restructured its publishing groups several times prior to selling to Random, and had signed publishing contracts with very many different corporate names, one of which was 'Reed Consumer Books', which was the group name that contained many of its companies, and for a while this included Secker & Warburg. The sale to Random included part of the assets of Reed Consumer Books, but not the whole company. Therefore authors whose contracts were with Reed Consumer Books (even though they might be published under the imprint name of Secker & Warburg) did have to be asked if they were agreeable to assigning their rights to Random House. Reed didn't want them – they were getting out of trade publishing altogether – but they were keeping parts of the corporate structure known as Reed Consumer Books. But they wouldn't be publishing novels, for instance.

Our agency, which only started in 1976 and so had just twenty years of trading at the time of the Reed sale to Random, nevertheless had several hundred contracts with more than forty different company names within the Reed group. This was achieved either because the company we had signed with had later been bought by Reed (Octopus and Hamlyn) or because Reed had reformed and regrouped its companies (so that Reed Consumer Books, say, became the contracting party, rather than Secker & Warburg). Some of those contracts had clear non-assignment clauses, and a few did not (even agents are less wise in their early years than later!). Some of my authors felt they would benefit by being published by Random, some did not (not because of anything inherently bad about Random, but perhaps because a direct competitor in their field was published by Random or perhaps because their Reed editor was not going to be working for Random).

This was clearly a very complicated situation, but initially most agents were at least pleased that the companies had been sold, and sold to an active and energetic publisher, because they had been offered for sale eighteen months previously by a company that clearly did not wish to own them, and the staff (and authors and agents) were very demoralized. At least now they were owned by Random House we could move forward and get on with good publishing.

The news of the sale hit the publishing community like a bombshell in the middle of the weekend before the opening, on a Sunday morning, of a very busy London Book Fair (three of us from the agency attending, all booked for half-hourly appointments from 8.30 to 18.00 every day) and in addition I had been performing, for the two nights previously, in the Publishing Pantomime that we do for charity every couple of years or so. More to the point, the Saturday night had not only been the second and last performance, but also the cast party, which had ended a little later than it should have. I was, perhaps, far from my best that Sunday morning.

I reached my table in the agents' centre and looked over the high balcony to the publishers' stands below. Coincidentally, the Reed companies and the Random House companies had been given stands next to each other. And very prominently displayed on the Random House stand was an eye-catching poster of one of my author's books . . . but it was a book published by Heinemann, a Reed imprint. And it was a contract signed with Reed Consumer Books, and I knew it carried a non-assignment clause. I was really furious at the arrogant assumption that the companies could buy and sell my author without consultation or consent and I asked them to remove the poster. I did not, though, as a highly coloured newspaper report had it at the time, 'tear it down from their stand', partly because I was aware that I didn't want to be accused of damaging their property, and partly because I was feeling a little too frail to contemplate such physical action! (One interesting point to note: anger clears a hangover very effectively.)

The chief executive of Random House came to my table in the agents' centre at the Fair and apologized personally. I made it clear I had no objection to Random House per se, but I did object to any publisher's assumption of ownership before consultation with the author. She invited me to lunch later in the week to discuss the implications of their purchase.

Then I really had to go to work. Sunday, Monday and Tuesday were Fair (and therefore also party) days and nights. Our lunch was set for Thursday. At the end of each Fair evening I and my assistant went back to our offices to prepare the paperwork for Thursday, reading, comparing and analysing every Reed contract in the agency files. We also spent Wednesday (and the evening) doing little else. When I went to Random House at lunch time on Thursday I carried with me three heavy lever arch files (one for me, one for the chief executive, one for her second-in-charge who was going to be handling the administration of the purchase) that analysed every one of our Reed contracts from several different viewpoints.

One section simply listed all the forty company names we had contracted with over the years. There was a column next to each name so we could mark whether all, or some, or none, of that company had been included in the Random purchase. Another section quoted the range of 'non-assignment clauses'. Another listed all the contracts by author, showing the status of the book (contracted but manuscript not yet delivered; manuscript delivered but not yet published; published and still actively selling; published, contract still current, but not actively selling; rights reversion requested but not yet received; and etc.). Another section was alphabetical by author and cross referenced all of the above under each of their titles.

The three of us sat around a large table in the Random House offices, and went through the piles of paper as we ate lunch. Rather than there being an atmosphere of hostility, it felt instead like an information-gathering exercise. I had brought so much detail with me because I didn't expect that they would have been able to get to grips with the individual contracts in the few days that had passed since the purchase was announced. They told me they had acquired some 20,000 contracts. I wanted to be able to talk specifics, rather than generalities, and the huge amount of work we put into preparing for the meeting proved very worthwhile.

We worked through the files, starting with the list of company names. Some of them came as a surprise to the Random executives. The first one on the list, they had never heard of and therefore had no idea whether it formed part of the purchase or not! If any ice needed to be broken, that did it.

It took a long time to sort everything out. Some of my authors were – and still are – happy to be part of Random House after initially signing with Reed. Some chose not to move to Random House, but all those who did move on, did so to follow their Reed editor to other houses.

The point of this long and anecdotal explanation, is that without a non-assignment clause, the authors who chose to move elsewhere would not have had the choice. It is vital, and I will not allow any contracts to be signed via our agency that do not carry such a clause.

By the way, I still have the poster that was removed from the Random House stand at the London Book Fair; it moved with us to our new offices. Not only is it an attractive poster, but I now feel it has sentimental value too!

If you do agree your publisher may assign your publishing contract, make sure that any document you sign to that effect makes it clear that the company they assign it to, takes on all the obligations in the original contract. It is not enough that they should simply acquire the rights and benefits: the paperwork must show that the new owner of the contract must perform, in every respect, according to the original contract. Some assignment documents are not clear enough on this point and you don't want to find yourself agreeing that, for instance, you will still be required to deliver a manuscript to the new company, but they are not tied to actually publishing the book, or paying you.

Reserved rights

This is fairly self-explanatory and should simply state that any rights not specifically granted to the publisher in the contract are therefore not owned by the publisher, but by the author.

My preferred wording is:

> All rights in the Work whether now in existence or which may hereafter come into existence not expressly granted to the Publisher in this Agreement are reserved by the Proprietor for his/her own use at any time.

This is very straightforward but you would be surprised at how many publisher-drafted contracts do not include a clause like this. Make sure it's in yours. I have even seen clauses in publishers' contracts' that say the opposite: that any other rights that may come into existence now or in the future will be owned by the publisher! Not something you'd wish to agree to, I suspect.

Arbitration

This is a clause that, as it is worded below, only applies to contracts signed within the United Kingdom, or, adapted, in any country that has an Arbitration Act on its statute books. The wording is sometimes part of the 'applicable law' clause, and it is a more contentious clause than it seems at first glance. Many lawyers (our agency's included) prefer for it not to be included any more because the arbitration process can be more time-consuming than going to law, and can also be very expensive. And you can find yourself going through the arbitration process only to end up going to law later as well.

But many contracts do still provide for arbitration, and some publishers like to include it. When it does appear, this is reasonable wording:

> If any difference shall arise between the Proprietor and the Publisher touching the meaning of this Agreement or the rights and liabilities of the parties thereto, the same shall be referred to arbitration in accordance with the provision of the Arbitration Act, 1950, or any amending or substituted statute for the time being in force.

I would prefer to omit the clause entirely. Omission does not mean you cannot choose arbitration if it suits you. Leaving it out means that you don't have to choose that route, but can instead decide according to the circumstances at the time.

Applicable law

A contract should always be explicit about which country's law pertains to it: in the event of a legal dispute both parties need to know what legal criteria must be applied to the dispute and where it will go to court if that happens. In the many cases where the author and the publisher are of the same nationality, there is no discussion: an Australian author signing a contract with an Australian publisher would naturally expect the law of Australia to apply to the contract. Where a Canadian author is signing with a British publisher, the publisher may insist that the law of England applies.

It is a simple clause:

> This Agreement shall be interpreted according to the laws of England (or Australia, Canada, whichever is applicable).

Where the relevant law cannot be agreed at the time of the contract, an uneasy compromise is sometimes to omit the clause altogether and agree to argue over it if the two signatories to the contract do eventually find themselves in a legal dispute. This compromise is used relatively rarely, and usually only when rights are being bought and sold between UK and US publishing companies, neither of whom will accept the other's law for the contract. Luckily, it is also reasonably rare for a publishing argument to become a legal dispute.

Another compromise that is sometimes used is to state that the law of the country in which the dispute arises shall apply.

Execution and delivery of contract

Sometimes it feels as though the entire publishing industry moves more slowly than treacle in winter. This clause is an effort to speed things up:

> This Agreement is not to be deemed effective unless payment of the advance due under Clause X is received by the Proprietor's agent within 30 (thirty) days of invoicing following signature of the Agreement by both parties.

It doesn't necessarily mean that the author would choose to repudiate the contract if the first payment arrives late; but it does give you a reason to jump up and down and make a fuss if they are taking their time about sending a cheque. And if you have managed to include a clause that makes the publisher pay interest on late payments, you get extra satisfaction when they do eventually pay up! Needless to say, a number of publishers refuse to accept this clause.

Editor clause

This is a clause that is quite rare (although more common now than in the past) and it is one that publishers are reluctant to accept. It provides for an author to be allowed to leave the publishing company and take the book elsewhere if the book's editor leaves. There are many versions of this, but the clause must be specific as to the terms under which the author may leave (usually dependent upon repayment by the author to the publisher of all monies received under the contract). It must also be specific as to when this clause may be brought into effect. On the relatively few occasions when I have wished to include a clause like this, publishers have usually wanted to make it clear that the author could move the book, if the editor leaves, only up to the point when the manuscript was delivered, or perhaps a very short while after delivery. This is to prevent a situation where the publisher has spent time and money on the editing and production process only to then see the book taken out of their schedule.

The clause also has to name the editor concerned.

Publishers don't like clauses like this because they see a book as being purchased by – and becoming an asset of – the company, not an individual employee. Individual editors do like these clauses very much, as the contracts containing them do, in effect, become personal assets. They can be valuable bargaining tools for the editor if they are looking to change jobs. It is only highly valued authors – and editors – who can get this requirement accepted by a publishing company.

Authors often feel very strongly about their editor, especially if they have worked together on several books, and they might hate the idea of being tied to a publishing company after their editor has left. Beware of signalling your allegiance to the editor, rather than the company. It can backfire if your editor leaves, but does not immediately – or for some time – join another publisher, or if they join a company you would not want to become your publisher, or if they join a company that you like, but which cannot afford your contract. Under any of those circumstances you could find yourself left friendless at your publishing house.

Payments

These are the clauses that lay out exactly what you will be paid by the publisher, both as an advance, and for sales and subsidiary rights sold. If the publisher has promised to spend a certain sum on promotion this clause might refer back to the sub-clause dealing with that, which would probably itself appear in the clause dealing with publication (discussed under 'Publisher Obligations').

Advance

This is the guaranteed payment that you will certainly receive so long as you deliver the manuscript, it is accepted by the publisher, and they do publish. It is called an advance because it is monies the publisher pays in advance of sales made. We talk of 'earning back an advance' because the publisher keeps records of every sale, and credits to the author's royalty account the contractually agreed royalty every time a sale is recorded. When the royalties earned (and the author's share of all subsidiary rights income earned) adds up to the amount of the advance, then the advance has been 'earned'. And every penny above the amount of the advance will be extra income for the author, to be paid to the author on the royalty reporting dates specified in the contract.

I always like to ensure that the advance is non-returnable: publishers often require wording to show that the amount paid on signature is returnable if the manuscript is not delivered or not delivered on time or is delivered but not accepted. It's hard to argue against these provisions but be careful with the definition of 'acceptance' as I have discussed under the 'delivery of manuscript' clause.

Agents sometimes successfully argue to drop the requirement of 'acceptance'; publishers usually argue to keep it as a protection for themselves against receiving what they might regard as a sub-standard manuscript. If you do have to allow an acceptance qualification, make sure that there is a detailed clause outlining what the book is that you have agreed to write, describing exactly what you have delivered so far, and that any material that is already delivered (such as an outline or synopsis and two or three chapters) is described, and defined as already accepted.

The amount of the advance and the payment stages will have been discussed when the deal was being negotiated but there are other variations to take care of unusual circumstances: all that is necessary is to make sure that the clause is clear, is not open to misinterpretation and reflects the understanding that was reached when you were negotiating.

Some typical wording of the advance clause would be:

> The Publisher will pay to the Proprietor a non-returnable advance of: £XX,000 on account of all sums accruing to the Proprietor under this Agreement (except if otherwise expressed in this Agreement), such advance to be paid as follows:
>
> £X,000 on signature of this Agreement;

£X,000 on delivery and acceptance of the manuscript;
£X,000 on first publication in hardback or within 12 months of delivery whichever is the sooner;
£X,000 on first publication in paperback or within 24 months of delivery whichever is the sooner.

The advance specified in this clause shall not be subject to repayment regardless of the number of copies of the Work actually printed or sold.

Escalator clauses

Sometimes deals are agreed that carry 'escalators', or 'top up advances' or 'bonuses'. These require extra payments to the author provided certain things happen, such as the opening of a film based on the book, or the book sells more than a certain quantity, or stays in the bestseller lists for a specified period of time. Examples are many and varied: they are usually offered when the publisher does not want to commit to a higher figure at the time they are negotiating, but does want to sweeten the deal in some way. Perhaps the publisher is trying to drive away a competitor, perhaps they really want to keep the author but are afraid that the book won't earn a bigger advance unless a film is made from it, or a television series. The clauses should always be specific about when payment is due.

Examples include:

an extra advance when a film made from the book opens (usually it is specified that it must open in a particular prime location or at a particular number of cinemas), for example:

> In addition, the following advance shall be paid: when a film based on the Work is distributed in the United Kingdom: £XXXX payable within 28 days of the film opening in London's West End.

an extra advance when a television series made from the book is aired (specifications here can include which television channel, how many episodes, prime viewing slots etc.), such as:

> When a television series of the work of at least three parts is shown on any terrestrial television channel: £XXXX payable within 28 days of broadcast of the first episode.

an extra advance on this book if and when the author's previous book earns back its advance:

> If, after returns, Book 1 has earned out its advance at the royalty accounting period immediately following the date of hardcover publication of Book 2, the Publisher will pay the Proprietor a sum equal to those excess earnings

an extra advance payable if and when sales on this book reach a certain level (in this instance the clause shows that the publisher will pay the extra advance on each format, not just on one – the wording would be changed accordingly if the publisher was only prepared to make one extra payment):

> If, after returns, the work sells more than XXXX copies in its hardback edition or more than XXXX copies in the Publisher's paperback edition, the Publisher will, within 28 days of such sales being reached in either edition, pay to the Proprietor the sum of £XXXX by way of extra advance against future income under this contract. Total extra advances payable under this clause shall be £XXXX x 2.

an extra advance if the book appears in a particular bestseller list (stipulations can include which position it must reach and how long it must stay there):

> The Publisher agrees to pay to the Proprietor the following additional advances within 28 days of the date on which the Work has:
>
> (a) appeared between positions 1 and 5 inclusive in *The Sunday Times* best-seller lists for four consecutive weeks in the Publisher's hardback, trade paperback or mass market paperback editions: £XXXX
>
> (b) appeared between positions 6 and 10 inclusive in *The Sunday Times* best-seller lists for four consecutive weeks in the Publisher's hardback, trade paperback or mass-market paperback editions: £XXX
>
> For the avoidance of doubt, the total extra advances payable under this clause shall be £XXXX.

Other escalator provisions can be devised, depending upon an agent's ingenuity and how badly the publisher wants the book and the author!

It is important to understand the difference between *additional advances* and *bonus payments*. All the samples I have given above have been additional advances which, like the original advance, will have to be earned back before royalties will be paid over to the author. If the escalator payments were defined as bonuses, rather than additional advances, then they would not have to be earned back by royalties: they would be simply extra payments. The original advance would remain as the only figure necessary to be earned by royalties. Obviously, authors prefer bonuses. Equally obviously, publishers do not!

To sum up, a clear escalator clause should answer the following questions:

— What is the event that will cause the escalator to be paid?

— Is there a time limit by which this must happen, to qualify for the escalator, and if so what is it?

— How much is the escalator worth and can it be paid more than once?

— When will it be paid?

Royalties

Royalties are the amount an author earns per copy sold. Royalties are usually expressed as a percentage of the recommended retail price, or as a percentage of the price that the publisher actually receives from a bookseller or wholesaler.

Agents always prefer to see royalties linked to the recommended retail price rather than the price received. The reasons are easy to understand: the recommended retail price is easy to ascertain but the price received is not. The price received depends on the negotiations between publisher and bookseller on their levels of discount, and the author has to take on trust the figure that the publisher puts forward. I don't want to sound paranoid here. I don't actually believe that all publishers are trying to cheat authors. But it is obviously simpler to police and check the figures if they are linked to the recommended retail price. Unfortunately this is not always easy to achieve.

Wherever possible try to negotiate royalty scales so that royalties are aggregated. This can make a great difference to the amount of royalties earned. Agents know which publishers regularly aggregate their sales and which do not like to: for instance, the Penguin group has a policy of not offering aggregated royalty scales. They are clear about this and are certainly not trying to pretend otherwise: their editors are always precise on this point when they make offers so when negotiating with them you know where you stand and so can argue for lower break points (the sales figure at which a royalty moves up to a higher level). But in some companies, editors themselves can be muddled about the basis for their royalties. I do strongly advise authors to be sure that the subject is discussed before agreeing a deal.

There is nothing worse than the confusion caused when the subject isn't discussed and the author is assuming royalties *will* be aggregated, and the publisher is offering on the basis that they *won't*.

Be sure that the clauses make it clear which territories are regarded as making up the home market. And if you are required to accept a 'royalties on high discount clause' (b. below), negotiate it so that it is expressed as a proportion of the original royalty, rather than, as many publishers try for, simply switching to 10 per cent of the price received. This clause has become common in British publishers' contracts in the last five years or so: as booksellers gained more muscle, their discounts became bigger. Publishers are getting a smaller slice of the retail price and have been pressurizing authors to accept smaller royalties on sales made at high discounts. Four-fifths of the normal home royalty level is a widely accepted level for high discount sales; what still has to be negotiated is the point at which it kicks in. At the moment an accepted level is usually above 50 per cent discount on hardbacks, and above 52.5 per cent on paperbacks.

This is a clause that causes much argument between publishers and agents. Publishers ask for variations on this formula, all, needless to say, more advantageous to themselves. These include the previously mentioned 10 per cent of the price received, or trying to agree an extra level of higher discount at which point the royalty goes down to three-fifths of the otherwise prevailing rate, or even switches to 10 per cent of price received, or trying to express the discounts as, say, '50 per cent and above' rather than 'at discounts above 50 per cent'. This may sound like a tiny point, but because these discount levels are regular watersheds in the trade, the difference of wording can make a sizeable difference in earnings.

Another word of warning on the royalties on high discounts clause: make sure that it applies only to home sales. If it is moved to a later position in the order of clauses, it could be applied to export sales as well. As export sales already carry a lower level of royalty, you could end up with very small earnings indeed on your export sales.

I have some sympathy for the principle that publishers are fighting for: after all, the portion of the retail price that they receive is small enough and getting smaller. But the author's portion is smaller still, and the author has to get by usually on only one book a year. Authors' mortgage payments and electricity bills never go down: I think it is unjustifiable that publishers should expect authors' royalty levels continually to diminish. The reality is that in well-run publishing companies their profits usually rise, so why should the authors' *proportion* be reduced?

Typical wording of author-friendly royalty clauses would be:

The following royalties shall be calculated on aggregate home and export sales:

(a) On copies of a hardback edition sold in the Home Market (the United Kingdom, the Republic of Ireland and the European Union):

10% of the UK recommended published price from 01 to 2,500 copies

12.5% of the UK recommended published price from 2,501 to 5,000 copies

15% thereafter

(b) On copies of a hardcover edition sold in the Home Market at a discount of more than 50 per cent of the UK retail price, the royalty specified in a. above shall be four-fifths of the otherwise prevailing royalty

(c) On copies of a hardback edition sold for the purposes of export (except in the European Union):

5% of the UK recommended published price from 01 to 2,500 copies

6.25% of the UK recommended published price from 2,501 to 5,000 copies

7.5% thereafter

(d) On copies of a trade paperback edition issued by the Publishers under their own imprint and sold in the Home Market (the United Kingdom, the Republic of Ireland and the European Union):

7.5% of the UK recommended published price from 01 to 15,000 copies

10% thereafter

(e) On copies of a trade paperback edition issued by the Publishers under their own imprint and sold overseas (except in the European Union):

6% of the UK recommended published price from 01 to 15,000 copies

8% thereafter

(f) On copies of a mass market paperback edition issued by the Publishers under their own imprint and sold in the Home Market (the United Kingdom, the Republic of Ireland and the European Union):

7.5% of the UK recommended published price from 01 to 25,000 copies

10% thereafter

(g) On copies of a mass market paperback edition issued by the Publishers under their own imprint and sold overseas (except in the European Union):

6% of the UK recommended published price from 01 to 25,000 copies
8% thereafter

(h) On copies of any paperback edition issued by the Publishers under their own imprint and sold in the Home Market at discounts above 52.5% of the UK recommended retail price the royalty specified in d. and f. above shall be four-fifths of the otherwise prevailing royalty

(i) On copies sold as sheets to a library supplier: 10% price received.

(j) On copies given away for the purpose of promoting the sale of the Work and/or replacement of damaged copies and such like purposes, no royalties shall be paid, but the number of copies free of royalty shall not exceed two hundred copies.

(k) In the event of VAT being imposed on books, the royalties will be based on retail price excluding VAT.

The sub-clauses dealing with paperback royalties (g) and (h) may well be repeated: once stipulating the royalties for a trade paperback (the larger format) and once for mass market. Trade paperback royalty levels are closer to hardback than mass market, but with higher break points; mass-market paperback royalty levels are the lowest rate of all and have the highest break points. The rates I have included here would be for a mass-market format.

In general, you can expect higher percentage royalty levels on sales of higher priced volumes, and lower royalties on lower priced books, but of course the print runs tend to be longer, and so the price to the public lower.

I do like to stipulate an upper limit for royalty-free copies (j) but not all publishers will agree to include this provision; others will but with a much higher figure.

Accounts

The clauses already discussed provided for what will be paid; this clause deals with when it will be paid. In the English-speaking publishing industry it is usual for publishers to send royalty statements, with monies due, twice a year. In the non-English-speaking countries it is more usual to receive annual accounting, although in some of the larger language markets this is changing slowly. Although some authors feel it is iniquitous that publishers should save up royalties and only pay them over twice a year, I do have a little sympathy for them.

The administration work involved in preparing royalty accounts is awesome: I know how much time my accounts department spend checking every line of the thousands of statements we receive every half year. If we were to move to quarterly accounting, and the paperwork were doubled, I doubt we would have completed the checking on one quarter's statements before the next started to arrive. One way around the fact that publishers hold money so long can be achieved by the inclusion of the sub-clause that starts towards the end of line four in the following clause. This provides for the publisher to pay to the author, within twenty-eight days of receiving it, any income due to the author from the sale of subsidiary rights, always provided that the advance paid to the author has already been earned back.

Here's my suggested wording:

> Accounts of sales of the Work shall be rendered semi-annually to 30 June and 31 December of each year, and statements shall be rendered and the amount shown due thereby paid on or before the following 30 September and 31 March respectively, but the Publisher shall pay all sums due to the Proprietor under clause XX [the subsidiary rights clause] within 28 days of receipt of all such monies less any part of the advance which the Publishers shall have paid to the Proprietor under Clause X [the monies paid as an advance] and which at that date shall remain unearned.

The dates quoted of end June and December for the closing dates for each set of accounts, and end September and March for delivery of the accounts to the author are the dates to which a large proportion of publishers in the English speaking world work. There are variations and there is no significance to be read into a publisher closing their half-yearly royalty accounts on different dates.

The gap of three months between the closing of the account and the delivery of the statement and the monies is simply the time needed to do the vast amount of work necessary to provide an accounting for every single active title on a publisher's stocklist. Whatever date a publisher does work to for the close of their royalty accounts, do make sure that the statements are due to you no more than three months later. Some publishers ask for four months but any longer than that is unfair on the author and their cash flow. If you are forced to agree a longer gap (because the publisher simply cannot physically produce the figures earlier) argue that they should pay interest on the sums due when they hold them any longer than three or four months.

Which brings me to a sub-clause I try to include in all of my contracts, but, not surprisingly, publishers argue energetically against including it. Here it is:

> (b) In the event of payment being late by more than one month from the due date, the Publisher shall pay interest on monies overdue at the rate of three per cent above the current bank base rate.

You can imagine the arguments put forward by each side. Publishers say it is not fair for them to be penalized if an administrative error occurs occasionally, and anyway, they are usually efficient. I will say that if an administrative error occurs only very occasionally it won't therefore end up by costing them very much in interest, and why should my client be penalized for an error on their part? And if they really are efficient, then it shouldn't bother them because they won't have to pay the interest, will they?

Most publishers *are* efficient payers. But not *all*. I have seldom had to bring this clause into play. I like to have it in contracts because it can prick corporate pride when it is invoked, and therefore helps to prevent delays on payments in the future.

Reserve against returns

It is an unfortunate fact of business life in publishing that booksellers are allowed to return unsold books to the publisher. Although it is certain that if it were to be swept away entirely, booksellers would order more conservatively and perhaps, overall, fewer books would be sold. Publishers do not want to pay royalties to an author on sales of books that later come back into the warehouse, hence the need for this clause.

Acceptable wording would be:

> The Publisher shall have the right to set aside as a reserve against returns a sum representing 10% (ten percent) of the royalties earned on the Publisher's first hardback royalty statement and 20% (twenty percent) of the royalties earned on the Publisher's first paperback royalty statement after first publication of the said work as earned during that period and to withhold this sum for a period up to and including the third royalty statement thereafter following which all monies due shall be paid in full at the time of the next royalty statements and thereafter the Publisher shall accept responsibility for the over-payments resulting from returns which occur subsequently.

Publishing companies have rigid policies on both the percentage levels they wish to hold in reserve (the figures I have quoted will be the best you can hope for currently) and the length of time they wish to hold them for. Here the wording provides for the publisher to take a percentage of the sales on the *first* royalty statement for each edition. For many books, this is likely to show heavier sales than any other period. This wording allows them to hold it for eighteen months (three half-year royalty periods) and then to pay it over on the fourth royalty statement. This is a system used by many publishers.

Another widely used method is to hold a specified percentage of sales income from the first royalty period and to return it in the next royalty period; then, during that second royalty period, to withhold the same percentage from the sales within that royalty period, and so on. This is slightly more complicated (but in fact straightforward to administer and to check) and is fairer to the author as the withheld income reflects a percentage of sales income for the current six months, as opposed to a previous royalty period: it reflects a sales pattern closer to the date of accounting.

Companies work to one system or another: they will not (and probably cannot) vary it for individual contracts or authors.

Some companies are notorious for always being late with their royalty statements. Occasionally there will be a good reason and some publishers will apologize, and some have been known to offer their payments with interest added. But some companies are late with statements because they are inefficient or because they have cash flow problems. Agents pay very close attention to habitual late payers and those publishers will find agents increasingly unwilling to do business with them.

Value Added Tax

In countries where a sales tax is added to services, authors will be obliged to charge VAT on their earnings, if they themselves are registered for it. This is the kind of clause you should expect:

> All payments, royalties and percentages set out in this Agreement are exclusive of Value Added Tax, which must be added by the Publisher, if required, according to the statutory regulations. The Proprietor's VAT registered number is: [fill in your number if you are registered].

This clause only applies in countries like Britain where services such as writing attract a sales tax. If you do live in a country where such a tax is applied, if you do not earn enough to qualify for registration, and you have elected not to register willingly, this clause can either be omitted or 'not applicable' can be written in place of a registration number. See the section on VAT in chapter 16.

Signature

Having waded through all that has gone before, it will be a relief to get to this part! It's almost unnecessary to say that each party to the contract should keep on file a fully signed contract original. Some agents keep their authors' original contracts, which has always seemed rather odd to me: we make sure that publisher and author each have a signed original and sometimes we do too. If not enough originals have been signed, the agency will settle for a photocopy of the finally signed document.

I have dealt more fully with the process of exchanging copies for signature earlier in this chapter.

Here is an example of a signature block; they don't vary by very much:

IN WITNESS WHEREOF the parties hereto have set their hands the day and year first above written

PROPRIETOR _____

Witnessed by _____

PUBLISHER _____

Witnessed by _____

Success: now you can invoice for the amount due on signature! And now the real work of publishing begins.

10 Preparing your novel for publication

Editors are like guides on safari, moving their clients through difficult country – George Plimpton

She'll save me from myself – Margaret Forster, on her editor

A professional writer is an amateur who didn't quit – Richard Bach

What does a publisher's editor do, and why?

An unedited manuscript is like the rough cut of a film: you may be able to see the talent and passion that formed it, but it may not be finely tuned. Editing polishes it. Experienced and tactful editors are a rare, disappearing, and precious breed of people. They are rare because the work requires talent and years of application to hone the skill. They are disappearing because whenever publishers try to save on costs, it always seems to be the editors who are 'let go' first, perhaps because their work is invisible when it is done well. They are precious because they can add enormous value to a manuscript, which an author and agent can reap benefits from when they sell on other rights to the book around the world. I wouldn't necessarily go as far as agreeing with Carmen Callil, the brilliant and aggressive Australian who founded the ground-breaking Virago imprint in Britain, who said in her speech at the Booker Prize evening in 1996 that, 'The editor has become no more than a corpse on which literary agents feed.' Strong words, which gives you an indication of how strongly people in the trade feel about the role of the editor (and agents!).

Authors, of course, feel just as, if not more, strongly about the role of the editor when it is their manuscript that is being criticized.

The title of 'editor' is used to cover so many different functions, but it is used indiscriminately in publishing so it's no wonder that authors can be confused as to who does what. There are basically three different functions, and at least two different jobs, which are all covered by the catch-all term 'editor'. These break down as follows, in the order in which an author would meet them:

1. The commissioning editor

The commissioning editor is a term that describes the person who buys books for the publishing house: the person who tries to identify that good book among the many others. Books are often also brought in to the publishing house by other staff members, but the commissioning editors are the people who are expected to provide the books that make up the publishing programme. This editor won't necessarily be the editorial director (who shapes and plans the publishing programme), although the editorial director may well also commission books of their own. They will make the decision to take the book to the editorial committee and to the acquisition meeting, this will be the person who has the costings prepared and makes the offer to the author or agent. This will be the person who steers the book through the publishing process, even though they may not attend to every detail themselves. The commissioning editor will brief the design department on what kind of look they want for the cover, argue for a prime position on the publication schedule and fight for a larger marketing budget, advertisements and a publication party. The commissioning editor is the main liaison between the author and the publishing company, the channel through whom all the information flows about the publication process.

This person is the most important link to the publishing company for the author and the book and it can be extremely difficult and frustrating for an author to lose their commissioning editor. When your commissioning editor leaves and you are passed on to – 'inherited by' – another editor in the company so much history is lost. Your original editor will often have become quite a friend so there can be sadness at having to start again with someone else. Their familiarity with you and your preferred work methods may have enabled you both to take short cuts in communicating with each other, to 'talk in shorthand', which will have to be rebuilt with someone new. And your first editor's awareness of your sales patterns to date, which books have done best where and why, which parts of the publicity and marketing worked best for you, will all have to be put together again. Obviously other staff members in other relevant departments will still be there with their knowledge of you and your books, but your commissioning editor really is the pivotal point for an author within the publishing company. Most authors will have to face changing editors at some point in their career and it always requires time and effort from all involved to make the transition comfortable.

Agents can and do play an important role at such times as this, particularly if the agent already knows the new editor. The agent can tell both the author and the new editor what they know of the other, and so help the new relationship to build.

2. Structural editing

Try to leave out the parts that people skip – Elmore Leonard

The next stage of work may well be done by the commissioning editor, but not always. This is the real editing, the work that deals with the content. This is the time when you get an editorial report that covers structure, pace and characterization. Sometimes this editor is a full-time employee of the publishing company, sometimes they are free-lance. This kind of editing is tremendously time-consuming and is often difficult if not impossible – to do during an office day while at a desk with all the normal distractions of an office around you, such as colleagues and telephone calls, which result in constant interruption. The result of this kind of work is always a written document, sometimes an overview, which leaves you to go through the manuscript again, working out how to solve the problems that have been highlighted, but sometimes done with incredible detail, with scene by scene comments. This kind of work requires great tact on the part of the editor if the writer is to benefit fully from it, rather than merely feel affronted that so much extra work is asked for.

I really believe that authors should be enormously grateful when this kind of work is done well on their manuscript. The author, after all, is the person who benefits from it when readers and critics admire the finished book and believe it to be all the author's own work. The author doesn't have to accept every editorial point: exchanges between editors and authors are often quite robust. An experienced editor will offer their advice, knowing that the author will have the final word, and that the author will be the arbiter who decides what to change and what to leave. But a wise author will pay close attention to a thorough editorial report because it can be the means to a better book. And smart authors can learn a lot from constructive criticism.

3. Copy-editing

When you catch an adjective, kill it – Mark Twain

Copy-editing may be done by the same editor who worked on the manuscript at the previous stage of structural editing, but is often a different person and this can be very helpful. Each new editor reading the manuscript with fresh eyes stands a better chance of spotting infelicities. I have worked with many books where the commissioning editor has deliberately invited other editors to also read through the manuscript towards the end of the editing process just to make sure that everything possible has been done to polish and smooth the text. Another reason to do this is to make sure that the commissioning editor's familiarity with the manuscript (they may have read it many times at different stages by now) has not caused them to miss anything.

The copy-editor is the last in line before the manuscript is sent for typesetting. Copy-editing is the nuts and bolts that mainly deal with presentation. This level of editing is the 'pencil on the page' time when spelling and grammar and publisher's house style is checked for. It is the copy-editor who will point out any timing inconsistencies (a character in one of the novels I represented seemed to be having a twenty-two-month pregnancy until the copy-editor got to grips with the manuscript!), and will check for factual errors or dialogue that contains modern idioms in a historical novel. This is the time when the manuscript is cleaned up and made ready for typesetting: your last possible chance to make changes before they become expensive. A reputable publisher will make sure that the author sees the manuscript again after copy-editing to check that they agree with all the changes made. I am certainly indebted to Tess Tattersall who copy-edited this manuscript and tidied it up considerably, thereby saving the reader from many repetitions and me from much embarrassment!

It is not unknown, but mercifully rare, for a copy-editor to get carried away with their task and to start rewriting text, a task that is way beyond their brief. One more read through by the author will ensure that the author is happy with the text that is to be printed.

Make sure that absolutely everything is checked and changed now. If you want to make changes once you receive proofs (apart from correcting mistakes that have crept in since copy-editing, which is all you should be doing at proof stage) the publisher may charge you for the cost incurred. You will probably find a clause in your contract that allows the publisher to bill you for charges if you make more than minimal text changes at proof stage.

Editorial advice and how to handle it

They may be mistaken about *what* is wrong, but if they comment
then something is wrong – Ken Follett, on editors

I have covered much of this subject in chapter 4, but there I was
focusing on editorial work and advice received prior to the sale of
your book to a publisher. Here I'm looking at the editorial advice you
receive after your book is bought by a publisher. If you are sent a long
and detailed critique of your novel, fight down the natural irritation
that comes from hoping that the only response would be: 'I love it!'
Instead focus on the pleasure of being able to improve your manuscript
before the reviewers criticize it publicly. What a privilege to be able to
polish your novel with all the wisdom that your editor can bring to it
as well as yourself. Editorial advice is hidden, in that the reader
believes what they are reading is all the author's own work, so the
author gets the full benefit of any suggestion they incorporate into
their work. If you receive little editorial criticism or even worse, none,
I would be worried.

One author I knew said to me recently, 'I'm delighted with my
editor's reaction to my latest manuscript. She doesn't want to change
a thing.' My heart sank: not because I disagreed fundamentally with
the editor, or because I thought the author should rewrite the novel
from beginning to end, but rather because of what that told me about
that author's attitude to the editing process.

That author likes to think of herself as the soul of reason, open to
any suggestions from her agent and her editor. In fact, over years of
working with her, her editor and I have come to realize that she is as
stubborn as a mule, but her demeanour is always that of sweet
reasonableness. When I or the editor, in the past, have suggested small
changes, perhaps to make the passing of time clear, perhaps to make
a passage faster when pace has dipped, perhaps to add depth to
characterization, the response has always been the same. In an
extremely friendly tone she discusses the point at great length, but
doesn't budge an inch. Furthermore, she manages to suggest to each
of us that the other has completely loved the manuscript as it stands
and thus the one she is now talking to is being unreasonable in
wanting changes. There is a fundamental flaw in this, of course,
because the editor and I do talk to each other too. But after talking us
both to a standstill (no mean feat to talk an agent into silence!) she
then thinks that she has proved that her first draft was perfect and
that's the end of the editing process.

She's delighted not to have to rewrite, and believes that this is good and that it makes her publisher value her more. In fact, the opposite is true and she is the one who is losing by showing such intransigence. Her editor has given up making editorial suggestions for improvements because she knows they will not be accepted and they will only lead to hours and hours of fruitless conversations. On several occasions I have followed up the editor's call and have made the same suggestions myself to no avail. Consequently that author does not get the benefit of suggestions that could actually improve her books. Luckily, she does write very well, and the suggestions were – and would be – minor. But wouldn't you think that she would want to improve her novels as much as possible?

The author's editor does tell me when she thinks a book should have had more work done to it. She believes that the author's novels are 'uneven' – i.e. some are stronger than others – and that this is stopping their sales force being able to lift her sales to higher levels.

If you have already completed your manuscript by the time a publisher buys it, then your agent, if you have one, will already have contributed their editorial advice and the manuscript will presumably incorporate it. But the publisher's editor will still edit it and may well ask you to rewrite all or a portion of it.

If you have sold your novel on the basis of a part-manuscript and synopsis, then your publisher's editor will almost certainly tell you what they like best and least, and might give you editorial notes for you to work with while you complete the rest of the book. They will be clear about what they think the strengths are so that you can emphasize them while you work on completing the book. Also, they will point out any weaknesses they have noticed so that you can remedy them as you continue writing.

Is there any point in your agent continuing to play an editorial role once your book is sold to a publisher? Agents take differing views on this point, with many stepping back entirely once there is a publisher's editor on board. At our agency we do continue to read our clients' work and to offer our editorial thoughts although I do hope that as an author forges a closer relationship with their editor, over several books, I will be able to retreat a little and will be able to contribute less editorial time.

Because we tend to sell rights separately to each language market rather than selling world rights to one publisher, I do have a broader view of the audience that the novel is destined for. The American, or Canadian, Australian or British editor who first buys your book will of necessity be tailoring the book for their own market, the one in which they are to publish it.

I know that once the manuscript is edited, I can then start work on the next phase of selling by offering the book overseas. So if I see aspects of the storyline that will be puzzling or incomprehensible to overseas readers I may ask the author to amend them or explain them a little more fully. Great care has to be taken with this so as not to render the novel bland. The wishes of the publisher who already owns it and has committed to it are always paramount, but if these are not compromised by making the story clearer to readers in other markets, then it is work worth doing. It occurs more often with non-fiction than with fiction, but an example I can think of was a thriller written by an author who had yet to break through to the US market. He sold well in Britain and had an energetic British publisher who edited him well. One novel was delivered, which was enthusiastically received by his British editor, but I felt that it was unfortunate that all the baddies were American. In other words, there were no baddies who weren't American, and there were no Americans in the novel except the baddies. I knew I would be submitting this manuscript to a range of US publishers and knew that they would all feel that their audience would find it hard to identify with a story in which every one of their countrymen was on the wrong side of the hero. To alter this slightly would not fundamentally change or compromise the storyline, and it made no difference to the British editor's enthusiasm for the novel, so the author made the changes and we did sell it to an American publisher.

I can hear the chorus of groans already emerging from some people who will think this is the most crass interference, by commerce, in something that should be viewed as art. I disagree. If my purpose is to manage an author's career, particularly if that author is writing commercial fiction, then I will certainly make suggestions that I think will enable a book to sell to a market in which it might otherwise be rejected. It is always up to the author to accept or reject suggestions of this nature, and so long as nothing else of importance in the novel is lost by incorporating a change that can improve the sales picture, then I think the suggestion is worthwhile.

The author, publisher's editor and agent should be able to work together editorially as a team. This may include more than one editor if the novel has been bought simultaneously in other English language markets. There is nothing more satisfying than several people working together on a manuscript that they love, and seeing it improve with each draft. When editor and agent and author work together harmoniously, each feeds off the other's enthusiasm and energy. I can think of several extremely satisfying teams of editors and authors that I work with in this way, where we all contribute ideas, discuss differences, and then agree the editorial changes amicably. To achieve this unity of purpose each of us must trust each other, we must know that we are all working towards the same end, and must share the same view of what we are trying to achieve. This may sound very obvious but it can take a great deal of tact to produce the ideal triangle. And first and foremost the author must feel comfortable with the work method.

Each of the group has slightly different priorities but should recognize the priorities of the other two. The book is, at the end of the day, the author's offspring and it is important that the author's voice and intentions for the story are not subverted. The publisher's editor must see the manuscript become a novel that can be sold successfully in the company's home territory and to its export markets and the editor will want to see it worked on until it's as good as the author can make it. The agent will also want to see it as a step in the building of the author's career and also as a book that can be sold widely in other markets. The first market that buys it will hopefully be only one of many.

Naturally, editor and agent sometimes produce conflicting ideas after a reading of a manuscript. Where I don't feel very strongly about a point, I will always bow to the editor. If the editor and I have strong differing views on a point (not something that seems to happen often at all), then all three of us will discuss it back and forth. It will always be the author's view that prevails anyway: editorial advice is always offered, not forced upon, a writer. So long as they produce a manuscript that, at the end of day, is acceptable to the publishing house, a writer can take or leave editorial criticism as they please. The most successful commercial writers do listen to their editors, and reap the benefit of stronger novels.

I can think of an unusual situation that happened with one of Maeve Haran's novels, *Soft Touch*. Little, Brown in the UK had published several novels by Maeve and she has a good working relationship with her editor. Maeve's novels sell well in the UK and its related territories, but there is no doubt she sells even better in her German translations published by Blanvalet and Goldman.

When Maeve first conceived *Soft Touch* she decided to have a much loved grandmother character die at the end. It made for a weepy, bitter-sweet ending and when she first wrote the outline, she discussed it at length with her editor and with me. We decided that was just the right way to end the novel.

When *Soft Touch* was delivered we all loved it: Little, Brown and I made some tiny suggestions for changes, Maeve swiftly did the work and the manuscript was put into production. We expected proofs in about six weeks. Normally that would be the point at which I start most of my rights offering to other markets, but some of the larger translating markets like to get the manuscript as soon as it's completed. This is certainly true with Maeve in Germany: her editors there couldn't wait to read it. I rushed it off to them and they made a handsome offer very quickly. We accepted, the deal was done, the contract signed: all very straightforward.

A few weeks later the Blanvalet and Goldman editors were in London and, having never actually met Maeve before, arranged dinner with her. I was sure they would get on tremendously well, and they did. In fact, they became so friendly that the editors felt emboldened to ask Maeve why she had chosen the sad ending? As they discussed it, Maeve realized that they really would have loved the grandmother to live, and the book to have a resolutely feelgood and upbeat ending.

We all talked the next morning: Maeve, her Little, Brown editor, and me. Maeve was willing to make the change if Little, Brown were agreeable. But Little, Brown liked it fine as it was, and they had a tight production schedule to keep. Maeve thought she'd redraft the ending anyway: if Little, Brown didn't want to use it she could always let her German publisher use it for their edition. But the German translator had already started work and the publisher would need the ending very quickly indeed if they were to stick to the same publication schedule as the UK publisher.

The next week, at the Frankfurt Book Fair, I saw her German editors at a party and told them they could have their upbeat ending. They were thrilled, and somewhat astonished that Maeve had agreed to do it, and amazed that she had been able to do it so quickly.

When I got back to London a few days later the first thing I did was to read Maeve's new pages: magic! The first ending was weepy and satisfying. The new ending was a real three-handkerchief affair, with a triumphantly satisfying, feelgood scene that had every strand of the storyline paying off beautifully. She had managed this in just twelve changed pages! The Little, Brown editor had read it before I returned and felt exactly the same way and quickly substituted the new pages in the manuscript that was being typeset. The proofs arrived on time with the new ending in place. The German publisher was ecstatic, and very grateful to Maeve for listening to suggestions from a market that seldom gets involved in the editing process of English language novels. And Maeve and I were grateful to them for being honest in their reactions to the manuscript. A win-win situation all round!

I can, though, also think of one or two instances where things have not gone so smoothly. On one occasion a publishing house had paid a very big advance for a book and was very keen to publish it quickly. After all, a publisher does not start to earn back their expenditure until it can begin selling books. The manuscript was delivered and was very impressive, but I knew that the author could make it even better if they worked on another draft. And if the novel became stronger, I would be able to sell it even more widely to other markets and rights. But in order to do more work, the author would need more time than the original publisher could afford if they were to publish in the lead-title slot that had been allocated to it. A dilemma, and one that needed a lot of tact and trust to work through.

I was worried that my feelings about the manuscript meant that if the author was going to do more work to it, the knock-on effect to the publishing schedule – and the marketing plans for the book – was huge. I became very nervous that I was making a fuss about very little, but then realized how much was at stake. We sell this author in more than twenty languages, and didn't want to risk losing any one of them. I didn't want to run the risk that the UK publisher might publish with a huge marketing spend, making enormous promises to the press and the book trade and the public that might not be completely fulfilled by the novel either.

No editor likes to think that someone else can see ways to improve a book they have worked on that they have not seen themselves. And no editor likes to delay a book in the publishing schedule if it means losing a hard-won lead-title slot, which may not be possible to obtain for that author at a later date. Coupled with the fact that the publishing house will have to wait longer to start earning money from the book, delaying a publication date for a title prominent in the schedules can be viewed as a disaster. But to my mind the more important issue is the author's career: each book has to be as good as the author can make it, and better than the last one, because each publication must take the author forward. Publishing worldwide is so very competitive that authors can't afford to stand still. And anyone who could improve a book but chooses not to is inviting disaster.

A situation like this can only be resolved if the author trusts the agent's judgement – and editorial suggestions – enough to be prepared to see the book moved to a different publication date. In this instance the author did. The author had been my client for more than a decade, and the editor was a good friend too so there was a good relationship and a lot of trust to rely on. Even so, the whole thing had to be handled with utmost tact.

The next step was for the author to show the publisher how the changes would improve the book. Having read the revised manuscript, the editor agreed that the revision was needed and had improved the novel, and the book was published a little later. It did get a lead position on the list, and it did receive all of the marketing spend and publicity that was promised. I'm pleased to say it also went on to receive terrific reviews, fantastic sales, and was published in many translations. Of course, it might have achieved all these anyway, but I hate my authors to take any risks with their career if they don't have to. And isn't it more satisfying to know that you have published the very best book you can write, rather than just a fairly good one?

Some editors can be suspicious of agents who read and edit their clients' work. This can be because the author/agent/editor team hasn't worked together before. It can be the result of a less than tactful agent, whose suggestions are seen as interference by the editor; it can be that the editor is inexperienced and feels as though they are being second-guessed by the agent; or it can be that somehow the editor and the agent have quite different views of what the author is aiming for. In any and all of these situations the only remedy is for the editor and agent to have a frank discussion to resolve the problems: nothing is achieved if everyone is not pulling in the same direction. The very worst outcome would be for the writer to be disturbed by tension between their editor and their agent. This could be very counter-productive. And this would be exactly the opposite of the ideal we are all striving for.

Many authors include their editors in their acknowledgements in the published book, which is evidence of the strength of the teamwork that editing can become. Indeed, some authors feel so strongly about their editors that they insist on 'editor clauses' in their contracts which allow the author to leave the publishing house if their editor leaves (see chapters 9 and 19).

You might think that only inexperienced writers would be open about acknowledging the help of their editors. But it is often the most successful authors who are most generous: success can breed confidence. I remember the American agent Al Zuckerman proudly showing me a present he had received from his client Ken Follett. The thriller writer had kept all the editorial correspondence between himself and his agent on a particular book and when the book was published, he had the inches-thick dossier of letters bound into several leather-covered volumes, and sent them to Al with a letter of thanks. Al was as moved by the thought behind the gift, as by the handsome volumes themselves.

Rewriting

Style and structure are the essence of a book; great ideas are hogwash – Vladimir Nabokov

I'm not sure that I agree with the great man above entirely, but style and structure are vital and can be improved with each new draft.

Why rewrite at all? I would say, so as to be able to take advantage of the clear-sightedness that comes from rereading the manuscript after putting it aside for a while, or the constructive criticism you receive from others who can be more objective than you, the manuscript's creator. Another person's reading can help you to make sure that your intentions are clear to the reader (which is why your agent and editor can be so useful if they were there at the novel's conception too, so know what your plans for the book were at that stage). And agents or editors, who have only your interests at heart, can help you to realize your best work. The more feedback you encourage from others for your synopsis and character biographies, the less likely it is that you will need major structural rewrites later.

As I've illustrated in the previous section, authors vary in their attitudes to rewriting. I sympathize with Jessamyn West who said, 'Writing is so difficult that I often feel that writers, having had their hell on earth, will escape all punishment hereafter.' She must have said that after being asked to rewrite a section of a book!

Revising and rewriting are done only for one reason: to make the book stronger. An obvious statement perhaps, but it's important to bear it in mind because too often you can become so involved in a piece of rewriting that it becomes a new creation, and as well as improving the parts that needed revision, what was good about the previous draft also gets changed and sometimes lost. I think it is incumbent upon editors to take as much care to highlight what is particularly good about a piece of writing that is to be revised, as they do to point out what needs changing.

If, for instance, you are rewriting a section because the pacing needs attention, it would be counter-productive to become so focused on speeding up the action that you force your characters into actions and dialogue that is quite out of character for them. Or vice versa – while trying to fix some characterization problems, you rewrite in such a way as to make the pacing go awry. Skill in these areas comes with experience.

Permissions

It is usually the author's obligation to make sure that anything in their work quoted from other sources is properly acknowledged, paid for if required and that permission has been sought for its inclusion. This is often a more onerous task for non-fiction writers, but novelists must be aware of the obligation. If you quote from other sources that are still in copyright, you must ask permission: if it is only a few lines, it is unlikely you will be asked for payment. But even if you are not required to pay for the use, you will probably be asked to acknowledge the source by mentioning author, title of the work and possibly the publisher. If you wish to quote more than a few lines you will be expected to pay a fee, usually payable at the time your book is published. After all, you would expect the same courtesy if your material was quoted by others.

It is obviously vital to know where the material comes from that you plan to quote. Keep meticulous records when you find material you think you may wish to quote. It can be very time-consuming trying to track down the source of a quotation you copied down years ago without keeping adequate sourcing details.

And a particular word of warning if you are thinking of quoting verses from popular songs: they can be *very* expensive indeed. There are certain songwriters who are notorious for quoting huge fees to anyone who wants to quote even a couple of lines from their songs. One very famous British group seems to be trying to make their fortune all over again judging by the fees they quote to writers who would like to quote their songs. One of my clients wrote a novel in which she wanted to open each chapter by printing a verse of a song made popular by this particular 1960s Liverpool foursome. She quickly had to abandon the notion when she discovered that the permission fees would have cost her about twice as much as the advance she was to receive from her publisher!

When you prepare to clear permissions, you need to decide whether to request clearance only for the market that your first publisher will publish in, or to clear permissions for the world in the English language, or world rights in all languages. Here you will have to take a view on the future possibilities. Your publisher and your agent can help with advice. It is obviously more expensive, but less work, to pay for the largest number of markets at once: this way you don't have to contact the sources every time you sell a new edition. It would be pointless, and expensive, to pay for markets that your book never reaches. A useful compromise is to pay for just the market that your first publisher will cover, but to ask the copyright owners to tell you what the other markets would cost. Keep detailed records of fees expected together with all names and addresses of the copyright owners, and it should therefore be fairly straightforward to send off payments in the future as your book is sold to other markets. Always file and keep the correspondence very carefully: some publishers will ask to see copies of the letters agreeing to use of quoted materials before they will go ahead with your book.

The simplest option is not to quote from copyright material owned by others at all! Copyright exists usually for seventy years from the end of the year in which the author died. There are variations, depending on the nationality of the original author.

Short passages, which fall under the heading of 'fair dealing' in the Copyright Act, do not require permission or a fee, but should always be acknowledged as coming from another's work by quoting author and title of the original work and must be used for purposes of criticism or review. The Copyright Act itself does not define this in any more detail, but The Society of Authors and the UK Publishers Association some years ago agreed that a definition would be a single extract of up to 400 words or several extracts up to a total of 800 words so long as no one single extract was longer than 300 words. For any other length or kind of quotation, permission is required. If in doubt, ask for permission.

It is best to write to the publisher of the work quoted initially. If they do not control the rights they should pass your letter to the rights holder – either the author or the agent or the overseas publisher from whom they acquired their rights. On a practical note, it is best to clear permissions as soon as you can. The later you leave it, the more likely you are to have to agree to high fees, if you haven't left yourself enough time to argue them. In order to know how to set the level of the fee, the rights holder will want to know what kind of book you wish to include the extract in, which markets you require the permission to cover, and approximately how long the print run will be for your book.

All writers must be aware when they are quoting from others. Quoting from other works without acknowledging the work and the writer is not only discourteous but illegal. Breach of copyright, plagiarism, passing off – these are all extremely detrimental to a writer's career, bank balance and credibility with publishers.

Libel

Defamation is called slander when it is spoken, libel when it is written. Libel is a statement that defames a person still alive, or a company still trading. It means that the statement has permitted them to be recognized and has left them open to ridicule or contempt. Although dead people cannot be libelled, if a statement about a dead person could be said to imply something libellous about their descendants, then a descendant would be able to sue on their own behalf.

Anyone suing for libel has to prove that they can be recognized by others from the text, and that the statements have caused them injury. It is not enough to claim that the libel was unintentional: it is the author's obligation to make sure that they do not libel anyone. Libel law differs from country to country. For British libel law, The Society of Authors publishes a very useful pamphlet in its *Quick Guides* series.

It is vital that novelists have a basic understanding of libel laws: many have been tripped up by assuming that it is only non-fiction writers who need to be aware of libel. In essence, you are guilty of libel if someone successfully upholds the claim that you have brought them into disrepute by something you have published. And because the definition of publication is a broad one, you are judged to have 'published' a libel if it is contained in a letter, so long as that letter has been read by someone else. If a manuscript is submitted to and read by an editor and it contains something libellous, you could be in trouble. Indeed, there was a lot of disturbance caused a few years ago by a book proposal. It was for a biography of a living person and one publisher to whom it was submitted showed it to the subject who promptly claimed that it libelled him. This situation caused many authors to worry not only about libel but also about the fact that traditionally, all submissions to publishers are treated in confidence, which was broken in this instance.

There are several defences against a libel claim. One is that it is true, but naturally you will have to be able to prove this. Another is for you to prove that your writing does not actually defame the person making the complaint. A third defence is that your statements constitute a matter of public interest, but if you were judged to have acted maliciously toward the person claiming the libel this would fail. An apology and damages – which can be high depending on the severity of the libel – are the usual penalties.

The warranty clauses in your contract (for a discussion of these see under 'Author Obligations' in chapter 9) carry wording by which the author indemnifies the publisher against loss or damages caused by an action for libel. Even if a case is settled out of court, there can be hefty legal bills to pay and sometimes a book containing libel must be withdrawn from sale. Very large sums can be involved. Although it is possible to buy insurance policies to cover libel, they are extremely expensive for individual authors. Publishing companies usually have insurance policies that can be extended to cover authors, but publishers are sometimes cagey about admitting to this for fear that authors will then be cavalier in their attitude to protecting against including libellous statements.

Houses that will cover their authors usually only do so for specific books. The publisher's insurance company will only extend cover if the author in turn gives many more assurances about the material in the manuscript, so it is necessary for them to include lengthy detailed paragraphs in your contract warranty clause section to be sure that your warranty to them mirrors the language in their insurance policy. These can result in very tight warranties indeed. Another feature of being included in the publisher's libel insurance is that they will always state that the publisher has to pay some of any amount claimed from the insurance company – the 'excess' – and the publisher will expect to pass that obligation on to you. If you think there is a danger of being sued for libel, and if your publisher is prepared to cover you with their libel insurance, always ask what this figure is. If it is very high it could completely negate the benefits of being covered by the insurance, especially if you have had to sign tighter warranty clauses as a result.

You can libel someone in a novel. The most obvious dangers are including real people in your novel and using their real names – always something to avoid, I would say, unless they are historical characters who lived long enough ago for their neighbours and immediate family to be dead, and therefore unable to accuse you of libel. For it is not only the famous who may sue.

If you say that Al Capone was a tax dodger, you can be sure that he won't sue you: he's safely dead and he was convicted of tax crimes anyway, so it's a matter of recorded fact. But if you imply that his whole family was averse to taxation, you might find that some ancient law-abiding Chicago librarian, long retired, pops out of the mid-west suburbs with a lawsuit – suggesting that you have brought them into disrepute because of their relationship to Uncle Al.

One of my clients wrote a novel loosely based on a real husband and wife who were spies for the Soviet Union in the 1980s. All the names of real people were changed, even though the couple were convicted of their crimes. When the publisher read the manuscript their lawyers queried the scenes where the author had suggested that the couple's neighbours probably knew what they were doing in the years before they were caught. The lawyer knew that the author had created the characters of the neighbours, but the problem was that not only might the real neighbours have sued because they believed that their friends thought the characters were based on them, but there was also the possibility they might have threatened a lawsuit just to see if they could win a settlement. Nuisance cases have to be defended in the same way as genuine cases, and can cost just as much. The author had to change the storyline.

A novel was written a few years ago that seemed to include the character of an ex-boyfriend of the author: he was by this time a reasonably well-known critic, and the character that might have been based on him was unpleasant. Proofs of the novel had been sent out to reviewers on magazines and newspapers, and an article was written (by a journalist who knew both the author and the critic) pointing out the similarities between the novel's character and the critic, and also having some fun at the critic's expense. The critic let it be known that he was very angry at his supposed portrayal in the novel and the publisher, believing he had the right to sue, refused to go ahead with publication.

Another publishing house took the book on and published it very successfully a season later. They had gambled on the fact that the critic, who had been made to look a little pompous and perhaps foolish in his reaction to the novel, would not want further publicity and would not actually sue: they were right.

This might have had a different outcome if the original publisher had gone ahead: publication of the novel so close to the unpleasant publicity of the original article might indeed have prompted the critic to sue. And the novel might not have been so widely reviewed when it was eventually published if it had not gained the notoriety of being dropped by its first publisher. We will never know, but there is no doubt that there was a very real risk that the critic may have sued, and may have been successful if he had done so. The second publisher knew they were taking a calculated risk and they were lucky. This was evidence that different publishers take different views on the libel advice they are given by their lawyers.

So you've written a novel containing no real names, you didn't base it on real people, and you've made up the entire storyline. No point in thinking about libel at all, is there? Wrong.

If you are specific about location, if you name a school, a yacht, a restaurant, a choir, a company, then be very careful that any naughty or nasty doing that you attach to your characters can't in some way suggest a real person who might work at a school with that name, own a yacht or a restaurant with that name, sing in a choir with that name, or own a company with that name.

One of my clients used to work in television and, not surprisingly, used the television business as the backdrop to one of her novels. The television business, like movies, has its fair share of larger than life people so she had no problem in filling her novel with memorable characters. When she finished it, she realized that life was imitating art. She had created a character of a television station boss and, by the time she finished the novel, someone with very similar characteristics was running one of London's television channels! So her wholly fictitious protagonist had to change from a tall, blond Australian to a short, dark Scot!

Some people, often in the public eye and with over-active egos, can be flattered by being portrayed in novels, however unpleasantly: but it's never worth the risk. If you are sued, even before a case is brought to court, it's possible for lawyers to succeed in obtaining an injunction against your book, which would mean it being withdrawn from sale. The injunction could last for months and, if the complaint were upheld, the book could be ordered to be pulped, and you could be faced with damages and with your own and your opponent's costs. This could be followed by a lawsuit from your publisher, suing for their losses and expenses, which might well include editorial costs, printing and distribution – not a great way to further your career as a novelist. It's far better to try to avoid libel problems at the outset.

Plagiarism

If you copy from one author it's plagiarism. If you copy from two it's research – Wilson Mizner

Despite the quote that starts this section, plagiarism isn't funny at all. Plagiarism is the act of using someone else's words and passing them off as your own. It is theft and, quite rightly, you can be sued by the copyright owner. Facts are in the public domain: plagiarism occurs when you use the same, or very similar words and word order as another writer, or when you copy a storyline. It is not enough to paraphrase or to slightly alter part of the plot. If the original copyright holder can prove enough similarities to convince a court that you must have seen their text before writing your own, then you will be judged guilty.

A cliché in publishing holds that only six original plots have ever been written, so an author could, when thinking about plagiarism, panic to the point of being unable to write again! This is where your actions must be governed by practicality. Every detective novel features a crime, a baddy who is going to be found out and our hero who is going to unearth them, so using that shape for your murder mystery will not necessarily leave you open to a charge of plagiarism. It is if you include sub-plots whose details closely resemble the other work, with characters who have similar mannerisms or names or backgrounds, and dialogue that echoes the novel too, that you will find yourself in trouble.

Several academic works have been written about the pre-existence of stories that suggest that every single play that Shakespeare wrote had a recognizable source in someone else's work, so he might be advised to be more careful if he were writing today. If you can prove that you have not read the material you are accused of plagiarizing, you may be able to establish your innocence. But bear in mind that it is extremely difficult to prove a negative, especially if there are close similarities between your work and another's.

Unconscious plagiarism can occur if you are read widely in the area in which you also publish, or if you had to read a lot to research your own book. This is more likely to result in copying aspects of another author's plot rather than whole sentences of their work appearing in your own. If you are, say, an avid reader of detective novels and also a writer of them, you do need to take great care that you do not reproduce parts of another writer's work in any form.

Correction of proofs

After the text of your novel has been edited and checked for all or any problems, the editor should let you see the copy-edited typescript for one last check. Once everything is agreed, the final version will be sent, via the production department, to a typesetter. If you supplied the book on disk and the copy-editing has been done on-screen, this will be in the form of a corrected disk with a clean printout, otherwise it will be a marked typescript plus uncorrected disk (or no disk at all if you didn't supply one). A lot of books are set to standard designs, or series styles, but if you're lucky you will get individual treatment. Before going for setting your manuscript will be given to a designer who will specify the text font and page layout, and style the title page, chapter openings, headings, extracts, etc.

After a while, you will receive proofs, which you will be asked to check by a certain date. Proof correction is a tedious business but vital. A good publisher will supply two sets of proofs to the author so they can keep one as a check and send one back, corrected. It is worth learning the accepted forms of proof corrections because it means there will be less room for error when the printer receives your corrected pages. Most of the publishing directories have a section on proof correction marks. Some publishing companies also supply helpful tips on how to mark the proofs.

Good publishing companies have the proofs read against the manuscript by a professional proofreader at the same time as the author reads them blind. But, as I've mentioned in chapter 9, authors and agents are disturbed by the current trend for publishers to cease to obligate themselves to carry out this task. It suggests that publishers who can't be bothered to pay a proofreader have little pride in the look of the books they publish. It can be argued that the words on the page are ultimately the responsibility of the author, but I would say that a responsible publisher should proofread too. Few authors will be as good as a professional proofreader. But it is important that you are assiduous in paying attention to correcting your proofs.

The marketing plan

If a publisher wants very much to publish you, and especially if they are having to compete with other publishers for the right to your novel, they will sometimes offer to – or be asked to – prepare a marketing plan, setting out how they intend to promote and sell your book. Although you would think that there are a finite number of ways in which design and cash, advertising and promotion can be used to sell books, the different ways they can be combined by clever publishers sometimes do seem infinite. I have seen hundreds of marketing plans and, although some items will be common to many, I am constantly surprised and delighted at the innovations that energetic and creative people can think of.

All publishers will have some kind of marketing plan for every book they publish, but most books will be given a very small – or no – specific budget to spend on promotion, and will be promoted by means of the regular marketing tools provided by the publisher, such as their catalogue, the regular sales information supplied to their bookseller and wholesaler customers, together with meetings and telephone calls, their sales conferences and, these days, their Website, if they have one.

But a 'big' book, by an author the publisher believes can achieve high sales, will be allocated an individual promotion budget and will have an individual marketing plan prepared for it. Whether or not you, the author, get to see this depends upon several ingredients.

If the publisher has bid for your book in an auction, they may well have sent a marketing plan to you or your agent as part of their effort to persuade you they are the best publisher for you. You might be lucky enough to see marketing plans from several publishers in this way. There is no doubt that when I ran the auction for Michael Ridpath's *Free to Trade*, the marketing plans from four publishers with similar monetary offers, influenced us very much when Michael and I had to decide which publisher to choose.

If the occasion is not an auction, but your publisher is planning to promote you so as to increase your sales, ask for a marketing proposal. I am in favour of authors and agents becoming closely involved in sales and marketing and believe that this can only increase the potential for success. It can be very interesting indeed to see what budget your publisher is proposing to spend on your book. And it is even more interesting to check that it is all spent as planned.

I keep all marketing proposals that are sent to me for my clients and file them with the contracts so that they can be checked regularly. If a publisher has been able to purchase a book by promising us a more impressive marketing budget than a rival publisher, it seems to me to be only reasonable that they should be asked to attach these promises to the contract, and that they should provide figures after publication to show us where and how the expenditure was used.

Keeping the marketing proposals can provide useful ideas in the future when you look back over them. I use them to provide ideas to overseas publishers when they come to promote the translated editions of the same book. The more impressive a campaign one publisher runs for that author, the more likely it is that I will be able to persuade others to do the same.

The items covered by a marketing proposal will include format, jacket, advertising (both trade and consumer), point-of-sale material for the trade, and author promotion.

Format

The shape and size of your book is part of the marketing plan. Publishers usually spend time thinking about the format in which they will publish before offering to buy a title. There are fewer formats used for fiction than non-fiction. For example, a 'landscape' format (broader than it is high) is often used for illustrated non-fiction but seldom for fiction. Formats go in and out of fashion as the trade reacts to price changes and successes and failures of the past season. As I've said before, the death of fiction in hardback has been predicted in every one of the many years I have worked in publishing, but still novels appear in hard covers.

At the simplest level, the larger the page size of a book, the more expensive it will be to print and the higher the retail price. It therefore follows that if a publisher proposes a smaller format with a consequent lowering of the sale price, one would look for a correspondingly longer print run to keep income at a reasonable level for both publisher and author. In paperback, what is known as the mass-market, or 'rack-sized' paperback is more properly called 'A' format: 181 x 111 mm. The next size up is 'B' format (198 x 129 mm). All the other, larger paperback formats are known collectively as trade paperbacks, or sometimes 'C' format, with the two most common being 'Demy' (216 x 135 mm) and 'Royal' (234 x 153 mm). These are approximate measurements that may vary slightly among publishers and printers.

These are conventions that the trade applies to formats. A very commercial mass-market novel is more likely to appear as an 'A' format paperback, while a more upmarket literary novel is likely to be published as one of the larger formats. Publishers choose formats with care and will be happy to explain the thinking behind their decisions.

Jacket

The jacket or cover is the single most important part of the selling of your book. Any advertising or point-of-sale material will be tied to it, and it is common for a jacket style, and sometimes the exact image, to be carried through from the first hardback edition to subsequent paperback printings.

Many people in the publishing company are involved in the design of covers. It may be the acquiring editor who first has an idea for the way it should look, but they will almost certainly consult with sales and marketing and publicity staff. Then the editor will brief the head of the art or design department, either in detail if they want to see a specific look, or in general terms if they know which part of the market they want the cover to appeal to, but wish for more input from the design team. The art department head will then brief a staff member or a freelance designer, who may in turn commission work from an illustrator or photographer. When the image is delivered, decisions must be made about colours, framing, lettering: there are many components that make up the designs that reach the bookstores.

A jacket is so important that a publisher may have a treatment in mind at the time they make their offer to buy the book. For this reason, I rarely agree with an author who wants to have cover *approval* in their contract because I believe that the people who are responsible for selling – the publishers – should have the last word on what it looks like. But I do believe strongly that the author should have the right to be *consulted* on what their book looks like. This means that the author's views should be sought by the publisher at a time when their comments can be taken into account. It is essential for the author and publisher to establish a good relationship from the start if this is to work well.

Publishers seldom want to publish a book with a cover that an author really dislikes, but it is important that authors remember that there may be reasons they are unaware of for the choices their publisher has made about their cover. If you are unhappy with yours, say so. Let your editor know what you think, but be constructive in your criticism and ask the publisher to articulate the reasons for their decisions. If what you want on the cover flies in the face of accepted wisdom in the trade you should think twice before pressing your case or you could damage your book's sales potential. Publishing is a collaborative process and nothing demonstrates this more clearly than the production of an image for a book's cover.

Author consultation on cover design

An instance where this worked well for us occurred with the cover design of a first novel by Anna Davis, *The Dinner*. Anna's editor at Hodder, who published the book in early 1999, briefed the cover designer in summer 1998. For a variety of reasons, the rough design was delivered later than any of us might have liked and when it arrived it was stylish, but – Anna and I felt – not quite right. The novel is literary, quirky, dark and contemporary, with a little magic realism, all of which contrive to leave the reader rather on edge as a dinner party goes hideously wrong. The first cover rough that we were shown, in August 1998, used bright colours,with an offbeat wine bottle design, but it didn't quite deliver the right message. Anna (a literary agent herself, with a professional's view of the trade) made some positive suggestions to Hodder and then we waited while they came up with another design. There were several people at Hodder who really liked the first design, but they were not so positive about it that they were not willing to try again in the hope of producing something that everyone thought was right.

Time passed and I started to get anxious because London always receives a stream of overseas visitors from publishing houses around the world during September, prior to the Frankfurt Book Fair in early October. I had to show them a cover image we hoped would be changed; Hodder themselves had to use that first design to sell-in to the bookshop chains. Anna became anxious that the publication date would have to be postponed. I worried that the pre-publication sales would be depressed. Anna's editor at Hodder started her maternity leave: still we didn't have a new design. The publishing world travelled to Frankfurt, and talked and partied their way through the Fair. Then a few days after we had returned to London, a new cover rough was sent to Anna and I – but not just one, two. We were unanimous: the surrealist fork with a hint of blood about it was preferred to the teacups – the novel was about a dinner party after all! The cover that the published book carried is absolutely right for it, and even those people who liked the first design were won over. An extremely tense few months resulted in a cover design in which everyone had confidence. A good outcome after quite a bit of worry: but it was handled with friendliness and grace on all sides, which meant everyone was pulling in the same direction. There was no feeling of confrontation at any point.

Author promotion

A speech is like a love affair. Any fool can start it, but to end it requires considerable skill – Lord Mancroft

The range of possibilities include interviews with magazines, newspapers and radio stations, both regional and national; bookshop events such as book signings and talks; book festival appearances etc. You can help enormously here by producing any and all items of interest from your life, and by remembering every useful contact you have ever made. Local newspapers are very useful, and local radio really does seem to sell books. But you have to be able to talk well and interestingly: you have to be able to give them something for their audience if they are to give you their programme or pages on which to promote your book. Too blatant a 'plug' for your book can be counter-productive: if you come over as a hard-sell you could turn off your audience instead of interesting them.

Humour bonds an audience to you more quickly than anything else but be careful of actually telling jokes unless you are very good at it. Gentle situation-based humour, or self-deprecating humour at which the British seem to excel, work much better in winning an audience to your side.

If you are not experienced at public speaking it is worth taking time to work on this. Local authorities run evening courses in public speaking and confidence building, and there are some very good specialized one-to-one public speaking courses that include radio and television training, but these are extremely expensive.

As with anything to be learned, practice makes a big difference. Record your voice on an audio cassette, get friends to help you video yourself while speaking. If you are able to criticize your own performance, you can learn a lot and improve the way you are able to promote your work effectively.

11 Selling to the publishing team

Think about human nature. Most of us naturally wish to reciprocate if someone has been pleasant to us, paid us a compliment or made a kind gesture unnecessarily. Exactly the same thing works in publishing. Although some writers seem to work to the principle of using the stick rather than the carrot, I believe that the stick only works in certain conditions. When you lose the upper hand a stick loses its efficacy at once. But if you are admired and liked, the chances are that will last for longer.

I heard two lovely stories that illustrate this, both about the same writer, the late actor David Niven. He was famous for playing urbane, sophisticated, witty characters and seemed to be one himself. Everyone who met him in publishing, through the very successful publications of his two volumes of memoirs, *The Moon's a Balloon* and *Bring on the Empty Horses*, had pleasant things to say of him.

The two stories involve different sections of the publishing trade: first, UK booksellers. Niven's publisher gave a party for publication of his first book, inviting staff members from Hamish Hamilton, booksellers from important chains and shops and reviewers from national newspapers. The actor was, as usual, charming and friendly to the people he already knew from the publishing company and then moved to talk to a group of booksellers. Apparently, for twenty minutes or more he kept them amused and entertained – and flattered – as he said things to them that suggested he envied them their jobs as they used their knowledge of the business to decide which books to back and which to ignore, wielding power enough to make or break titles. Hamish Hamilton reported that some of the buyers from the bookshops present at the party then doubled their initial orders.

The next story involves the American publisher of the same book, Putnam. Niven was being escorted by a senior executive of the company to a drinks party for him in their offices, but before arriving at the boardroom where the guests awaited him he asked to be excused for a minute or two. He went back to the reception desk and asked the way to the post room, where he chatted to a number of quite junior staff. Then he joined the executives for drinks. Apparently, every time he visited Putnam's office after that, he would pop in to the post room, greet people by name and ask about their family members. There are two lessons to learn from this. First, that David Niven was a gregarious and charming man. Second, that he was very, very smart: even though he was the kind of person who would chat naturally to people, he knew that this would be helpful in selling his book. Like the fact that the UK booksellers increased their orders, there is a pay-off to the Putnam story too. Some time later, his Putnam editor took a call from the biggest US television chat show: if they could have a copy of Niven's book rushed to them that evening, they might give him the main spot on their show the next day. Putnam's office was just about to close, it was pouring with rain and staff members were streaming into the elevators on their way home, yet every-single post-room person who was still around – and several secretaries who had met the author – volunteered to take the book across town!

If, without seeming unctuous or ingratiating, you can make friends with staff in your publishing company, it will only be helpful, even if, at the time, you can't see how any direct benefit could come of it. I would think this was too obvious to write down if I hadn't, over the years, personally witnessed authors doing just the opposite.

I have represented clients in the past (note that phrase!) who have alienated my staff by being obnoxious to junior members. It's plain bad manners on one level, and very silly professionally at the other end of the scale. Receptionists, secretaries and assistants wield an enormous amount of power, out of all proportion to their job titles. If you want to speak to their boss, don't be rude to them! I hate the kind of bullying that allows someone to be rude to a junior staff member because they know that person can't answer back. Assistants rarely tell tales to me about rude clients, but I often find out because of a chance remark, or because I notice, say, that people make faces when a particular person telephones, and are not anxious to take the call. It's a very different situation when some of our other authors call or drop in to our office.

Being friendly, polite and charming makes all kinds of social situations more pleasant and the same ingredients work wonders in a business environment.

Head office

Selling yourself and your book to the publishing company's main office staff is begun when the first submission is made to the editor. I always give editors information about the writer, as well as about their writing. It's only natural that editors are interested to know what authors are like, what their family situation is, how they handle publicity events etc. The more personal details I can give that are relevant to the author's eventual publication success, the better. If I have positive press cuttings about the author from previous publications I send those too, and a list of foreign sales of their previous books, all of which presents the author as a successful professional.

If you haven't been published before, information about your current career can be helpful: authors who have been successful in other fields are always looked upon favourably. I know that the editor will share all the information at their disposal with other departments who are necessarily part of the equation when they are putting their offer together, such as sales and marketing and publicity.

Once you have accepted an offer from the publisher and as you get closer to your publication date, you will start to meet other people who are part of the publishing team. Always take care to remember names: if you're hopeless at it (as I am) admit it and ask for their business card. One easy way to collect cards is to carry some yourself and proffer them when you are introduced to someone new: they will almost certainly give you theirs in return. But if they don't, it is certainly not considered rude or odd to take a moment to write down their name and job title. This is your new profession and these people will have a great influence on whether you make a success of it or not. They will only be flattered that you are taking so much care to remember them.

With junior staff this is not such a good ploy, and they are unlikely to have printed business cards. So make a point, once they have left the room, of asking someone such as your editor for the name of the secretary who called you a cab, or the assistant who was particularly helpful. You'll probably speak to them several times during your time with the company and they will be flattered and pleased if you can remember their names. You'd be surprised at how effective this will be in making people want to do just that little bit more for you, and your book.

In my experience, Americans are much better at this than any other nationality, perhaps because they are brought up to believe that ambition is acceptable, even laudable. The British, on the other hand, are worse at networking than any other nation I know of, perhaps because they are brought up to believe that success is somehow vulgar. I'm with the Yanks on this one.

Obviously, it's pleasant, and perhaps flattering to you, if you are introduced to the very senior staff, or the directors of the company. But don't push for this at once if there is no good reason. There is nothing worse for a writer fairly new to publishing to gain a reputation for being 'pushy'. You might think that is an odd thing for an agent to believe as agents are often caricatured as the epitome of pushiness. But I believe that the greatest form of salesmanship is to make someone want what you are selling – whether it's a manuscript, a box of soap powder or yourself.

If word filters up to the people at the top of the company that you are a talented writer, you behave professionally, and – my goodness – those who have met you really like you too, then you can be sure the managing director is going to want to meet you at some point. This may well be less haphazard than it seems. Your editor knows that if they are working with an author that their boss likes and admires, they stand a better chance of being successful when they press for advertising monies, or a bigger print run, or a bigger advance for your next contract, so it may be the editor who makes sure that the board members know how much you are valued.

If you do not find that you are gradually meeting a wider range of other people in the publishing company, suggest to your editor that you would like to, or have your agent broach the subject. You will certainly need to meet at least the publicist who has been assigned to you, and, depending on how big their launch plans are, people in the design department, and sales and marketing for both home and export.

Remember to share information with your agent and your editor. If you do anything yourself that brings you visibility, keep everyone informed. Many of our novelists also write short stories for magazines and newspapers. We make sure that the publisher knows well in advance when a story will be published. They are thus able to let the sales force and the bookshops know. And because we arrange for the magazines always to mention the author's latest novel, an extra piece of publicity is achieved. If you are contacted by a local group and asked to give a talk – let your publisher know. The more information you share, the greater the chance of it being useful.

Several of our novelists also publish journalism: the regular columns written by authors like Joseph O'Connor and Sheila O'Flanagan keep their names in front of potential buyers of their fiction.

I also keep my clients' editors up to date on overseas sales of their books, and of course on news of film or television sales. Even though another contract for a translated edition will have little direct impact on the English language sales, and the sale of film or television rights may well occur years before the film or series reaches the public, positive news about good things happening for the author and their book help to keep the author in the publisher's thoughts and promote the image of a more and more successful author.

If we've had a particularly wide range of rights sales for an author I will sometimes write to the head of the company or other department managers, and if an overseas publisher has had a particular success or has done something really innovative for my author, I will let the marketing director or the publicity director at the UK house know about it. Shared information never does any harm, and it can sometimes be very helpful.

One thing that I find extremely effective is a meeting, arranged by the editor, where the publisher's plans for the book are explained to the author, some months before publication. I go with my client, which leaves the writer free to listen and look while I make copious notes. If the author has not been published before, they won't have anything to which to compare the launch plans; but I have been to dozens of meetings like this, and will be able to ask questions at the time and give my view of the plans – and my notes – to the author afterwards.

These meetings often involve the people who will be responsible for designing the cover, planning the publicity campaign, designing the advertisements, and selling to bookshops at home and abroad. It's an ideal environment for the author and the publishing team to get to know each other, but can only happen for the relatively small number of authors who are published with some prominence.

Not all authors, by any means, will have the luxury of this meeting, and if there is little planned, asking for such a meeting would be counter-productive. It's a matter of tailoring your expectations to the relevant situations.

If you don't often get a chance to visit your publisher but know that you will be able to visit their office at a particular time, let your editor know your proposed date in advance and ask if you can drop in to meet a few people informally.

We have a number of South African writers as clients, many of them represented by Isobel Dixon, herself South African. One of her clients, a novelist called Deon Meyer, knew he would be visiting London at a time when his first novel had just been bought by Hodder, so this was a good opportunity for him to meet his editor.

Isobel arranged with his editor for a number of informal meetings with a range of people at Hodder who were involved with Deon's book. He is modest and charming, and ended up spending a considerable amount of time in Hodder's offices as each person kept him longer than the schedule called for. We heard from another Hodder editor that Deon's progress around the offices could be charted by the hubbub that followed him as each meeting got larger: people were reluctant to leave him and were following to the next meeting!

I was in Hodder's office myself that same day with another client, Glenn Meade, the Irish thriller writer. He also has a considerable fan club within Hodder (and at his American publishing house where there is much competition in the publicity department to work on his campaigns!), but on this occasion Glenn and I found our marketing meeting was a little held up as a couple of people had to be prised away from Deon!

I'm not suggesting that charm school tactics should be laid on thickly to achieve a successful publication. But normal good manners and courteous behaviour can achieve much more than many people give them credit for.

It's so easy to complain about things that go wrong. But remembering to thank a designer for a particularly striking jacket, or a publicity department staff member who waited with you until your overdue train eventually arrived, is always remembered gratefully. Don't underestimate how much it can do for your career.

The sales team

I am keen for my authors to get to know staff in the sales force, and vice versa. These are the people at the sharp end of the trade, the people who really do make a difference to the day-to-day sales of the book. If you, the author, can strike up a working relationship with the sales person responsible for, say, your local area, that can be directly helpful to you. They might be able to introduce you to booksellers near to where you live, which could result in bookshop events, or a display card announcing your book to be 'by a local author'. Every piece of promotion can result in more sales.

The sales team have no illusions: they know how hard it is to sell to bookshops and to the consumer, day after day. So listening to them if they offer constructive comments about promotion, or covers, or when they have feedback from booksellers about your title, can be extremely informative.

If managers or directors in the sales and marketing departments get on particularly well with an author, they will put a little more effort into the book, and every extra effort makes the whole publication package just that bit bigger and more effective.

I asked a number of sales and marketing directors recently what single thing they thought an author could best do to make a difference to the way their book sold. Without exception they all said the same, and it wasn't original or startling: an author should be prepared to do their bit for publicity and behave well. A triumph for common sense.

Occasionally authors are invited to visit bookshops with someone from the sales department. This is separate to bookshop events, where the public are invited to meet the author, and where the author might give a talk or sign books. Visits to shops with a sales person usually involve informal chats with the bookshop manager, the signing of copies from the shop's stock for sale later, and may well involve conversations about other books and authors the shop is selling – or being persuaded to buy – from the publisher. These opportunities are ideal for forging a bond with the sales person and also for getting to know bookshop staff. But remember how many books the publisher and bookseller have in common: believing you are their only concern can lead to a blow to the ego!

The more you are asked to be involved with the sales team, the surer the sign that the publisher values you and believes in your book. Possibly the highest accolade is to be invited to attend a sales conference.

The sales conference

A sales conference involves the publisher bringing together all or part of the sales team, together with staff from the editorial, publicity and marketing departments, to exchange information. Editors will present their books scheduled for publication in the next season; the publicity and marketing staff will present their plans for the titles to be promoted; and the sales director and his team will set sales targets per title by geographical area or customer. Many companies bring key staff over from important export markets. In a well-run company all of them will listen to feedback from the sales team themselves.

Companies organize their conferences in a variety of ways. Most will have one large one, involving everyone, for each publishing 'season', which in the UK tends to be spring and autumn. Many will also have regional sales conferences, smaller ones for each main geographical area. Some companies will takes their staff to exotic locations, with extravagant social events organized for the evenings. Some organize single day presentations of key titles from their forthcoming publications.

Transworld in the UK gained quite a reputation for flying their staff to sunny resorts in the middle of the British winter for their main sales conference of the year. But I heard that it was obligatory to take part in a fancy dress party at each conference. Well, they say there's no such thing as a free lunch! Actually, to be fair to Transworld, everyone always reported that they were highly enjoyable, with additional fun to be gained from the fact that the most senior staff always threw themselves into the games with gusto. There are few things more pleasurable than seeing your boss being prepared to make a complete idiot of themselves in public.

Most publishers will use sales conferences as opportunities to introduce star authors to their staff, and vice versa. This can only happen for a relatively small number of writers. If you are invited it is an honour, so don't think of refusing as one of my clients told me she was planning to, some years ago. I gave her a good talking to, and she changed her mind. She should have known better as she was an ex-publisher. In the event, she went, thoroughly enjoyed herself, and was much praised for her speech and general graciousness.

For an author to have access to so many people from the publishing company is a terrific opportunity to network, make friends, find out even more about how the company works and the details of exactly who does what, and how they are planning to do their bit for you.

An author at a sales conference is often asked to give a short speech, which is an opportunity to say a little about the book, about themselves, and perhaps an occasion to thank the publishing company for the effort they are putting into the publication. Your editor or publicist should brief you on what is wanted, how long you should speak for, and exactly who else will be attending. If they don't offer this information, ask for it before the conference.

Some publishers invite authors to a part of their presentations during the day, other invitations may be to a dinner when the presentations have finished. Sometimes an invitation extends to both.

Most writers invited to a sales conference dinner will be offered a room at the conference hotel so that they can stay overnight. A word of warning: publishers, and those in sales in particular, have been known to have a drink or two after a sales conference dinner. They sometimes invite authors to join them. Doing so can engender feelings of bonhomie and immense well-being – until the next morning. It is better to stop drinking before you forget that these people have the success of your book in their hands. If you do drink too much try not to do or say anything outrageously unpleasant to anyone sober enough to remember it. And take comfort in the fact that the liver is the only organ in the body than regenerates itself!

If you do get the chance to meet so many members of the publishing team under these favourable conditions, don't waste the opportunity. Listen carefully to everything you are told, not only about your own marketing, but any other authors' books, whose presentations you may hear. Information about your relative importance can be put to good use. Interesting promotions for others might give you ideas for suggestions you can make to your editor or agent for your own title. Don't hesitate to ask questions, but do try to be constructive rather than negative. Nothing is more wearing, and counter-productive in the long-term, than an author who continually complains, or who shows their jealousy at what is being done for other authors. Positive suggestions, rather than constant moaning, are far more likely to get favourable results.

12 Who sells where

In America only the successful writer is important, in France all writers are important, in England no writer is important, in Australia you have to explain what a writer is
– Geoffrey Cotterell

Export markets for books in English

The English language is one of the few languages that is regularly divided between publishers. Others are French (France itself, and French publishing Canadian publishers), Spanish (Spain, Mexico and South America) and Portuguese (Portugal and Brazil), although it is still more usual for publishers who work in these languages to buy world rights in that language, to print in one place and ship to the other locations. Only books expected to achieve really big sales will be able to achieve more than one contract for these languages.

Most languages, these included, tend to be published worldwide by only one publisher. German language publishers, for instance, will buy worldwide rights in German and will export their own edition throughout the German-speaking world: to Germany, Austria and Switzerland.

The English language has bred several major centres of publishing. In order of size they are: America, Britain, Australia, Canada and South Africa. It is likely that many commercial novels will be bought separately by publishers in Britain and in America: but only very successful authors find they can sell their work separately to Australian, Canadian and South African publishers as well. To publish separately in any or all of these smaller markets, the books must be highly commercial and capable of sustaining print runs large enough to make it worthwhile printing separately in these locations, or must be of very special local appeal to these markets.

Australia is capable of selling huge quantities of books but the number of non-Australian authors who are separately published and printed there is small. Most non-Australian authors' books will be exported to Australia by their UK or US publishers and sold by

Australian publishers as part of the distribution arrangements they have with UK or US houses.

Many of the publishers in Australia, Canada and South Africa are successful because they publish local authors: they will only buy in authors from overseas in exceptional circumstances.

If you live in Australia, Canada or South Africa is it well worth-while approaching local publishers first: they will know you are available for publicity, and if your novel is set locally it is more appealing to a publisher. If the book is successful there, that publisher will either belong to a larger group, and so can perhaps recommend publication elsewhere through their own group offices, or will have contacts with publishers overseas and so can either sell, or recommend, your book to others.

Most writers in the English language will find themselves being published by either an American or British publisher, and therefore having their book sold by this originating publisher to the markets around the world that make up the export market licensed (with the home territory) to that first publisher. Chapter 9 has more explanation of territories.

Who sells you where is determined by the first contract you sign. In the past, UK and US publishers were prepared to divide the world between themselves in a civilized manner. The UK publisher's home market was usually the British Isles (England, Scotland, Wales, Northern Ireland and the Republic of Ireland, known as the 'home market') plus, as their exclusive export market, Australia, New Zealand and South Africa. There are other, smaller parts of the 'old' Commonwealth usually included as well.

If the author is British and the British publisher is buying rights before an American publisher has committed to the book, the British publisher will argue strongly to include Canada in their exclusive export market. The author or the agent then has to decide whether they think they have a good chance of selling American rights (and including Canada in the American publisher's exclusive export market) or if it is likely they will be able to sell English language rights in Canada to a Canadian publisher. If they think it unlikely that they will accomplish either of these rights sales, then obviously it would be wise to let the British publisher export to Canada. It is in no one's interest for the book to be excluded from sale in Canada, but you might sometimes find you have to take a view on this earlier than you would wish, and before you have had time to explore the overseas markets in sufficient depth. This is where an agent's knowledge of the international publishing scene becomes so useful.

The US publisher would expect, as their home market, the United

States of America, its territories and dependencies, and the Philippines. They may also argue for Canada to be included as their exclusive export market (see previous paragraph).

The respective strengths of particular UK and US publishers in Canada is something that an agent will know and can discuss with their client, as well as the different income an author can expect to receive when Canada is paid for as an export market by the different English language markets. Obviously, the ideal is to sell Canadian right to a Canadian publisher when you will then be paid a home royalty on the Canadian retail price. But this is seldom possible as the small publishing industry in Canada can only absorb relatively few overseas authors published by Canadian publishers, as opposed to being distributed there on behalf of their UK or US publishers.

Other territories that UK and US publishers may say they require exclusively (with varying degrees of success depending on the policy of the house, the size of the house and therefore their arguing power, and the balance of power in the deal between the publishing house and the author) can be Israel, Egypt, Hong Kong (especially now that it has passed out of British control) and India.

Europe is another issue: this is dealt with in chapter 9. International legislation is impinging more and more on agents' day-to-day work and authors' rights to license their work. The European Union single market policy, intended to create a freedom, has in practical terms become a market restriction for English language publishers wherever they are located. EU law says that any commodity that may be sold in any part of the European Union territory, must be available throughout the EU territory – there may be no restrictions within it – the market may not be divided. Anyone who has the right to sell anything within *any* part of the European territory may sell that product *throughout* it. This has meant that with Britain being a part of the European Union, UK and US publishers face a dilemma.

Every territorial agreement for an English language book now has to address this issue afresh, as British publishers, rightly and legally, I believe, argue that EU legislation means they must acquire exclusive sales rights throughout Europe (or at least the countries that are members of the European Union) in their contracts. If the British publishers do not control Europe exclusively, and continue to sign contracts in which Europe is a non-exclusive market for both UK and US editions, any American edition that enters Europe (legally if the Americans have the right to sell their edition in Europe) may, under EU law, also be shipped into Britain, which would violate the British publisher's right to their home market.

Because EU law supersedes the laws of each member state, British publishers would not be able to sue under their own contract. And unless they had bought the British rights from the American publisher, there would be no one to sue anyway. If the British contract was with the author, there would be no point in the British publisher suing the author because the author was not in breach: the argument would be with the American publisher. But if the British publisher had no contractual relationship over the title with the American publisher, there was nothing to accuse them of: catch-22.

British publishers take the view that they must obtain exclusive Europe because EU and British lawyers have advised them they would be breaking the law if they accepted a contract that split the EU.

American publishers argue that this is nonsense and they should continue to have the right to sell their books, in English, alongside the British publishers in what used to be the 'open market' of Europe where the UK and the US have traditionally competed with each other (and, of course, with the locally published translations in each individual European language market – Dutch in Holland, Italian in Italy, Norwegian in Norway etc.).

In this argument British publishers have been aided and supported by British agents. The Americans argue that the Brits have interpreted the legislation to suit themselves. If the American publishers were able to maintain their right to entry to Europe, EU law could be used to allow them free and unencumbered right of entry to the whole of the British Isles: American books could sell alongside British books in Britain and the British publishers would no longer have any exclusive home market whatsoever. How would American publishers react if the situation were reversed, and British editions started to make their way into the United States?

This became a huge issue in the early 90s. Tempers ran high as publishers and agents argued every day over the interpretation of European Union law for every contract that was negotiated with British or with American publishers. British publishers and agents were told by their lawyers, and by lawyers in Brussels – headquarters of the EU – that anyone signing contracts that divided the EU territory (that could include publishers and authors) could face a fine, which at one point was set at 1000 ecus (the European Union common currency before the euro was introduced) *per contract, per day*.

In an attempt to reconcile the trade, I wrote an article to try to persuade publishing groups with imprints on each side of the Atlantic to start a dialogue at least within their own groups, so that New York and London would take the same view of a single contract if the publishers were within the same group. When the article appeared in *Publishing News*, one of the two weekly UK trade papers for publishing, the international marketing director for Bantam Doubleday Dell in New York harangued me on the telephone for two hours! He *didn't* think that American publishers were being unreasonable, he *did* think that British publishers, British lawyers and Brussels lawyers were all wrong-headed, reading the legislation wrong, and resistant to change. When I suggested mildly that perhaps it was in the interests of American publishers to take this view because it gave them access to a larger market in which to sell their editions, he was furious that I was in some way insulting the honour of his company. As he was actually Welsh, I would have found it funny if it hadn't been such a serious issue for the industry, and its writers. The more time we all spent arguing the issue, the longer it took to get contracts signed, and therefore authors paid.

Still today, not one transatlantic group that I know of has produced a unified policy on this subject. Some years ago, I tackled the then chief executive of Penguin Books worldwide, Peter Mayer, on the subject. He looked rueful, and said that when he was in Britain he thought like a British publisher, and when in America like an American; and his view changed about halfway over the Atlantic as he flew back and forth. I told him I thought that was a terrible abrogation of responsibility when publishers and agents had to continue to reinvent the wheel every day as the same topic was approached wearily with every contract. It produced tedious, time-consuming and money-consuming arguments that went around in circles and never reached a conclusion that could be applied to the next deal. He agreed, but said he couldn't see a way to solve it: the two nations were each so entrenched in their views that the other was interpreting the legislation wrongly.

Since then the situation on this issue has calmed a little. Publishers seem to have resolved for themselves when the issue is worth a fight and when it isn't. The issue isn't settled, but is being circumvented. When UK houses are the first to buy a UK author, they fight for and get the EU as an exclusive market, so long as they pay UK home royalties on that market. When US houses buy a UK author after the UK house has signed up, the US publisher is usually prepared to accept that the EU is not available to them. But the American publisher will then expect to be offered Canada as an exclusive market in return for not being allowed into Europe. You take something away, you must offer something else in return.

My regret is that the Canadian market has become a bargaining tool between the American and British publishers, which means it is less likely to become a market one can sell independently to Canadian publishers. Canadian publishers are also less than happy about this, as you can imagine.

So: once the markets are allocated in the primary contracts, what happens to the markets that are designated as 'export markets'? They are treated in one of two ways. Either the originating publisher has a sister or subsidiary publisher in that market, or they have an 'agent' relationship with another publisher. Either way, the UK publisher will hope to receive orders for copies of their own edition from that export market.

If your publisher is part of a worldwide group, they may have an associated publisher within the group in the export markets.

If, for example, you sign up with Penguin UK, your export sales to Canada and Australia and South Africa will be handled by the Penguin companies in those markets.

If you are contracted originally to Penguin UK, and they have the exclusive right to sell your book to Canada, Australia and South Africa, they will treat those markets as export sales (with your contract having already provided for lower royalties in the export markets than in the home market) and their co-operating companies in those markets will act as sales agents for Penguin UK. This means that your originating publisher remains Penguin UK, who will direct the way you will be published, the look of the package, the extent to which they will promote you and the book etc.

The export sales department at your UK publisher will negotiate to sell your book to those 'export agent' publishing houses at export rates. Big discounts to the UK publishers' sister companies overseas mean lower royalties for you, even if it can look to authors and agents as though sales within a group, from one geographical location to another, is like the left hand selling to the right hand but taking a profit while doing so.

Let me be clear about the difference between your original contracting publisher *distributing* you in overseas English language markets, and your book being *published* separately in those same overseas English language markets. Although it may look as though the same things are happening – books shipped overseas, the title appears in the overseas' company's catalogue, books sent to reviewers in that market, some advertisements placed etc. – it is the structure of the deal with the writer and often the degree of effort that differs in the two different cases.

Distribution on behalf of another company means that the distributing publisher has not contracted with the author for the book. They do not print or design the book or cover, but take the package that has been produced by the originating publisher with whom they have a distribution agreement. This agreement will usually give them the right to be the exclusive importer of all of that publisher's books to their market, although they will not necessarily import every book on the publisher's list.

Pan Macmillan, for instance, will ship their books (including this one, I hope!) to Pan Macmillan Australia, and to Macmillan South Africa. But those companies will have views on what quantities they require of the titles on offer, and may not wish to take every title that Pan Macmillan in the UK has to offer, if they feel that some will not sell well in their market.

The UK publisher and their co-operating companies in the export markets will negotiate hard over the prices at which books are bought and sold, with the originating publisher often pushing for higher unit sales and a higher unit price than the distributor overseas is willing to commit to.

If the UK publisher really believes a book can be made to work well in export markets they will sometimes contribute to the cost of a promotion, or to taking the author to that market. They take advice from the overseas distributor about how the title and author suit that market.

One significant change in English language publishing in the last few years is the co-ordination of publication dates worldwide. Until a few years ago, the export editions of UK published books would come out in Canada, Australia and South Africa some two or three months after UK publication. Now, with the change of laws in some countries (Australia and more recently, New Zealand, in particular) and with on-line selling breaking down territorial boundaries, UK publishers must see their books published simultaneously in all the exclusive markets they control or risk losing sales to the American editions of the same book.

The Australian copyright law change at the beginning of the 90s shook up publishing considerably. Briefly, the Australian Government, having been lobbied energetically by Australian booksellers, passed a law that was intended to give their booksellers the right to order any overseas edition of their choice if the overseas publisher who controlled Australian distribution rights exclusively (usually, but not always, the British publisher) did not distribute copies in Australia within thirty days of the book first appearing in English in any market in the world. The act is a lot more complicated than this massive simplification, but for most books that is the effect of it.

This meant British publishers had to become much more aware of first publication dates of books they were buying from America, Canada or South Africa (the British publisher had to publish at the same time if they were going to protect their rights to the Australian market) and it meant that the British publisher had to prepare for simultaneous publication of their own edition in the UK and Australasia or risk seeing American copies being ordered by Australian booksellers.

British publishers (not always the first to embrace change, it has to be admitted) were alarmed, fearing that Australia was trying to put itself into an open market situation, i.e. one in which UK and US editions competed freely, as happens in Europe. And this was a scare that spread to authors and agents too. It is generally accepted in the publishing community that exclusive markets provide the atmosphere that persuades publishers to invest in authors, promotion and distribution. Publishers do tend to sell more intensively in their exclusive territories and that benefits authors too. Non-exclusive markets, where more than one edition of the same book competes for an audience, seldom receive the same degree of publicity and promotion effort and even more alarmingly, can see price wars break out as UK and US publishers reduce the price of their own editions in the hope of achieving a larger market share. This is detrimental to their own profits and greatly detrimental to the author who sees their royalty per sale diminishing with each price cut. The author can benefit if sales volume rises dramatically but a lower on-sale price does not come with a guarantee of huge extra sales volume.

The Australian Booksellers Association said:

> The changes that have been made to the Copyright Act are not designed to produce an open market for the importation of books but rather the Act has been amended to improve access for Australian booksellers and the Australian public to overseas publications as soon as they are published in their country of origin.

With simultaneous publication of many titles around the world in English it can become awkward to arrange author tours as one author can't promote in several continents at once! Publishers must negotiate with an author or their agent for the author's time, and some publishers must accept that the author promotes in their market some weeks after the actual publication date if they are busy promoting in another market at the time.

It can be enormously effective if an author who is good at publicity is given the chance to make promotional trips to overseas markets. When I visited publishers throughout Australia recently I spent some time telling them about my clients they were already distributing. Two of my writers have visited Australia since and we have increased sales to show for it.

Every part of the export market needs attention if an author's career is to build, book after book.

13 Selling other rights

Once you've sold volume rights to your first publisher you can start to think about other ways to exploit the potential of your novel. There are many other rights to sell, some of which will be organized by your publisher, some by yourself or your agent. Subsidiary rights sales bring you extra income after the first contract, but require no more writing time. These sales really can buy you time to write your next book. Extra rights sales for one book may continue for years if properly managed, and the income from them can be extremely beneficial to your career.

I will declare my own strong interest here: I firmly believe that publishers should sell books and agents should sell rights. In other words, I don't think that it is necessarily in an author's interest to have their publisher acquire a large package of subsidiary rights. I believe that a publisher's focus should be on maximizing sales of the book itself. Once they have the right and the ability to make money from the book by selling rights to other publishers and other media, their urgent need to earn back the advance by selling their own print run is lessened. I'm not suggesting that when publishers acquire a large rights package, they give up on their efforts to sell books, that would be too simplistic. I do prefer to think that a publisher should concentrate all of their efforts on the selling of the book itself. The smaller the rights package that a publisher controls, the more effort they must put into selling books.

Publishers often justify their wish to acquire as many rights as possible by saying that it is necessary to prevent competition with their own editions, or that a secondary publisher needs to work very closely with them when acquiring production material (on an illustrated book, for example). These are usually excuses to justify the fact that the real reason why publishers like to control a large package of rights is because it is convenient and profitable for them to do so.

There is a reasonable argument for publishers controlling those rights which, if licensed by others, might produce editions in conflict with their own (such as a hardback publisher who wishes to control paperback rights). I can see no reason why an author can't retain control of these rights provided they consult with the publisher as to the manner and timing of the licensing of them.

I don't expect many publishers to agree with me. Their main consideration in discussions about the size of their rights package is the income they can generate – and hold on to – by licensing rights to others. As most subsidiary rights income is held by the publisher until the advance has been earned back, it can be of considerable benefit to the originating publisher to own rights they may sell to others.

When deciding how big a rights package to include in your license to your original publisher, consider the following:

— Are they good at selling the rights they are asking to control?

— Will they put the details of the deals to you for your approval before completion?

— Will they pay monies from subsidiary deals to you without waiting for the royalty period to end?

— Will they return to you unsold rights they have failed to sell after an agreed period of time?

When your publisher is making their case for purchasing a large rights package, it is quite reasonable for you to question them about their ability to exploit those rights, whether it be by their own publication, or their rights department staff licensing it to others. How skilled are they at this? How many international trade fairs do they attend? How many other foreign trips do they make? If they want serial rights, ask them how many major serials they sold from their books in the last year. When deciding whether to be published by a particular publisher, you can take a view of their publication list by looking at their catalogue; but to judge their skill at rights selling you need more information from them: don't be afraid to ask for it.

When your publisher does control rights that they may sell to others, insist on a clause in your original contract that requires them to seek your approval on rights deals. If you are on fax or e-mail, there is no reason why they can't be obliged to get your written approval. Publishers may ask for the phrase 'not to be unreasonably withheld' to be added to such a clause: resist it if you can, as I have discussed in chapter 9.

With some subsidiary rights, sales can bring in large sums. Ask the publisher to agree to pay over to you your portion of the subsidiary income within twenty-eight days of their receipt. Even if you have to agree to this only for sums received after the advance has been earned back, it can be a considerable help for your cash flow. But not as enhancing to your cash flow as selling the rights yourself: if you or your agent sells subsidiary rights, you become the contracting party, licensing rights directly to the purchaser, and the income goes straight to you or your agent.

Always try to include a clause that limits the time during which the publisher may control rights that remain unsold. Ask that unsold rights should revert to you after an agreed period of time. If they have failed to sell certain rights after one or two years, it is highly unlikely that the rights department can afford to spend more time concentrating on them: their attention will have moved on to newer titles.

It is extremely important, once you start to amass a range of deals and contracts for the same book, that you take great care that none of the rights you are licensing overlap with each other. You must take care that you do not, through lack of attention, put yourself in breach of contract. For instance, when licensing the same book to a UK publisher and to a US publisher, it is vital to make sure that the territories you are licensing are complementary to each other: that you are neither licensing the same territory to each of them, nor leaving a territory out of each contract so that no one ends up with the right to sell your book there. Because subsidiary rights granted to a publisher may only be exercised by them within the territories you have licensed to them, make sure that the two clauses work together.

A word of caution: when you negotiate your contract initially, take care that it contains a short clause making it clear that the split of income stipulated against each right that the publisher controls is based on 100 per cent of the monies from the sale of those rights. If the publisher employs a third party (a freelance rights sales person, or an overseas agent selling on their behalf) any commission due to that person should be paid by the publisher. Some publishers try to pay their freelance rights person or agent from the 100 per cent, and then divide the *rest* between the author and publisher. There was one contract that I saw an unagented author had signed, in which the publisher's contract provided for their own freelance rights agent to be paid for entirely out of the author's proportion of the income! Needless to say, that publisher's contract was somewhat deficient in other ways too.

There isn't sufficient room in this volume to provide sample contracts for subsidiary rights but I will try to cover the method of selling and the variable deals. For much more detail on rights selling, see Lynette Owen's *Selling Rights* (Blueprint).

I'll describe and discuss the rights in the five groups: domestic, international, audio, visual and merchandising.

Domestic

Some of these rights will always form part of your grant of rights to your initial publisher, so it is the publisher who will do the selling (despite my misgivings about rights controlled by publishers!). Others may be licensed to the publisher or kept back and sold by yourself or your agent.

Paperback

These days, paperback editions are much more likely to be published by your publisher themselves, so your income from a paperback edition will come to you without being shared with the hardback publisher. Of course, it is quite possible that your book will be published straight into paperback without having had a hardback edition first. In each of these instances your earnings will be provided for by the royalties clause in your original contract, which should state exactly what royalty you are to be paid for each format.

Even if your publisher intends only to publish a hardcover edition themselves, it is usual for them to control paperback rights. It would be very unusual indeed if they were to agree to buy just hardcover rights and allow you to retain control of paperback rights because it could be argued that a separate license for paperback rights might conflict with their own edition and so they must have the right to control the timing of such an edition.

If your publisher does license these rights there are a number of ways of dividing income. Up to about fifteen years ago, paperback income was nearly always split equally between the hardback publisher and the author; 60 per cent to the author and 40 per cent to the hardback publisher is now the norm, although it is quite possible for established authors to negotiate more favourable income splits. Some contracts can provide for a sliding scale such as 60:40 up to a particular level of income, and 70:30 or 80:20 for further income.

Licenses to paperback publishers will always stipulate a period within which they must publish, usually defined as not earlier than a certain date (say, twelve months after hardback publication) and not later than a later date (such as twenty-four months after hardback publication).

Large print

Large print editions are just that: books printed with extra large print for the benefit of the partially sighted. These are often found in libraries, hospitals and old people's homes, but some will be found in larger bookshops. A few trade publishers do publish in this format, but most license to specialist publishers. If they publish their own edition, but also have the right to license to others, you will need two clauses in the contract: one to cover the royalty they would pay you if they published in this format themselves, and another to cover the rights income split if they license to another publisher.

It is common for trade publishers to control this right. The income is low (£1000 to £2000 is the range for most large print advances) and the split with the original trade publisher is usually 50:50 or 60:40 in the author's favour. It is unusual for the large print royalty rate to be higher than 10 per cent of recommended retail price.

Contracts will usually restrict the publication of the large print edition so that it may not appear before the initial hardcover edition.

Serial

Serial rights will usually be part of the discussion with your domestic publisher when your deal is initially agreed. Serial rights may be either part of the publisher's package for them to sell, or they may be retained for you to sell yourself.

Serial rights are defined as two separate kinds: pre-publication ('first serial'), meaning any that begin before first publication, and post-publication ('second serial'), which refers to any that begin after first publication.

Both are sold according to strict territory definitions according to the distribution of the publication buying the rights. It is possible to sell extract rights simultaneously to several separate markets. So long as the negotiations and contracts are clear, serials from UK published books can be sold separately to UK, Australian, New Zealand and South African publications, and sometimes also to papers or magazines in Scotland, Wales, Ireland etc. In America, where few national newspapers are published, it is possible to sell several different serials to a range of newspapers whose distribution areas do not overlap.

When buying a book, a publisher will always try to include serial rights in their license. I used to retain serial rights in order for us to sell them on behalf of our clients but that was when magazines and newspapers fought with each other to pay high figures for these rights. Publishers would seldom add a huge extra figure to their advance in return for having the serial rights, so it seemed better for me and my author to keep them ourselves and sell them when the manuscript was completed.

Serial rights are no longer as valuable as they used to be (show business memoirs and politicians' autobiographies still fetch high prices though) so I tend to take the pragmatic view that publishers may as well control these rights and use them as a publicity tool. Publishers may sometimes be persuaded to add a little to the guaranteed advance (sometimes they will add a lot, depending on the nature of the book) and my author may as well have the money as a guarantee, as part of the publisher's advance, instead of having to wait until nearer to publication time to offer the serial, with no guarantee of success.

If we feel that the serial rights may be particularly valuable then we do fight to keep them out of the publisher's package of subsidiary rights if they are not willing to increase their advance in return for including these rights.

Some books that sell as extracts to newspapers or magazines don't achieve large fees, but the resulting exposure can turn into healthy extra sales so long as readers of the serial feel there is more to be gained by buying the book. It is vital, when selling serial rights, to be sure that you stipulate the maximum amount of material they can use.

First serial rights

This is a term used for any series of extracts whose publication begins before publication of the book. These rights can bring in large sums of money, although that is more likely for non-fiction than for fiction. Newspapers and magazines who buy serial rights have specialist staff who scout for material. They buy their serials many months before publication, although newspapers also purchase rights at the last minute.

Publishers and agents maintain close contacts with the literary editors and feature and fiction editors who buy serials because successful sales depend upon those editors being prepared to read the manuscripts. It is a very competitive market: so many books are published annually, yet few will be serialized. And the papers and magazines are often competitive amongst themselves for the few, high profile, serializable books that appear, so those that do sell first serial rights may do so for very high fees indeed.

Few publications serialize fiction now, certainly many fewer than fifteen years ago.

There has always been considerable debate within publishing as to whether the appearance of book extracts in newspapers or magazines helps or hinders sales. It's a question that is unlikely ever to be resolved but opinions can be strong. Some argue that the larger the number of people who become aware of a book through the licensing of serial rights, the better it must be for book sales. Others feel that two or three extracts, taken from the most interesting parts of a book, can make potential book buyers feel they have read all they want.

When your agent or your publisher sells first serial rights the serial contract will always impose a timing restriction upon the buyer so that the extract or extracts appear at a time to suit the book, such as around the book's publication date. The hope is always that the publicity from the serial's publication will help to sell more copies of the book, so other restrictions in the contract will deal with the number of extracts, and the maximum number of words to be used as well as setting out the exact wording for the credit to the author and the book. If the author had retained serial rights, it is not unusual for the book's publisher to have included a clause in their contract with the author stipulating that wordage and timing of a serial must be subject to consultation with the publisher.

It is common for papers who have bought serial rights to demand an undertaking that the author will not give interviews to rival publications to appear before their own publication of the serial. A deal for first serial rights will often require the author to grant an exclusive, first interview to the purchaser of the serial rights.

The timing and presentation of first serials, especially for non-fiction titles, can cause enormous rows and upset particularly if the material is previously unknown or secret, or involves prominent personalities. Rival newspapers often try to publish a 'spoiler' – a piece that spoils the impact of the serial owned by another newspaper – and sometimes run an article about the book in the guise of a long review. Thankfully few of these problems attach themselves to the selling of serial rights in fiction, although the down side of that is that the income these rights produce is correspondingly lower. Getting agreement from the newspaper or magazine to show their extracts (and proposed headlines) to the seller for approval can be the subject of a heated debate: if the material is controversial it is worth arguing this one.

One extra facet of timing with regard to first serial sales is that, with very newsworthy material, a paper may insist on an undertaking that books are not distributed to shops until after its first one or two extract-carrying issues have appeared. It is more likely that this will be achieved if it is the publisher co-ordinating the sale of rights and the distribution of books. This can be an argument for publishers to control and sell first serial rights to books likely to be affected in this way.

If this is the case, when you agree your initial deal with the publisher, negotiate that they either increase their advance to take account of the expected income from a serial sale, or that they agree to pay over to you immediately upon receipt, all serial monies less their agreed commission. Publishers will be more likely to agree to do this only once the advance they paid you is earned back.

When publishers control serial rights, 90:10 is the usual division of income for first serial, although many publishers will ask for a greater proportion.

Second serial rights

This term applies to any serial or extract whose publication begins after publication date of the book. These rights are far less valuable than first serial rights because the information is no longer new or exclusive and the book is in the bookshops. Few newspapers buy second serial, although quite a few magazines do. It is possible to sell both first and second serial rights for the same book to different publications, so long as their publication date requirements can be made to fit with each other.

These rights are usually, but not always, controlled by the publisher, even where first serial is handled by the author/agent. When a publisher does control second serial, the split should be 80:20, or 75:25, certainly never more generous than that for the publisher.

Condensation

Usually these rights are part of the publisher's package. The purchaser of these rights is usually Readers' Digest, who publish bound volumes for their members, containing three or four slimmed-down novels. They pay an advance based on the size of their expected print run for that volume and a very low royalty per copy for each author, in the range of 3 or 4 pence per volume. Publishers have been trying to push Readers' Digest's royalty levels up for years but Readers Digest argue that with three or four authors to each volume, the total royalty is the figure that must be considered. Stalemate.

Readers' Digest publish from, and buy rights for, several different offices around the world, in many languages. They buy English language condensed book rights for many separate pieces of the English-speaking world including the UK, Australasia and Hong Kong. Once one of their offices picks up a title, others will often follow.

Most authors and publishers view Readers' Digest editions as extra readers and income, rather than seeing the volumes as competition for the trade publisher's edition. Although the condensations are prepared in a sensitive manner, some authors have been known to object in principle to their books being condensed.

Maintaining a good and close communication with your publisher can result in you being shown the edited versions of your text that the publishers of these kinds of condensed texts plan to use. There can be a provision for this kind of consultation and/or approval in your original contract (which only then works if the provision is in turn inserted into the license from your publisher to the condensed book publisher or the audio book publisher) but in my experience this is rare. Some of my clients have been shown their edited-down manuscripts, usually because of particularly good relationships leading to close communication between the author/agent and the publisher's editor, the publisher's subsidiary rights department, and the company obtaining the license to condense.

One of my thriller writers, for example, is so admired and liked by everyone in this communication chain, that he is regularly sent his condensed texts for his approval before their use, even though there is no contractual obligation to do so. Everyone at Readers' Digest takes great pride in the fact that they are producing new versions of his work that please him.

Newspapers and magazines will sometimes, though rarely, run a condensation of an entire book. Publishers prefer to control these rights, again on the basis that such a license would be competitive to their own publication and so must be controlled by them.

Condensation rights are usually divided 50:50, or 60:40 in the author's favour.

Book club

Book clubs sign up members who guarantee to purchase a minimum number of books over a set period of time, usually something like four books per year over two years. In return for that guarantee, the clubs sell books to their members at a discount.

As a rough rule, you can expect that a club will wish to sell to members at approximately 75 per cent of the recommended retail price of the publisher's own edition. This relationship between the retail price in shops and the club's price to members has been pretty constant over a number of years. In Britain, book clubs have had to fight hard to maintain their membership numbers now that books are regularly discounted in bookshops and the club prices look less attractive . They rely upon their members wanting the convenience of having a range of titles selected for them, some of which may neither be readily available nor discounted in bookshops.

Book club rights are almost always within the publisher's rights package. There are two different ways of selling a title to a book club.

One way is a rights sale, with the club paying an advance and royalty, based on the selling price to their members. They will then print the book themselves, paying a separate offset fee to the publisher for the use of the text, and a fee to use the artwork for the jacket design.

If they are planning to use a title as a main choice – the title recommended to members by the club editor for that month – they will expect to sell a large quantity and will almost always try to buy a license for that reason.

The income from a book club rights sale is usually split 60:40 between the author and the original publisher, although higher proportions for the author can be negotiated.

Another way to sell to book clubs involves the original publisher printing copies for the club, usually as part of the publisher's own initial print run. This is advantageous for the publisher as it lowers the unit cost for all the books printed at that time, including their own. On deals like this, it is usual for the publisher to quote a unit price to the club for each copy supplied, which will be calculated to include a fixed percentage of the unit price as the author's royalty.

Given that the clubs price their editions at about three-quarters of the price of the publisher's own retail price, they like to buy from the publisher at no more than one-quarter of the publisher's recommended retail price. This squeezes profit margins, although no publisher is going to want to do a deal that doesn't actually make any money for the company. Publishers seldom offer an author more than 10 per cent of the price received from the club on these kinds of deals, although it is sometimes possible to push it up to 12.5 per cent. On paperback book club deals the author's royalty usually goes down to 7.5 per cent of price received.

Even with the large quantities that can be involved, authors make very little money at all on book club deals. The clubs themselves, and book publishers, argue that these should be seen as *additional* sales, made to an audience that is entirely extra to those reached by the original publisher. I'm not sure that I agree with this because I know plenty of heavy book buyers who frequent bookshops and who also belong to several book clubs. They will buy from the clubs for the discount when they can't find that book at that price in shops.

Agents believe that publishers make a bit more profit on book club editions where they are printing for the club than they like to admit, because of the reduced production costs for their own edition. But, like the debate about selling serial rights, this one is unlikely to be satisfactorily resolved.

International

As you will know by now, I believe an author should retain foreign language rights and not license them to their English language publisher. But even I license world rights deals occasionally if that is the only way to obtain enough funding at the outset to provide what the author needs.

A word of caution if you do license world rights to your publisher: make sure every aspect of the foreign deals include you. You should have approval over every deal so that – at the very least – you know that the deal has happened. You should be able to approve the publisher and the details of the deals, and you should receive copies of all signed contracts. And you (or your agent) should certainly check your royalty statements very carefully indeed to make sure that you receive the right proportion of income from foreign sales and receive it at the time it is due to you.

I like the publisher who is responsible for the selling of the rights to send us copies of royalty statements from the foreign publishers' licensees for all the same reasons as above. And of course they should send you most of the printed books from the foreign editions that they receive, keeping just one or two file copies for themselves.

I think it's reasonable to provide some interim feedback when a publisher controls your rights. A brief report on progress after a major trade fair, or some indication of submissions after a foreign trip made by a rights executive would all help to persuade the author that their book was being looked after well.

USA

As I have said elsewhere, I have no objection at all to related companies buying the same book. When HarperCollins UK and HarperCollins US publish the same book, they can do a fine job for the author, getting them into every English language market around the world. Likewise, other worldwide groups such as Random House or Little, Brown. And often the purchase by a publishing group of world English language rights is fine, so long as it is clear how the advance is split between the two geographical areas and how the royalties are accounted against the advance.

A problem can be caused when one part of a worldwide group offers for world English language rights without having first sought a publishing committment from their counterpart in the other market. If that partner rejects the book, the publisher who bought world English language rights has to try to sell the remaining market to a publisher outside their own group. This can make the rights look unattractive because other publishers will know the book has been seen and turned down by the publisher within the group.

If, having bought world English rights without consulting their partner, the originating publisher arranges a deal with their own company overseas, it will pay you to look at the figures very carefully. The rights manager of a London publishing house (which owns an American publishing company) published an article in *The Author* where she looked at rights selling to associated companies. She wrote: 'The role that agents often play is a valuable one in that they can ensure that rights deals negotiated "internally" are as good as third party ones.' She's right, but I find it worrying that a publisher will accept that agents need to play this policing role. It suggests that rights departments, in remembering their loyalty to their employer, can sometimes fail to realize that when licensing rights on behalf of an author, the company owes a debt of responsibility to the author as well. The rights manager who wrote that article is now an agent. I don't find that surprising.

A good publishing rights department knows that they are working for both the publisher and the author. There are times when this produces a conflict of interests. If a publisher wants to buy a title from an associated company but offers less than it is thought might be available from others, does that publisher get the book? At such times it is rarely the author's wishes that are uppermost in the minds of the publisher's employees. Before I started our agency I used to run rights departments and I recognize these situations only too well. An honourable solution would be for the rights department in the originating publishing company to offer the book elsewhere in that market and let the associate publisher compete for the rights with anyone else who wanted to make an offer. This would have the merit of achieving the market price for the book and author and would ensure that the book went to the most enthusiastic house. If a publisher wishes to sell to an associate at what they fear might be less than the going rate, I think they must put their arguments fairly to the author and accept the author's wishes with regard to the sale.

When a publisher licenses another English language territory, income should be split 80:20 in the author's favour. Publishers will sometimes ask for a greater proportion but I can think of no good reason for allowing it.

Translation

Publishers and agents can both be very good at selling translation rights. Some sell through sub-agents located in the foreign markets, some sell direct to publishers overseas, and some do a mixture of both. That's how I operate our foreign rights business. In twenty-four markets, I work with co-operating agencies overseas, in the rest I sell direct, either because there are no good agents in those territories, or because I prefer to handle a particular market myself.

I've always joked that I handle Dutch rights myself because a) Dutch publishing contains a large number of very handsome men and b) I love Amsterdam's shoe shops. Both those things are certainly true, but I handle Holland myself because I love doing foreign rights deals in a hands-on manner and Holland is a market that's easy to stay in touch with from London. There are many good rights agents in Holland (and many terrific female publishers too!), but with Amsterdam being so accessible from London, I can see Dutch publishers regularly either in their country or mine. I wouldn't be able to cope with the workload though, if I tried to handle all the overseas markets without the co-operation of agencies in many other markets, and many publishers find the same.

A British publisher's financial director once admitted that their company found it very difficult to administer the income from foreign rights deals: they didn't have enough systems to track and chase monies that were due. An employee in the rights department of a large American publishing house once told me that they had to handle so much more work than they could cope with, that they had an account, into which they put cheques from overseas that they couldn't identify.

This account contained a vast quantity of dollars, which couldn't be allocated to the authors it belonged to because they couldn't match the cheques with contracts. It just sat there, earning interest for the publisher.

Scary, but true, so be alert if you do allow your publisher to handle translation sales. If they do control these rights, again an 80:20 split in your favour is the norm. And with these rights in particular, check your contract carefully to be sure that the stated percentage is of the whole, and that the split of income is not being made *after* payment to their sub-agent.

The form of contract with overseas publishers for translation rights is similar to an English language contract, but perhaps a little simpler. It will provide for an advance, royalties, the licensing of subsidiary rights by the publisher, regular reporting of sales and earnings etc. While the copyright in the original work remains with the author, the copyright in the foreign language translation, paid for by the foreign language publisher, will be vested in the overseas publisher but they are circumscribed as to the ways they can use it by their original license from the author.

Audio

This comprises a range of rights, exploited through different media. All can be retained by the author, although publishers often wish to control them.

Radio

There are two separate exploitable rights for books with radio: straight reading of the text and dramatization rights.

Straight readings are usually – but not always – controlled by publishers. They are licensed for use language by language, and there are fairly standard fees per minute of broadcast time for their usage, although well-known authors may be able to negotiate better rates.

Dramatization rights in all forms, including for radio broadcast, are more likely to be retained by the author. There are no standard fees and payments will vary a great deal based upon how well-known the author is and whether the title itself achieved bestseller status, although there are accepted minimum rates.

Few subsidiary rights are granted to broadcasters with dramatic rights. They will be allowed to repeat the programmes, with levels of payment for each broadcast provided for in the contract. The BBC does require audio cassette rights for a set period of time for education programmes, but not for dramatized fiction.

Radio programmes that read or dramatize fiction do give full credits to book title, author and publisher within each programme.

Cassette tape

There are several ways in which books are licensed to cassette: in full length, single-voice readings that contain every word of the book ('unabridged') or in shorter, abridged forms, or multiple voiced dramatized forms. They carry very different selling prices and sell to different audiences. Abridged versions usually end up on two cassette tapes and sell through bookshops at a retail price close to that of a mass-market paperback. Unabridged cassette sets can run to fourteen or sixteen tapes or more, costing sometimes twice or three times the equivalent of a hardback book. These tend to be institutional purchases, bought by libraries, hospitals, prisons and homes for the elderly.

Dramatized versions on tape tend to be recordings of radio dramatizations and are usually marketed by the broadcaster. The BBC has an extensive range of cassette tapes in this area.

Some book publishers have audio divisions that tend to publish abridged versions rather than unabridged. They can then sell the tapes to the same customers who are buying the book in its printed version.

If the trade publisher wants audio rights included in their rights package and intends to produce tapes themselves, be sure that the contract makes it clear that they not only have abridged cassette rights, but they are obligated to produce the cassette version as well, and within a specified period of time. My view is that even if they are producing their own abridged cassette version, the agent can still control unabridged rights on behalf of the author. The contract needs to be clear on this point.

If the book publisher owns an audio publishing division but does not want to commit to an audio version at the time of signing the book contract, they will sometimes ask for an option on audio rights. I have no objection to this provided they agree to make up their minds early enough. I often include an audio option clause that obligates them to give their decision within four or six weeks from delivery of the full manuscript to the book division. This means if they decide not to go ahead with an audio version, our agency can offer the rights to others shortly after delivery of the full text. If they do decide they want to do an audio version, these rights become the subject of a fresh contract with an advance and royalties provision.

In addition to trade publishers' audio divisions, there are dedicated audio book publishers who sometimes market only one form, sometimes both.

Most unabridged books-on-tape are produced by companies who specialize only in that, and they buy licenses from book publishers or agents and authors. Houses such as Chivers, Isis and Soundings will sometimes compete with each other for these rights purchases.

Even with competing offers, audio cassette rights of either kind bring in limited income. The advances fall usually between £1,000 and £2,000 although for a well-known author they can rise beyond that. Royalties tend to be a flat rate of either 7.5 per cent or 10 per cent of the selling price, or wholesale price sometimes for unabridged rights. Some companies have better distribution than others: take care not to license a bigger market to them than they can adequately service.

If your publisher controls these rights and intends to license them, a reasonable split of income would be 80:20 in your favour. This is a widely accepted level.

Visual

Visual rights are divided between dramatic (film, television, inter-active electronic) and non-dramatic (television readings, electronic read-only text).

These are the most complex categories of rights to sell and contract and I would not advise any author to try to sell these rights for themselves without professional advice.

Compared to the number of books published, very few are sold for film or television rights, and of those sold very few are actually made. We had one of our author's books turned down by someone in Hollywood with the words, 'I very much enjoyed the novel. However, in consideration of how tough the market place here is on non-high-concept, character-driven pieces that don't lend themselves to theme park rides and lunch box marketing, I find it to be a hard sell.'

There are two areas of specialization with regard to these rights: the selling of them and the contract negotiations. I would not attempt to do either, myself.

Film and television

Hollywood executive: Sometimes you just option a book because your gut tells you this is a book that has to be butchered
– *New Yorker* cartoon, 1998

Film and television contracts are the stuff of legend: film and television negotiations can be the stuff of nightmare. Half our agency works only on film and television rights, with one of our directors also being a qualified barrister. And still we use the services of a specialized media law firm for all of our film and television contracts.

It is usual for publishers to control these rights only on behalf of unagented authors. Most publishers also acknowledge the complexity of handling these rights and employ the services of specialized agents. To sell these rights effectively an entirely different world of contacts must be built up and sustained, a range of trade fairs and festivals attended that do not overlap with the book world, and experienced specialized lawyers used for the actual contracts.

There are a variety of categories of purchasers for visual dramatic rights: independent production companies, broadcast companies, individual producers, directors, sometimes even scriptwriters or actors. Usually you will receive a larger sum of money for the rights if you sell to an independent production company or producer than to a broadcaster, but then the chances of the film being made will be less because the independent company will have to raise the finance to make the film or television series after they have purchased the rights from you.

Often these rights are purchased in two stages, an option (for a specified period of time, often renewable once or twice) followed by the full purchase. A film option, for example, might be for a year, renewable for another year. The full purchase price will be agreed at the outset (and the full contract negotiated and attached to the option contract for signature later if and when the rights are purchased) and the fee for each year's option might typically be 10 per cent of the total purchase price. The option fees may or may not be offset against the total purchase figure.

While you retain copyright in your original work various other copyrights will come into being connected with the film, and all will belong to others: script, the film itself, music etc. Once the full rights purchase is exercised, it usually means film rights are sold for ever, whether or not the film is made. There can be provisions in a film contract for rights to come back to the original author, but in reality that hardly ever happens.

Once you have achieved a sale, my advice to my clients when selling dramatic rights to their work is to not spend the cheque until it's cleared through the banking system. The *only* bounced cheques I have ever had experience of, in more than thirty years of rights selling, have been from film or television companies! I tell clients not to expect anything else to come from the deal (so many options sold, so few turned into films!). And if they are eventually invited to watch a film or television series based on their book, they should view any similarity between their original book and the dramatized version as a bonus. This might seem cynical: I prefer to think of it as realistic!

It would be highly unusual for the author of a novel to have any approval rights at all in the way a film or television series adapts the book, unless the author were already a big name. Even big name writers can feel left out when their books are turned into films. Tom Clancy, author of several books that have been turned into big box office films such as *The Hunt for Red October*, *Patriot Games* and *Clear and Present Danger*, was quoted as saying 'Selling film rights is like pimping your daughter.'

Despite the huge figures that are sometimes paid for film rights, most dramatic rights sell for modest sums. Even if film or television rights in your novel are sold for a small deal, extra books sales around the world made as a result of a film or television series could mean substantial extra earnings. If you don't like the version that has been made from your book console yourself with thoughts of the extra book sales you will doubtless enjoy. And remember that your book still exists in exactly the same form as you first published it for those who want to read it as a book.

After a film or television series has been aired, the dramatization could be released on video. Video rights will usually have formed part of the original dramatic license.

Electronic

Technology is moving so fast that this area of rights is the most confused. Publishers want to control electronic rights because they fear a license in this area could produce a product that will take the place of a book sale; authors wish to retain control of the rights because they fear losing control of unknown areas of rights that have yet to be invented or developed.

The range of rights covered by this catch-all phrase is wide: from straight text displayed on a read-only screen, which most agents now agree should form part of the book publishers' license package, all the way through to inter-active multimedia games. Some publishers do produce material in these areas, and some have expert and specialized staff to license the rights, but most do not and for that reason agents are seldom happy to include these rights in book contracts. Many agents will employ specialist companies to license and contract these rights and I would not advise any author to license in this area without the advice of an agent or lawyer with specialized knowledge of the field.

When licensing rights in this area take the trouble to discuss how limited the license can be: it is good advice to license very restrictively and selectively.

Merchandising

Again, complex rights to sell and negotiate and rights that will be licensed for a very small number of properties. Merchandising is the term that covers the licensing of a character or design into a different medium, and can involve any number of linked products, such as dolls and soft toys to tie in with children's books (usually after they have been made into films or television series). It covers such oddities as a license that Penguin agreed once for the name of Wainwright, their author who wrote dozens of guides to the Lakeland area, to appear on a range of walking boots, the Beatrix Potter porcelain, dozens of products featuring Enid Blyton's Noddy. More merchandising rights are licensed from characters or designs linked to films than to any other medium, even though the original may have been a book.

Merchandising rights are divisible and are licensed separately, although a range of linked items may be licensed to one manufacturer. Royalty rates per sale may be low but volume high, with advances based on the expected rate of sale. It is important, when entering into the merchandising rights arena, to think carefully about the mix of your copyright and the item the merchandiser plans to link to it, and important too for the copyright owner to have some approval rights over the product.

The licensing of merchandising rights is labour intensive because it requires knowledge of and contacts in so many varied fields. There are agencies who specialize in merchandising and most publishers, literary agents and authors would be well-advised to employ their services. Merchandising is an area that attracts a lot of copyright fraud and piracy. As with electronic rights, license merchandising rights very restrictively if possible, by time period and geographical area. Not all products are appropriate throughout the world and these licenses can reflect that.

Part Three

PUBLICATION
AND BEYOND

14 Publicity

A book shut tight is but a block of paper – Chinese proverb

The shelf life of the modern hardback writer is somewhere between the milk and yoghurt
– John Mortimer, *Observer*, 1987

Writers should be read – but neither seen nor heard
– Daphne du Maurier

How to generate publicity yourself

You've written the book. You've even sold it to a publisher. Now comes the hard part: convincing the public to buy it. You can't afford to sit back and assume that this is the publisher's job. It is their job, but it is yours too: if you wait for your public to come to you, you'll wait a long time for sales and earned royalties.

A publisher has dozens, hundreds, sometimes many hundreds of books to promote in a year. You probably only have this one. Who has the greater motivation, the most to gain from working hard on *this* book? You do. So get out there and work hard for it. Daphne du Maurier was living in a gentler age. Publishers and the public now expect to hear from writers, to have books brought to their attention, to know something about the writer and the book that makes them want to go into a bookshop and ask for the novel. Books have to compete – for time, attention and money – with so many other forms of entertainment, and the return on time and money invested (by both author and publisher) is so much lower than with music, video, films and television. Therefore everyone's approach to the effective marketing and promotion of books must be that much more creative.

Authors must subscribe to the feelings that Oscar Wilde had when he said, 'There is only one thing in the world worse than being talked about, and that is not being talked about.' If John Mortimer's comment is close to being true, then the more active the author can be on behalf of their own book, the better.

Writers are sometimes nervous about doing publicity for their book themselves. I know many who are shy and feel they cannot face their potential readers. This is a real drawback for a writer and something every author must to try to overcome. There are very good courses you can attend on public speaking, but even without such training, it is possible to help yourself to overcome inhibitions of this kind. If you have little experience of addressing an audience, make sure that you introduce yourself gently to it by speaking to a small group first. Go to other authors' talks and see how they do it. Talk to them afterwards and ask for tips: most people will be helpful.

Publicity managers with publishing companies can be helpful in offering practical advice on public speaking and there are very good books available.

All of the points I made in chapter 2 about networking for authors apply when it comes to generating publicity. Use your membership of any group to spread word about your book, introduce yourself to your local bookshop manager and ask if they will be taking copies, or displaying a 'local author' showcard, or if they are interested in involving you in any publicity events centred around their shop.

Make sure that your local newspaper is sent a copy of your book and perhaps offer to write a piece for them to coincide with publication. Strong local sales can often lead to bigger things nationally. Regional radio is another useful weapon in spreading word about your novel.

Elizabeth Chadwick, an author I represent, who writes wonderfully vivid historical novels set in the medieval period, belongs to a historical re-enactment society. She uses this to publicize her novels, giving talks in medieval dress and getting newspaper coverage for the events. She sends me photographs of her and her family in medieval dress, which I forward to her publishers in other countries, and to our agents in markets where we haven't sold her books yet.

Persuade friends to post reviews of your book on the Internet. There are many bookshop sites where readers' comments are welcomed. If you write feature articles or short stories this is the time to use them well. Prepare ahead, because magazines need to buy stories many months before they publish them.

Be sure to set these up professionally. One of our clients had a friend who worked for a regional newspaper who offered to publish a piece by our author to coincide with publication of his book. The author forgot to tell us until the piece came out, didn't get paid for the piece and insult was added to injury when he saw that there was no mention of his book at all. The article was organized with the best of intentions, but in publicity terms it proved worthless.

Another of our clients is wonderfully enthusiastic and always agrees exuberantly to projects intended to publicize her books, but seldom tells us or her publisher in time for us to make the events or newspaper articles useful. This kind of uncoordinated publicity at best is only half-useful, and at worst can actually stop other more useful press pieces if it overlaps with something set up by your publisher.

It is easy to make colour postcards featuring the cover of your book. They are not very expensive, and can be used for every kind of casual correspondence, as well as for specific book publicity. I particularly like sending notes to publishers on cards advertising my authors who are published elsewhere! Several of my authors have made postcards for their books, either to supplement the publisher's efforts, or because the publisher was doing little themselves. It's a small investment for constant reminders of your title and its cover.

If your publisher has not produced a press release, there is nothing to stop you making one. It is easy to generate a single sheet 'flyer' on a computer, or to have your local copy shop make colour photocopies of the book's jacket and then print some selling copy on the reverse side. Ask your newsagent, corner shop, dry cleaner, restaurant or delicatessen if they will display it in their window or slip copies into customers' shopping bags with their groceries.

Create your own Website. There is no doubt that display sells and putting your cover, review comments and blurb on to the Web can certainly sell books. If you consider this you may need to pay for a company to design and produce it for you, and you must be willing to update it and spend time on it. Readers like to be able to communicate with writers whose work they like. Writers I know who have their own Websites have all said they find them useful sales tools, especially if they are set up to receive browsers' comments and e-mails.

The American publishing paper *Publishers Weekly* carried an interesting story in October 1998. The Starr Report on the Clinton scandal had appeared. The entire report was available on the Web, and also in two book editions, one from Pocket Books (as an inexpensive mass-market paperback) and another from PublicAffairs in a more expensive trade paperback. It might have been expected that either no book edition would sell well because the material was freely available on the Web, or that the cheaper book edition would sell best. But Amazon.com, which sells on-line, reported that the more expensive edition was selling fast, and best. The reason, it seems, was because it was the PublicAffairs edition that was featured on the Amazon.com home page. *Publishers Weekly* commented: 'Even though it is very easy to search out other editions on the Web, customers seem willing to accept the first one they see.' Display sells.

An essential thing to remember about organizing your own publicity, is that once you have set something up, be sure to tell your publisher with as much notice as possible. I can't stress enough how much communication means here: setting up the event is only half of it. The publisher must know so that books are available at the venue or can be sent to the paper or radio station in advance.

Some authors consider using their own freelance publicists. If you have the means to finance this, choose your publicist with care, and explore the subject tactfully with your publisher first. It could be seen as a criticism of the publisher's publicity team so be careful to present the idea as adding to their efforts, not replacing them. When choosing a publicist, be clear-sighted about what you expect to achieve and ask them to tell you frankly what they think they can achieve and how much time and money they think they will need to make an impact.

Publishers and agents will know a range of publicists who specialize in book promotions and may well have experience of working with several they will be happy to recommend. Good freelance publicists will be realistic about what they try to achieve for you: be wary of any that promise you the earth and are vague about what they will charge.

Even without your own publicist, there is much you can do to capitalize on publicity you have received. John Harvey, author of the Resnick detective novels, is a model of efficiency in this regard. He produces his own regular newsletter, *In a Mellotone*, containing news of his novels internationally, extracts from reviews, recipes for Charlie Resnick's trademark delicatessen sandwiches, playlists for Charlie's favourite jazz tracks, some of John's poems, details of publicity events and tours and much else.

It is written in an informative tone (*not* overheated press release language), is well designed to a professional standard, and is sent to a mailing list he has built up over the years. He supplies me with fifty copies of each newsletter, which I send to his many publishers around the world and to our agents overseas.

Above all, be organized about publicity: start early, keep copies of everything, plan in detail, inform everyone and don't leave anything to chance.

What your publisher will – and won't – do

Authors and agents can become very jaded about publishers and publicity. Like book covers, everyone has an opinion, everyone could have done it better, and with publicity no one is ever satisfied that there is enough.

Douglas Gibson, former editorial director of Macmillan Canada, wrote an extremely funny and cynical, but horribly true memo about publicity, which he used to hand to new authors when their book was about to be published. Called 'Don't Look for your Book in the Bookstores', he said the initial reaction it provoked was amusement often followed by thoughtful letters some six months later when the authors had experienced most of the disappointments he listed. The memo covered publication day (no one will notice it), booksellers (they will blame the publisher for lack of stock), reviews (there will either be none, or they will appear too early or too late to be useful), friends (who will give you a list of misprints in your book) and interviewers (who will not have read your novel).

While it was intended to be amusing the subtext was a warning to authors not to expect too much. But it is human nature to want your book to be noticed.

Advertising

Advertising is like learning: a little is a dangerous thing
– P. T. Barnum

On the whole, publishers will vote more money to a book's publicity budget if they think the book will sell a lot of copies than if they think it will achieve a small sale. You might think I am a master at stating the obvious. But it is worth thinking about that fact quite carefully. I know authors who, even though they are aware that the publisher has only printed 2,000 copies of their book, will still make countless telephone calls to try to persuade a publicity manager to throw a party on publication or to take an advertisement in a national newspaper.

It is not fair, but well-known and bestselling authors will always be given bigger publicity budgets than authors who haven't yet sold well. Of course, it is possible to argue that this policy is entirely upside down; that it is the authors who are not selling well who really need the publicity. There is no doubt that is true, but the bigger issue is that it is impossible to prove if advertising – or which advertising – sells books.

Publishers will always spend more money advertising books that are already selling well. Does that sound like nonsense? Books for which they have limited expectations will receive no advertising at all. A title with an estimated sale of 2,000 copies will not be worth advertising because even if they were to increase its sale by 50 per cent, another 1,000 copies sold will not add greatly to a publisher's profits.

If, on the other hand, publishers have a John Grisham novel that has sold 100,000+ and advertising boosts that by only 10 per cent, they have nevertheless added an extra 10,000 sales. Even with the cost of the publicity, an extra 10,000 sales will be profitable for the publisher, especially when they have sold 100,000 already. And it is more likely that a novel already proved to be appealing to a broad audience can be made to sell more by the simple process of telling people of its existence. Not a comfort to an author without an advertising budget, but it does make good business sense and it does explain publishers' attitudes to advertising.

Another factor is that the entire publishing industry spends less on advertising than a perfume manufacturer might spend launching one new brand. The reasons for this are quite clear: the book business produces hundreds of thousands of brands, or products – books – a year and the industry does not generate enough money to launch any of them like a new French perfume. With limited resources, publishers feel it is better to advertise only those books where they can spend enough to create some impact.

If you know your book is to be advertised, the advertising will form part of a larger marketing plan and I would hope you had been involved early in the process of planning it (see chapter 10). While I don't believe it's easy to persuade a publisher to advertise a book they had not been planning to advertise, it is easier to persuade them to do more advertising for those for which advertising has already been allocated. Make sure that you see the advertising copy before it is used so that you can prevent any mistakes or muddles getting into print. Publicity departments are hectic, and they are dealing with many titles and authors at once. If you read your own book description, author biography and quotations from reviews that they are planning to use, you can be sure you won't be embarrassed by the finished material. If the publisher has not commissioned a recent photograph of you and plans to use one you are not keen on, have your own taken and supply them with copies.

Publication parties

Few publishers think that publication parties sell copies. When they do give parties it is to please the author, which means it is entirely celebratory and that they believe the book will sell sufficiently to sustain the cost of the party anyway. Many publishers can be persuaded to contribute a cheque, or a venue towards a party. Don't be offended if the publisher won't pay for the entire party. Instead investigate how much impact you can achieve by using their cheque to buy drinks, and your own house, or local bookshop, or art gallery or wine bar as a location. If they offer you their boardroom, it's then for you to decide how much of your publication payment you want to spend on refreshments. If you do have a party, think about the guest list very carefully. Don't just invite friends and family. Extend invitations to booksellers, newspaper and radio journalists, your children's teachers, your accountant and bank manager. Every articulate person you introduce to your book can become an advocate for it. Make your party work for your book.

Bookshop signing sessions

These can be a double-edged sword. They enable you to get to know bookshops and their staff, but unless you are sure that efforts will be put into publicizing the signing session, you could find yourself embarrassed if only a trickle of people come to buy your book. Always ask about the plans to publicize any signing session that you agree to do, and once you have agreed to do one, have your publicist call the shop on the previous day to be sure that copies of your book have indeed reached the store. Don't leave anything to chance; if you have relatives or friends in the area of a shop signing, persuade them to come!

Point-of-sale material

At the very least, most publishers will produce a showcard for your local bookshop, and for you to take to any talks you arrange yourself. At best, and as part of a major publicity campaign, publishers will produce a weird and wonderful range of material, limited only by imagination. I like to have copies of particularly imaginative pieces of point-of-sale material produced for my authors' work. Displaying them in our office is useful when overseas publishers visit, and we sometimes photograph them to send to the authors' other publishers and to our agents in the overseas markets.

There is a school of thought now among publishers that much money spent on point-of-sale material is wasted because bookshops, inundated with it, have little room to display it, and much of it is never unpacked. Recently more and more publishers are saving their money to put into chain booksellers' own promotions, which do carry a guarantee of display in the shops belonging to the chain (see below). HarperCollins in particular have been open about their switch towards consumer advertising and away from point-of-sale material. They feel bookshops are in danger of being buried in cardboard display pieces and glossy brochures that they don't and can't use.

Chain bookseller promotions

The bookshop groups, the 'chains', are more interested in promotions that link successful books and authors to their own company name and image than they are in joining in with promotions organized by publishers. Recent years have seen the bookselling chains become much more proactive with promotion and, as competition between the chains accelerates, they are all doing more to stamp their name rather than their competitors' on the public consciousness. Descending to the London underground train network, you could be forgiven for remembering only the name 'Dillons' or 'Books Etc.' from the often-repeated advertisements that line the escalators, rather than the titles or author names connected to the range of titles featured.

Most authors are surprised when they discover the cost to the publisher of joining these bookshop promotions. The process works like this: the bookselling chain announces their promotions for the coming year, and the cost for each participating title, and invites publishers to nominate books for inclusion. The chain chooses a few from the many submitted, using a range of criteria – cover, publication date, price, content and author's profile.

Once a title is chosen, the publisher pays into the scheme and in exchange gets a guarantee of a substantial order from the chain (supplied at a hefty discount and still with the right to return unsold copies to the publisher) and display space in the chain's shops. Many chain bookshop promotions also carry a guarantee of inclusion in the bookshops' own advertising. The more the chain does for the book, the more it costs the publisher.

One head of a bookselling chain told me that they like to be self-sufficient; they base most of their buying around their own promotions and rely very little on promotions organized by publishers.

A publicity tour

Only big publicity campaigns include an author tour. Indeed, with modern technology, it's possible for you to stay in one place but be interviewed and publicized in a wide variety of locations. If you are asked to embark upon a tour, do not underestimate how gruelling it can be. Authors are often given schedules that might include seven or eight events in a day, including interviews with the press, radio and television, readings in bookshops, signing sessions and other 'meet and greet' opportunities. Days as full as this can finish with a dinner with half a dozen booksellers, or perhaps with a train or plane journey to another location where it will all begin again.

This might sound like nirvana to a struggling novelist, but tours can be intimidating and exhausting. Always ask for a schedule before setting out and think through the logistics very carefully. Publicity staff can be very skilled at putting together these kinds of promotion trips but they don't always think of everything. If you are the one who has to be able to look calm while giving a talk to a room full of people, you will want to be sure you have time for lunch, for calls home to your children, for getting from the train station to the radio station without sounding breathless as the broadcast begins.

The need to be charming and upbeat despite the pressures of performing day after day can wear anyone out and it is important to remember that the only point of a promotion tour is to *promote*. You must remember to mention the book title in every interview, to turn up to every talk as enthusiastic as if it were your first, and to be pleasant to even the most idiotic or insulting questioner. Mordecai Richler tells a story of a promotion tour he did for his Canadian publisher. A man approached him and said, 'Let me shake your hand. I've read everything you've written. I think you're wonderful.' The writer thanked him but then the fan went on, 'Now let me ask you a question. What do you do for a living?'

In the busy publication seasons of spring and autumn, bookshop audiences can become jaded and as a consequence thinner. Try to come up with innovative ideas for providing something different that draws people and gets your book talked about. For several years, John Harvey has organized unusual bookshop readings that involve a jazz trio and another author. The mixture of music, novel readings, poetry and drama has proved very popular. In October 1998, Anne Rice, the American novelist, decided to combine her bookstore appearances with a call for blood donors. Booksellers made links with hospitals, and fans who donated blood could go to the head of the queue for book signings in the bookshop, wearing a lapel badge that read: 'I gave blood to the VAMPIRE ARMAND'. No prizes for guessing the book title at the centre of the promotion!

It is a real asset if an author can deliver humour well. Joseph O'Connor, a literary novelist we represent, also writes humorous journalism and has had several collections published in book form. The readings he has performed for these books have been wonderful to see, gaining extraordinary audience reaction whether the events are consumer or trade based. These work so well because Joe does write very funny pieces indeed, but also delivers them with a particularly effective understated style that adds enormously to their impact.

Interviews

Authors want to be interviewed. Interviewers only want to do interviews with people with a *story*, and seldom do they think that the fact that you have written a novel is story enough in itself. If you want to be a successful interview subject, work on finding angles that will help to produce good copy for the journalist. Research the publication before you give the interview and keep in mind the readership you are addressing.

When you are interviewed by a newspaper or a magazine, ask the journalist to let you know when it will be appearing. When you visit a radio or television studio, take an audio cassette tape or a video tape with you and ask them to tape your interview. You can then take the tape when you leave and know that you won't run the risk of missing the broadcast. Have a friend tape it for you too, just in case! We keep taped interviews with our clients on file as we keep print interviews: it's all helpful when selling the authors to other markets, or to another publisher in the home market should the author choose, or need, to move.

Reviews

Never demean yourself by talking back to a critic, never. Write those letters to the editor in your head, but don't put them on paper – Truman Capote

Insects sting, not in malice, but because they want to live. It is the same with critics, they desire our blood, not our pain – Friedrich Nietzche

Reviews are exciting and useful when they do appear and are positive; depressing and infuriating if they either don't appear or are negative about your book. *Under no circumstances* ever reply to an unfavourable review. You will certainly feel like doing so. Indeed, writing a scathing response can be enormously enjoyable. But once you have finished it, throw it away: don't send it. Refuting a critic's comments always looks small-minded, whereas ignoring them conveys the impression that you have risen above those who may only be motivated by jealousy.

Your publisher should certainly send out review copies to newspapers and magazines, and you should ask to see the list before publication. If you know of any potential reviewers, or outlets for reviews, tell your publicist in good time. Always keep all positive reviews: your agent and your overseas publishers will be able to put them to good use and if you change publishers you will be able to use them to show what you have achieved. Reviews are less transitory than other forms of publicity: bookshops use them to promote books they believe in and building up a good review file is the easiest way for an author to show what their books have achieved.

Authors are often asked to become reviewers themselves. This is good because you get your name in the paper, you are given free books and they pay you (a little) for the review. But think carefully before agreeing to review novels in the field in which you write yourself, which is likely to be the kind of fiction they will want you to review. If you agree, you could find yourself committed to review a book by someone you know, which is fine if you like it and can say so. It becomes awkward if you know the author but dislike the book or don't like it enough to praise it. One of my clients was in this position recently and found herself in a dilemma: should she write a negative review and risk offending her friend, or risk being judged unprofessional by the newspaper if she didn't deliver the review as promised? Luckily, she knew the review editor quite well: she explained the delicate situation and didn't send in a review.

Reviewing does take up a disproportionate amount of time for its rate of payment: you would probably spend your time better writing more pages of your next novel!

Bestseller lists

Bestseller lists, like reviews, produce strong feelings. When your book is included in the lists you may feel euphoric, but when you expect to open a paper and find your novel listed and it isn't, the disappointment will be sharp. At such times it won't be much consolation to know that bestseller lists are compiled from sample stores only, which often reflect only a small proportion of total book sales. Despite the money and technology devoted to bestseller lists, most people in publishing have their own stories about the fallibility of them.

When your book does appear in a bestseller list, be sure that you keep copies of the printed lists, that all your foreign publishers are informed, and that you try to persuade your publisher to do all they can, by way of extra publicity, to keep it there.

There are two main companies compiling and analysing sales data that produce bestseller lists in the UK: Whitaker BookTrack and Bookwatch. They each collect figures on a weekly basis from a range of outlets including independent bookstores, small to national chains of bookshops, supermarkets and mixed multiple stores, and they each weight them to produce bestseller lists, which are supplied to different publications. Each company sells their data to companies and publications who pay for the lists, and each believes their figures to be more accurate than the other's. All the consumer sees is a variety of lists that at times differ surprisingly.

Publisher websites

Many publishers maintain their own Website. Ask if your book is appearing, offer material they can include, suggest that extracts from reviews appear. Publishers update their Website regularly and may only feature you around the time of your publication unless you remind them of other opportunities for inclusion, such as a particularly good review that could be quoted.

Once you achieve big enough sales, the publisher may create and manage a dedicated site for you. This takes the onus off the writer, and means that you do not have to spend time responding to the public who contact the site. It seems to me to be a little like having the publisher manage your fan club!

Don't forget that publishers do spend a large proportion of their marketing money on items that are probably more effective than advertising, but which many authors may be unaware of: partial funding of the discounts to consumers off the retail prices of the books, buying display space in bookshops, putting their titles into bookshop promotions and catalogues – these are all heavy expenses.

Lastly: the ego and how to contain it

Politicians are like monkeys: the higher they get up the tree, the more revolting are the parts they expose
– Attributed to an anonymous past Home Secretary

I have deliberately opened this section with an offensive quotation expecting that you will read 'writers' for 'politicians'. I've done this because I find it's often only by imagining potential extremes of behaviour that one can be alert to the beginning of problems in this area. I'm sure we can all think of celebrities in many areas who display breathtaking degrees of arrogance and antisocial behaviour. On the whole, publishing escapes the worst of these excesses, but some authors do have a tendency to believe their own publicity, and their attitude to others in the publishing industry can become boorish. This can be enormously detrimental to a fledgling career. Maurice Valency said, 'Failure is very difficult for a writer to bear, but few can manage the shock of early success.' Unfortunately, ego-driven problems are not always restricted to beginners.

Ego plays a role in how we all respond to criticism. A certain amount of ego is healthy and probably essential in the make-up of a writer: after all, you must think your writing is of interest to others or why else would you be offering it for publication? But maintaining the right balance between a healthy regard for yourself and your work, and the arrogance that can steal upon writers – especially successful ones, is vital. Hemingway once wrote: 'The most essential gift for a good writer is a built-in, shock-proof, shit detector. This is the writer's radar and all great writers have had it.' He was referring to the ability of writers to criticize their own work, but he could also have had in mind the way an author handles their own image, and their ego.

Many stories that circulate of uncontrolled ego in publishing are probably apocryphal. There is the story of the bestselling American author who allegedly insisted on changing the publicist who was accompanying her on a book tour 'because I'm not feeling enough love'. Many of these stories do have a ring of truth about them. A celebrity chef who was asked to sign an expensive bottle of wine that was to be auctioned for charity, drank it instead.

A prominent novelist refused to leave a bookshop until his latest book was moved into the display of 'This Week's Top Ten Titles'. When the manager protested that the novel wasn't in the display because it wasn't a top ten seller in that store, the novelist asked how many it would have to sell to achieve that. When he had the answer, he stayed in the shop until he had personally persuaded that number of shoppers to buy it, and left only after the top ten display had been changed. The author did indeed achieve sales but also behaved in an overbearing manner toward the shop's staff. If he had handled them in a more friendly fashion, he might have been able to get them to collude with him, rather than leaving them feeling as though he doubted their professionalism. Rather, it was his professionalism that was in doubt.

Another story involves a hugely selling novelist who liked to hire her own van and drive to bookshops unannounced. She would offer to sign their stock of her book (once books are signed, they cannot be returned by the bookshop to the publisher for credit) and then would suggest that they didn't have nearly enough stock and she could let them have a few more. She would leave them with an extra box of (signed) copies. She made sure the publisher's invoice followed. The bookshop had been backed into taking an extra order of books they couldn't return.

These are fairly mild cases of arrogant behaviour, and somewhat amusing. The last two, in particular, resulted in extra sales, so where is the harm? The harm is not in persuading people to buy books, but the way it is done. It's human nature to feel bad when you have been manipulated, and blatant manipulation is unlikely to make those booksellers feel motivated to put that extra bit of effort into either of those authors in the future.

Most aspects of ego-related behaviour often start small but can cause bad feeling nevertheless. I always find my alarm bells are set off if I hear of a client I had believed to be civilized and polite, being rude to the secretary who has answered the phone. It's the act of a bully to be rude to someone whom you know probably won't be rude back to you. If I hear of circumstances like this (and one of the problems of stopping this kind of behaviour early is that sometimes I don't hear of it) I will probably call the author right away and ask them why they had a problem in the previous call. I don't relish making these kinds of confrontational telephone calls, but someone who gets away with this kind of bullying tactic on junior staff will do it again and again if they are not challenged. Each time the effect on a staff member is more upsetting, more demotivating: and that's my point, that authors who behave poorly towards other people in the business end up harming themselves, which is something I'm sure they seldom take into account.

I have always taken the view that part of my role on behalf of my clients is to speak frankly and bluntly to them under any and all circumstances. If this takes the form of trying to save the client from the consequences of their own actions then so be it. If an author is paying me to give them advice as to how best to conduct their career, then I will always speak up if I feel the author is doing something detrimental to their career. This may be uncomfortable to put into action, but it is necessary and important. It's been said that publishers and agents can 'create monsters' when we combine to help an author become successful and famous. I believe it is in my clients' own interests to have someone on their side who is willing to tell them the truth. Arrogant 'monsters' make enemies of booksellers and publishers alike.

By contrast, one of our most successful clients takes care to remember the names of shop assistants at signing sessions, and writes notes of thanks to the local sales rep, all the bookshop managers and the publisher's publicity staff after promotional tours. One author called me with praise of my staff when we had completed a serial sale to a newspaper, and wrote a note of thanks for every new translation deal. Everybody is made to feel good by actions like this. Consequently everyone is highly motivated to do even more for those authors, who incidentally will be the ones who know the name of each staff member, even to the most junior.

Long-term, carrots work better than sticks in this business! Politeness and good manners have a place in business. Success does not automatically equal an ego out of control.

Most publishing houses and agencies are busy all the time. We always have more to do than time to do it. If there is a choice of several authors for whom to do something new (compiling their review list, mailing their free books, chasing their French publisher, who promised to make a decision on their book last week) it's unlikely that you will choose to work on the book by the author who was rude to you yesterday. That work will get done, but perhaps not immediately and perhaps not with the same degree of enthusiasm as the other tasks. It's human nature.

It's also human nature that pushes authors into these kinds of predicaments in the first place. Back to the old adage that publishers and agents are 'in the business of creating monsters'. When the publisher's publicity machine cranks out fulsome praise of you and your work, advertisements repeat the most extravagant phrases from reviews, interviewers queue up to talk to you and signing sessions are arranged in bookshops because your public prefers to buy a book they have watched you sign, it's hardly surprising that your ego can become inflated. Most sensible authors will manage to remember that they are mortal and will stay the same as they were before the hype happened: grateful for their talent, friendly to the people who promote them and sell them and buy them and with their sense of humour intact.

It's only a tiny proportion who behave as if a Hollywood bratpack actor or an old-style rock star was their role model, brutal to anyone who doesn't agree with them or who doesn't immediately gratify their latest whim, savage to those who they deem unworthy of attention, and pleasant only to those they think they still need. It's people like this who will be rude to my assistant, but polite to me; sarcastic to our office junior, but fine with our finance director (who sends out the cheques and who is, incidentally, famed for her blunt speaking!).

Egotism is a horrible character trait that I'm pleased to say is not shared by all successful writers: indeed the really big stars are often the most gracious. I usually steer clear of representing show business 'stars' because I'm too short-tempered (and indeed bad-tempered) to bow to famous egos all the time. And I have an old-fashioned and healthy respect for words on the page, so rarely want to represent those who need someone else to write 'their' books.

When I was first introduced to Jane Asher (stage and television actress, cake maker *extraordinaire*, author of books on bringing up children, editor and presenter of her own style magazine and television series, the advertising face of biscuits and bakeware, newspaper columnist, renowned beauty, wife and mother) I thought it was highly unlikely that I would be the right agent for her because I assumed she was simply the public face for work done by others. But very quickly I was impressed by her total involvement in the many projects she undertook and charmed by her naturalness, although that word certainly belies her accomplishments.

When she joined us she had several very good, practical, non-fiction books behind her and has gone on to write several more. I am pleased to have represented her first novel (and to have had a hand in persuading her to try fiction in the first place) and was thrilled that it was so good. When *The Longing* achieved such good reviews I think I was more proud of them than Jane! She's become a friend, but the point I'm making is that she's a terrific role model for authors' behaviour. She has more reason than most to act the 'star' but, perhaps because she is secure and level-headed, never does. She just gets on with the job in hand, delivers everything on time, remembers people's names, arrives on time for appointments, and thanks people when they do things for her. Just good manners, of course, but we're impressed because people constantly in the public eye often lose good manners when they become famous.

Two of the biggest-selling authors I have ever represented have been with us since their first books and are still with us. They are kind and gracious, have impeccable manners and are warm and accessible to anyone who deals with them. Of course, they are wildly talented and wouldn't be selling the millions of books they do without that talent. But, without wishing to play down their sheer writing talent, I have no hesitation in saying that being a complete delight to deal with has undoubtedly contributed to their sales. Every person who comes into contact with authors like Barbara Erskine and Michael Ridpath wants to put that little bit more effort into their part of the process. The editor will read the new draft a little quicker because they know the author will be happy to discuss editorial changes openly and without rancour or irritation; the marketing department will find a little more in the budget for that extra brochure or poster; the publicity chief will spend more time on an innovative campaign in order to please a favourite author; the agent will squeeze in a few more meetings at the next Book Fair because the author's work hasn't yet been sold in Estonia – and so on.

Remember the good cop/bad cop routine: authors (good cop) and agents (bad cop) can use this very effectively so long as they present a reasonably united front to the publisher.

Contrast that with a politician who wanted to join our agency. He was planning to write about a particularly sleazy episode in British politics and, as far as I knew, had never had any writing published. My assistant told him that I always asked to read something before arranging a meeting. A couple of hours later I heard raised voices in our reception room and discovered the politician arguing that he had an appointment with me and wanted to see me immediately. Our receptionist wasn't coping with his sarcasm well, and my assistant was politely explaining that, as she was the one who had taken his call, she knew that I wasn't expecting to have a meeting with him at that time. When I joined them he turned to me and said, in a most ingratiating tone, that he supposed my assistant had omitted to tell me that she had fixed this appointment, and could he now talk to me about his book? My assistant was wide-eyed and open-mouthed by this time. I had great pleasure in telling him that I was quite sure she certainly had not arranged such a meeting. He countered by asking if I could read his synopsis while he waited, and when I said no, he was most reluctant to let me have it. I made it clear that if he didn't leave it with me, I couldn't read it, and if I didn't read it, I couldn't represent him, never mind have a meeting with him.

He left the material with me, tried to make me promise to telephone him the next day about it and left our offices. I wonder if he was pleased with the impression he left behind him? Nothing on earth would have persuaded me to represent such a self-important and charmless individual. If he could be that overbearing to people in a company he was presumably trying to persuade to work with him, what would he have been like once we had said yes? Later I saw his book announced as a last-minute addition to the catalogue of a very small publisher. I don't envy the publicity department that had to promote it and him.

Authors who behave badly perhaps believe that being pleasant is a form of weakness. One author admitted as much to me. We had worked with him for several books and seen his sales rise in a gratifying way. We had reached a point where we'd had big auctions for his next two books in the UK, the US and Canada and expected that success to be repeated in all his foreign editions. We took him to a major book fair as our guest, gave a party on our stand for him and about sixty guests, and a dinner in a restaurant for twenty. No mean investment (especially at Fair prices!) but well justified by our faith in his writing and by the level of sales we expected for future books.

This was a public relations exercise and we were happy to show him off to his many overseas publishers and our many co-operating agents around the world. Except that he started off exhausted (a very early flight meant little sleep the previous night) and drank too much. Tiredness and too much alcohol quickly turned him into an aggressive drunk who seemed determined to behave as badly as possible, especially towards us, his agents and hosts. He flew home early the next day and we soldiered on through the rest of the Fair, which included a few awkward conversations with publishers and agents who had witnessed unpleasant scenes.

Julian and I drove back to England talking all the way, as we always do after a busy trade fair. This time we weren't only discussing all the deals we'd done and all the deals we expected to do as a result of the agency's 200 plus meetings, we were also discussing what to do about Author X. We decided that we had to discuss things frankly with him. To have ignored the situation would have made us very nervous of public events with him in the future, and I am sure would have resulted in us becoming resentful of his attitude.

We asked him to come to the offices for a meeting and had a very blunt conversation. He was initially shocked, but we were able to talk about it openly and we never had to worry about a similar situation again. He had felt enormously important, surrounded by dozens of publishers and agents, and was obviously high on adrenaline, ego and too much champagne. When we showed that we would rather resign from representing him than get into a relationship where we had to apologize to his publishers for his behaviour, he immediately saw how self-destructive his behaviour had been. We were able to clear the air and put it behind us. That happened thirteen years ago. We still represent him, and I count him a close friend.

Ego is a necessary evil in the writing business. But it's a wise author who knows how to control its effects.

15   Royalty statements

Authors and agents love royalty statements when they arrive from the publisher with cheques. Who wouldn't? Some agents, apparently. One in particular is on record as saying that if he receives royalty earnings for his clients he feels he has failed them because he should have got them a bigger advance to start with. I have no patience with that attitude: that kind of short-term thinking doesn't take into account the fact that most authors want their writing to be a career. If an author is happy to agree a deal, and still receives more earnings later, that seems a pretty successful outcome to me.

Can you understand your royalty statement?

Apart from the cheque that sometimes accompanies a royalty statement, any other consideration of them often produces groans of dismay. Dismay from the author who sometimes feels a little stupid because they can't readily understand the royalty statements. Dismay from the agent at the vast amount of work necessary to check every line of every page of thousands of statements that arrive within a four-week period. Dismay from the publishers who have to prepare these incredibly detailed documents twice a year for every one of their titles with active contracts.

Royalty statements *should* be easy to read. They are the documents publishers are obligated to provide regularly that ought to be able to tell us much interesting and useful information about your book. So why aren't they easy to understand?

They are not easy to read, partly because they do contain many and varied figures. But it is possible to learn to read them, once you have become familiar with the format. And that's where the theory can come unstuck, because it's jolly difficult to become familiar with the format as every publisher's royalty statement differs. They differ in shape and size: any files holding hard copies of royalty statements from a variety of publishers will always look a mess with different paper sizes and shapes spilling out. They differ in the way they use different coloured inks and highlighting and shading: publishers obviously do not think forward to the point when the author or agent is photocopying the statements (for each other, the tax office, a lawyer). Some colours do not copy well at all, making the text difficult or impossible to read, and where a publisher uses colour or highlighting alone to indicate a fact, that can be lost entirely when they are copied. The statements differ in the quantity – and quality – of the information they display, and they differ in their reliability! This is all quite apart from whether the publishers send them out on time or not.

Surveying royalty statements

When I first became President of the Association of Authors' Agents some years ago, I decided that I would organize a project: something that I could leave behind that would improve an aspect of the business, and preferably one that would improve conditions for authors and agents. I thought a survey of royalty statements would be the right project. The member agencies of the Association would share the task of providing and checking a selection of randomly-chosen statements, and I would do the analysis.

It was a minefield. Any criticism of royalty statements makes publishers defensive. Another organization had previously run a simple survey assessing whether publishers delivered statements on time or not, and almost without exception each publisher whose statements had arrived late had produced excuses as to why theirs had been late on just that one occasion: I've not heard of so many sick royalty managers or local postal strikes before or since!

I preferred to compare the information that publishers supplied in their statements, so whether or not it was correct was deemed irrelevant. Our survey would be a list of facts with which the publishers would not be able to argue. What we were trying to do was to produce a list of facts that we thought should be available to every author in every statement, and one way of doing that was to highlight those publishers whose statements were in some way deficient.

As soon as publishers heard about our intentions, I and my other committee members found ourselves being lobbied by them. They were worried that because they were small companies they would be picked out for unfair criticism; they were worried that because they were large companies they would be picked out for unfair criticism; they were worried that their statements would be made public so others could see what they paid their authors. I thought that if so many publishers were worried about the survey even before we had started to collect data, this was bound to be an interesting project.

Collecting the data

Naturally we didn't intend for specific statements to be made public: agents are bound to keep their clients' financial affairs completely confidential. We certainly didn't want any authors to feel they were being used to confront publishers. My intention was that we would make a list of as many different publishers as we wanted to include, and we would also have another list of the items we thought should be included in the statements. I devised a simple sheet that had space for the publisher's name at the top, and a series of headings down the left-hand side of the sheet, with boxes to be filled in against every one We would take a royalty statement at random from each publisher, and mark it off against the items on the other list with a tick, a cross or one of several other codes. The checklists did not name the author or the book.

The royalty statements used to produce the checklist would only ever be seen by the agent who represented that deal, although the agency would undertake to keep that particular statement available should there be queries that had to be checked later. The agent would send me a sheet for each publisher for whom they had checked a statement.

We decided to restrict the survey to publishers in Britain and we came up with thirty-one publishing companies (which covered many dozens of imprints), and forty-three items of information that we intended to look for. Not one publisher provided all the information we thought was necessary, and many fell far short of even providing rudimentary facts about the state of sale and income. Indeed, I commented in the article I wrote about it for *The Author* that some publishers only seemed to reveal information on a 'need to know' basis. Agents of the Secret Service have always worked on this principle: agents for writers – and the writers themselves – often find themselves needing counter-intelligence skills to decode royalty statements. Yet the only reason for royalty statements is that they are supposed to provide information!

The kind of information we thought essential to include in royalty statements ranged from those so obvious that we had initially not put them on the list (such as the author's name, and the publisher's name) to some rather more esoteric facts that had been on my 'wish-list' for years (such as cumulative sales figures or export sales shown separately and broken down by each market).

Publishers had seldom sought agents' views when planning how their companies provided information to authors. I thought the results of this survey might help the industry towards more author-friendly royalty statements, both in the quality and quantity of what they contained and in their presentation. While we were gathering the information, two large UK publishers – HarperCollins and Penguin – were actually preparing to change their statements and the computer programmes that produced them. They did want to consult with the agents' body, especially once they knew we were working on a survey of statements.

HarperCollins telephoned to consult me *thirty minutes* before they were to hold a crucial internal meeting on the subject. Penguin were obviously more serious: they said they could wait two days for a response. Unfortunately I was in New York on business at the time, with eight appointments a day. Neither publisher had allowed any time for proper consultation with the people who receive the statements. I think their calls were prompted more by a desire to find out how we were going to comment on their own company's statements, rather than a genuine wish to involve agents in their plans to change their documentation.

I know that computer programmes are difficult, expensive and time-consuming to change and I am reminded of that afresh every time we upgrade those in the agency, but when an author or an agency's royalty manager calls a publisher with a query, it costs *both* parties money. The fewer pieces of information provided on royalty statements, the more calls there will be. Clearer statements would make for more trust in the publishing partnership and would actually save on overheads long-term. All the information we included on our list *could* be incorporated into software programmes for royalty statements: a leading software company that I contacted confirmed that. Their manager also told me that the stumbling block was that many publishers either did not want to change their programmes, or simply didn't see the need to provide the extra information.

We organized our 'wish-list' for royalty statements into three separate sections: the first was simple facts relating to the book and the statement's presentation; the second dealt with information about the publishers' own editions; the third covered sub-licenses from the publisher to others. The items of information that we felt should be included on all royalty statements were then, and still are, as follows:

Are these shown clearly?

Publisher's name and address; Author's name
It seems incomprehensible that either of these would be omitted. They usually are included, but each of them has been left off some statements. One large university press only supplied the authors' surnames: a scholarly oddity!

Proprietor's name (if not the same as the author's)
Some authors, often for tax reasons, form their own companies; some rights are purchased from another publishing company rather than an author. In each of these cases the proprietor's name should be shown, and so should the author's. Fifteen of the thirty-one statements we checked did not: nearly 50 per cent.

Statements addressed to the agency
When an author or proprietor is represented by an agency, the contract will call for the royalty statements to be sent to the agency on behalf of the author. Some publishers will address their statements (and the envelopes in which they are mailed) only with the author's name. Many literary agencies have their offices in buildings that are shared with other companies. If an envelope is addressed to their building, but only with the author's name, it might not be delivered to the agency. Two of the publishers covered by the survey did this.

Imprint indicated
Thirteen of the statements we included in the survey were for books published under multiple imprints by the publisher supplying the statement: four of the thirteen did not indicate the imprint for each separate edition.

Multiple book contracts
It is not always clear as to whether they are jointly or separately accounted. This often causes difficulties, where the publisher has put the figures together as though the books were all on one royalty account, but the contract calls for separate accounting. If there is a clear indicator as to which is required, there would be fewer mistakes. It is vital to get this right, or monies due to an author could be withheld for many more royalty periods than necessary.

Total advances shown (including those not yet paid)
Some statements only show the amount paid so far by the publisher. If, for instance, the book was not yet published, you would not yet

have received the amount due on publication. If a significant amount of money had already been received by the publisher (say, from a sale of serial rights) your portion of that income when shown on your statement against the part-advance you had so far received, might make it look as though you were due to receive money from the publisher. They, however, depending on how your contract is worded, may not be required to pay you anything until earnings total more than the entire advance due to you. If this figure is clearly shown, fewer misunderstandings arise. Of the thirty-one statements we checked in the survey, twenty-one did not show the total advance (and on one other statement it was 'not applicable', because the publisher had not paid an advance!), meaning that only nine did provide the figure.

Last figure from previous statement carried forward on new statement

The last figure on a statement will be the balance of the account: either a sum due to you because earnings have exceeded advance, or a minus amount showing how much advance has yet to be earned. Statements that open with the balance figure from the last statement are much easier to check because you know the position you are starting from. If the figure is not there, the author or agent has to check it from the last statement. Actually, we always check the last statement, even if the figure is there, just to be sure it's the right figure. Agents are paid to be suspicious! Most publishers in the survey did provide this figure, but four did not.

Separate statement per author

This might seem obvious, but one publisher simply ran together all their statements due to the agency. I know of another company, not in the survey, who publishes specialized editions (large print books, books on audio cassette tape), who would send us one long royalty statement that covered all the deals we had ever done with them. They seemed surprised when we said this made it impossible for us to provide clear paperwork for our clients. We were having to do 'cut-and-paste' jobs on the photocopies to separate one client's figures from another: the copies we were having to supply to authors looked like the result of a hectic day in a craft class for eight-year olds! They did, in time, change their reports.

Each title on a separate statement

If each title receives a separate statement less muddle is likely. If a title is part of a multiple book contract that is jointly accounted, it is simple to provide an additional summary sheet to link them. Companies who prefer to run together all of an author's titles can, sometimes, cause chaos. We represent a prolific client who has dozens of published books. His British publisher used to provide dozens of pages of statement, which would list the books alphabetically by title. They identified different editions by ISBN only, without naming the format. The author joined us after having been with three other agencies over a long period of time. When we received the first statements for his range of titles we couldn't make head or tail of them: nothing seemed to fit the contracts.

I was negotiating a new deal for that new client with the managing director of the company and needed to be able to read the statements because I had to know what his books were earning. I told the publisher my problem: he invited me to his office so that we could discuss the statements. I spread them out on his desk: he couldn't understand them. He invited his royalty manager to join the meeting – he couldn't unravel them either.

As we worked our way through the pile of pages, it gradually became clear that the publisher had, without discussion or agreement, moved portions of unearned advances from one title, over to another title that had already earned its advance. It is only permissible to 'set-off' one book's advance against another if they are a) both part of the same multiple book contract and b) the contract states the books are jointly accounted. My author had several single book contracts, several two-book contracts, and several three-book contracts. Some of the multiple titles were jointly accounted, some were not. Regardless of what the contracts stipulated, the publisher had moved advances not only *within* contracts, but *across* from one contract to another.

This had been happening over a period of years, had never been spotted by the author's previous agents, and was complicated and time-consuming to remedy, but we did get it sorted out in the end, and were rewarded with a cheque for the author that came with interest added to the amounts that should have been paid in previous royalty periods.

Months between accounting period and date statement is due

Most publishers close their accounts at the end of June and December, and provide statements for that half-year in the following September and March respectively. Some work to different dates, but the gap between the end of the sales period and when the publisher is expected to produce the report is usually three months. Of the thirty-one publishers covered by the survey, six allowed themselves four months, and one had the nerve to ask for five. This is, in effect, the period of time during which publishers may hold on to monies due to authors. Why should some publishers expect to have these interest-free loans for one or two months longer than their competitors?

Opening and closing dates of royalty period

Agents like these dates to be stated clearly because there are, as I've said above, a range of dates on which publishers produce their royalty accounts. Having the period set out clearly at the beginning of the statement makes it easier and faster to check that no statements are missing in a royalty file. It's only by reading a sequence of royalty statements that a sales and income pattern can be established for a title. These dates were missing from nine statements checked in the survey.

Currency of statement

Only thirteen of the surveyed statements carried a clear indication of currency. Most statements provided only figures without even a currency heading above the money columns. This can produce confusion, since many publishers publish in different territories, using the same name but different currencies.

We had a situation in which we were dealing with three publishers with the same name: one in Britain, one in America and one in Australia. The British publisher identifies themselves with their address on the statement, but it also carries the addresses of all their overseas offices in the British Commonwealth, which includes Australia; the American one does not carry an address but just the company name and logo; the Australian one has an address printed in tiny type. The British statement (which also shows the Australian address) pays in pounds sterling but nothing on the statement says so. The American statement, computed and paid in US dollars, does state a currency but only as 'dollars'. The Australian statement is computed and paid in *Australian* dollars, naturally, but again, their statement, while showing a currency, also calls the currency simply 'dollars'. One name for the currency, but two quite different values! Thank goodness we didn't also receive statements from their Canadian and Hong Kong offices, which would also have been in 'dollars', and would have provided two more different values.

Is the failure to denote currency cultural imperialism or a lack of foresight? When checking your statement (indeed, when banking your cheque!) make sure you are aware of its currency. Twelve of the thirty-one British publishers in our survey had no mention of a currency on their statements. For the British recipients this would have caused no confusion at all, but as we are only too aware, publishing is an international business and a significant proportion of royalty statements will go to overseas authors and other proprietors. Now that many European countries are trading in the Euro as well as their own currency, this is an even more important issue than before.

Key to codes provided
Some publishers use a code to indicate certain pieces of information. In our survey, seventeen of the thirty-one publishers involved used at least some codes on their statements, yet only eight provided a key. Two provided a key to *some* of the codes they used and seven used codes but gave no clue at all about what the codes represented! Obviously, telepathy would be a useful skill to acquire for authors published by these houses.

Statement photocopiable?
Four of the thirty-one statements we checked in the survey could not be copied well on reasonably sophisticated office photocopy machines. This figure did not take into account those statements delivered on large and unwieldy sheets that could require individual handling. My medium-sized agency has to handle formidable quantities of statements. Those on A4 (or, to accommodate the Americans, quarto) sheets can be put through the automatic document handler and copied so much faster (and more cheaply) than the awkward sized pages that have to be copied by hand.

Money due for book purchases
If the author or the agency has bought copies of the author's book from the publisher, and the publisher has agreed to take payment from monies due on the royalty statement, that item should be shown clearly for what it is, not just taken off the final balance with some vague description such as 'deductions', as I have sometimes seen. One or two publishers make our lives easier by attaching to the statement copies of the delivery documents so that we can match up the deduction with our order and receipt of the books.

Each author's final figure kept separate
This is obviously needed to be sure that there is no confusion between who is owed what when the statements arrive at an agency. On the whole, publishers do this well, but in our survey one publisher's statements were unclear on this vital point and on whose money was whose.

Publisher's own edition

Publication date per edition

Having the publication date for each edition displayed clearly is helpful for several reasons: if there is no other indication of which edition is relevant, at least the date helps you guess! It also tells you how many statements you should have received for that edition (two a year, usually), which makes it easier to check if you are missing a statement. When reading through statements, sometimes years after their receipt, it's helpful to be reminded of how much time has elapsed between initial publication and the royalty period you are looking at. Fifteen of the thirty-one statements in the survey did not carry publication dates.

Retail price

As with the last section, this is a guide as to which edition's figures you are looking at. It is also helpful to have to know when different printings of the same format go through price changes. As almost all home royalties are linked to recommended retail price, there is a very good argument to say that this should be shown on every royalty statement, without fail, particularly as some publishers change their retail price without sending the author or agent copies of the new edition. Sometimes a royalty statement containing this information will be the only means by which an author or agent will know the retail price has changed, or that a new printing has been authorized.

Total copies in print and copies left in stock

These are two categories that relate closely to each other. From the thirty-one publishers' statements we checked, *only one* gave the figure for the total number of books printed, and that was a relatively small independent publisher who is now owned by a company whose core business is in a much less supplier-friendly industry than publishing . . . do not be surprised that this no longer appears on their statements. *Not one* publisher showed a figure for copies in the warehouse.

Some editors maintain close contact with authors and agents, calling with excitement every time a new printing is authorized. Some do not.

Once you know how many copies have been printed and how many copies are in the warehouse, the difference between the two figures will tell you exactly how many sales ought to have been accounted for on your sequence of royalty statements. The technology certainly exists for providing these figures on every statement, but perhaps the willingness of publishers to provide it, is what is lacking.

Oh dear, perhaps I've stumbled on something . . . Actually, although I love a good conspiracy theory, I don't really believe that there is a cabal of publishers agreeing how much information they will withhold from their authors. I think the lack of these figures can be put down to the fact that publishers are naturally reluctant to spend time and money changing their computer programmes, and authors and agents have not lobbied hard enough to have these items included.

Cumulative sales figures
Only three of the thirty-one statements checked carried cumulative sales from one statement to another. If an author or agent wishes to know how many copies have been sold altogether of a book that was published three years ago, they will need to find and add figures from six statements, carefully subtracting the figures for returned copies. Apart from their own reasonable curiosity, authors are asked to provide sales figures for a variety of reasons: a foreign agent needs a little bit more ammunition to persuade an undecided overseas publisher to make an offer; an American editor is writing a persuasive in-house memo to aid their argument to bring the author over for a promotion tour; a film or television company wants to prepare a press release for the Cannes Film Festival; the author is giving a speech and wants to be able to quote figures. It doesn't matter why the figures are needed: they can easily be provided and should be.

Sales and returns shown as separate figures
No one likes to see books returned, but they are a fact of publishing. If they exist, then authors and agents should be given the information. I like a statement to show one line for sales, and a separate line for returns. That way the royalty statement is providing evidence of the ebb and flow (or rather the flow and ebb) of sales.

Some publishers declare only the result of books going back and forth between warehouse and shop. Without showing both figures on the statement, they subtract returns from sales, and show only the figure for the difference. While producing an accurate figure for royalty reporting purposes, this can give a misleading picture of the sales pattern, both for books that are selling and for those that are not.

For some books this reporting method could suggest too much good news. If a publisher, who does not let you see the figure for returns, shows sales on a royalty statement of, say, 12,000 copies, you would be forgiven for thinking that was only good news. If that publisher had, though, in that royalty period, shipped 25,500 copies to stores and had taken 13,500 back, the picture would not be so rosy.

Or, to interpret the same figure another way: again you receive a royalty statement showing 12,000 sales. But the reality is that 12,500 were shipped to stores and only 500 returned. This suggests a very high sell-through from shop to consumer, and would be a cause for rejoicing by both publisher and author.

A statement prepared in such a way that showed '(500)' or '–500' – both ways of indicating that the 500 figure was negative – could mean either that all that happened in that royalty period was 500 copies returned; or, rather differently, that 25,500 copies went to shops but 26,000 came back in the six months covered by the royalty statement (which means that not only did all the copies shipped in that six months come back, but some that were shipped in a period covered by an earlier royalty statement did too). Knowing exactly what quantity was ordered by shops and what was returned does not make the final picture any more palatable, but it does make it more real, and you and your agent need real figures, and real sales patterns, in order to manage your career.

Export sales markets shown separately

Many more publishers break these markets down now than previously, but more information is still required from a large number of publishers. Royalty statements are still, for many authors, their only source of sales information.

Inter-company transfers differently shown from export sales

Most publishers treat sales to related companies overseas as though they were made to non-related companies. Agents have long argued that this is left-hand selling to right-hand and that authors should not have to accept the same low level of royalty when sales are made within an international company as for when sales are made outside the group. We have not yet won this argument, and publishers seldom show inter-company transfers separately.

How much held as a reserve and for how long

A 'reserve against returns' is an amount of earned royalties that the publisher holds in reserve because they expect bookshops to return some copies at a later date. Rather than pay monies over to the author and then be out of pocket themselves, they hold back an amount of earned royalties for several royalty periods to take care of royalties that must be repaid to them to compensate for returned books.

Most British publishers will agree how many royalty periods they will hold reserved royalties for and will stipulate this in the author contract together with the proportion of earned royalties they will hold in this way. Very few American publishers will agree these specifics, insisting instead on a clause that vaguely refers to them being allowed to hold 'a reasonable reserve for returns' with no time limit imposed.

Most of the statements we looked at in the survey withheld the correct proportion but some were unclear in the way they stated this in the documentation.

Hard/soft editions with separate imprints covered on the same statement

It is important that when more than one edition of a book has appeared, it is easy to identify which is which on the royalty statement.

Altered retail prices in particular overseas markets shown

English language publishers sometimes reduce the selling prices of books in certain markets in order to compete more effectively with another edition. In Holland, it is quite common to see British and American English language editions carrying stickers proclaiming a 'Special Low Price for Holland'. Not surprisingly, this infuriates the publisher of the Dutch language edition and reduces authors' earnings per copy sold when the export royalty is based on the price received. About half the publishers' statements did not clearly show when a retail price had been changed.

Special royalty rates separated out and explained

There can be many different levels of royalty rates, not only because the rate increases as sales volume increases, but because it can decrease as discounts to booksellers increase. At the time of our survey few publishers presented this information clearly enough, but now statements have become easier to read in this respect, although there is still room for improvement.

Indication that the book is out of print

Only five of the statements in our survey showed this information. Few publishers have a computer system that can provide this so it is up to authors and agents to query if the book is still in print when they receive a statement showing no – or low – sales.

VAT added automatically

Six of the publishers' statements did not add VAT automatically and required an invoice from the author after receipt of the royalty statement. This is a cumbersome process, and can result in authors receiving income and VAT in different tax periods, resulting in an author being expected to pay the VAT before they have actually received it.

VAT date (payment date rather than end of royalty period) indicated

This is a complication because the end of the royalty period will always be three or four months at least before the payment of the royalties is made. Thus the VAT date is the date of the payment and needs to be shown clearly on the royalty statement. Four of the royalty statements in the survey did not make this clear, which could result in problems with the authors' tax inspector as to when the tax portion of the payment was received.

Payment without need for an invoice

Five of the publishers required the author or agent to send them an invoice for the amount due before they would pay over monies. This should be unnecessary as payment of royalties is a contractual requirement.

One balance given for hard/soft deals

Where the author has received an advance against all editions of the book, and the publisher has published more than one format, it makes the statement much easier to read if there is a single figure showing the balance of total sales earnings against total advance contracted. Two publishers did not provide this although most do now.

European sales separated out where home royalties are payable

At the time of our survey, hardly any publisher showed European sales separately because the EU legislation was relatively new. Penguin were the first to introduce market-by-market sales figures and agents were extremely pleased to see them. More – but not all – publishers now provide this information, but few in such detail as Penguin. It is important that total sales in EU territories be reported if the royalty rate is to be checked. Separating out each and every part of the EU, and other export markets, is not always necessary from the point of view of the royalty statement checks, but it is helpful information for the author and agent to have about sales patterns.

Sales quantity given as well as monies received, where royalties are based on receipts

Too many publishers still show only the royalty earnings when they are on a 'price received' basis. This gives the author no information about the numbers of books sold. If the royalties for home and export are aggregated, it can be impossible for the author to check if the correct royalty rate is being applied. This is still a problem with quite a few publishers' statements.

*Title out of print but selling (e.g. from remainder sales or
subsidiary rights)*
Only four of the surveyed statements produced this information, and
things have not improved in recent years. Publishers seldom ever state
a book is out of print, either because their software isn't set up to
produce this fact, or because they don't want to admit that the author
could ask for a rights reversion if the publisher's own edition is no
longer actively selling.

Sub-licensed editions

State 100 per cent of monies received
Some publishers show the amount they receive from their overseas
agent (which will be less the commission the agent takes for making
the sale) rather than the total paid by the overseas publisher. This can
be very confusing because the author's percentage should always be
expressed as part of the whole, not the 90 per cent (or less) paid to
licensing publisher. In the statements covered by our survey, thirteen
did not show the entire amount, and one publisher who did show it,
did not have the right to sub-license that right anyway!

Percentage of income, as well as money, to author
Some publishers, who have the right to license overseas editions, show
only the amount of money that they are paying over, rather than also
including information about the percentage of the whole that it
represents. This means that to check it the author must always refer
to their original contract, and must of necessity enquire of the publisher the amount received from the overseas publisher.

When subsidiary monies were received by publisher
Few publishers show a date of receipt for sub-license income. Agents
like to know when income reaches the publisher. If it is a publication
amount, for example, it is an indication of that edition's publication
date; if it arrived in a foreign currency it is possible to check exchange
rates on the date it was received (see below), and if it arrived much
later than the contract suggested it should have, a protest can be
lodged that might persuade them to collect monies more efficiently in
the future.

Subsidiary monies paperwork attached
Only one or two publishers provided the back-up paperwork with
subsidiary income, such as the royalty statement from the licensed
edition, or the payment slip that they received when the monies were

sent to them, which would enable the author or agent to tell when the income arrived (see previous heading). Some publishers' contracts do allow for an author to request subsidiary deals' royalty statements, so long as the request is made within a specified period of time.

Currency and conversion rate given
Of all the statements included in the survey, only one, HarperCollins', stated the currency in which the income was received, but they did not state the conversion rate. This is an area that can give much cause for concern, especially at times of currency fluctuation. Without knowing the currency of the payment, the date it was received or the conversion rate applied, the author is required to take on trust that the publisher is paying over to them the correct amount.

One item we did not include but which I would want to add if I were running this survey again, would involve publishers who license overseas editions to countries that impose a levy, or tax, on authors' monies leaving their country. Those publishers should obtain, from the overseas publisher, an official certificate showing that the amount withheld has been received by that country's tax office. The author then uses this certificate to obtain a refund against their own taxes. I would like royalty statements to clearly show if any portions of monies due to the author have been withheld in this way, and also to indicate if they are providing a certificate of tax paid.

The results

Nine agencies volunteered their royalty manager to mark statements that were all chosen from the same royalty period. They sent the filled-in sheets to me, our agency put them into a chart and then I started to analyse the answers. The chart made fascinating reading.

We really did find some statements that didn't give the author's name, and one that didn't have the publisher's own name on it. I wondered if that was the ultimate form of corporate arrogance (or modesty!). At the other extreme, Penguin used to supply statements on paper that had a five centimetre high company logo on the centre of each page, which effectively obscured several lines of sales figures. It used to photocopy black, thus blocking out the figures entirely. Mandarin, the now-defunct paperback imprint of the Reed group, issued statements that superimposed a coloured band over all the columns containing the figures. That photocopied solid black too, so that not one figure showed up on the statement once it had been copied.

I am pleased that quite a few publishers, including some of the biggest, did use the results of our survey to improve their statements to authors. At the time, in the article that accompanied the survey, I was able to comment that HarperCollins, Headline and Hodder (before these last two became one) all stood out as providing the clearest and most informative statements, but even those could be bettered. Penguin, who were upgrading their software while we were doing the survey, did take note of the list of items we thought should be included, and their statements were the first to improve. Their revamp included showing separately, market by market, sales from the major export areas. They were the first publishers to do this. And they did remove the offending logo that obliterated lines of sales figures!

Many publishers' statements have improved tremendously since this survey was carried out in 1993, but many haven't changed at all. Curiously, one of the effects of the whole European Union situation has been to improve some publishers' statements. Many publishers now provide sales figures broken down for each separate export market so that they can differentiate between export markets that attract export royalties, and export markets – the EU – that attract home level royalties. Previously these were all reported as one total under the heading of 'export'.

How to read a royalty statement

Carefully, has got to be the first requirement! Carefully, and with a copy of your contract at your elbow, or a digest of the salient points to hand or called up on the computer screen.

If you find figures or computations of income from sales that you can't make sense of, or figures that seem to be arrived at using royalty rates that don't match with your contract, you must approach the royalty department of your publisher (or have your agent do it for you). If you are represented by an agent, this checking work will be done by them on your behalf, and should be done before the statement is sent on to you.

The royalty departments of most publishing companies are staffed by hardworking individuals who are striving to produce order from, sometimes, millions of figures and thousands of contracts. They didn't devise their royalty statement form, they don't make policy about what facts and figures are revealed and what are concealed, and they do not take pleasure from inserting errors into the statements they send out, yet every six months they have to prepare a mountain of time-sensitive documentation that they know will produce queries they will have to answer.

The solution to getting your own queries sorted out swiftly and simply is to make yourself easy to deal with. What I am about to advise is only common sense, and some of the points in the chapter on troubleshooting with your publisher might also be useful. But remember, at the outset, that you do not yet have a *complaint*, but a *query*. If the answer to your query is unsatisfactory, then you might be justified in feeling you have a complaint. Put yourself in the place of the publisher's royalty manager. They know that, a short while after they have sent out royalty statements for every single active contract with the company, they will be bound to receive a barrage of calls and correspondence from people who think they have found mistakes. Some of these will be aggressive, some will be polite. Which would you rather deal with? Quite. Over the years, our agency's accounts department has had to raise thousands of individual queries about figures in statements and they know they will have to do so every six months. They know that there is no point in antagonizing the publishers' staff when they will probably be dealing with the same people for years to come.

If you have to raise queries yourself, I would recommend that you send a polite and businesslike e-mail, fax or letter simply stating the problem you think you have found and asking for their response. Allow ten days or two weeks to elapse before chasing because of the weight of work concentrated around these times of the year. If you don't receive a reply, or it is unsatisfactory, repeat your query with a little more forceful language. If another two weeks pass without satisfaction, I would say that is when you appeal to your editor for their intervention.

If you find a problem with figures on a statement, but that statement still shows an unearned advance, it is still worth raising the query so the statement can be corrected. At some point in the future the book may achieve sufficient sales to provide extra earnings: if an incorrect figure is left in the sequence of royalty statements, it might take you longer to reach that desired moment.

Royalty statements often look daunting to those not used to them. It is worth learning how to read them because they are the source of so much information about the sales of your book. Take them slowly, use the checklist in this chapter to work through the facts you are seeking, and ask questions of the publisher or your agent when things are not clear.

16   Understanding your income

Turnover is vanity, but profit is sanity – Old saying

Whenever I'm asked what kind of writing is the most lucrative, I have to say, ransom notes
– H. N. 'Swanny' Swanson, legendary Hollywood literary agent

I always start a book for money. If you're married five times you have to – Norman Mailer

Projected income

To give yourself an indication of when to expect payments from your writing, list your contracts against a calendar, being as realistic as possible about when you expect to receive your portion of the income.

Your home market deal

One contract, say, from your British publisher, might provide an advance that looks very attractive, but it is vital to remember that it will be paid to you over a long period of time. Even a large advance, perhaps for a three-book contract, can look less than exciting when broken down into its separate payment stages.

A contract for three books might have the payments divided into ten portions: one on signature (which I would hope, in size, would be equivalent to three signature payments being one for each of the titles on the contract), followed by payments for each book on delivery of manuscript, publication of the hardcover (or first) edition, then publication of the paperback edition. If you will need a year to deliver the first manuscript from the time you sign the contract, and a further year for each of the two publication dates to come around, the payment stages from this one contract could stretch forward for several years. Any delay – in delivery of manuscript, in a changed publication date – could result in a later payment. One delay of this kind could also have a knock-on effect, because one delayed publication date might well cause all the others to be moved on as well.

Remember that payments always come in some time after they are contractually due. If you are signing a contract with most (but not all!) English language publishers, it is reasonable to assume that payment will be with you between three and six weeks after the contracting parties have exchanged signed contracts.

The payments due on delivery of manuscripts may take several months to be paid because the publisher's editor will read the manuscript – and perhaps even require rewriting from you – before putting through the authorization for the payment to be made. All payments, once requisitioned, will take a few weeks to be mailed to you or your agent. Large companies sometimes do cheque runs only once a month, or operate monthly invoicing cycles. If you require a payment urgently it may be possible to have your editor speed things up through the company, but not always. It is important to be realistic about the time that payments may take to make their way through a company.

This is a very simple cash-flow income projection for one three-book contract.

Month	Event	Payment
1	Signature of British contract	
2		Signature payment, contract
12	Delivery of manuscript, Book 1	
14		Delivery payment Book 1
24	Hardback publication, Book 1	Publication payment Book 1
25	Delivery of manuscript, Book 2	
26		Delivery payment Book 2
30	Paperback publication, Book 1	Publication payment Book 1
36	Delivery of manuscript, Book 3	
	Hardback publication, Book 2	Publication payment Book 2
38		Delivery payment Book 3
42	Paperback publication, Book 2	Publication payment Book 2
48	Hardback publication, Book 3	Publication payment Book 3
54	Paperback publication, Book 3	Publication payment Book 3

Home market subsidiary sales

Naturally we hope that contract won't be your only income. Let's be optimistic, and just look at the first book of the three: serial rights are sold two months after you deliver your manuscript, and that contract is paid half on signature (which means four to eight weeks after both parties have signed and you or your agent has invoiced for the amount due) and half when the magazine or paper can publish (that will be the same month as publication, but again in real terms, the money will be paid to you four to eight weeks later than the invoice date).

Audio cassette rights are sold seven months after delivery of your manuscript and that buyer pays you half on signature of the contract (six weeks after the sale is agreed) and half on their issue of the cassette tapes, which will be a month after the book's first publication date.

Foreign language sales

Foreign rights start to attract buyers when your English language proofs are available, which will be perhaps four months after you deliver your manuscript. For the sake of this illustration I am assuming that your agent is selling the rights and that the monies will come to you via your agent as soon as they arrive from the foreign publisher, rather than being paid to your home market publisher, who might hold on to them until a royalty statement is due.

A deal is agreed for Dutch rights two months later (six months after delivery of manuscript) and the exchange of contracts takes two months, followed by a month for the payment to arrive: this is a market that does not require a double taxation document (see below) and does pay the whole advance on signature of contracts.

Another translation deal is agreed, this time with Germany, a month after the Dutch one (three months after proofs have arrived, seven months after delivery of your manuscript) and this time a double taxation document is required (see below). The contracts take three months for all parties to sign and your tax office takes another month to send you a stamped form. By this time we are eleven months on from when you delivered your manuscript and being realistic, you will not receive the signature payment from this contract for another two months at the earliest. Some deals with German publishers are all paid on signature of the contract; some, particularly if they are large, are paid half on signature and half on German publication. For the sake of this illustration we'll assume the payment comes in two instalments.

Two more small deals with Eastern European markets (Poland and Hungary) are agreed two months after the German deal: they don't require tax forms to be supplied but the bureaucracy in their own countries means the monies take a long time to come through. It will be a small amount from each country but it will all be paid on signature of the contract.

Now the cash flow forecast for just the first of the three books sold to the home market publisher looks like this:

Month	Event	Payment
1	Signature of British contract	
2		Signature payment, contract
12	Delivery of manuscript Book 1	
14	Serial rights sold	Delivery payment Book 1
16	(Proofs available)	Half serial rights payment
18	Dutch deal agreed	
19	Audio deal agreed	
19	German deal agreed	
20		First half audio payment
21	Poland deal agreed	Dutch payment
21	Hungary deal agreed	
24	Hardback publication Book 1	Publication payment Book 1
25		Second half audio payment
26		Second half serial payment
27	First UK royalty period ends	First half German monies
		Hungarian monies
29		Polish monies
30	Paperback publication Book 1	Publication payment Book 1
33	First UK royalty statement arrives: no extra earnings (only covers first 3 months hardback, months 24–27)	
39	German publication	
40		Second half German monies

It is very pleasing to see how extra deals, for just the first book, and which have involved the author in no extra work, have greatly increased cash flow. Adding extra deals for the other two books sold to the UK publisher would improve the author's income projections considerably.

It will take longer for overseas monies to reach you for a number of reasons. Some foreign language markets have a number of official and bureaucratic obstacles placed in their way by their own governments, when they wish to make payments overseas. It can take six to twelve months, for instance, to receive monies from Greece, and that is not entirely about the efficiency or otherwise of the publisher (however, there are publishers in markets afflicted by this kind of red-tape, who will take advantage of the delays and will pay later than they need to).

Foreign publishers, who may not know you personally, and who may be dealing with you through several intermediaries – such as your own agent (or publisher) and a subsidiary agent in their own country – will not worry, as your English language publisher might, that they may meet you soon. They are less likely to have personal contact with you. This can lessen their concern about timely payment.

Most literary agents work through co-operating sub-agents who are located in the overseas markets to which they are selling. If this is the way your agent operates then payments will be made by the foreign publisher to the foreign agent, from the foreign agent to your primary agent, and thence to you. Each agent must make sure that the payment has cleared before paying it on.

Double taxation exemption agreements

Quite a few overseas markets (among them France, Germany, Japan, Italy and Spain) have government regulations requiring their publishers to deduct a sizeable percentage for tax (10–20 per cent usually but it can be more) from payments due to be sent out of the country. The only legal way to prevent this is for the person or organization to whom the payment is to be made (you, the author) to show evidence that they pay taxes in their country of residence. To do this it is essential to fill in and sign a document called 'a double taxation exemption form'. You then send it to your local tax office in order to have it stamped by them, which they will do if they can verify that you pay your taxes in a civilized manner. That form is then sent back to you, you send it to your literary agent, who sends it overseas to the foreign publisher. Only on receipt of this authorization is the overseas publisher allowed to make full payment without deductions for local taxes.

In Japan there is another catch: even with a correctly authorized double taxation exemption form the Japanese publisher is required by law to pay 10 per cent of the transaction to the Japanese tax authorities rather than to you.

If you cannot obtain a double taxation exemption form (for instance, South Africa does not have reciprocal agreements with some European countries), or in the case of the Japanese situation described above, you must insist that whoever is responsible for selling your translation rights to the market in question, obtains for you a certificate from the tax authorities in that overseas market, confirming that the overseas publisher has paid the withheld tax to their tax office. Once you have that document, your own tax office should allow you to withhold exactly that amount from the taxes you are required to pay at home. This method is efficient eventually, but hard on your cash flow, because tax is deducted at source from the payments you receive often quite a long time before you can claim it back against your own tax bill.

Agents will take their commission from the whole because it is only the author, the beneficial owner of the rights, who can reclaim the taxed amount withheld.

When you are calculating your own cash flow, don't forget that the payments to you will be less any agents' commissions incurred and less any agreed expenses deducted by your agent (the cost of buying the proofs from the publisher, for instance).

Buying you time

This might look like a gloomy picture full of delays and procrastination, but view it from another direction. Once you have written and delivered your manuscript, apart from the time it takes to check the proofs and, later, to do publicity and promotion around publication time, you are free to start work on your next book (indeed you have to if you are to meet your contracted deadline!). It is your publisher or your agent who puts in the work to sell additional editions, and the income that results from these sales comes in without you having to do any more writing. Now do you see why I am so keen on selling foreign rights?

An irreverent – but perhaps not irrelevant – although certainly vulgar – joke comes to mind here. Selling additional rights to an author's manuscript makes me feel like the little old lady who decided, in her old age, to run a brothel because it was such a satisfying form of business: 'You've got it, you sell it, you've still got it, and you can sell it again.' What joy!

Taxes – and accountants

Only little people pay taxes
– Leona Helmsley, American hotelier, allegedly said to her maid *before* she went to prison for tax evasion!

The hardest thing in the world to understand is the income tax
– Albert Einstein

As the old saying goes, 'Only two things in life are inevitable: death and taxes', and of the two, tax is the only one you can plan for and lessen the impact of. If you are efficient and have a good accountant, you can make this a little less painful too.

Agents are not a substitute for a good accountant. Agents will not be aware of all the financial aspects of your life, and are not qualified to give tax advice. I do recommend that all authors should have an accountant who understands the peculiar nature of an author's income flow with its irregular patterns and payments. After all, if Einstein had trouble understanding taxes, it's no wonder they give the rest of us pause for thought.

Accountants are invaluable in helping an author to make choices that can, legally, save on taxes. They will keep up to date on tax legislation, choose an accounting date for you that is helpful, offer bookkeeping services, prepare budgets and cash flow statements, establish pension schemes and other tax-efficient arrangements and help you to deal with VAT, tax auditing, overseas tax forms, insurance, wills and inheritance tax.

Another very valuable service provided by accountants is advice on how to spread tax. By the very nature of the work, novel-writing produces income in different years to those in which the work of writing the novel took place, as my simple cash flow list amply demonstrates. Careful accountants can persuade tax authorities to take this into account when assessing authors for tax payments. Authors who are earning a reasonable income from their writing may benefit from setting up a company into which their earnings are paid, and which then pays them (and perhaps their spouse) a salary. These are tax-efficient schemes that can be complicated to set up, but simple to run. They certainly require an accountant's input at every stage.

The Society of Authors organized a survey of authors' attitudes to accountants and published an article by Michael Legat in their summer 1995 issue of *The Author*. They pointed out that a few accounting firms who specialized in media clients did seem to represent a number of the authors who responded to the questionnaire, but most authors did not choose specialist accountants. The results of the survey were diverse but did provide the Society with a long list of accountants they are happy to recommend.

The area in which an author can best help themselves with regard to taxable income (apart from simply earning more!) is to pay careful attention to expenses and to be meticulous in keeping receipts for these. Authors can usually claim for expenditure on secretarial and proofreading help; money spent on research and researchers; telephone and stationery; magazines and books for research; travel to meetings with agents, publishers, researchers; subscriptions to societies; press cutting agencies and many other household expenses that may be apportioned. These could include lighting and heating, rent and television and video costs. Here an author must be careful not to claim too high a proportion of total costs: some of these will be for personal – not professional – use.

Always keep statements from your agent carefully: these will be required by your accountant and will be evidence of both income (monies from your publisher) and outgoings (commission charged by the agent, and any allowable expenses such as book purchases).

Value Added Tax

This tax, which is applied in many countries under a variety of names, seems complicated at first, but isn't too daunting once you separate it into two columns: VAT you are spending, and VAT you are charging. Regulations, the levels of the tax and the items it applies to vary not only from country to country but from year to year as governments change the tax level and the items to be taxed.

The principle of a value added tax return, is to set out what you have spent on VAT, to set it against what you have charged for VAT, and to compute the difference. If you have spent more than you charged in any tax period, you may demand a cheque from the Revenue. If you have charged more than you spent, you must send a cheque to the revenue.

You may only charge VAT (on your services) if you have registered with the tax authorities. In Britain, you must register if your income is over a certain level. The level is set by government and can change. If you are earning below that level, you may register if you wish. Some authors will choose to register, even if their income is low and therefore registration not compulsory, because they gain the right to have the VAT they spend refunded to them. Agents' services are taxable for VAT, which means that an agent's commission has to have VAT added at the current rate. This should be shown clearly on the statement that an agent sends to their client.

An agent's statement to an author (accompanying a cheque for a payment from a publisher less our commission) may have two separate items of VAT: one showing the VAT the publisher added to the gross amount they paid to the agent on behalf of the author if the author is registered for VAT, and a second showing the amount of VAT the author is being charged by the agent on the agent's commission. The first VAT amount is passed straight through to the author: that is a VAT amount that the author has charged the publisher. The second VAT amount (which will be much smaller) is one of the author's outgoings. If these two are the only VAT items that the author has to report on a VAT form, then the author will be sending the Revenue a cheque.

Here's an illustration to make it clearer. This is what the agent's statement to their author might look like:

Received from Publisher A

Amount due on signature of contract for		
FREDDY'S FIRST FICTION		£1,500.00
Less		
Commission to agent @ 15 per cent	£225.00	
VAT @ 17.5 per cent	£39.37*	
Total deductions	£264.37	£264.37
		£1,235.63
Plus		
VAT from publisher @ 17.5 per cent on £1500		£262.50†
Cheque attached		£1,498.13

From this statement, looking only at the VAT, you have received £262.50† (from your publisher), and you have been charged £39.37* (by your agent). Therefore you owe the Revenue £223.13, which is the difference between £262.50 and £39.37. In practice, you will have many other items to declare on your VAT form but I hope this illustration makes the principle clear. The VAT element of the agents' statements is another reason to keep them carefully with your accounting paperwork.

Happily, it is not required by the British Government that VAT is added to the retail price of books (and long may that continue) although many other countries do have to add it. In some Scandinavian countries, for instance, it is as high as 28 per cent and pushes the prices of books to astronomical levels. If you are receiving royalties from a country where VAT is charged on books, the publisher would pay your royalty based on the price of the book excluding the book's VAT.

Happiness is positive cash flow

Whoever said money can't buy happiness simply hasn't discovered the right place to shop – Bo Derek

I don't like money, actually, but it quiets my nerves – Joe Louis

One of the least impressive liberties is the liberty to starve. This particular liberty is freely accorded to authors – Lord Goodman

'Don't give up the day job' is advice I often give my clients. Many authors are keen to become full-time writers far too early in their career. It worries me if I see authors deciding to exchange salaried work for the uncertainty of relying upon income from their writing when neither their deals nor their income has settled into a pattern that can be relied upon. I can appreciate that it is frustrating to have to go to work, perhaps to a job you don't love, when what you really want to do is to stay at home and write all day.

Take care to remember how difficult it could be to get another job if the income from your writing either dried up or slowed down. It's far better to be cautious at the outset, even if it does mean that it takes you longer to finish your novel, or you find yourself having to get up an hour earlier or go to bed an hour later in order to fit in more writing time.

Cash flow and profit are quite different. Cash flow is the shorthand term for the pace and regularity of your income set against your outgoings month by month: it ebbs and flows like the tide but unfortunately not always so regularly. More cash in than out equals a positive cash flow; more cash out than in, is negative (and depressing). Profit (in its simplest definition) is the difference between your income and your outgoings at the end of a tax year. You might find you make a profit from your writing at the *end* of every year, but still experience periods *during* the year when there is more money going out of your account than coming in. Writing produces income in irregular patterns, so learning how to manage your cash flow is essential.

An agent can draw up a cash-flow projection for you based only on your earnings from your writing (which will therefore only be flowing in one direction: in), but you will need an accountant to help produce a household cash flow that takes all of your expenses and income into account. An accountant can also help you to compute profits and loss if you supply them with enough facts.

Agents can advise clients as to when they have reached – or might reach – the point when it is safe to rely on income from their writing alone, but it is the author who must make that decision for themselves. A very small percentage of published writers can survive on the income from their writing. Most writers must supplement their book earnings with income from other work.

Cash flow for your beneficiaries

A will is an essential part of any financial planning. Copyrights, and the income from them, are a writer's assets: remember to make provision in your will so that it is clear who will benefit from the income from your writing. Also remember to appoint a literary executor, someone who will make the decisions about what to license and who will sign the contracts. You might want to appoint your lawyer, for example, but with instructions that they should continue to use your literary agency to do the deals. Quite a few of our clients have appointed the agency as their literary executor.

Few writers that I know like to spend much time thinking about tax, expenses, cash flow or pensions and I can't blame them. But some time spent on setting up systems to take care of these areas, early in your career, will pay off throughout your career.

17 Troubleshooting

Your attitude, not your aptitude, will determine your altitude
– Zig Ziglar

Publishing, like any business, will go wrong sometimes. The art is in knowing how to get things to go right again, and much of this lies in the way you complain. Complaining can be cathartic: you shout at someone, throw out a few sarcastic remarks, slam the telephone down and generally feel better. Complaining as a route to putting right a wrong, or persuading someone to your point of view must be done with more subtlety.

Take this exchange between an author angry and his would-be publisher. A novelist had insisted on an immediate decision on his manuscript, saying that he had other irons in the fire. Michael Joseph (the man, who founded the publishing company of the same name) cabled back: 'Suggest you extract irons and insert manuscript.' The author got his answer but not what he really wanted, which was an offer to publish the novel.

Know what you want to achieve before you begin to complain and keep it in mind all the time. Simply moaning may make you feel better but it will do nothing for your relationship with the publisher or your agent, and may not solve your problem either.

When you have a problem, start low and progress higher. In other words, deal directly with the person who seems to be causing you the problem, before moving on to their superior. Complaining to someone's boss may solve the problem quickly, but probably creates another in its wake because you then have to repair your relationship with the person whose boss you brought into the argument.

Be brief and succinct, keep copies of letters and faxes and make notes of points discussed in telephone calls together with relevant dates. Then you can retrace the way the problem has been dealt with if you need to.

Problems with your publisher

Business is a combination of war and sport – Andre Maurois

These days it is unusual to see an author and publisher partnership last for the entire career of a writer. Unusual, but not unknown. Dick Francis has been with Michael Joseph for all of his writing life and, from what I know of the relationship, is likely to stay there for ever. He joined Michael Joseph decades ago, and his editor was originally Anthea Joseph, Michael's wife.

Back then, the trade reacted well to an author who delivered novels regularly and sold a few more copies with each publication. A first novel was not expected to set the world alight. Publishers, while always hoping for a big success, would nevertheless continue to publish an author if the first novel sold about three-quarters of its first print run, if there was a review or two, and if the booksellers expressed faith in the author's future. So long as sales increased a little with each new title, the publisher would continue to offer new contracts.

Publishing has changed a lot since those days. The business of publishing is a much bigger one now; there are few independently owned publishers and booksellers. The majority of publishing companies and bookshops are parts of a much bigger whole, and the owner is likely to be not an individual, but a group responsible to shareholders. The introduction of shareholders to the publishing scene is one of the ingredients that has radically altered the way publishers evaluate the business. Shareholders and overseas owners will view the group as a whole, and each part of the group – publisher or bookshop – must make their contribution to the group's profit.

This puts pressure upon every department of the publishing company to continually improve their financial performance by spending less or making more. Few publishers now want to add an author to their list who isn't perceived as 'big'. Authors feel this pressure: editors ask for a 'break-out' book from an author who has been steadily building over a number of titles, or they drop authors whose books have not increased their sales, title after title.

A sour comment often heard when agents discuss the issue is that it has become almost easier to get a huge advance for an unknown author than it is to obtain a smaller one for an experienced writer. 'An unknown author hasn't failed yet', to quote a cynical industry catchphrase.

The financial mechanics of publishing are not simple: it is not a straight choice between paying Martin Amis half a million pounds, or publishing a hundred first novels with advances of £5,000 each.

Publishing is an area where people matter: relationships can be strained by inefficiency or neglect. Now that most publishing companies are so much bigger than they used to be, the number of people involved in publishing an author's book is correspondingly larger and there is more potential for problems.

Against this background of financial and performance pressure, it is no wonder that problems occur. Publishers are often heard to deplore the fact that authors seem to have little loyalty to their publishers any more. I would be expected to take the authors' part in such an exchange, but I do believe that it is not simply that authors have become greedy and will chase the highest advance offered, but rather that the nature of publishing itself makes it hard to know just who or what an author is supposed to be able to feel loyalty toward.

Should they be loyal to their editor? Most authors I know have had several changes of editor forced upon them, even if they have stayed with the same company. Perhaps the company? How do you define 'the company'? Is it the imprint name that appears on the spine of the book? Hardly, when editors can find themselves with the right (and obligation) to buy for maybe eight imprints within a group, and the imprint may be just one of dozens reporting to a British head office, which itself reports to another group in New York, which itself reports to an even larger group in Germany.

In an age when company ownership has become impersonal and publishing contracts have become confrontational, it is perhaps no wonder that authors find personal feelings such as loyalty sometimes redundant in their dealings with publishers.

Close bonds like this have, perhaps, been transferred to agents. It is when authors face problems with their publisher that they often value their agent most.

Given the immense complexity of many publishing groups now, I am sometimes surprised that authors don't encounter more problems than they do. When I was President of the Association of Authors' Agents I heard about many disputes between authors and publishers that could have been resolved if the contracts had been better drafted. An argument about the acceptability of a manuscript that was different to the storyline the publisher thought they were buying would have been unnecessary if a description or synopsis of the novel had been included with the contract at the outset.

If your publisher is sold from one group to another and you are not sure that you really want to be part of the new group, again your original contract can be a help if it contains the right clauses (see chapter 9).

Other problems can arise for which no contract can help. It is interpersonal skills that will be required if you want to change editor or publicist, or need to persuade the company that the cover they want to use isn't right, or that the title you wish for your novel is preferable to the title they have suggested.

The problem an author often encounters with a publisher is that of speed, or lack of it. Many large publishers have large contracts departments but still too much work to cope with; many small publishers just don't have enough staff, or enough skilled staff. Books take a long time to be published once the manuscript is delivered, and it can be daunting to wait a year for your publication date when you have been working to your delivery date deadline.

Publishing is slow and any author who constantly rails against payments coming in three weeks after publication date rather than on publication day itself, or who insists on a particular month for publication despite the best advice from their publisher that two months later would put it into a more advantageous season, is always going to be unhappy. You will have to adapt to trade practice. No author can single-handedly change the business. But that doesn't mean you must be complacent. When there is real cause for complaint take a while to think through what will be the most effective procedure for putting things right.

If you have an agent, they should be your first port of call. Talk things through and listen to advice that probably comes with a lot of knowledge about the way your publisher works. If you don't have an agent, The Society of Authors can help, particularly if it is a matter of trade practice. If the problem is purely legal, or financial, your lawyer or accountant may be useful.

But first I would always advise talking to the relevant person at the publishing company. Always try to deal with the problem at its source before bringing in others.

One of the most awkward problems to deal with is if you wish to stay with the publishing company but would prefer to move to another editor. This must be handled delicately, and is much easier to handle through an agent than trying to do it yourself. But if you get on well with someone else at the company whom you can trust and can talk to confidentially, ask their opinion and ask for a recommendation as to which senior publisher you should approach for help in arranging the change.

If you wish to change publicists within a company, it's your editor whom you should be able to ask for help.

Many of the problems you are likely to encounter with your publisher are dealt with under the relevant sections of this book: accepting editorial criticism, negotiating a deal, assessing their offer, dealing with publicity or the lack of it, understanding royalty statements, getting rights back when your novel goes out of print.

Many authors might be surprised to see that the next section on problems with your agent is actually longer than this section! This is partly because the entire book is approached from the point of view of the author and their agent and so potential problems with your publisher are highlighted in each chapter. To find specific areas do use the chapter headings or the index.

Problems with your agent

Changing agents is like changing deck-chairs on the Titanic
– Old actor's advice to a young one

There are others you can go to for help in dealing with publishers. But many authors feel quite helpless when they encounter problems with their agent.

As an agent, I hope for long-term relationships with my clients, but inevitably there will be some that founder. The important consideration is to try to solve problems in such a way that you can still deal in a productive fashion with the agent with whom you are having a dispute, whether you stay with them or not.

Problems and trying to solve them

Authors and agents fall out far less often than authors and publishers but it does happen and can cause authors real emotional turmoil, particularly if the relationship has been a close one in the past. Reasons for author–agent relationships breaking down range from the relatively minor 'She always takes two days to return my phone calls', to a major crisis if you believe your agent isn't accounting to you on time, or at all, for payments made to them on your behalf. Or, and more difficult to remedy (without leaving), is if you believe your agent is not advancing your cause sufficiently, not selling you well enough.

Whatever the problem, I would always counsel prudence initially. Talk to the agent about the problem, perhaps sending a letter (or fax or e-mail) first, outlining the problem that you want to discuss. This can be a way of diffusing the anxiety for you of bringing up the subject in the first place, and can help lower the emotional intensity.

This may sound as though I am overdramatizing, but I know that authors and agents who have worked together for many years do often feel extremely nervous if they have to confront a problem that may well call into question the whole issue of trust perhaps misplaced.

I have seen authors take hasty decisions to leave agents without necessarily having talked through the problem first. In publishing, we are all in the business of communicating and sometimes communications can go haywire. It can be a great pity for authors to leave long-term agenting situations because of a problem that could have been solved by sitting down and discussing it. Things could improve once you have aired the problem.

If you have a problem you can't solve and you need help to deal with an agent, there are several bodies who will advise and sometimes also take action, depending on the problem. If the agent in question is a member of the Association of Authors' Agents, contact their president or secretary, in writing, with a summary of the problem, perhaps having first read the Association's Constitution (see Appendix 6). The Association can be very helpful in sorting out problems between client and agent, and if the agent is at fault in a way that transgresses their Constitution, the Association will take prompt action.

Alternatively you might call on the services of The Society of Authors. If you are a member they will advise you immediately and might also help you draft a letter, or suggest what your next step should be. If you are not a member, this would be an obvious time to join.

But sometimes there is no solution except to leave the agency.

Deciding to change agents

If you feel that there has been such a breakdown of trust and communication, or a dereliction of duty that makes it impossible for you to continue to be represented by your current agent, then you have a number of decisions to make.

If you can't bear to deal with your past agent any longer it will be difficult to deal with matters that they will continue to handle, such as royalty statements on past contracts, so whatever the nature of your complaint, try to deal with it in as businesslike a manner as possible. A dignified exit is more becoming – and more conducive to civil relations in the future – than a row. This is a business matter after all. No matter how high the feelings have been running, try to put them to one side and concentrate on what has to be done to tie up loose ends.

If you do fall out with your past agent to the point where relations are very strained, you might feel that they have little motivation in taking care of your affairs and under those circumstances it might well be best to have your publisher make separate payments to the agent and to you. Then you may have to take responsibility yourself for chasing the publishers for action and material, checking your own royalty statements, chasing your own payments. Your agent should still be doing this, but if you can't bring yourself to deal with them any longer, you won't be able to find out if they are.

There is seldom an obvious time to move agencies, seldom a moment in a writer's life when things have 'stopped'. Your previous book may be contracted but not yet delivered, or delivered but not yet published, or published in your home market but not yet signed up overseas, etc. But all of this can be dealt with calmly and professionally so long as the leave-taking is orderly. By orderly, I mean that each publishing step has been thought through and discussed, and each member of the chain – author, previous agent, new agent – knows who is responsible for what.

Usually the agent who negotiated a contract continues to handle it, and to collect their commission, for the life of the contract: raising invoices where necessary, collecting monies due for delivery of manuscript, publication etc., checking that finished books are received from the publisher, receiving and checking royalty statements. This means that you must remember to tell your previous agent when you do things that require action but which, as they no longer represent you, they might not otherwise know. If you have left your agent after a contract is signed but before you have delivered your manuscript, you must remember to tell them when you do deliver it. As it might no longer be delivered via their office, your agent needs to hear from you when you have sent it to the publisher so that they call in the money due on delivery. It's no good berating a past agent for not collecting your delivery money on time if they had no way of knowing it was due.

Sometimes an author will move a past contract to a new agency, having agreed with both past and present agents to do this, and having agreed on the terms of the move. The usual arrangement in such circumstances is for the new agent then to take over all the business on the past contract (the author must inform the publisher of this arrangement in writing, preferably with a copy of the letter to each agent) and for the new agent to collect all income for the future and for the two agents to split the commission equally. When the new agent receives income under the contract, they will send half the commission to the previous agent.

But what if, having left your past agent, you are deciding to do without an agent for the foreseeable future? Your choice is then either to leave the contract with that past agent or, if you really cannot sanction your income passing through their office, to come to an arrangement whereby the publisher splits all future payments due under the contract, paying commission to the agent, but the rest directly to you.

It is an unfortunate fact that relations do sometimes break down when clients move, but they don't have to. Last year a client left me to go to another agent. I can live with that without getting too upset about it. My rationalization to myself is that she has unrealistic expectations anyway, and no one is going to be able to achieve what she thinks she deserves! Be that as it may, I still like her personally (and love her novels) and am good friends with her new agent. She left just before the paperback publication of her second novel and her publishers gave her a party to celebrate. When I received my invitation I rang her to check if she knew I had been invited: she did. I love parties, and saw no reason not to go to this one so we all had a jolly evening together, a *ménage à trois* of my past client, her past agent and her new agents.

That's what happens in the best of worlds but I'm realistic enough to know it doesn't happen like that all of the time. I have one past client who complains every time they see an opportunity: if royalty statements seem to be a few days late, if foreign editions turn up late, or get damaged in the mail, if a publisher lets one of their books go out of print, if a telephone call isn't returned the same day, if I'm on holiday or abroad on a business trip when they want to speak to me, in other words if any occasion occurs in which they think they can feel slighted. This is tedious, but one gets through it as best one can. I think that an agent has to be even more scrupulous in dealing with the affairs of past clients to prevent such nit-picking and irritating behaviour. If someone is looking to catch you out, it's much more irritating to them if you behave with extraordinary meticulousness!

Most authors will feel more secure leaving an agent if they already know which agent they are moving on to. This brings me to a potential minefield. Part of the Constitution of the Association of Authors' Agents states firmly that agents should not 'poach' clients from each other. I have no trouble adhering to this as I've never approached a potential client in my life, but it does impose an obligation on agent members of the Association to be sure that they know the agenting circumstances of any potential client they are speaking to. I am of the opinion that if an author approaches me and sounds me out about the possibilities of me acting for them, and that if they admit they are

presently with another agent but are intending to move, it is honourable to continue the discussion. Authors must have the right to choose
and this includes the right to move as and when they wish. All
meetings of this kind are confidential, as they should be. I always ask,
when a potential client first approaches me, to read some of their
writing before organizing a meeting, and to be told of their current
agenting situation.

I would advise authors when choosing an agent initially, and when
moving from one to another, that they should sound out several and
not make a decision until they are absolutely sure they have got it
right. I can hear groans at this point because I do know how difficult
it is to get an agent. But particularly if you are already published, and
you are moving from an agent, there is a strong possibility that there
will be several agencies prepared to offer you representation. Making
a decision in a hurry can be regretted later on if you make the wrong
decision. Even if your publisher is about to offer for a new book, you
can ask them to hold on until your agency situation is clarified. There
are rarely such urgent time-conscious matters happening in publishing
that can't either happen anyway via your previous agent, or wait until
you have made a move.

Once you have decided who to move on to, tell your previous agent
immediately. There is nothing worse than for the agent to hear from
someone else in the business that you are leaving. At that point you
should discuss what rights stay where. Most agents' agreement letters
call for a specific notice period. This is to allow the agent to finish off
negotiations and submissions that are in progress. Some agents require
one or two months: three should be the maximum. All members of
the Association of Authors' Agents sign letters of agreement with their
clients. If your agent did not sign one with you, make sure that at the
point of giving them notice, you also suggest a notice period after
which you may take any unsold rights away, if you so wish.

We had a situation recently where a client was joining us from
another agency. She had published five novels, none of which had
been sold to anyone other than her British publisher. She wanted to
move the unsold rights in these books to us and I was keen to take
them over. I judged them to be saleable – still – to publishers in
translation. Her previous agent, angry that she was leaving at all,
would not countenance these rights being moved, despite the fact that
they belong to the author, not the agent. He corresponded with her
most aggressively, accusing her of being ungrateful for all his past
work, and argued that in order to pay him back for all his years
of work on her behalf, her translation rights had to stay with him
for ever. Needless to say he was not, and is not, a member of the

Association. The author had to endure several angry letters which only stopped when she wrote a very firm letter, pointing out that she had withdrawn from that agent her authority for him to act on her behalf, and sent open copies to me and The Society of Authors.

She had never been offered a letter of agreement to sign with him, and he was employing bullying tactics, plain and simple, to try to get his own way. It was shocking behaviour: no author should be intimidated in this way.

If you do move your unsold rights to your new agent you will have to be able to supply the new agent with copies of your past books (enough to make fresh submissions) and also, preferably, information on past submissions. In the example I've quoted above, the author was able to give me enough copies of her books, but we have never been able to get any information out of her previous agent about submissions made in overseas markets. I think, perhaps meanly, that this is because there have been few submissions and he doesn't want to admit that. But he has been so obstructive in every respect that he may be withholding information anyway. I have had to make submissions to overseas publishers without knowing which of them have seen her work before.

Not all agents wish to take on the selling of old titles. One agent I know and respect is very open about not wishing to do this. She feels that the motivation of her own agency and her co-operating sub-agents overseas can never be high for offering old books, and she would always rather start from the new title. Under those circumstances an author has no alternative but to leave their past books with their past agent, even though that agent's motivation to go on offering them will also have dipped once the client has moved on.

If your past agent does continue to offer some rights for you, make sure that both agents are quite clear about the demarcation lines. Agency work is all detail, and it behoves authors to master this when they are dealing with two agencies. Muddle at the point of handover will be to the detriment of the author and their work, either because of lost sales or lost time.

Moving to a new agent means you, the author, must be responsible for briefing that new agent on the state of your publishing affairs. It helps if you type a chronology of all your books, all their editions, complete with editor and publisher names, year of publication, and copies of all the contracts you can lay your hands on, together with information as to which editions are in or out of print, and copies of as many royalty statements as you can supply for reasonably current books. I am continually amazed by how few authors can supply information of this nature without getting into a muddle. I have had many meetings with potential new clients where I have had to debrief them verbally and have spent hours taking down details, sometimes given in a very haphazard fashion.

Remember that so-called 'electronic' rights can be practically indivisible once a licence has been granted for any of them. Contracts for film rights, even options, can sometimes promise all or part of these rights when even the most astute agent is negotiating. Make sure that your new agent reads contracts you have signed through your past agent because otherwise they could negotiate new deals for you that impose upon rights already granted. As you are the signatory, it is you, the author, who would be in breach of contract if you ended up selling the same rights to two different parties.

It is important, as a regular item of good housekeeping, that agents should request reversion of rights when books cease to be actively sold by a publisher. We do this when we receive royalty statements and see sluggish – or no – sales in any period. If your past agent was slow or negligent in doing this, it may be the first thing that your new agent does for you. It can be a bit depressing, having moved to a new agency, to receive a regular flow of reversion letters but don't be daunted! It is much better that the files be tidied in this manner. If a publisher is not actively exploiting your book, rights should certainly be returned to you. Thus, if you suddenly receive a film rights offer on one of your past novels, and the book rights have reverted to you, when the film is being made you can sell the book again, rather than simply letting the previous publisher reprint when the film comes out. When you obtain a reversion of rights on a contract negotiated by a previous agent, that ends the agent's involvement in the contract and title. At that point the rights can be handled on your behalf by the new agent. Of course, there's nothing to say that the new agent will be able to re-sell an old book, but it is better to have as much as possible of your career handled by one agency.

During the notice period, your previous agent will collect answers to submissions already made and it is possible that offers could result. You are free to accept them or reject them in the normal way. Once again, if you accept an offer from a submission made by your previous agent, then the previous agent will put through the contract and be entitled to commission. If you decide against accepting an offer that comes from an agent you are about to leave, it is not honourable to reject it and then try to accept it through your new agent. Your new agent ought to advise you against this anyway. Nor is it acceptable to reject an offer made via an agent and then try to accept it yourself, without using an agent.

I did once hear of an exaggerated version of this. An author who is a household name had a three-book contract via a well-known and large agency. The author asked the agent to negotiate a release for him from the contract. The agent did so and the contract was nullified. Shortly thereafter the author left the agency. Some time later the agency heard that the author was again signed up with the same publisher, for what looked suspiciously like the same three-book contract. The author had used a blatant subterfuge to try to get out of paying commission to the agency on the future payments under the long-term contract. The agency instructed a lawyer to sue for their commission on the grounds that the contract was materially the same as that which the agency had negotiated. The agency stated their case sufficiently strongly and the author settled out of court.

But most authors who chose to leave an agency manage to do it with relative ease, even if they do find it a worrying time. It is your right to move and if you are unhappy with your representation you should seek a change. It may not have happened to you before but it almost certainly has happened to your agent. They will survive it. And so will you.

Joining a new agency

When you decide to approach another agent, send a confident (and confidential) letter outlining your career to date. In fact, any communication between prospective (and indeed current) client and agent should be treated in confidence by both parties. If you are a published author with a backlist, the more information you give the agent about your past work, the better they will be able to assess what they could do for you in the future. Include a full rights list (each book title, with publication date, and each edition in English and translation listed with publishers' names). If you have a record of advances paid and sales figures you should include these too.

Give an indication of your future plans and say whether you are approaching more than one agency. One drawback of a multiple submission to agencies is that some agents, me included, will not read material in competition with other agencies. For a fuller discussion of this see chapter 2. An upside of multiple submissions is that you might get faster responses if an agent knows there is competition. But most agencies are working at full stretch all of the time. If your only criteria is initial speed of response you could be missing out on the best agency for your work.

Don't be surprised if the agent you have contacted asks for material – and time – to read some of your work. The agent may already have read your books, but if they haven't, it's only professional of them to assess your work before offering to meet you. Meeting a writer before reading them can be a complete waste of time in case the agent doesn't like the writing. And no self-respecting writer should want an agent who isn't interested in their work.

The best sample of unpublished writing consists of the first two chapters, and a synopsis of the whole book. If you are published, send a copy of at least your most recent book as well.

At your first meeting with a new agent, don't take your spouse, nanny, dog or neighbour. Think about your first day at school: did you really want your mother to take you? There's very little difference. This is a professional meeting: treat it as such. I can only think of two clients I have ever taken on who have chosen to attend our first meeting with their other half. It often makes me feel they are unconfident, distrustful of their own ability to make decisions.

Talk to your new agent about a range of relevant subjects: the way you like to write, your and their attitude to editorial collaboration; their relationship with your editor, your publisher; how they handle American and translation rights; who their other clients are; who their staff are and how long they have been together; and of course their commission rates. All this will have a bearing on your decision to join them or not.

Ask your new agent to show you their letter of agreement with clients as soon as you are in a dialogue with them. All member agencies of the Association of Authors' Agents (AAA) are advised to offer agreements to their clients. These are clearly stated documents that set out simply who does what and for how much. There can be no misunderstanding about business relationships when you've seen and signed such a document.

Ask your agent if they belong to the AAA. Non-membership could simply mean they have not been trading long enough to qualify, or that their income isn't big enough. But membership means that you know they adhere to the AAA Constitution, and that there is a Committee you can talk to or complain to if you run into problems with your agent.

When you do sign up with a new agency, in addition to the copies of previous contracts, I would suggest that you also give them a file of your press cuttings and copies of previous books. And remember to let them know when the notice period with your previous agent runs out. Moving from one agent to another can be done smoothly, provided all parties behave in a professional manner.

18 Your next book

Finishing a book is just like you took a child out in the back yard
and shot it – Truman Capote

It is by sitting down to write every morning that one becomes a
writer. Those who do not do this remain amateurs
– Gerald Brennan

Instead of mourning the loss of your past book and its characters
(whether this is because it is published, and therefore public property,
or because you can't sell it and have decided to move on), take
pleasure in starting the next.

You might be forgiven for thinking that, after the battle to get your
first published, starting the next will be easy, and anyway something
you can put off thinking about until the time comes to start it. Wrong.

Because of the huge problems to be overcome in launching a new
author, once a publisher has decided to offer for your first novel, you
may well find that they make an offer for two at the outset, particularly if you have actually completed the first one at the time of the
sale. Indeed, they may put off making an offer for the first because
they want to see a synopsis for the second. They want to be sure you
have more than one book in you. Agents often feel the same.

So it is worth spending some time thinking about your next book
before you offer the first. This is not to suggest that you should simply
prepare to write a sequel to the first. This is something that so many
inexperienced authors do, and it is somewhat off-putting. Planning a
sequel involves making all kinds of assumptions about the first and its
level of success. Unfortunately it's been proved time and again that
sequels seldom sell more than – or even as well as – the first. I know
we can all think of exceptions to that rule, but it is more usual for
series to diminish in sales if the first has not been a huge success.
Locking yourself into a sequence of novels (unless it's a well-defined
genre like detective novels where series do work well) can be dis-
astrous.

If you like the idea of continuing the storyline or the characters, it's far better to produce the sequel as your third or fourth book in response to eager suggestions from your publisher. By that time the hardback and the paperback of the first will have been published and the sales can be assessed. That way you have written book two, seen it published and perhaps delivered the manuscript of book three without relying on an audience for a sequel to the first, which you couldn't predict at the time you embarked upon the second or third. If your sequel only makes sense to those who have read book one, it's hard to see how it can sell more than book one.

What should you write as book two? Certainly something that will appeal to the same kind of audience you expect for your first novel. To change genres this early could be a mistake. You are trying to make a name for yourself, and the way to do that is to continue to please your core audience and to add to the numbers with each novel. Your publisher will have endeavoured to establish your name with a particular group of readers. That's what you must build on. I am often amazed when authors approach me with plans for a sequence of books as diverse as a children's novel, a science fiction story, a literary historical novel and a thriller. It happens, but I am hardly ever tempted to take them on.

It's not necessary to repeat yourself. John Grisham uses his own background of the law to write legal thrillers; they are all different, but the audience who like them expect to like the next one. Michael Ridpath does that with financial thrillers. Barbara Erskine does it with contemporary women's fiction that blends a ghostly element from the past with a central character in the present.

If you have signed a one-book contract for your first, you will have finished that and be thinking about the next well before your first book is published, and so therefore well before the publisher has any kind of sales figures or feedback from bookshops. This is another reason to plan your next book to please the readers of the first: a publisher will find it very alarming to contemplate launching a writer in two different areas, one after another. If your publisher should turn down your second book because it is so different to your first, you might have a hard time relaunching yourself with another imprint. It's not impossible, but it is very tricky.

You don't have to feel compelled to write the same thing for ever. Once you have become successful you can hope that your audience will be such devoted fans that they will buy whatever you write. But I would still preach caution: make small changes from the style of one book to another rather than writing something completely different. This is one of the areas where commercial and literary fiction differ:

literary writers who are read more for their language than their storyline alone can expect their audience to be more receptive to the writer changing direction between books. The audience for commercial fiction is less forgiving of abrupt changes in genre. One exception is the very commercial Ken Follett. His books are often extremely different to each other but his sales have remained consistently high – an example of how you can manipulate your audience, once you have a large one.

Of course, it's quite common for writers to use more than one name to differentiate between writing styles. Joanna Trollope writes also as Caroline Harvey; Ruth Rendell as Barbara Vine. When the writer becomes famous under their own name, publishers often wish to put both names on the pseudonymous novels as happens with both of these writers now hence: 'P. D. James writing as Barbara Vine'. By the time publishers are happy to identify the writer behind the pseudonym, the pseudonym has simply become a signal to the reader of which kind of novel they should expect from each writing name.

Another and different example of a writer's name acting as a 'brand' is the author Virginia Andrews. She wrote a number of bestselling 'gothic' family stories that sold hugely around the world in many editions. She died many years ago but her family approved her American publisher's use of a pseudonymous author (someone who had already had a number of novels published under his own name) to keep the Virginia Andrews name and sales going. The author credit is now 'The New Virginia Andrews TM' (trade mark).

And finally . . .

For a dyed-in-the-wool author nothing is as dead as a book once it is written . . . She is rather like a cat whose kittens have grown up. While they were a-growing she was passionately interested in them but now they seem hardly to belong to her – and probably she is involved with another batch of kittens as I am involved with other writing. – Rumer Godden

Whatever you decide to do for your next novel, get on with it. Write something every day. No writing equals no book, so even if you don't feel like it, write something; you can always revise it tomorrow. Writers who procrastinate will find lengthening periods between books cause problems with marketing, selling, publicity, and eventually demotivates your publisher.

A writing life should be an enjoyable one too. But there are pitfalls, and to help you be aware of them, in order to overcome them, I pass on this advice from a writer who knows. When you become a writer you are advised on royalties, given hints on craft, offered editorial advice, but here are:

Ten vital things nobody (especially your editor or agent) will tell you . . . by Maeve Haran

1. *Your weight will balloon overnight*
   It's all those snack attacks that are so hard to resist when you're based at home with nothing but a word processor to stare at. 'I think I'll just have another chocolate biscuit while I'm downstairs putting the washing machine on . . .' is how it starts.

2. *You will elevate displacement activity into an art form*
   Dusting skirting boards previously ignored for years will suddenly become an essential task, study-tidying is an old faithful and once when I was really desperate to avoid work I tidied my daughter's dolls' house!

3. *You will lose your friends . . .*
   Either because they think they're in the book or because they fear they aren't.

4. *You will experience a dark night of the soul around page 64 . . .*
   This is the moment when you start thinking, 'I'm hating this and if I hate it how can I ever expect anyone else to read it for *pleasure*?' This is entirely natural and happens to everyone. Ignore and plough on.

5. *Even if you previously had the generosity of Mother Teresa, you will suffer from envy*
   You will especially start to hate anyone described in the review pages as 'the new Joanna Trollope'. You will scan Alex Hamilton's fast sellers list (which you had never heard of before you became a writer) with hate in your heart.

6. *Going into a bookshop will never be the same again*
   Now you will simply worry whether your book is on show and, if so, is it in a good enough position? If they are sold out is this because your book was in desperate demand, or because it sold so slowly they haven't reordered?

7. *You no longer have a personal life*
This has to be dredged annually for the PR trail . . . the ideal writer has a darker past than Lucrezia Borgia and should be ready to mine it every year for all the little slots that newspapers specialize in. You know the kind of thing: 'Me and My Abortion', 'The Hometown I Couldn't Wait To Get Out Of' . . .

8. *You need the thick skin of a rhinoceros or an Ivana Trump*
Reviewers can be kind or cruel. For some reason it's only the cruel ones you will remember. The *Sunday Times* said my first book was interesting but the main problem with it was that not only could you not imagine my heroine being big in television, you couldn't imagine her being big in home-made chutney!

9. *You have to be game for anything*
While promoting my books I have had to debate women and work in a shopping centre in Argentina, be interviewed about the nature of drama while in a jacuzzi aboard the QE2, and eat stone-cold vegetable tempura cooked for me an hour earlier by Robert Carrier for a TV programme. All to sell books!

10. *It's all worth it!*
Writing is the most enormous pleasure and privilege and we're incredibly lucky to be allowed to do it and be paid.

Every writer I have shown that piece to has recognized most, or all, of those feelings!

So – back to the computer – to write!

Part Four

APPENDIXES

Appendix 1

Publishers who have negotiated minimum terms agreements with The Society of Authors and The Writers' Guild

Andre Deutsch, 1992
BBC Publications, 1984
Bloomsbury, 1987
Faber&Faber, 1992
HarperCollins, 1992
Hodder Headline, 1994
Penguin, 1990
Random House, 1993
Transworld, 1995

Agreements had also been negotiated with the following: Chapmans and Journeyman Press, which are now out of business; Hamish Hamilton (no longer used now they are part of Penguin); Metheun and Sinclair Stevenson (no longer used as they are both now part of Random House).

Currently negotiating with Macmillan (1999)

To obtain copies of these agreements (which differ slightly from publisher to publisher) write to The Society of Authors.

Appendix 2

Awards, bursaries and prizes

Up-to-date listings for authors' awards can be obtained from The Society of Authors.

Publishing News organizes the annual publishing trade awards, called 'The Nibbies' (the awards are in the shape of a fountain pen nib). The awards are voted for by an academy made up of leading trade people from all aspects of the industry and presented at a glittering awards night each February. The trade magazine can provide you with a list of past categories and winners.

Book Trust Guide to Literary Prizes is published by Book Trust (see page 362). Awards for fiction include:

Authors' Club – *Best First Novel Award*
The Secretary, Authors' Club, 40 Dover Street, London W1X 3RB.
Tel: 0171 499 8581. Fax: 0171 409 0913.
Annual, for a novel published in the UK by a British author.

The James Tait Black Memorial Prize
University of Edinburgh, Department of English Literature,
David Hume Tower, George Square, Edinburgh EH8 9JX.
Tel: 0131 650 3619. E-mail: www.ed.ac.uk/~englitw3/jtbinf.htm
Annual, for a novel published in the UK.

The Booker Prize
Book Trust, Book House, 45 East Hill, London SW18 2QZ.
Tel: 0181 516 2973. Fax: 0181 516 2978.
E-mail: www.booktrust.org.uk
Annual, written in English by a citizen of the British Commonwealth, Republic of Ireland or South Africa and published for the first time in the UK by a British publisher.

British Science Fiction Association Awards
Chris Hill, BSFA Awards Administrator, The Bungalow,
27 Lower Evingar Road, Whitechurch, Hants RG28 7EY.
Annual, best novel and best short fiction.

Commonwealth Writers Prize

Book Trust, Book House, 45 East Hill, London SW18 2QZ.
Tel: 0181 516 2973. Fax: 0181 516 2978.
E-mail: www.booktrust.org.uk

Annual, best work of prose fiction (including short stories) and best first novel or first collection of short stories written in English by a citizen of the Commonwealth.

Crime Writers' Association Awards

Crime Writers' Association, P O Box 6939, Kings Heath, Birmingham B14 7LT. Tel: 0121 444 2536.
E-mail: www.twbooks.co.uk/cwa/cwa.html

Annual, a range of awards for crime writing.

Encore Award

The Society of Authors, 84 Drayton Gardens, London SW10 9SB.
Tel: 0171 373 6642

Annual, best second novel published in the UK in the English language.

The *Guardian* Fiction Prize

The *Guardian*, 119 Farringdon Road, London EC1R 3ER.
Tel: 0171 278 2332. Fax: 0171 713 4368.
E-mail: www.guardian.co.uk

Annual, novel or short story collection published by a British or Commonwealth writer.

The Hawthornden Prize

The Administrator, Hawthornden Trust, 42a Hays Mews, Berkeley Square, London W1X 7RU.

Annual, best work of imaginative literature by a British author.

David Higham Prize for Fiction

Book Trust, Book House, 45 East Hill, London SW18 2QZ.
Tel: 0181 870 9055.

Annual, first novel of short story collection written in English by a citizen of the British Commonwealth, Republic or Ireland or South Africa.

International IMPAC Dublin Literary Award

The International IMPAC Dublin Literary Award Office, Dublin City Public Libraries, Administrative Headquarters, Cumberland House, Fenian Street, Dublin 2, Republic of Ireland.
Tel: 00 3531 661 9000. Fax: 00 3531 676 1628.
E-mail: dublin.city.libs@aol.ie

Annual, fiction published in English or translated into English.

The McKitterick Prize

The Society of Authors, 84 Drayton Gardens, London SW10 9SB.
Annual, first adult published or unpublished novel by author over the age of 40.

The *Mail on Sunday*–John Llewellyn Rhys Prize

The *Mail on Sunday*–John Llewellyn Rhys Prize, c/o Book Trust, Book House, 45 East Hill, London SW18 2QZ.
Tel: 0181 870 9055.
Annual, best English language work by a UK or Commonwealth citizen under the age of 35.

Orange Prize for Fiction

Orange Prize for Fiction, Book Trust, Book House, 45 East Hill, London SW18 2QZ. Tel: 0181 870 9055.
Annual, published fiction by a woman of any nationality in the English language.

Romantic Novelists' Association Awards – *Parker Romantic Novel of the Year*

The Old Bake House, 36 East Gate, Hallton, Market Harborough, Leicester LE16 8UB. Tel: 01858 555602.
Annual, best modern or historical novel by a UK citizen.

The Sagittarius Prize

The Society of Authors, 84 Drayton Gardens, London SW10 9SB.
Annual, first novel by writer over 60.

W. H. Smith Annual Literary Award

W. H. Smith Group plc, Nations House, 103 Wigmore Street, London W1H OWH. Tel: 0171 409 3222. Fax: 0171 629 3600.
E-mail: www.whsmithgroup.com
Annual, for a Commonwealth or British citizen who makes the most outstanding contribution to literature.

W. H. Smith Thumping Good Read Award

W. H. Smith, Books Department, Greenbridge Road, Swindon, Wiltshire SN3 3LD.
Annual, for a 'page-turning good read'.

The Betty Trask Award

The Society of Authors, 84 Drayton Gardens, London SW10 9SB.
Annual, first work of a romantic or traditional, rather than experimental nature by a Commonwealth citizen under the age of 35. The winners are required to use the money for a period or periods of foreign travel.

Whitbread Literary Awards
Karen Earl Ltd., 2–3 Ledbury Mews West, London W11 2AE.
Tel: 0171 243 0064. Fax: 0171 792 1220.
Annual, five categories including: Novel and First Novel. Overall winner is Whitbread Book of the Year.

Appendix 3

Bibliography

Many of the subjects below are also covered by the *Writers' and Artists' Yearbook* and *The Writer's Handbook* (see under 'Reference') and by The Society of Authors in their *Quick Guides*. For Australia, *The Australian Writer's Marketplace*, first published in 1998 and expected to be updated annually, is published by Innervision Communications, Victoria.

Agents

Greenfield, George. *A Smattering of Monsters*, Warner, London, 1997. Not a guide but a hugely entertaining memoir by a distinguished British agent: full of stories of famous writers and publishing characters.
Legat, Michael. *An Author's Guide to Literary Agents*, Robert Hale, London, 1995. One of the few guides to literary agents.

Copyright

A Guide to Royalty Agreements, 5th edn, Agreements Committee of the Publishers Association, London, 1972. Dry but reliable.
Flint, Michael F. *A User's Guide to Copyright, 4th edn*, Butterworths, London, 1997. Readable guide by an expert.
Skone, James E. P. *On Copyright*, Sweet & Maxwell. The standard work but unreadable except by lawyers, I would have thought. I recommend Flint above.

Film and television

Friedmann, Julian. *How to Make Money Scriptwriting*, Intellect, London, 1999. The second edition of my business partner's guide to becoming a professional scriptwriter.

Libel

Rubinstein, Michael (ed.). *Wicked, Wicked Libels*, Routledge & Kegan Paul, London, 1972. Anecdotal rather than a guide to the law. Entertaining (and frightening!), by a leading libel lawyer.

Negotiating

Balkin, Richard. *A Writer's Guide to Contract Negotiations*, Writers Digest, Ohio, 1985. A robust American approach.

Legat, M. *Understanding Publishers' Contracts*, Robert Hale, London, 1992. Accessible beginner's guide.

The Writer's Rights, A&C Black, London, 1995. A good guide for authors.

Owen, Lynette. *Selling Rights, 2nd edn*, Blueprint, London, 1994. More for industry insiders: perhaps too detailed for writers.

Promotion and publicity

Bostock, Louise. *Speaking in Public*, HarperCollins, London, 1994. A good basic guide.

Smithies, Dick. *How to Speak in Public: A winning way with words*, Unwin, London, 1985. Old but still relevant.

Publishing

Baverstock, Alison. *Are Books Different? Marketing in the Book Trade*, Kogan Page, London, 1993

How to Market Books, Kogan Page, London, 1993. The two Baverstock titles on marketing in publishing make some important points

Butcher, Judith. *Copy-Editing: The Cambridge handbook for editors, authors and publishers*, 3rd edn, Cambridge University Press, 1975. The standard work but probably more than most authors need to know.

Gross, Gerald (ed.) *Editors on Editing: What writers need to know about what editors do, 3rd edn*, Grove Press, New York, 1993. American editors talking about their own work: extremely interesting.

Owen, Peter (ed.) *Publishing Now*, Peter Owen, London, 1993. An independent English publisher's view of 1990s publishing.

Unwin, Sir Stanley. *The Truth about Publishing, 8th edn*, Allen & Unwin, London, 1976. The classic insider's guide, even if it is now rather old.

Self-publishing

Finch, Peter. *How to Publish Yourself*, National Small Press Centre Handbook (published by National Small Press Centre, Middlesex University, White Hart Lane, London N17 8HR

Stanley, Trevor. *Publishing Yourself*, (Co-ordinator of The Association of Little Presses). The above two titles are helpful and practical.
Wynne-Tyson, Jon. *Publishing Your Own Book*, Centaur Press. By an independent publisher: a different viewpoint.

Writing

Bird, Carmel. *Dear Writer: Advice to aspiring authors*, Virago, London, 1990. Practical and inspirational.
Bishop, Leonard. *Dare To Be a Great Writer*, Writers Digest, Ohio, 1992. American take on the same subject.
Block, Lawrence. *Writing the Novel from Plot to Print*, Writers Digest, Ohio, 1986. Very practical American guide to getting published.
Brande, Dorothea. *Becoming a Writer*, Papermac, London, 1983. A book which, deservedly, has a huge following.
Brown, Rita Mae. *Starting from Scratch*, Bantam, New York, 1988. American novelist gives advice on your early writing career.
Carroll, David L. *A Manual of Writers' Tricks*, Paragon House, New York, 1990. American advice on short cuts to success.
Crofts, Andrew. *How to Make Money from Freelance Writing*, Piatkus Books, London, 1992. By a very successful ghost writer.
Fowler, H. W. *A Dictionary of Modern English Usage*, Oxford University Press. The classic work.
Frey, James N. *How to Write a Damn Good Novel: The hard-hitting handbook for everyone who wants to write like a born storyteller*, Papermac, London, 1987. One of the most practical and accessible books on the subject I have ever read. I recommend it highly. Out of print but perhaps obtainable from libraries.
Geraghty, Margret. *The Novelist's Guide: Powerful techniques for creating character, dialogue and plot*, Piatkus Books, London, 1995. Prescriptive help on specific aspects of writing fiction.
Gibbs, Alison. *Writers on Writing*, Robert Hale, London, 1995. Anecdotal rather than prescriptive, but makes interesting reading, particularly if you are interested in the writers interviewed.
Haffenden, John. *Novelists in Interview*, Metheun, London, 1985. Like the Gibbs above.
Higgins, George V. *On Writing: Advice for those who write to publish (or would like to)*, Bloomsbury, London, 1991. One of the few books on how to write by someone who is an international success at it himself.
Keating, H. R. F. *Writing Crime Fiction*, A&C Black, London, 1986. Another successful practitioner who knows what he's talking about.

Legat, M. *The Nuts and Bolts of Writing*, Robert Hale. By an ex-publisher who now publishes widely on the trade.

Partridge, Eric. *Usage and Abusage: A guide to good English*, Hamish Hamilton. A classic work.

Saunders, Jean. *How to Research Your Novel*, Allison&Busby, London, 1993. Takes the hard work out of research.

Vogler, Christopher. *The Writer's Journey: Mythic structure for storytellers and screenwriters*, 2nd edn, Pan, 1999. Although aimed at scriptwriters, this is an invaluable guide to powerful narrative, by a story executive with 20th Century Fox. Highly original approach.

Whale, John. *Put it in Writing*, Dent, London, 1984. A collection of very useful newspaper columns. Old but not dated.

Whitelaw, Stella. *How to Write and Sell a Synopsis*, Allison&Busby, London, 1993. Learning the essential first step to success.

Zuckerman, Albert. *Writing the Blockbuster Novel*, Little, Brown, London, and Writer's Digest Books, Ohio, 1994. An American literary agent with Ken Follett among his successful clients. A very practical book on how to write commercial fiction.

Reference

Bolt, David. *An Author's Handbook*, Piatkus, London, 1986. Practical and readable.

Directory of Publishing, Cassells. Reliable but not interesting. I would rather recommend the two Turner's below.

Writers' and Artists' Yearbook, A&C Black, annual. The standard reference book for the trade and layman alike until the much more opinionated Turners appeared. Now seems rather dull.

Turner, Barry. *The Writer's Companion*, Macmillan, annual
The Writer's Handbook, Macmillan, annual. The two Turner volumes have established themselves as the most readable and reliable guides to the trade for the writer and insider alike. I love the essays and opinions even if I don't agree with all of them. At least they are *interesting*!

Appendix 4

Trade papers and publications for writers

Australia

Australian Bookseller and Publisher. Monthly. D. W. Thorpe,
18 Salmon Street, Port Melbourne, Victoria 3207.
Tel: 613 9245 7380. Fax: 613 9245 7395.

Britain

The Bookseller. Weekly. 12 Dyott Street, London WC1A 1DF.
Tel: 0171 420 6000. Fax: 0171 420 6013.

Publishing News. Weekly. 39 Store Street, London WC1E 7DB.
Tel: 0171 692 2900. Fax: 0171 419 2111.

Writers News. Monthly. P O Box 4, Nairn IV12 4HU, Scotland.
Tel: 01667 454441. Fax: 01667 454401.

Canada

Quill and Quire. 70 The Esplanade, Suite 210, Toronto, Ontario,
Canada M5E 1R2. Tel: 416 360 0044. Fax: 416 941 9038.

South Africa

At the time of writing there is no South African trade magazine.

USA

Publishers Weekly. Weekly. 245 West 17th Street, New York,
NY 10011. Tel: 212 463 6758. Fax: 212 463 6631.

Appendix 5

Trade organizations

Authors, The Society of
84 Drayton Gardens, London SW10 9SB. Tel: 0171 373 6642.
Fax: 0171 373 5768. E-mail: authorsoc@writers.org.uk
An independent trade union with more than 6,000 members. Organizes meetings with speakers, publishes a magazine and guides to publishing for writers. Will advise on negotiating, help with complaints, and take legal action on behalf of members. Reads and comments on contracts, has various specialist groups within the Society and administers a range of awards. In conjunction with The Writers' Guild has promoted and negotiated Minimum Terms Agreements with a number of publishing companies.

Authors' Agents, The Association of
c/o The Secretary, 62 Grafton Way, London W1P 5LD.
Tel: 0171 387 2076
A British group whose committee of seven members, each serving for three years, is made up of working agents who give their time to the Association on a voluntary basis. Members adhere to a Constitution and a Code of Practice and meet quarterly in London. All member agencies must agree to sign a 'terms of business' letter with their clients if they are to qualify for the group negotiated professional indemnity insurance. The Association acts as an industry lobby group on behalf of issues that affect the agent community. To qualify for membership of the Association, agents must have been trading for a minimum of three years at a minimum commission rate of £25,000 per year. In directories such as the *Writers' and Artists' Yearbook*, agencies who are members of the Association are identified as such. See Appendix 7 for the Association's Code of Practice. There are associations of authors' agents in America, Australia, and South Africa.

Authors' Licensing and Collecting Society Ltd (ALCS)
Marlborough Court, 14–18 Holborn, London EC1N 2LE.
Tel: 0171 395 0600. Fax: 0171 395 0660. E-mail: alcs@alcs.co.uk
A non-profit making collecting society that collects and distributes income due to authors from collective rights such as photocopying,

electronic rights, off-air recording, rental and lending rights (but not British Public Lending Right: see below), retransmission of programmes over cable and many others. For further information or to register, contact their offices or view their Website at http:/www.alcs.co/uk Membership is free to members of The Society of Authors and The Writers' Guild and the National Union of Journalists.

Booksellers Association of Great Britain and Ireland

Minster House, 272 Vauxhall Bridge Road, London SW1V 1BA.

Tel: 0171 834 4577. Fax: 0171 834 8812.

E-mail: 100437.2261@compuserve.com

Represents over 3,000 members' interests to publishers, authors and the rest of the trade as well as to the Government. Offers training courses in all aspects of bookselling, marketing and management, administers some literary prizes, publishes directories and surveys and organizes World Book Day with the Publishers Association.

Book House Training Centre

Book Trust, Book House, 45 East Hill, London SW18 2QZ.

Tel: 0181 516 2977. Fax: 0181 516 2978.

E-mail: www.booktrust.org.uk

An educational charity to promote books and reading. Offers a book information service that is free to the public and administers many literary prizes and organizes surveys of reading habits etc. as well as publishing reference books.

The British Council

10 Spring Gardens, London SW1A 2BN. Tel: 0171 930 8466.

Fax: 0171 839 6347.

Exists to promote Britain overseas, through literature, the arts, science and technology. Organizes groups of writers to travel overseas to promote their own work.

British Science Fiction Association

1 London Row Close, Everdon, Daventry, Northants NN11 3BE.

Tel: 01327 361661. E-mail: bsfa@enterprise.net

Exists to promote science fiction and to help members contact each other. Publishes magazines and newsletters, and organizes writers' workshops for an international membership.

Clé (The Irish Book Publishers Association)

Cultural Office, Temple Bar, Dublin 2, Republic of Ireland.

Tel: 00 3531 872 9090.

Promotes Irish publishing and provides training for the industry.

The Copyright Licensing Agency Ltd
90 Tottenham Court Road, London W1P OLP.
Tel: 0171 436 5931. Fax: 0171 436 3986. E-mail: cla@cla.co.uk
Jointly founded by the Authors' Licensing and Collecting Society and
the Publishers Licensing Society Ltd. Administers copyrights' rights,
such as photocopy, which would not be economic for publishers and
authors to administer themselves. Issues licenses and distributes fees
via ALCS and the PLS.

Crime Writers' Association
60 Drayton Road, Kings Heath, Birmingham B14 7LR.
Professional crime writers only may join, and agents, publishers and
booksellers who specialize in the genre may join as associate members.
Meetings with speakers are held monthly in London and frequently
around the country via its regional chapters. Publishes a newsletter,
organizes conferences and presents annual awards.

The Guild of Erotic Writers
CTCK PO Box 8431, Deptford, London SE8 4BP.
Tel: 0973 767086.
Promotes the genre, provides contact between members, publishes a
newsletter and tip sheets and organizes a manuscript-reading service.

Independent Publishers Guild
25 Cambridge Road, Hampton, Middlesex TW12 2JL.
Tel: 0181 979 0250. Fax: 0181 979 6393.
Its members are independent publishers and packagers. Holds meetings, organizes conferences and seminars and publishes a bulletin.

Irish Writers' Union (Comhar na Scríbhneoirí)
19 Parnell Square, Dublin 1, Republic of Ireland.
Tel: 00 3531 872 1302. Fax: 00 3531 872 6282.
Protects the rights of, and promotes, writers in Ireland.

The Library Association
7 Ridgmount Street, London WC1E 7AE. Tel: 0171 636 7543.
Fax: 0171 436 7218. E-mail: info@la-hq.org.uk
A professional body for librarians. Publishes reference books and a
magazine for members. Has a Website at http://www.la.hq.org.uk

National Association of Writers' Groups
The Arts Centre, Biddick Lane, Washington,
Tyne & Wear NE38 2AB. Tel: 0191 416 9751.
Fax: 0191 431 1263.
A registered charity open to all writers' groups. Publishes a newsletter,
organizes writing competitions and an annual festival.

National Literacy Trust
Swire House, 59 Buckingham Gate, London SW1E 6AS.
Tel: 0171 828 2435. Fax: 0171 931 9986.
A registered charity that exists to improve literacy standards and to encourage reading and writing. Provides training, runs seminars and conferences and publishes a magazine. Organizing the 1999 National Year of Reading for the British Government. Has a Website at www.literacytrust.org.uk

New Science Fiction Alliance (NSFA)
c/o BBR Magazine, P O Box 625, Sheffield,
South Yorkshire S1 3GY.
Exists to help new writers by promoting small press publications around the world. Publishes a magazine and a newsletter and offers sample magazines to members.

P.E.N.
7 Dilk Street, London SW3 4JE. Tel: 0171 352 6303.
Fax: 0171 351 0220.
Part of International P.E.N., which is an association of published authors against censorship and oppression. Organizes talks, publishes a newsletter and has one international conference a year.

Professional Authors' and Publishers' Association
292 Kennington Road, London SE11 4LD. Tel: 0171 582 1477.
Fax: 0171 582 4084.
An organization that provides self-published authors with facilities such as an imprint name and a production and marketing service. The authors own the books and receive profits on the sales.

The Publishers Association
1 Kingsway, London WC1B 6XF. Tel: 0171 565 7474.
Fax: 0171 836 4543.
A trade association for UK publishers that represents their interests to the Government and overseas. Publishes reference works and organizes conferences.

Publishers Licensing Society Ltd
5 Dryden Street, London WC2E 9NW. Tel: 0171 829.
Fax: 0171 829 8488.
Administers the licensing of photocopying on behalf of member publishers. Works with the Copyright Licensing Agency.

Publishers Publicity Circle
48 Crabtree Lane, London SW6 6LW. Tel/Fax: 0171 385 3708.

A networking group for publicists. Holds monthly meetings that are open to journalists and television and radio producers. Publishes a membership directory.

The Romantic Novelists' Association
1 Beechwood Court, The Street, Syderstone, King's Lynn, Norfolk PE31 8TR. Tel: 01485 578594. Fax: 01485 578138.
Membership consists of published novelists and serial authors. Publishers, agents and booksellers may join as associate members. Authors who are not yet published may join the New Writers' Scheme provided they submit a manuscript each year, on which they will receive an editorial report. Organizes members meetings with speakers, annual awards, and publishes a newsletter.

Royal Society of Literature
1 Hyde Park Gardens, London W2 2LT. Tel: 0171 723 5104. Fax: 0171 402 0199.
Organizes lectures, poetry readings, and two literary prizes.

Science Fiction Foundation
c/o Liverpool University Library, P O Box 123, Liverpool L69 3DA. Tel: 0151 794 2696. Fax: 0151 794 2681.
An academic body to promote studies of the genre. Publishes a magazine and has a reference library at Liverpool University.

Scottish Publishers Association
Scottish Book Centre, 137 Dundee Street, Edinburgh EH11 1BG. Tel: 0131 228 6866. Fax: 0131 228 3220.
E-mail: enquiries@scottishbooks.org
Promotes members particularly with regard to joint marketing of their books. Publishes catalogues, directories, membership lists and newsletters. Organizes training and market research.

Society of Authors in Scotland
24 March Hall Crescent, Edinburgh EH16 5HL. Tel: 0131 667 5230.
Scottish branch of The Society of Authors (see above). Organizes meetings and events for its Scottish members.

The Welsh Academy
3rd Floor, Mount Stuart House, Mount Stuart Square, Cardiff CF1 6DQ. Tel: 01222 492025. Fax: 01222 492930.
The English language section of the National Society of Welsh Writers that exists to promote English literature in Wales. Organizes readings and an annual conference. Publishes a newsletter, reference works and directories.

Welsh Books Council/Cyngor Llyfrau Cymru
    Castell Brychan, Aberystwyth, Ceredigion SY23 2JB.
    Tel: 01970 624151. Fax: 01970 625385.
Exists to promote Welsh literature and authors. Offers advice to authors on how to get published, and offers editorial marketing and distribution services to publishers. Publishes a magazine.

Women in Publishing
    c/o The Bookseller, 12 Dyott Street, London WC1A 1DF.
A networking group to promote women in the industry. Organizes training courses and meetings and publishes a newsletter.

The Writers' Guild of Great Britain
    430 Edgware Road, London W2 1EH. Tel: 0171 723 8074.
    Fax: 0171 706 2413. E-mail: postie@wggb.demon.uk
A trade union affiliated to the TUC open to writers in film, radio, television, theatre and publishing. The Guild negotiates the terms upon which writers' contracts with television broadcasters are based, as well as those with independent producers. They provide advice on contracts and all aspects of life as a writer, and organize meetings and publish a magazine. Has a Website on www.writersorg.uk

Young Publishers, Society of
    12 Dyott Street, London WC1A 1DF.
A networking group that also provides associate membership to those over 35. Organizes meetings and publishes a newsletter. Has a Website at http:/www.thesyp.demon.co.uk

Appendix 6

Author–agent relations

Association of Authors' Agents
Constitution and Code of Practice

1. AIMS

   The aims of the Association shall include:

   i) To maintain a code of professional practice to which all members of the Association shall commit themselves.

   ii) To discuss matters of common professional interest.

   iii) To provide a vehicle for representing the view of authors' agents in discussion of matters of common interest with other professional bodies, the media industry and to the public.

2. STRUCTURE

   The Association shall comprise eligible and duly elected members. Such members shall in turn elect a Committee which shall be responsible for making and implementing day to day decisions in relation to the affairs of the Association and on its behalf. The Committee shall consist of seven members, four 'Officers', being a President, a Vice-President, a Secretary and a Treasurer, two 'Ordinary Members' and the Retiring President (or sometimes an additional Ordinary member).

   Members of the Committee of the Association shall be elected at the Annual Meeting of the Association at three-yearly intervals and shall serve for three years on a voluntary unpaid basis. The President may not serve two consecutive terms. The Vice-President, Secretary and Treasurer may be re-elected to the Committee but not to the same office, and may not serve on the Committee for a consecutive term of more than six years unless elected to the position of President. The Ordinary Members of the Committee may only be re-elected for two consecutive terms if they are re-elected as Officers. No member may serve for more than six consecutive years, except in the case of a seventh year as ex-officio President.

   All members of the Committee shall be elected by written ballot by a majority vote of those agencies represented at each Annual Meeting of the Association, each agency having only one vote. Unless expressly authorised at the Annual or Extraordinary Meeting of the Association, no two members of the same agency shall be elected to the Committee at the same time. Any agent of a member agency shall be eligible for election as President so long as he/she has been a full-time authors' agent for not less than seven years, and any agent of a member agency shall be eligible for election as any other officer on the Committee so long as he/she has been a full-time authors' agent for not less than five years, such restrictions to be subject to the discretion of the Committee.

In the event of the resignation, death or incapacity of the President mid-term, the Vice-President shall automatically become President and elections for Vice-President shall be held at the next meeting of the Association. Upon the resignation, death or incapacity of any other Committee Member(s) other than the President mid-term, election(s) shall be held at the next meeting of the Association.

The President, or in his/her absence the Vice-President, shall preside at all meetings of the Association. At the Annual Meeting of the Association, the President, or in his/her absence the Vice-President, shall present to the meeting a report of the activities of the Association during the year. This shall include a summary of matters recommended for action by the Association.

The Secretary shall give notice of no less than two weeks of all meetings of the Association, keep the minutes of such meetings, and conduct the correspondence and keep the records of the Association. Such records shall be passed on to the Secretary's successor and other Committee Members shall also pass on relevant correspondence and documents to the Secretary within one month of leaving office.

The Treasurer shall keep the books of the Association, collect all dues, pay all outgoings, and render a proper annual account of the Association to the Annual Meeting.

The Constitution of the Association may only be changed by a 3/4 majority in a ballot of members of the Association present at any general meeting with a quorum of not less than half the number of member agencies. Any proposed changes shall be notified in writing to all members in advance. Actual changes shall also be confirmed in writing to all members.

3. MEMBERSHIP

Any agency or individual independent agent who has been actively engaged in representing authors and other individuals engaged in the profession of creating copyright works ('clients') for a period of three or more years shall be eligible for membership. Applicants for membership must have a place of business within the United Kingdom although exceptions may be made at the discretion of the Committee and must be able to give satisfactory evidence to the Committee of their ability to offer the full service of an authors' agency in the handling of all literary, drama, media, subsidiary and related rights. Each applicant should have a list of clients who are actively engaged in writing and who produce a level of business averaging not less than £25,000 (or such figure as may be determined from time to time at an Annual or Extraordinary Meeting) in commissions for each of the past three years. An agency or agent who is also employed by publishers or purchasing principles, other than for selling rights, shall not be eligible for membership.

Applicants shall furnish the Association with a statement of their commission rates and, if elected, notify the Association of any changes in such rates, which shall be recorded by the Committee.

Election to membership of the Association shall be approved by a majority of the full Committee. The Committee reserves the right to refuse membership to any agency or individual who may qualify technically under the conditions set out above. Any applicant for membership who does not technically qualify under the conditions set out above may in exceptional circumstances be accepted for full membership or may be given Observer status if such an applicant is approved by a majority of the full Committee. If a member of an agency who has been an agent for three years with a member agency establishes his/her own agency he/she may apply immediately for a membership of the Association and acceptance shall be at the discretion of the Committee. Observer status shall not confer an automatic right to future full membership.

Payment of the annual subscription shall constitute acceptance of the Association's Constitution and Code of Practice.

4. DUES

An annual subscription of £50 shall be payable on or before the first day of January of each year, by standing order to the Association. The subscription may be changed subject to a quorum of half the number of member agencies at any full meeting of the Association. The Association's bankers are Lloyds Bank PLC, 472c Fulham Road, London SW6 1DD, account number 0299 49302: sort code 30–99–02. Cheques drawn on the Association's account may bear the signature of any one of the four officers of the Association.

5. MEETINGS OF THE ASSOCIATION

The Annual Meeting of the Association shall be held on a Wednesday in January in each year. Ordinary meetings of the

Association shall usually be held on a Wednesday in the months of March, June and September. Extraordinary meetings of the Association may be called at any time by the President or within two weeks' notice by no fewer than nine members. The committee shall meet by arrangement and may also appoint special subcommittees of the Association to consider and report on particular questions of interest to members.

6. CODE OF PRACTICE

(a) All members are required to act in such a way that the reputation of the Association of Authors' Agents is protected and enhanced and to observe the Code of Practice set out in the following paragraphs. Members shall pay due heed to such other non-mandatory standards and guidelines to good practice as may be proposed by the Committee from time to time.

(b) No member shall knowingly represent the client of another agency, whether or not that other agency is a member of the Association. Failure to enquire as to a client's agency relationship shall be considered a violation of this rule.

(c) No member shall restrain a client from leaving his or her agency. In the event that a client does leave a member agency, then that agency shall have a continuing right to full commission on contracts which it has already negotiated. The original agency shall, unless otherwise agreed, release to the client all unsold rights and any rights that subsequently revert from licensees.

(d) All members shall by cheque or bank transfer account faithfully to their clients, within not more than 21 days of clients' monies being cleared in the member's bank account for all sums due to their clients unless instructed otherwise by their clients or otherwise agreed.

(e) All members shall furnish promptly to their clients any information and material which the client may reasonably request in connection with his/her business. A member shall allow his/her clients at all reasonable times the right to verify and authenticate any statement of account concerning that client and shall submit promptly and regularly to the client full details of any transaction handled by the member.

(f) All members recognise the continuing right of other members to commission on contracts already negotiated.

(g) No member shall act for a client after the client's authorisation to do so has terminated, except that
   i) no member shall be debarred from continuing to act in specified areas if so instructed in writing by the client and

ii) the member shall continue to receive commission in respect of the agreements entered into previously with third parties on the client's behalf and appropriate commission in respect of negotiations carried out on the client's behalf and which are consequently concluded by the client or a new agent.

(h) No member shall charge a reading fee or any other fee to a client beyond his/her regular commission as notified to the Association without the client's or prospective client's prior consent in writing.

(i) No member may without informing his/her client in writing in advance, represent in any transaction both his/her client as vendor of services or copyright material and any other interest as purchaser and/or representative of purchaser of such material and must declare to the client in writing any proprietary or profitable interest in any contract apart from that of a normal agency commission.

Members may in exceptional circumstances make special commission arrangements with a client provided that they obtain the client's prior consent in writing. Members are strongly advised to consult the Committee if they are in any doubt whatsoever as the propriety of any such special arrangement. The Committee shall have power to decide on the acceptability to the Association of any such special arrangement which comes to its notice and to require the member in question to amend to its satisfaction any such arrangement which in its view it deems unacceptable. The member may elect to withdraw from membership of the Association upon receiving notice that a particular commission arrangement is unacceptable in the Committee's opinion.

(j) No member shall use or communicate to others information relating to a client's affairs confidentially given to him/her except as required by law.

(k) All members shall establish for their clients' monies a bank account separate from the members' general business and personal accounts and shall deposit clients' monies in that account immediately upon receipt or as directed by the client.

(l) All members shall at all times act honestly, and in such a manner that neither clients nor third parties are misled. Members shall keep their clients appraised of relevant information and offers that they receive. Members shall not knowingly or recklessly disseminate false or misleading information.

(m) No member shall knowingly, recklessly or maliciously injure the professional reputation or practice of another member

(n) All members shall promote and protect their clients' best interests and maintain regular contact to keep them informed as to work undertaken on their behalf.

(o) All members shall conduct their business lawfully.

(p) All members shall notify new clients in writing of their terms of business.

(q) All member agencies shall hold adequate provision for Professional Indemnity Insurance to a minimum level adequate to the requirement of the member agency's trading.

(r) Members who are sole traders shall make adequate legal provision for the protection and disbursement of clients' monies in the event of resignation, incapacity or death.

All complaints made against members for alleged violation of any provision of the Code of Practice shall be considered by the full Committee of the Association who shall have the right to expel any member against whom a significant and material breach of the Code of Practice is upheld. Such a decision must be taken unanimously by the full Committee. Any member against whom a complaint has been lodged shall have the right to appear in person before the Committee to hear and/or answer such complaint. In the event of a dispute between member agencies over a matter of professional practice, the Committee may, if requested by the parties, act as arbitrators.

Blake Friedmann client–agent agreement letter

The Association of Authors' Agents recommends that all member agencies sign a 'terms of business' letter with their clients. Here is the wording that the Blake Friedmann Agency uses:

Dear _____,

I'm very pleased that we will be working together, and I would like to outline our conditions and terms. This letter, once signed by both of us, will be an agreement between us.

In addition to the confidence and trust that we must have in each other for a satisfactory working relationship, this agreement does give us both protection. I would like to emphasise at the outset that should you wish to terminate our representation you can do so at any time.

The letter spells out the details of the agreement. If any of it is not clear please do not hesitate to talk to us about it. If you are in agreement with the terms and conditions laid out below, would you please sign both copies of this letter, keep one copy and let us have the other for our files.

We are very pleased that you wish us to act as your exclusive worldwide literary agent. You will refer all approaches regarding your works to us. We shall represent your interests to the best of our ability, using sub-agents where we consider this appropriate, in relation to the exploitation of all your works, but we will not commit you to any agreement without your approval.

You warrant that you are the author and sole owner of the works you ask us to represent and that the works are original and contain no matter unlawful in content nor do they violate the rights of any third party and that they are in no way whatever an infringement of any existing copyright, that the works contain no blasphemous, indecent, defamatory, libellous, objectionable or otherwise unlawful matter, and that all statements contained therein purporting to be facts are true. You undertake to indemnify Blake Friedmann against loss, injury or damage occasioned to Blake Friedmann in consequence of any breach of this warranty. You warrant that the rights granted hereunder are free and clear and that you have the full power to grant such representation to us.

We will do all we can, short of seeking help from lawyers – which will only be done by arrangement with you – to collect money due to you under contracts negotiated through us and we will remit to you promptly money which we collect after deduction only of our commission, any expenses incurred by us on your behalf, and any other money which may be due to us from you.

Our commission (to which VAT must be added) will be a percentage of the income arising from all contracts for the exploitation of works you create entered into during the period we represent you (and after that only to the extent mentioned below) at the following rates:

Books, serials and columns, UK	15%
Books, serials and columns, overseas	20%
Radio, television, film	15%
One-off journalism and short stories	25%
Audio, abridged and unabridged, British	15%
Audio, abridged and unabridged, overseas	20%

Our commissions cover editorial advice and the preparation of presentation material where we consider it appropriate. We will (in consultation with you) do as much editorial work as we feel necessary on outlines and manuscripts, whether developing projects for publishing or for film, television or radio.

If you are registered for VAT you may reclaim the VAT paid on the commission. Should you receive any income direct we shall be entitled to receive from you our commission plus VAT where applicable. If you have a VAT number please enter it here:

_____. Please be sure to inform us if your VAT status changes.

You, in turn, undertake with us that (so far as is reasonably practicable) all contracts relating to the exploitation of your works entered into whilst we are your agent (whether or not negotiated through us) will include a provision whereby the income payable under them is to be paid to us, both during and after our agency period. You authorise us to make the deductions from the income referred to above.

Please remember that it is your responsibility to ensure that you read and fully understand any contract negotiated by us on your behalf and that your signature to any such contract shall be deemed an acceptance of the terms of that contract and of the deal negotiated by us. If there is anything contained in any such contract which you do not understand or do not wish to accept, it is your responsibility to make this clear before you sign the contract.

We shall be entitled to charge you for the following concerning works written by you:

i) books and proofs bought by the agency for promotional purposes and for submission to publishers abroad
ii) photocopying of manuscripts and sales material (press cuttings etc.)
iii) couriers
iv) other exceptional expenses which may be incurred with your prior approval

No administrative, postage, telephone, telex, fax or other overhead costs will be charged to our clients.

Our agency will continue until terminated by either party on giving not less than 30 days written notice to the other whereupon, unless we both agree otherwise, we will cease to represent you but we shall continue to be entitled to commission in respect of all income arising from contracts for the exploitation of your works entered into while we represented you and from all extensions and renewals of such contracts. We shall also be entitled to commission where the income arises from a contract following a submission we made to a publisher before we ceased to represent you where that contract was signed after we ceased to represent you.

Whilst we take all reasonable care of the manuscripts, outlines, illustrative material, books and other property which you may entrust to us, we will not be liable in respect of their loss or damage.

All manuscripts and outlines that come to us should be in duplicate and we do advise you to be sure to keep copies for yourself.

The meanings of the terms 'works', 'exploitation' and 'income' used in this letter, and of the terms used in their definition are set out in the Appendix, together with some information on our staff and our international arrangements.

Our agreement shall be governed by English law and the English courts shall have non-exclusive jurisdiction.

Please confirm your agreement to these terms by signing and returning the enclosed duplicate of this letter.

Yours sincerely,
Carole Blake
Joint Managing Director

Endorsement on duplicate

Date: _____

Dear _____ ,

I agree to the terms set out in your letter, of which this is a duplicate. I acknowledge that I have read and understood the letter.

Yours sincerely,

_____

The Appendix

'Works'

means every literary, artistic or dramatic work, whether intended for publication in book form or as a contribution to a book or as an article or other contribution to a newspaper, magazine or other periodical and including a script for any play, film or other entertainment intended for any Media Format devised, created or written by you whilst we represent you, or which was so devised, created or written at any time prior to our representing you to the extent that the rights in it are not now subject to any subsisting agreement with any literary agent or for exploitation and also every literary or dramatic work so devised, created or written after the expiration of this appointment where the same has been put under option to any person under the terms of an agreement entered into whilst this appointment is in force.

'Media Format'

includes radio, television (including cable and satellite television), the making and distribution of films, video and audio cassettes and disks, their performance or publication in a form suitable for entry or storage in any electronic information system now in existence or hereafter invented, publication in written form, and every other means of dissemination now or hereafter invented.

'Exploitation'

includes every form of exploitation of the copyright in any work including without limitation the assignment of such copyright and the grant of the right to do any of the following things in respect of the work, namely its publication of the same in book form (in any format) or other Media Format, the serialisation of the same in any newspaper, magazine, journal or other periodical or other publication or by other Media Format (whether by the grant of first or second or subsequent serial rights) the publication of abridgements, condensations, adaptations or extracts of any work, its adaptation into a play or film or strip cartoon or other picturisation including its subsequent broadcasting or publication by any Media Format and the grant of Merchandising Rights.

'Merchandising Rights'

means the right to exploit characters, items and events in any work through the manufacture, licensing and/or sale or other distribution of goods or services.

'Income'

means the entire consideration received from the publisher or other holder of any right or licence in relation to the exploitation of each work in respect of such exploitation before the deduction of any overseas withholding tax and commission and any expenses payable to us hereunder and whether or not the relevant consideration is receivable by you or by any third party to whom you have transferred the work or the income thereof or any rights in respect thereof other than by normal exploitation contracts at arms length.

The singular shall include the plural and the masculine shall include the feminine and the neuter, and vice-versa in each case.

'Overseas Rights'

We represent our clients at major international book, film and television fairs and festivals around the world and make regular selling trips to America and Europe. We have agents working for us around the world (their commission is paid by our agency) and at present they are as follows:

USA *non-fiction and thrillers* – Stuart Krichevsky Inc
  other – Carole Blake, London office
Brazil – Sarah Nundy, Andrew Nurnberg Agency
Bulgaria – Katalina Sabeva, Anthea
Canada – Bella Pomer Agency
China – Lily Chan, Tuttle Mori China
Czech Republic – Olga Bendova, Dilia
France – Maggie Doyle, La Nouvelle Agence
Germany – Eva Koralnik, Liepman AG

Greece – Nelly Moukakou, J L M Agency
Holland – Carole Blake, London office
Hungary – Katalin Katai, Katai & Bolza
Israel – Ziv Lewis, Ilana Pikarski Ltd
Italy – Roberta Oliva, Natoli, Stefan & Oliva
Japan – Various, depending on author
Korea – Mi Sook Hong, KCC International
Poland – Maria Strarz-Kanska, Graal Ltd
Portugal – Sarah Nundy, Andrew Nurnberg Agency
Romania – Simona Kessler Agency
Russia – Natasha Sanina, Fontanka
Scandinavia – Anneli Hoier, Leonhardt & Hoier Agency
Slovak Republic – Various, depending on author
Spain – Sarah Nundy, Andrew Nurnberg Agency
Taiwan – Lily Chan, Tuttle Mori Taiwan
Thailand – Jitpanga Varasiri, Silkroad Agency
Turkey – Kezban Akcali, Akcali & Tuna

Where appropriate we also use film and television agents. We reserve the right to change our agents at our sole discretion.

'The Agency'

For your information here are the names of the current Agency staff:

Carole Blake – Book Rights, Joint Managing Director
Julian Friedmann – Film & TV Rights, Joint Managing Director
Barbara Jones – Finance Director and Accounts Manager
Conrad Williams – Film, TV & Radio Rights Director
Isobel Dixon – Book Agent
Kate Wilkinson – Books Assistant
Jane McRae – Film/TV Assistant
Beverley Jones – Director and Office Manager
Helen Cousans – Accounts Clerk
Elli Colebrook – Office Administrator

Please do not hesitate to call any of us or arrange to come in and see us. We are here to work for you.

Index